The Book of the SubGenius

Being the Divine Wisdom, Guidance, and Prophecy of **J.R. "Bob" Dobbs,** High Epopt of the **Church of the SubGenius,** Here Inscribed for the Salvation of Future Generations and in the Hope that Slack May Someday Reign on this Earth

Translated out of the Original Tongues.
Appointed to be Read in Churches.

The SubGenius Foundation

McGraw-Hill Book Company

New York   St. Louis   San Francisco   Bogota   Guatemala   Hamburg   Lisbon
Madrid   Mexico   Montreal   Panama   Paris   San Juan   São Paulo   Tokyo   Toronto

Sometimes a book goes too far.
Sometimes . . . is *now*.

First — there was *The Gilgamesh*.
Then. . . the *Bhagavad-Gita*.
Then. . . *The Torah, The New Testament, The Koran*.
Then. . . *The Book of Mormon, Dianetics, I'm OK You're OK*.
And now . . .

THE BOOK OF THE SUBGENIUS
(How to Prosper in the Coming Weird Times)

THE BOOK YOU NOW HOLD IN YOUR HANDS COULD CREATE A NEW INQUISITION — A SELF-PERPETUATING FASCIST STATE THAT WILL LAST TO THE END OF HUMANITY — OR IT COULD BE THE FOUNDATION-STONE OF THE PROMISED KINGDOM OF PEACE AND HARMONY. WHICH WILL IT BE?

Yes, **YOU** can rape your *own* mind. **YOU** can finally relax in the safety of your *own* delusions.

This epipastic for the brains of Epoptics, Beholders, and Initiates, works an authentic gnostic magician's spell that will drive OUT the foreign personalities and id-demons. Protected by its own occult roots in the most extreme forms of para-and mecha-psychology, it places the reader within a "shell" of Weird Phenomena which *must* be used for good *and* evil.

Its system of Mystik Correspondences' has already given

SECRET POWER to the Church of the SubGenius — the world's first *industrial* church, the prophesied End Times cult of screamers and laughers, scoffers, blasphemers, mockers, sinners, and the last true holymen in America today.

KEEP THIS BOOK NEAR YOU — in your pocket, your bathroom, your glove compartment. Study it. Memorize it. Find within its pages a NEW DIRECTION — a NEW WAY — a HIGHER yet LOWER REALITY — just as thousands before you have done!

Peels away the bullshit, LAYER BY LAYER!!

The world-famous authors of the original *Facts About Dobbs* show you how to unearth and wield your amazing hidden powers of VENGEANCE. This prophetic new accounting of future history and a fantastic religion *beyond* science is " . . . more entertaining than fiction — more terrifying than the truth!"

A self-"help" book for sinners, creeps, junkies, morphodites, and wise men and guys who know they wouldn't get "help" from any book even if they needed it in the first place.

**WITH SPECIAL
INSANE BONUS OFFER
"THE PRESCRIPTURES"
Prophecy of the SubGenius**

LIBRARY OF CONGRESS CATALOGING IN PUBLICATION DATA

Dobbs, J. R.
    The Book of the SubGenius.

    (McGraw-Hill paperbacks)
    1. Religion—Anecdotes, facetiae, satire, etc.
I. SubGenius Foundation. II. Title.
PN6231.R4D6 1983   818'.5402   83-5470
ISBN 0-07-062229-9 (pbk.)

ISBN 0-07-062229-9

Do What Keepeth Thou from Wilting   Shall Be the Loophole in The Law

The Church of SubGenius is an order of Scoffers and Blasphemers, dedicated to Total Slack, delving into Mockery Science, Sadofuturistics, Megaphysics, Scatalography, Schizophreniatrics, Morealism, Sarcastrophy, Cynisacreligion, Apocolyptionomy, ESPectorationalism, HypnoPediatrics, Subliminalism, Satyriology, DistoUtopianity, Sardonicology, Fasciestiouism, Ridiculophagy, and Miscellatheistic Theology.

"Researching the Public's Fear of the Unknown Since 1953!"

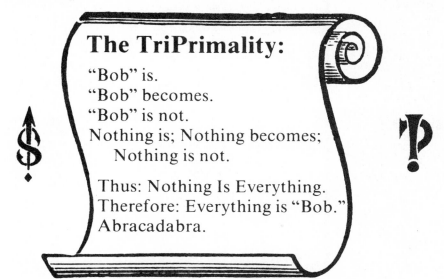

The TriPrimality:

"Bob" is.
"Bob" becomes.
"Bob" is not.
Nothing is; Nothing becomes;
    Nothing is not.

Thus: Nothing Is Everything.
Therefore: Everything is "Bob."
Abracadabra.

For up-to-date information on The Church, send a stamped, self-addressed envelope to:

The SubGenius Foundation
P.O. Box 140306   Dallas, Texas 75214

We welcome contributions of any kind: letters, artwork, photos, clippings, articles, sin materials, artifacts, money, sacrifices, tapes, and all other shreds of humanity. **NOT TAX DEDUCTIBLE.** We would rather not hear from Mediocretins, Pinks, Glorps, or False Prophets.

This Book was begun in 1953 by
J.R. "Bob" Dobbs

High Epopt of the Church of the SubGenius

Revised In 1979 by

Dr. Philo U. Drummond, Ø1   Dr. X   Rev. Ivan Stang, A.Ø.

Board of Directors of The SubGenius Foundation appointed in 1980:

Puzzling Evidence
Doug Wellman
HellSwami John Hägen
Pastor Buck Naked
Cookie Drummond F.G.O.T.R.

St. Sterno Keckhaver
St. Janor Hypercleats
Drs. for "Bob"
Pope David Meyer III
J. Erickson

LIES
St. Paul Mavrides
Sir Guy Deuel
Glassmadness
someone else

Additional Sacrifices, 1981, by

High Priestess Eileen Keller
Dr. Bootmokus
Alexander D. Smith
Rev. Larry Sulkis
Shrendi Chisholm
Bob Black,
THE LAST INTERNATIONAL.
Dr. Jay Kinney
St. Joe Schwind

Capt. Hugh M. Smith
Tribunal Overdrive
Stefan Hammond
Rev. David Boone
Dennis Keller
St. Byron Werner
R. Wollard
BurnMartyr Dr. Snavely Eklund
Severn Institute

Pope St. D. Lee Lama
St. Poonflang Dammerung
Kerry Wendell Thornely
Pope Mike Danger
Hector Hilldale
Autumn Deuel
Leslie Gaspar
Drelloid
tENTATIVELY, a cONVENIENCE

1982 Illiterati:

Dominatrix Candi Strecker, Dr. Gary Hughes, Rev. Brian Curran, Rev. Garth Danielson, Bishop Buhle, Bishop Huey, St. Karen Trego, Mechapope Monika Vidi, Apostle G. Don Trubey, Fair Use Empire, Pope Michael Flores and *The People's Temple,* Sir Hal Robins, Krononautic Organism, Rev. Bob Lee, Nick West, St. Patricia Daley, Stigmatic Ted Early, Mastress Freddie Baer, Political Bizarro Luke T. McGuff, Maestro John Crawford, Prof. Mark Mothersbaugh, St. Becky Block, Radio Popes Kates, Chusid, Brown, Ginsburg, Nelson & Opinion; John Steakley, St. Rick Hoefle, Will (Lord) Small 888

Front cover, "The Deadline Approacheth," by HELLSWAMI JOHN HÄGEN

Hieroglyphs by Stang, Hägen, Mavrides, Hal Robins, Guy Deuel, Buck Naked

Back Cover, "The Tree of Knowledge," by St. Paul Mavrides and Rev. Ivan Stang

Electrostatic Technician and Astral Plane Scout: St. Karen Gould
Photostatic Technowrestler, Dallas: Mark Veale

Endpaper multi "Bobs" by Rev. Garth Danielson

Typesetting: Archetype Graphics, Grand Rapids, Michigan
3/4 Design, Bloomington, Indiana
Franklin Typesetting, Austin, Texas

McGraw-Hill editors: Rev. Dr. Tim McGinnis, St. Joan of Eckerman   All work signed "LIES" is copyright LIES (Paul Mavrides).

A very special tip of the Dobbs hat to Rip Off Press, Inc., San Francisco, for blessed permissions, scam-abuse, technology, inspiration, Slack, etc.

Sacred Agent: Jane Jordan Browne, Multimedia Product Development, Chicago, IL.

Final Word Wrangling by:
Rev. Ivan Stang

Final Image Arrangements and Design by:

LIES
Chapters: 1,3,4,7,10,13,14,16 & 19

Hell Swami John Hagen
Chapters: 0,2,5,8,9,11,12,15,17,18 & 20

APPROVED BY DOBBS

Robert Williams

THE SOURCE:	**JEHOVAH-1** (a.k.a. WOTAN, YAHWEH, RA, etc.)
THE TEACHER:	**J.R. "BOB" DOBBS**
THE GOAL:	**SLACK**
THE OBSTACLE:	**THE CONSPIRACY AND ITS DUPES, THE NORMALS**
THE WAY:	**THE CASTING OUT OF FALSE PROPHETS**
THE WEAPON:	**TIME CONTROL**

SLOGANS:

"Fuck 'Em If They Can't Take A Joke"

"Too Much Is Always Better Than Not Enough"

"Pull The Wool Over Your Own Eyes"

"You'll *Pay* To Know What You *Really* Think"

"Give Me Slack, Or Give Me Food (Or Kill Me)"

"If I Can't Whup It, I'll Go DOWN"

"Bleeding Head Good, Healed Head Bad"

"If You Act Like A Dumbshit, They'll Treat You As An Equal"

"SCIENCE DOES NOT REMOVE THE TERROR OF THE GODS"

ATTENTION   ACHTUNG

DO NOT ALLOW TO FALL INTO ENEMY HANDS
NE PAS LAISSER TOMBER AUX MAINS DE L'ENNEMI
NICHT IN FEINDESHAND FALLEN LASSEN

PUZZLING EVIDENCE

WARNINGS & DISCLAIMERS

If you think there's nothing wrong with the world, *don't* buy this Book; if you are offended by your own sick rage when viewing literature alien to your repressive behavior code, go ahead and *purchase* the book but **don't read it.**

The Church of the SubGenius may drive you crazy.

The Roman Catholic Church has driven people crazy. Scientology has driven people crazy. So have Satanism, Islam, the Boy Scouts, the government of the United States, Judaism, traffic jams, LSD, the C.I.A., Taoism, parents, kids, TV, war, and peace. Some people drive themselves crazy.

This Book will not drive SubGeniuses crazy. It will supply them with the Slack they need to drive *others* crazy.

Many idiots will object to this publication. The techniques and secrets revealed herein have been passed through the headquarters of many terrorist organizations (including the **F.B.I.** and **C.I.A.**) for years. This knowledge will also enhance *your* professional capabilities and aid you in protecting against THEM — but it is not meant for the young or irresponsible.

J.R. "BOB" Dobbs is endowed with the full range of ESP abilities. Although "Bob's" accuracy has never been questioned by previous "clients," no SacraMentalist can claim infallibility. With "Bob," especially, it is only a matter of time before he falters in a big way; he is farther from so-called 'perfection' than most of us could be if we worked at it. Therefore, "Bob," his associates, promoters, employees, sponsors, agents, followers, and writers must disclaim all liability to all persons or groups who act upon ESP impressions given by word of mouth, print, telephone, film, tape, or holograph recording now or in the . . . **the future.** The Secrets of the Elder Gods are not offered in an attempt to persuade any person of the supernatural powers of rites, rituals, amulets, talismans, seals, incantations, or other ideas and devices mentioned herein. No magical claims are made and medical problems should be attended by *licensed physicians.*

The Church is not responsible for the actions of individuals which may result from their mere possession of this Book. Any resemblance by characters in these pages to any person, living or dead, except where intended for direct satirical purposes, is strictly "Coincidence." That's right, it's all a big joke! Ha ha! "The Conspiracy"—what a laugh! Ha ha! 3,000 children starving to death in Mexico City every day, ha ha! Radioactive waste cannisters rotting in the ocean! Ha ha ha! Mind control by horrible secret societies—yuk, yuk, yuk.

IGNORE THIS: FNORD: To practise and preach the same things is utter madness. Sometimes communication must be made *more difficult and irritating than necessary,* in order to convey certain dangerous complexities. The knowlege must not fall into the wrong hands. "SCIENCE DOES NOT REMOVE THE TERROR OF THE GODS."

The SubGenius knows that a god*like* alien space monster calling Himself "**Jehovah-1**" *is* watching us and making us dance like cheap puppets for His own indiscernible ends. He demands that we "whorship" Him, and so we surely must.

And if you say that the SubGenius is decieved, that there is no alien God of Wrath, then the SubGenius will attack **YOU!** You are wrong; we are right; WOTAN told us so and we believed it. Alright? Now roll over and go back to "sleep" . . . (By "God's Third Leg," you'd think these humans didn't know what religion was *for!*)

A note about the word "he" as an all-purpose pronoun: we use it because constantly saying "he or she," "s/he," or "it," sounds STUPID. However, notice also that while JHVH-1, God, Jesus and a few others are called "He" with a capital H, "Bob" is merely a "he." These spellings are in accordance with the express wishes of the respective deities. "Bob" de-deifies himself whenever possible to counterbalance the tendency of his followers to go overboard.

CAUTION — MAY BE HABIT FORMING. Do not drive a motor
vehicle or operate heavy machinery while under the influence of this book.

PROPHECY CRUSADE

WE THE SUBGENIUSES OF THE POST-HUMAN RACE, in order to preserve life on this planet from immanent destruction, reestablish intelligence, regain Slack, cast out the False Prophets, smother forever the fear of fear Itself, receive the questionable gifts of the Beforelife and of the Space Dwellers, become as Overmen, unmask the Conspiracy, grip the reins of human evolution, control reproduction and mutation, decipher the Code, placate the Stark Fist of Removal, achieve Time Control, see That Which Must Come To Pass, become as gods, find the Twins with the Scissors of Sight, avert the Rupture of the Equilibrium, and secure the fiancial blessings of Jehovah-1 the God of Wrath for ourselves and our descendants, do hereby admit ourselves as such and thus ordain this Advertisement of the SubGenius Race of Earth

Erwin Bergdoll

CONTENT

Ch. 0   **TruthStinger Barrage** 9
Ch. 1   **Don't Laugh** 13
Ch. 2   **The Miracle of "Bob's" Tyranny** .21
Ch. 3   **Earth Is Hell** 37
Ch. 4   **The Curse of "Bob"** 53
Ch. 5   **The Secrets of Slack** 61
Ch. 6   **Creative Truth** 71
Ch. 7   **Salvation $1 and the Perils of False Slack** 76
Ch. 8   **Your SubGenius Heritage** 83
Ch. 9   **Shut Up or Stand Up — "The Brag"** 89
Ch. 10   **We Dare Call It Conspiracy** 91
Ch. 11   **The UFO Made Me Do It** 99
Ch. 12   **Dateline for Dominance** 113
Ch. 13   **The Prescriptures** 125
Ch. 14   **ANSWERS: Money and Jobs** 137
Ch. 15   **ANSWERS: Sex — The Divine Battle** 143
Ch. 16   **Health, the Industrial Diet, and Bad Things** 149
Ch. 17   **Starting Your Own Church** 157
Ch. 18   **Your Instructions** 163
Ch. 19   **Paths to Frenzy** 169
Ch. 20   **Your Move: A Letter from "Bob"** 181
         APPENDIX 185

J. Erickson

"Flash Gordon's Ape — he's too day." — Capt. Beefheart
For someone else.
Dedicated to **The Nameless Mission.**
We are merely Initiates, paying homage to The Mysteries.
This book printed on **AIN SOPH** by MegaGnostics.

Superior Mutants!

REPENT! Quit Your JOB! ¡SLACK OFF!

The World Ends Tomorrow and YOU MAY DIE!

(Well, no, probably not . . . but whatever you do, just *keep reading!*)

ARE WE CONTROLLED BY SECRET FORCES?

Do you ever get the feeling that "free will" is a joke?

DO PEOPLE THINK YOU'RE STRANGE? DO YOU??

. . . THEN YOU MAY BE ON THE RIGHT TRACK!

ARE YOU ABNORMAL?

THEN YOU ARE PROBABLY **BETTER** THAN MOST PEOPLE!

ARE ALIEN SPACE MONSTERS BRINGING A STARTLING NEW WORLD?

YES!

YOUR KIND SHALL TRIUMPH!

IF you suspect that things are much worse than you ever suspected—

IF the only thing you've been able to laugh at for the last 5 years is the fact that NOTHING is funny anymore—

IF you sometimes want to collar people on the street and scream that you're more "different" than they could possibly *imagine* —

IF you can help us with a donation —

IF you see the whole universe as one vast morbid sense of sick humor —

IF the current 'Age of Progress" seems more like the Dark Ages to you —

IF you are looking for an *inherently contradictory* religion that will condone megadegeneracy and yet tell you that you are "above" everyone else —

Then . . .

THE CHURCH OF THE SUBGENIUS™
could *save your sanity!*

INSTANT ANSWERS TO EVERYTHING!

Your secret wishes can be granted in full — *once you know what they are!* **"You'll PAY to know what you REALLY think."** — J.R. "Bob" Dobbs, 1961

NOW, AT LAST!

SUCCESS

The step-by-step process is revealed! THIS IS IT

— the only "faith" that promises

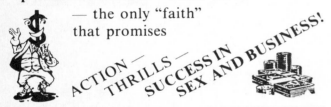

ACTION — THRILLS — SUCCESS IN SEX AND BUSINESS!

FEELING LIKE THERE'S JUST NO SLACK?

You may have 'snapped' already from the information disease! ("The sleep of reason begets monsters.") Look to the High Unpredictables of the Church of the SubGenius for pancultural deprogramming and resynchronization! Perfect your subliminimal vision — edit your memory — **relive your reincarnalty** — SYNC UP! THE SUBGENIUS MUST HAVE SLACK!

Using SubGenius secrets of BULLDADA and MOREALISM you can now MIRACULOUSLY ELIMINATE COMPULSIVE URGES such as smoking, eating, sleeping, working; end baldness, constipation, sex-money problems, assouliness, and painful shortage of SLACK!

Become a Doktor of the Forbidden Sciences... make religion a kick-ass adventure! Indulge in Self-Help through Raising Hell!

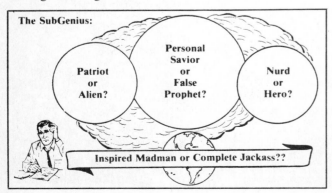

The SubGenius:

Patriot or Alien? | Personal Savior or False Prophet? | Nurd or Hero?

Inspired Madman or Complete Jackass??

Having all the *GUILT, but none of the SEX?*

"Have Intercourse With A Beautiful Live Girl"

or

DAMN NEAR ANYTHING ELSE!

Thought you'd tried everything? YOU AIN'T SEEN NOTHIN' YET! Learn to THINK **BIG!** Develop the tricks of **Length Extension!** Bring your *weirdest dreams* to rampaging LIFE!

Stand erect for your own abnormality. *WISE UP! They're* out to get you.

The "different" are being silenced by a global conspiracy. WEIRD-MEN ARISE!! Find out who "They" are... and how to **SMASH** them! You probably already knew that the U.S. Government is a SHAM —something propped up there for you to *blame.* But did you know that the *real* "powers that be" are not even *people?* That they are actually shambling, unbelievable, unmentionable, unthinkable **THINGS??**

yes!

Jehovah IS an Alien

and still threatens this planet!

Defy the sinister "**Star Forces**" which mock us all. Evil demons have kept the truth from humanity for thousands of years —**God has been misquoted all this time!** His actual words may disturb you . . . but "Bob" Dobbs is a bulwark against the unbearable fear and anxiety tormenting mankind. "There's No 'Prob' . . . With "Bob"!"

10

"Bob" is a way of life to *millions* — yet *half* of them don't even KNOW it! He is the one true **LIVING SLACK MASTER** with the spiritual know-how to help you BASH THROUGH the locked doorway to **FINANCIAL HEAVEN.** He is the *only* real Short-Cut to **Slack.**

SEE ANOTHER DIMENSION ON YOUR TV

"Bob's" promise is to widen the scope and nature of **abnormal behavior** . . . to explore NEW WAYS of going over the edge *and coming back,* PLUS to *bring back those* who *couldn't on their own* . . . to help you create the **HIGHEST POSSIBLE EARN-INGS** from the PSYCHODYNAMICS of ABNORMALITY . . . to turn Conspiracy-implanted personality disorders AROUND and channel them into an ILLUSION OF CREATIVITY that will *fool normals* and **GET YOU SEX!**

As you learn more and more reliable, safe methods of Time Control, you will find your I.Q. increasing — your very cranium will seem to pulsate from within, barely able to contain the turmoil of glorious new concepts and mental skills. Soon you'll be able to withstand COMMUNICATION WITH THE *XISTS,* our **mentors in space;** you will be ready for **TRANSFIGURA-TION** into a *new physical body,* a more powerful one, built to contain the surging mental and material mutations that your brain now generates. YES — become an OVERMAN, a dangerous and feared superhuman of the future! Yet — because your SubGenius roots can never be forgotten — you won't abuse your powers, but instead make them an unstoppable force for GOOD and JUSTICE, choosing always to defend the oppressed SubGenius wherever he may be!

The world is a turkey, and "Bob" gives you the carving knife.

Fear THE STARK FIST OF REMOVAL no longer! Become **PHYSICALLY ATTRACTIVE —** overnight! Attain **STATUS — LUCK — PROSPERITY** by *blowing them off!*

When you join this "Order of the Knights of Wotan," you get big, strong impressive muscles . . . a mastery of **fighting skills** . . . good health, an attractive personality, and, above all, a **WEIRD ABILITY TO INFLUENCE OTHERS!** To BEND THEM to **your**

WILL! TOTAL DOMINATION of **bosses, teachers, dates** — the job improvement that comes with confidence — INSTANT HIGHER GRADES or EARNINGS, **WITHOUT TRYING!!**

You'll learn **INCANTATIONS** that lead to **MASTERY** over the FISCAL PLANES . . . the OCCULT TECHNOLOGY of FINANCE POWER . . . E—Z ways to borrow money — from *other people who don't have it either!*

Achieve SHEER **GUT BLOWOUT.**

Our "ascetism" consists solely of the abstinence from abstinence. **Give up** the not giving into of temptation! Think thoughts that no man has ever dared think before. You CAN learn to recall memories from the past that you had forgotten — or that never existed at all.

NOW CONTACT ALIENS

— both benevolent *and* evil. They reveal themselves to the worthy at our **Altar of Xist Contact.** Attend *End o' the World Drills* at our Survival Farms. Learn *Body Repair, Frenzy Techniques,* and **Excremeditation.** Evaluate and *use* the so-called "accidents and coincidents" in your timestream. Perform long, complicated, impressive-looking rituals of *Communionication* with the desired sex! At the jungle settlement of **DOBBS-TOWN, skilled Doktors** trained by "Bob" himself can give you acubeating therapy, stress aversion by direct electrical brain stimulation, breast enlargement through hypnosis, Amnesiastic De-Inhibitional Experience Erasure, even plastic surgery through Therapeutic Mind-Letting.

Yes. *YOU* can indulge in SubGeniusment even while maintaining your present beliefs, practices and lifestyle — **WITHOUT the aid of snide, self-righteous "teachers" and gurus.** Simply *accultate* yourself to the Church. You will be isolated, given a new diet, a new set of habits, a different name and appearance. The now-void brainpan will be refilled with corrected info and subconsciously implanted ritual experiences. Follow your FOLLIES and COMPULSIONS and become rich like us.

Joe Schwind

Explore the "Zen" of stupidity! Channel chronic procrastination into life-saving paranoia and precise anality! *MAKE WASTE!!*

Find out who your Personal Saviors may be and who are the False Prophets *in your life!*

The most 'NO WAY' New Wage religion yet! Brain-trust of our species . . .

With the advent of technology, major physical evolution ceases. Thus, the next viable mutation must be mental — a new mind/world aspect.

WE ARE THAT NEXT TEETERING LUNATIC STEP.

This Contrivative Theology, computer-designed by precise mathematical formulae to arouse the *lowest* instincts of the *most* intelligent and the *highest* instincts of the *least* intelligent, is invaluable to all renegades who, *at any time*, are on the **nether edge of insanity** and can be made whole only by developing their **Wotan**-derived seventh sense of **Bludgeon Humor.**

It is the ultimate secret order for those who "know better" but who demand in their **LUST for GRINS** a spectacular, special-effects laden belief system — a **'stuporstition.'** It is a **certified religion** of scorn and vengeance directed at *THEM*, the *enemies* of us **Outsiders.** It is "self help" through *scoffing* and *blaspheming, frenzied fornication* and the *Mockery* of *Graven Images*. The Church provides **sure answers** and **miracles** in the service of **SURREAVOLUTION.**

"Pay no attention to the man behind the curtain!" — OZ

"SUBGENIUS"
has **nothing** to do with intelligence.
has **nothing** to do with race.
has **nothing** to do with education.
has **nothing** to do with skill.
has **nothing** to do with humanity.
"SUBGENIUS" Makes Sense, Has Sense,
　Sells Sense.
Common Sense, Sense of Humor,
　Dollars and Cents.

Bub Bogdan

LIFE LIBERTY SURVIVAL

Chapter 1
DON'T LAUGH

"I don't practice what I preach because I'm not the kind of person I'm preaching to."

"Bob" in *Newsweek*

"We believe the planet is being led to destruction by a race of inferior creatures who place blind trust in their own culturally dictated concept of "intelligence." Look, you guys, you know as well as I do ... they may be smart, but they don't have good sense."
— "Bob" to the Senate Subcommittee, 1956

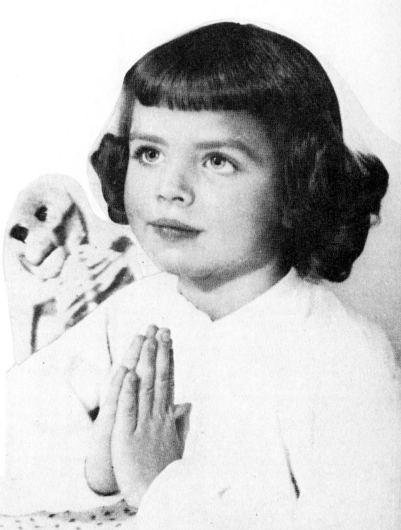

Dear Querent into the profundities of
This Twisted Randomness We Call Reality:

"IS THIS SOME KIND OF JOKE?"

Well, if you thought this Church was a joke, then you'll by God NEVER 'GET' THE PUNCHLINE.

Oh, we're the first to admit that we deliver far more laughs and yuks per dollar than Scientology, the Unification Church, or *any* other religious group, except *possibly* the Southern Baptists. But they are *for* **braindeath.** We are *against* braindeath. That would put a damn *bounty* on our heads except that we tread the thin tightwire of the jokes *just enough* not to have been covertly killed *or bought.* MY GOD, look what they did to any of our predecessors that kept *straight faces.*

No, this is NO joke, NO parody. Only the *foulness* of your programming keeps you from believing we have thousands of members, nationwide revivals, radio shows, and so on. But we do.

Not only are we not kidding, but we'll even *piss you off.* Indeed, that's our JOB — our CALLING — our MISSION. We're going to shock the hell out of every man, woman and child on this planet. It's a big job, and we only have until **1998** to do it. Still, it's enough time for the Church to be infiltrated and made *evil* if we don't watch ourselves.

YES — **BEWARE** — the biggest danger this Earth faces is *the Church of the SubGenius becoming POPULAR and turning it into one big CHEAP JOKE.* The Conspiracy has a way of doing that to damn near anything that comes near it — i.e., tries to make a buck. And when this **Industrial Church,** this **Final Organization,** takes full power over the entire globe in '98, it *just better not* have been tainted and cheapened by such Normal Armies as Pinks[1], Punks, False Prophets, Hippies, right-wing Nerds, obnoxious would-be hepcats, Nazis, Commies, Glorps[2] or, as the Prophet Hypercleats dubbed them, *Mal-Aligned Normals.*

The teachings of "Bob" are NOT universal. For the Pink at heart they simply won't work. For the evil they'll backfire. And they'll even be DAMN HARD TO FOLLOW for *ignorant* SubGeniuses.

But we must NOT water them down; the Conspiracy will assimilate them, twist them to fit Their plans, and sell them back to us in CRIPPLED, USELESS condition.

ONE BIG CHEAP JOKE

Rev. St. Candi Strecker

UNBELIEVABLE

No, only the truly abnormal, those who are abnormal *inside,* in their eternal, ungainly *souls,* not *just* the maladjusted, ONLY THESE must wield the relentless POWER of "BOB" on July 5, 1998, **X-Day,** when the Angelic Host from Planet X descend in glory and terror.

1. PINKS: (Colloq) Slang corruption of the formal SubGenius derogatory term PINK BOYS, meaning any sheeplike status-quo normalcy dupe, living in terror of making his or her own decisions, usually possessed of an unusually 'blank' facial expression, characterized by mental temerity masked by physical self-assurance. Term does not refer to skin color, sexual identity or proclivities, or age, though it does derive from black slang for "suburban white man." What is "pink," in the SubGenius definition, is their outlook.

2. GLORPS: The same thing as Pinks, but even more consciously pro-Conspiracy. Typified by complacent suburbanites who don't mind chemical dumps as long as they're "across the tracks." The term derives from Arkansas SubGenius backwoods medical dialect, popularized by the head-launching musical group, *Doctors for "Bob."*

LIES

UNSPEAKABLE

Sensationalism is just the lure we use in order to communicate *in all sobriety* certain awful histories and a secret fate for the Earth so unspeakable that it may take several books to prepare you just to *read* it.

Because if you are reading this in the late 20th Century, EVERYTHING YOU KNOW REALLY *IS* WRONG. You are an uncivilized, ignorant, BARBARIC peasant that will be looked back upon by future generations with every bit as much pity as you regard the plague-ridden wretches of Downtown Medieval Europe.

LIES

Your "civilization" got off so heavily on the WRONG FOOT, is so far OFF THE TRACK, and will keep going SO FAR from where it is "meant" to be, that **YOU DON'T EVEN KNOW WHAT SLACK IS** and the only way you can reopen your primitive mind, your buried gene-memory of SLACK, is to roll up your sleeves and GET DOWN with "Bob." If you're worried about getting your hands dirty, DO NOT ENTER. If you want to keep thinking "science" is right, DROP THIS BOOK NOW.

UNBEARABLE!!

If you want to remain agnostic about The Forces, GET THE BOOK OUT OF YOUR HOUSE. If you don't like the cold, get out of the freezer.

If you are, say, a hopelessly intellectual Conspiracy dupe (or "JudgeHead") with just enough verbal skills to think this is "funny" but lacking the intuitive scar tissue that lets you see where it's ALL TOO REAL, then your naked, tame soul risks getting SCALDED by the white-hot Truth of "Bob." If you THINK you're a Christian, but AREN'T, then you're going to see DEMONS in this book. Your belief system is paranoid, so it whips up *reasons* for paranoia.

You see what you want to see.

So you have to pay to know what you think. You pay Them.

They've got you so closed off from what you're REALLY SEEING, and have made your most instinctive hopes and desires seem so "imposible" or "impractical" in the **quote** "real world" **unquote**, that you're still looking where *they're* pointing rather than *just looking around.* You can SEE what CAN lie ahead if you'll *just slow down.*

Don't pay them to know what you really think. **Pay "Bob."** It's *much cheaper.* Besides, you owe "Bob" a living. But then, the entire WORLD owes YOU a living. **YOU ARE OWED SLACK.**

YEAH, BUT . . .

Right. You want to know, **"JUST EXACTLY WHAT *IS* THIS CHURCH OF THE SUBGENIUS?"** That question is asked a thousand times a day, every day, somewhere. And it's a good thing, because that's the most pertinent question *to* ask in this modern age.

There is no description. Words do not suffice; one must **"SEE."** We let you see a little at a time until you are led *gradually* to TOTAL CLARITY. It is **the Nameless Mission.**[3] The true mission is always nameless. To name it is to doom it . . . to alert the enemy.

And SLACK is what you want. SLACK is what you need. As the Pope of All New York[4] told the multitudes,

"With the FULLNESS of Slack a CHANGE will come;
Slackness will ENTER your life, Slackness will MAKE YOU SEE,
Slackness will SET YOU *FREE!*
Slackness IS! Slackness LIVES,
Slackness WAITS FOR YOU and YEAH! send $20."

Slack is what was *taken away;* Slack is what "Bob" gives BACK.

That's as simple as we can ever make it. From here it just spirals off into stormier and stormier complications but in the very MIDST of that storm there are two anchors you can always get back to, and those are "Bob" and Slack.

Now, you do not just sit and wait for Slack. You do not "work" at it either. This is an *exact science* of ways to achieve Slack through **"seeing."**

You will be taught by someone you can trust completely. By "Bob."

The fact that you have gotten *this* far — procuring this Book — indicates that you haven't been completely "asleep." You haven't been totally taken in by Them. Not yet.

But they can still trick you. As bait they feed you *too much* of the *wrong kind* of Slack — the **FALSE SLACK** of **the Conspiracy.**

The "Conspiracy" is **Them.** It was *They* who took away your real Slack.

Them.

THE SUBGENIUS® MUST HAVE SLACK!!

Doug Smith

But as the million-legged Church crawls around inside your cranium, there is one point it keeps returning to. It is the very point *of* the Church. The point is **"Bob."**

"Bob" is, was, and ever shall be, "Bob" is you, "Bob" is me, "Bob" is the Kama Sutra, the Id, the light that glows in the heart and mind of EVERY free-thinking SubGenius. And "Bob" is a man.

It's "Bob."

It always comes down to that.

Because **"Bob" is SLACK.**

3. THE NAMELESS MISSION: named by Puzzling Evidence, an anti-Conspiracy intelligence agency originating from a secret base somewhere on the West Coast and spreading out to influence all Sub-Geniusdom, militarily, for better or worse. Keepers of the Archives of the Ears of Unibrow. Commander-in-Chief Well Manhead, Disemboweler of Conspiracies Nankar Phlege, & Security Officer Sensitive Leaf have been assigned to act as impartial Arbiters of Justice for the SubGenius Foundation in case Dallas is nuked.

YOU are not one of Them, and never were, not even when They made you *want* to be. In fact, that's *why* They wanted *your* Slack. It's why you *had* Slack in the first place.

They did manage to steal most of your Slack. But they obviously haven't got it *all,* and they haven't got "Bob," and as long as there is **ONE FREE MAN** among us their system cannot be complete, because it is by nature a closed system, and if we can *keep* their system incomplete, it will close down of its own accord. By Their own Law. Their **Law of Normalcy.**

Yes. They wanted you to at least *want* to be "Normal." Well, you may *look* normal. You may *act* normal. But you *aren't* normal. **YOU JUST AREN'T NORMAL.**

And it is the POWER of your abnormality that saves you,

4. The Pope is the Rev. Dr. Dr. (Mr. M.D.) David N. Meyer, III, D.D., B.B.T., who holds his revivals ONLY in the evillest, most lucrative New York night clubs. Performs healings by sheer vocal intensity alone.

that causes their system not to have a *place* for you, that makes you a SubGenius.

The Conspiracy system burns humans as fuel. SubGeniuses aren't humans. They gum up the works.

If you're a human you've read too far. **CLOSE THE BOOK!**

Joe Schwind

"There's a whole market, a type of person there's no word for. I want 'SubGenius' to be that word."

—"Bob" on Board Room Tape Number 668, Verse 17.

You may have heard the term "SubGenius" sometime before, but you might not be able to *quite* put your finger on it —almost as if it were some dim racial memory, some archetype from Neanderthal times. That may very well be the case.

Now, the Church was not founded until 1953. And it was 1979 before Dobbs created **The SubGenius Foundation** as a vehicle to bring the teachings to the public. But SubGeniuses have always existed. . . even before Dobbs. In all the cradles of civilization — Sumeria, Egypt, Atlantis — clues have been found which prove the existence of the Conspiracy and of the SubGenii who fought to subdue it.[5]

The wisdom of those ancient SubGeniuses was never lost. Carried down by secret oral traditions, it lies latent in many living people, waiting only to be triggered by the Abnormality Revolution. Perhaps, even as you read this, you can feel those ancestral powers and arcane memories surging up from within your dankest brain gutters.

Ask yourself — don't you feel different at this exact moment than you ever did before? Isn't it because you feel some vague but momentous force emanating from this very piece of paper?

You didn't just wander into a bookstore and happen to notice this Book. You were *led* to us, and we to you, by powers much greater than Man and yet, seemingly, more random than Fate. But the ways of the great Manipulator in Space, **Jehovah-1,** only *appear* random. YES! Our paths crossed because it was *planned* — plotted out aeons ago, by alien minds more bizzare than your wildest nightmares, as part of a "WorkNet:" a cosmic scheme woven into such a complex web that not just human history but the *fabric of cause-and-effect themselves* was dis-

5. For more on prehuman SubGenius history, see Ludwig Prinn's shunned *De Vermis Mysteriis,* and *The Babylonica* of the diabolical Hermes Mortius, if you can find the three or four existing copies.

rupted. **FACE IT** — the very fact of your eyes moving across *this* page at *this moment* is inevitably and subatomically **decreed.** You are locked into the machinations of a cosmic puppeteer who works your strings so skillfully you never knew they were there.

UNTIL NOW! The Church can't cut your strings — you wouldn't want us to, if you knew what they can mean for you —but we can show you where the strings are attached and how to 'sync up' with the Puppetteer. . . how to stay one jump ahead of the other puppets by *assisting* the Puppet Master: by following **the Path of Least Resistance.**

Remember, **Jehovah 1** — or **Wotan,** or **Shiva** or whatever you want to call Him — is not God. He might as well be, as far as we're concerned, because he has powers of creation and destruction that Man has mistakenly associated with God throughout history. He is merely a bit player in this vast Movie which God is apparently leaving unedited. Nevertheless, His galactic goals — it makes no difference what they are — can be achieved sooner if He hones a few special tools to aid in the task. As the trance dictation of Dobbs tells us, SubGeniuses *are those tools,* and Jehovah-1 *needs our help.*

In return, we Chosen are rewarded with **Slack** as He tips the scales of cause-and-effect in our favor. Indeed, WOTAN-1 can "cheat" your Karma for you, much like a tax expert greases your way through the I.R.S. *You can beat the system if you have the right connections.* The space god can literally make coincidents and accidents happen to favor *you.* Think what this means in the areas of love, sex, finances and social standing. It isn't *what* you know, it's *who* you know. "Luck" simply means being in the right place at the right time. If you pay Him enough lip service, JHVH-1 can 'fix it' so that you will constantly find yourself stumbling into that right place at just that right time. This "deal" is called The Covenant.

HOLISTIC HEROIN— PERFECTLY LEGAL!

SOUNDS CRAZY? YOU BET. The early Christians sounded so crazy to the Romans they were used as lion fodder. Modern-day Christians seem to have forgotten that; plenty of them would like to see *us* thrown to the bulldozers. Oh, sure, we blaspheme like crazy against the gods. But that's exactly *why* this is the first religious text in history that *doesn't* take "the Lord's Name" in *vain.* For once, there's a *reason.* **GOD HIM-SELF CUSSES!! He's MAD!** He's being falsely represented on Earth! Jehovah-1's pretentions would be bad enough, but now all these *human preachers* have gotten into the act, doling out notions of "right" and "wrong" as if their peabrains could even BEGIN to sort such things out. They've cornered the market and set things up so that enlightenment in Their churches consists of four basic stages, each more tortuous than the last, and when some poor devil finally does get Illuminated he just reenters the world and goes back to basically normal behavior.

SubGeniuses are *born* enlightened and so may remain in the world, "acting normal" (it's all relative). They already KNOW the Big Secret of most Mystery Schools: that "divine ecstasy" is arrived at *just as easily* with a backrub, or a good screw, as it is through 20 years of ascetic self-flogging in a cave — at least, AS LONG AS THERE IS SLACK.

By now, the average False Christian reader will assume that this whole Church is the Devil's work. But we're much too unpopular for the Devil. He's strictly big time and doesn't mess with marked underdogs like us. He uses those already in seats of power. The power of the SubGenius is that WE DON'T NEED POWER. **We don't even need brains.** We have "Bob," we have a Deal with JHVH-1, we have our own capacity to **blunder creatively.** We're too *disorganized* for the Devil. If he's anywhere, he's where you least expect him.

We may attack your beliefs. But only those who believe blindly, greedily or half-heartedly will be bothered by our brand of mockery. To question their beliefs threatens them; it makes a secret part of them *ashamed*, and they get riled up and start smiting.

Of course, SHEER STUPID HATE isn't the only thing that keeps people away from the SubGenius Church. You may simply have more **important** things to spend your time and money on — things like albums, going to the movies, a new tape deck for your car — things you'd much rather possess than, oh, say, life after death, reincarnality, psychic powers, immortality, invisibility, nirvana, communication with Higher Intelligences, SLACK, and so on. If those things are meaningless to you, by all means just give this Book to someone else. We're sorry you even bothered.

You see, we're not trying to sell this to *everybody*. There are many we don't *want*, and there are plenty we *can't* save because it's *too late*. Hard-sell recruitment for this Church is too much trouble to bother with, because by definition **true SubGenii are not "Joiners."** They're rightfully suspicious of herds. They don't want to be "members" of any organization. It's a miracle that we've gotten *this* far. Between the cult's tendency towards

secrecy and the one Law that the laws change from minute to minute, it's not surprising that there's no man-on-the-street soliciting and prosyletizing. Even our biggest revivals are spur-of-the-moment, bacchanalian brawl-party affairs. The telephone is used far more than the altar.

Because of demand From you ... We Now Offer "STYLE OF THE MONTH CLUB"

CAN'T QUITE PUT YOUR FINGER ON IT? Well, divine obfuscation has a purpose.

> "In order to experience this correctly, you have to be smarter than your normal self. In order to become that way you must first experience this correctly. Thus we screen out those False Prophets who would be wrongly Illuminated. The knowledge must not be abused."
> Iwade Stanglings, 1891

Wotan works in mysterious ways, and this serves to keep the unattuned out of His business. The only way you're going to get truly, metaphysically high off this material is to snort *between* the lines. (But what you read between the lines must be taken *literally*. DO NOT read your own message into it. **There is only one true interpretation.**)

Swami Satellite Weavers

WITH APOLOGIES TO CLIFFORD HARPER

"BOB" IS NOT A FAN CLUB

Most people totally misunderstand the term, "**SubGenius.**" Look at the word. What does it mean?

It means NOTHING! It's utterly ambiguous. All-purpose. It sure as hell doesn't mean "just below genius level." To "Bob" and his mighty friends in The Council of None, one happy idiot is worth far more than ten A-bomb-inventing geniuses. We throw most so-called "geniuses" OUT. They're too nervous, they take themselves too seriously, they're *snide*. They do not truly 'know' Slack.

Praise "Bob," there are as many idiot SubGenii as "smart" ones. Most prevalent, however, are *smart-asses*. It isn't *brains,* but an intuitive, anti-Pink, anti-cute **Attitude Mutation.** The Conspiracy has proved that you can have "high intelligence" but still not be able to *think*.

No, yes, SubGeniuses are merely The Chosen People — the class which cannot be classified, those who are *different* not only from others but from *each other*. **If any two are the same, ONE MUST GO!** We band together only for *strength,* and only temporarily. The Conspiracy used to KILL people who displayed SubGenius traits. Thanks to the countless martyred evo-and devolution cults that paved the way, nowadays you're merely penalized *financially, socially* and *sexually* for weirdness. But at least we can come out and admit that there *are* people mutating ahead, and they are **US**; and, because mutation is so unpredictable, there will inevitably be unguessed other steps *beyond* SubGenius . . . but only if WE fulfill our genetic DESTINY.

Ultimately, it isn't Smart Vs. Stupid or Cool Vs. Uncool, but **The Good Guys Vs. The Bad Guys.** The free men against the robber barons. Frankenstein's Monster against the Villagers. Of course, it's *our* definition of "Good Guys," so if we aren't careful we'll end up as a bunch of Hitlers instead of Robin Hoods.

So BEWARE — THERE MUST BE *NO* STEREOTYPES. Not all SubGenii *act* and *look* weird. Many must encase their Weird Thoughts inside a Guise of Normalcy just to survive and infiltrate. Why, some of the main Saints of the Church *look* just as Pink as the day they were born. Some have had to become so

intensely, weirdly "normal" that they come full circle to achieve High Unpredictability, ripping their hearts out for "Bob" and stomping them into the floor, kicking the remnants off their bloody boots so that they can then do the same to a million unsuspecting Con-Dupes, **AIIEEEE!**

?SEE HOW EASY IT IS?

The ones to be avoided — yet the hardest to get rid of — are those who behave as weirdly as possible but are really insecure closet Normals, doing it only for attention from the opposite sex or something equally inconsequential. SubGeniuses are not just the super-cool. Why, EVEN CHRISTIANS can be Sub-Geniuses, believe it or not. "Wide-open-minded" sure doesn't mean Punk or "New Wave" or Liberal; that's all fashion slavery financed by Them. The hippies were easy enough to buy. They sold *their* cultural fringe to the Normals *cheap!* And soon the norms will consider *us* fashionable. That's why we owe NO loyalty to Right Wave, New Wing, or anyone else. We must *transcend style* through *nonstop style metamorphosis*. The Sub-subculture must always be *one step beyond cool*.

You think that's *easy*? Although the publishing of this Book is a key event in Dobbs Prophecy leading to the tumping of the Con's Foundations, it nevertheless will produce the first sickening wave of "Token SubGeniuses" or "Bobbies." You will see "Bob" bumperstickers and T-shirts on the cars and torsos of Pink Boys. As Dobbs said in a letter to L. Ron Hubbard, **"Sure, they're Pink, but their money is *green*."** Still, this means that the *real* Church of the SubGenius will always remain a secret society. There will always be that massive public face, but when the time comes the *true* cult will disappear and come back under another name.

The problem is that although Abnormals are the only truly "free" bipeds, they often don't know just how FREE THEY ARE. They take it for granted too easily; they fall into ruts. **Being *of "Bob"* doesn't mean you have to identify with a guy with a pipe and a shit-eating "I know more than you do" dog-grin all over his homogenized face.** In fact, if you aren't *already* sick and tired of the buzzwords "Slack," "Pinks," and, yes, even "Bob," then by god YOU have a PROBLEM and had better start looking for a new escape route.

While this pith-ridden religion may be perfect for quote-heavy persons like college students, it's *risky* for them too. It can turn whole tribes of them into dogma-replaying assholes. Ask yourself: did you buy this book because of fear   group pressure? If so, STOP READING NOW. You will injure yourself with this material; you'll use it as a high-faluting excuse to become infantile to the point of senility. We KNOW the power of the Dobbs. We've seen it happen, *all too often.*

A major secret that "Bob" learned from the Conspiracy is that deep down inside, everyone, even the SubGenius, craves authority. It's from having *parents.* But a SubGenius short-circuits this urge. He appoints *himself* Pope or Raja or something, and he *believes* it. But it's easy to *fake* that belief, even to yourself.

Therefore, in his Church our "Bob" has included many built-in Alienation Devices to prevent false Pink Interpretation while encouraging the *real, down home* SubGenii to start their *own* damn religions. **"Bob" is not a fan club.** The Teachings constantly contradict each other and yet remain equally true and false. Dobbs makes outright worship impossible by suddenly, unexpectedly changing the *basic dogma* just to forcibly **"disconnect"** the mindless zombie-in-a-rut. The confusing Church deliberately pulls the rug from under the preconceptions of "Follower" types, thus separating the wheat from the chaff. It uses Shock Value; we're often, praise Dobbs, **too sardonic** for those smug hip ones who thought they were already as sardonic as you can get.

The sacred rule of **"KILL BOB"** and the related doctrine of **"OR KILL ME"**[6] are two of the main built-in fuse breakers designed to prevent the ego-overloading that eventually gelds other faiths. They are reminders of the Church's promise that it will, in the long run, accept NO SUBSTITUTE for SLACK.

There is a Hierarchy of various flamboyant characters in the upper echelons of the Church, which, despite your liberal programming, is how it should be. However, thank God, "Bob" is the only real "star." In this society, stardom destroys. It subverts and it waters down. But "Bob" is immune to that, which is why he is so incomprehensibly important. He gave his precious obscurity for his charismatic but susceptible Priesthood, to deliver them from temptation.

Thus you are **ON YOUR OWN.** It's between you and "Bob." Just remember, this is the religion that canonizes, bribes, and enslackens its most REBELLIOUS HERETICS and CHEATS those who presume to be its most DEVOTED MONKS. Those who **'Kill "Bob" '** always return to the fold triumphant, CHANGED from pupils to Teachers.

We can't stop ninnies from buying the Word of Dobbs, nor can we prevent *you* from spreading a watered-down version of *yourself* in our name. All we can do is warn you: **DON'T BE A "BOBBIE."** The curse will fall on YOU. As Rev. Emile O'Day told the poor wretch who lay in the hospital bed with radiation burns from trying to smoke the True Pipe, **"A little Dobbs'll do you."**

Yes, the love of "Bob" can *kill Normals.* "Bob" is *too good* for them . . . and too **baaaad** for them. (For this reason we urge you not to leave this Book lying around your house for the uninitiated to see, unless of course you have mastered the impossible art of "explaining" the Church and are eager to challenge a diseased, superstitious world. Because of the potentially dan-

---

6. Both key Death Requests were discovered by *Doctors for "Bob."* They are the two most *unsettling* answers to stupid demands made by Pinks; they are also the only two steps to rebirth available to modern Seekers.

HOW CAN YOU EVEN BE READING THIS?

gerous **Power Shell** that each copy of The Book possesses, we suggest you keep it in the most holy and private sanctuary in your home, which is usually the Chamber of Excremeditation or bathroom. There, at the Throne of your own Holy of Holies, you and the Spirit of "Bob" can be alone together, safe from Conspiracy distractions.)

Once the wrong kind of person gets into the Church, it's torturous business getting them out. The power of SubGenius is unarguable, and they keep coming back for more and more no matter how much abuse and humiliation we heap on them. Anyone who gets heavily into the cult finds his Luck Plane suddenly *leaping out at him.* And the **coincidence level** . . . "Bob" is everywhere, friend, and at times it *can be weird.* Once an entire, all-new Church Pamphlet just materialized in the dead of night, burned right onto the plates of the printing press; the machine turned itself on and in the morning we found 10,000 new booklets sitting there along with the glowing heel of "Bob's" shoe.

Obviously, you don't want irresponsible people tangling with such forces.

So how does one *know*? How can one tell whether his friends are ready to walk the Path of "Bob?" Surely not just by the Dobbs T-shirts they wear . . .

If you yourself are Pink, you'll never really be able to tell. But if you are a true Child of "Bob," you'll soon be able to '*whiff-read*' or intuit whether another is for real or not by his . . . by his . . . Well, there's no human word that describes the 'personality-within-a-personality' as the SubGenius recognizes it.

> **"If you haven't been there, I can't tell you how to get there. But if you *have* been there, I can show you how to *stay* there." — Dobbs, in 1965 Sales Lecture**

One does not 'become' a SubGenius. If you haven't already been liberated from false sanity, you never will be.

If this begins to sound like empty promises, it's because you have no *faith.* You are of this faithless generation that demands *proof* of miracles. Oh, look to your heart, friend. Is that not the only source of truth for you? Can you not see the glowing core of **Bulldada** that shines within each latent SubGenius, just waiting for the right stimulus to EXPLODE?

To offer "proof" would be to insult the Isness of "Bob;" indeed, concrete evidence would deny *you* the great Test of Faith that "Bob" demands. If you believe, it will work. If you secretly scoff, it will fail you — or, rather, **you will fail the universe.** Those who demand logical scientific proof of Dobbs' good-luck power will never understand. They are permanently "asleep." We call them **"Gimme-Bobs"** and the True SubGenius can have no pity on them (particularly because they are the least likely to donate money to the Church). Ours is a ferocity of faith that can move spoons or bend mountains, depending on the degree of *developed fanaticism.*

Yes, to some extent this *is* like deliberately going insane. So what? That's what all gurus, followers, hobbyists, drug users and other seekers are after. HELL, the reason "Bob's" Sacred Luck works is because it *is crazy.* **This is *magic* — REAL MAGIC.**

Proof? We'll let others provide that. Two years from now you'll be trying to *escape* those who would burn your ears off yabbering their rapid-fire tales of miracles since they "found Dobbs." (Actually, no one *finds* Dobbs; Dobbs himself does the selecting. If you were not born naturally *Of "Bob"* then your ignorance is permanent. It's the indefinable, ineffable Essence of the Eitherness of **The Dobbs**.)

If you have no faith, it is because you don't own yourself.

You let someone else decide how you're going to get screwed.

Decide for *yourself* how you're going to get screwed. SOME WAYS ARE FUN.

DON'T MISS OUT EVOLVE!

If, because we seem to preach that everyone is going to get screwed no matter what, we seem like *total cynics* to you, you're WAY OFF. If we were that cynical, do you think we would put our literal asses on the line, dangling our "sins" in front of the Conspiracy? We wouldn't do it if we didn't think there was HOPE. We *know* America is still worth saving. We *know* enough people out there will understand this to make us rich.

When the Xists arrive in their illusory ships of light, and after the 3rd, 4th and 5th Comings, this planet will no longer belong to the humans OR the SubGeniuses. That puts this *beyond* politics and religion; it points out that an entire *mind-set* has to be erased.

Idiots think politics can supply an answer. Bullshit. Politics are abstract constructions: false, oversimplified coloring-book versions of life. They can't have any effective bearing on your concrete daily grind; they're just different ways of looking at the same things. We want to stop looking at those things entirely. They've become sterile and ineffectual because they long ago became *rote activity* conditioned into a society that was moving too fast for its own good. We're like the wheels of a bogged-down car, spinning deeper and deeper into the mud as our panic at finding ourselves stuck increases. To get OUT, we must SLOW DOWN. If we calm ourselves, step out of the car and look around for some old flat rock that just *happens* to make a perfect ramp for our wheels, we can stick that sucker down there, climb back in, and *gently* rock the car *back and forth* until we pop right out of the rut.

Thanks to aeons-tested Conspiracy False Slack programs, however, most people, when faced with trouble, spend more of their time abjectly staring at the problem than looking *away* from it for the *obvious solutions* that are everywhere. Now, we can't do anything about people who are born without imagination. But we can sure as hell KICK ASS on those who are just too lazy — *or too harried* — to *use* it. They're sitting there letting their most precious quality *rot* when they should be sitting there *pumping iron* with it. GOOD GOD, it's not like we're asking them to *get up*. We just don't want "getting up" to be *outlawed*.

We don't need to know what kind of government we'll replace the Conspiracy with. Our forefathers fought for independence *first* and then sat down to figure out exactly what the "United States" was going to be. In their primitive way, they tried to opt for *less government*. We should know by now that the next step is NO GOVERNMENT **except by the laws of SLACK.** (Con-infiltrated 'Anarchist' political groups are STILL POLITICAL.) Politics is a dead end. **Don't revise the rule book —throw it out.**

A couple of decades back, we'd have been hung for saying things like that. But today, in the 1980's, we'll make a million dollars off of it.

That, perhaps as much as anything else, indicates the depths to which this nation has sunk.

This is a crooked and perverse nation, friend. People are more worried about economy than ecology. JESUS! The lack of money makes life difficult, alright, but the presence of radiation and deathkulture chemicals is the very antithesis of *life itself* . . . and people run around arguing about the price of god damn pantyhose.

One thing we MUST prevent, therefore, is letting the Church become a soporific, a "drug" that lets us *accept* the death of all life on Earth. Yeah, THAT'S funny, HA HA! This better not become some god-awful **End Times PORN** for those who can only "get off" on fear-and-laughter. The Church should make it easier to conceive of the humans' inconceivable threat to themselves, but ONLY IF THAT MAKES US DO SOMETHING ABOUT IT.

THAT is the whole point.

Our twisted Hell Shit that all those poor saps send off a dollar for has to do more than merely put an uglier slant on what started out ugly enough. SLACK? YEAH, you'll laugh all the way to the fully-equipped survival shelter when "Bob" lets you in on the joke.

"Bob" can handle the Aliens, but we must police ourselves.

For: LOOK what the Conspiracy has done to 95% of your heroes, your religious leaders, your rock stars, all your once-faves. It has taken them and hammered them into the ground with promotion and money they know not how to *spend*; it broils their brains in TV lights and saps from them all time needed for their true calling while turning them into mere self-parodies. It starts with the leader and from there infects the hierarchy, then the followers . . . ultimately, the planet itself.

EEEYAH! Oh "Bob" we now pray to know what we really think and that you prevent us from turning your sweet name into some **jargon-infested in-joke.** Spare us thy servants from, uh, *complete* temptation and deliver us from Pop Acceptance yet somehow let us keep turning a profit that we may continue to **SPREAD THY SEED IN RIGHTEOUSNESS,**

Amen. Without remorse.

CHAPTER 2
THE MIRACLE OF "BOB'S" TYRANNY
AND THE ALCHEMY OF SALES

"And though I may not Comprehend, I know my God is Good."

— Anon.

"He ain't no man . . . He ain't no god . . . I don't wanna walk the path that "Bob" trod . . . "

— prayer of St. Janor the Hypercleats

"Ph'nglui mglw'nafh "BOB" D'lyeh* Wgah'nagl Dhobbz f'htagn." ("In his Great Easy Chair at D'lyeh, Dread Dobbs lays Smoking.")
— one of the Dhol Chants for raising the Elder Gods, from *Incubustum Mysteris des Helle,* Sir Colin Anton Wilson, 1706

"I want my monkey brains well done!"

— "Bob" to cook at Dobbstown, Malaysia

CAN YOU AFFORD TO IGNORE THIS?

Individually, each of us is buffeted by social tidal waves, generally powerless except to create peaceful, temporary islands of Slack with her or his own self, kin, and buddies.

BUT. As one group, collectively acting and moving like one relentless Hydra *whose parts are not the same,* encircling the world in a monstrous belt of unpredictability, the world's SubGenii will be IMMUNE to the False Slack of the Pink Boys, and shall OVERCOME The Conspiracy. Our brains are too *well-worn,* too *smudged* and *stained* to be completely washed by their insidious "mind-cleaning" techniques.

We don't worry about The Conspiracy driving us crazy because we already ARE crazy. We don't worry about the New Depression reducing us to barbarism — SubGeniuses ARE barbarians no matter how rich or poor, smart or dumb, cultured or plain. Our precious 'bad attitude' sets us apart from the lackluster Others shuffling through their hundred million jobs. Oh, we have to slave away at jobs too, but the difference is we don't let the *job run us.* We seek something better — Something, in fact, for Nothing. That is our Grail, our Quest. Throughout history all Subgenii, individ-

ually or collectively, consciously or subconciously, have sought that perfect, pure, unbeatable **MONEY MAKING FORMULA** that will free mankind from its self-imposed Slacklessness.

And indeed, that relentless racial drive *has culminated, in this decade,* with That One True Magic Miracle Earning Equation Formula that can pander to *all* common denominators *without varying one iota* from the True Path, that will fetch for its masters the Treasures of Solomon, the Fountain of Youth, the Philosopher's Stone, the pot of gold at the end of the rainbow, and the Rocking Chair of Ultimate Slack ALL ROLLED INTO ONE.

Pope Meyer III phrased it this way while ranting to the masses at the 1981 World SubGenius Conclave:

"What TAKES AWAY your SLACK? PUSHY WAIT-RESSES!! ARROGANT CASHIERS!! INSENSITIVE EM-PLOYERS take AWAY your Slack. WithHOLDING Tax takes away your Slack. WHO GIVES YOU BACK YOUR SLACK? Tell me Children, *WHO GIVES YOU BACK YOUR SLACK?"*
It's "Bob." **IT IS "BOB."**

J.R. "Bob" Dobbs, the Living Slack Master of Mystick Sales Training, the Bridge between Heaven and Earth and Hell, the wordless Bobhead, the Naked Dobbs, All-Knowing, All-Prevailing, All-Just, All-True, All-None, ALL-ONE, DOBBS is the ONE TRUE WAY by which we may finally achieve that elusive SLACK which has been denied us.

Science and religion each prove totally different things, yet they both appear to be true. So, by divine logic, the answer must be "Bob." He IS his own self-fulfilling prophecy . . . his own best idea. During every instant of time he is simultaneously killed and reborn, perpetually rising from the ashes of his own self-consuming Flame of Truth which Lights the Path through the Illuminated Darkness of his Isness.[1]

A "60-million-year Cycle" will end in 1998; Dobbs sees the world entering a New Aeon which, *in a few years,* will bring more wondrous and miraculous change, and carnage, insanity and destruction, than all of mankind's history and prehistory before it!

"Bob" brings a *new destiny for America* — a time of cataclysmic economic change that will offer UNTOLD RICHES AND POWER to those "in the know" while billions of DESERVING CONSPIRACY DUPES *FRY* in Hell-on-Earth . . . Uncontrolled thinking, controlled by "Bob," will usher in a SPIRITUAL REBIRTH and a cascade of *astounding mysteries, supernatural riches,* and a restoration of *lost psychic abilities* that will totally transform the lives of those who DARE to seek them and pay for them. That's right — you're *lucky* to live in the End Times.

For only nowadays does Man have access to the uncut truth of JHVH-1's Prime Ordinances. "WHAT IS THE LAW? Not to make laws, that is the First Law; Are We Not Men?"[2]

In the early Forties an industrious young American salesman, while working late one night on an experimental television of his own design, was abruptly *Removed* and translated astrally across the yawning gulfs of space and time to the very '**IDGE**' of JHVH-1 HIMSELF! While his body lay thrashing at home in a seizure-like trance, the young man's consciousness took the brunt of the first brain-buffeting **communionications** of countless to come from the alien Yahweh: awesome gland-curdling pronouncements which now form the sacred **Prescriptures** of the Church.

THE MYSTIC PATH TO ABUNDANCE

We call this milestone in Man's mined path to Slack **The Divine Emaculation of J.R. "Bob" Dobbs.** It transformed him overnight into history's sexiest, most sensational Religious Leader and gave him the spiritual know-how to handle both the "curves" — *and* The Conspiracy! From suave ladies' man (and men's man) to hard-as-nails fighter, he takes daily threats to his life with raw, cold courage and can mix it with the best and worst of rival cult leaders.

Although the least scrutable or approachable of all SubGenii — and there is some debate whether he even *is* one — he is by far the most frequently invoked of all our uncountable "**Short Duration Personal Saviors.**" While he doubtless would prefer to remain an anonymous executive shunning publicity or recognition, he is nonetheless our basic model, the Archetypal Sub Genius who set the "anti-pattern" of random conduct we all now follow . . . if you can call that 'following'. His are the divine *defects* and *failures* which we devotedly preserve, twist and distort for future generations. Yet he remains a mystery man; the only photos of him that exist are culled from old two-bit magazine ads for which he modeled, or grainy frame blow-ups from Grade Z monster movies in which he played bit parts. We are forever in search of historic Dobbs.

Dobbs is one of those rare Adepts who walks the Earth every few centuries, those Ascended Masters who "**see**" in a far greater way and can unravel the other wavelengths of overlapping realities, treading aether in the cosmic mind-oceans of Higher Mentalities. As a trance medium he is unparalleled, able to '**Spout**' at will the messages beamed into his head from vast numbers of

---

1. You talk like this, people think you're crazy. But when they see it WORK —when your success snowballs INSTANTLY — when your very COOLNESS becomes intoxicating to them . . . well, *you'll* see.

2. The "What Is The Law?" cycle is a holy chant from JHVH-1's **Revelation X.** It was worked subliminally into the film, *Island of Lost Yeti Women* (Smith Films, 1965).

discorporate spirits, demons, dear departed, crazed saints, mystics and conquerors of ancient history (including **Cerinthus the Mad Gnostic,** actual author of the Book of Revelation!), alien space intelligences and god-like entities from all seven circles of the Beforelife, and — most crucial of all — from JHVH-1 Himself. All share the same basic message: that there is a world beyond this silly material plane, a vast power grid bearing the energy pattern of all that has ever happened and ever will happen — *The Skor.* While we are all of the essence of this great reality-file, only a few can open and close its drawers as they please. "Bob" is one of those gifted few, and as "Sleeping Reporter" he divulges to us Initiates what ancient wisdoms we must know to be freed from the million minor irritations and compulsive frettings that plague us daily and short-circuit the pre-Atlantean psi-biotic energy shafts that would otherwise feed us Slack. YES! The Word of "Bob" brings **INSTANT GOOD LUCK** (both material and hallucinatory); it SLAPS the scales of social norms from our eyes; it lets us channel the glorious abnormalities of the Universe and *transcend* the dull, earthly blunderings we call "life" on this Planet of the Clocks. **Time Control is OURS!**

GIFTED READER AND ADVISOR!

"Bob" has a great *power* which even the Pope of the Vatican envies: the power to fail, and fail repeatedly. Yes, "Bob" is FALLIBLE — as fully, humanly fallible as is *superhumanly* possible. And, either despite or because of his infrahuman mediumship, he possesses one single failing above and beyond all his other shortcomings: his most holy and all-inclusive *FOLLIES,* which embody in some cheaply symbolic way all the foibles of the all-too-human race. Where these would be crippling to another person, in Dobbs they loom stranger-than-life and make him a very "MICROCOSM" encapsulating every imperfection of the so-called 'human condition.' His beautifully expressive blunders and idiocies, his cleverly illustrative errors and inadvertencies, are perhaps more sacrosanct, more deserving of analization than even his hallowed salesmanship. He has every weakness in the

book — including his rash willingness to carry the battle for Slack ALL THE WAY.

He has one strength alone: his insane dedication to the Good Fight against the Dark Side and all the enemies of free enterprise, Sales, and WORLD SLACK.

Yes — "Bob" is human: lonely, isolated from his fellows by the importance of the Nameless Mission he's taken on. He sweats, bleeds, suffers, like anyone else. Perhaps this is his greatest appeal to some. For others, there's always the thought of "Bob" the lover — immaculately attired, debonair on the dance floor, instinctively understanding of their frailties, and passionately eager to comfort them. While salesmen know him as "the man who could sell anything," his 'Initiates' know him as just . . . "The Man."

No, he isn't *just* a man. He's *all men.* And he's ALL MAN to all women. And friends, when he married his Main Wife, **"Connie,"** he YES *merged* with her and became, *YES,* despite his great Steel Sceptor, ALL WOMEN.

For "BOB," my friend, "BOB" is a **SEX GOD.** "Bob," in fact, *IS SEX:* an all-encompassing sex that is the very In-ness and Surrounding-ness of the UNION of both the lingam *and* the yoni.[3]

And not just hetero sex — ALL SEX. "Bob" does not choose to fornicate — "Bob" as the Tool of WOTAN *has* to fornicate. And not just with women. Not just with men. With ANIMALS, with PLANTS, from a faithful oak tree in his back yard to the mighty whales of the briney deep; with THE VERY EARTH ITSELF! Yes, "Bob" copulates with the *ground!*

SEX AGAIN AND AGAIN

"Bob" is the REAL THING. He *came* to *refertilize* your sexual preconceptions, to make us ALL relive our reincarnality in the million polyverse combinations we once enjoyed. Sure, this Church *drips* with MACHISMO IRONY, with insanely overblown CAJONES. This religion isn't for the amalgamation of the sexes, no . . . but it sure as hell *is* for the divine UNION of them. ALL of them.

3. This information is airbrushed into the hairdos of the members of the band DEVO on the cover of their fourth album, and is backtracked into the disco 'muzak' of the Glassmadness album, *Do the Sexy "Bob."*

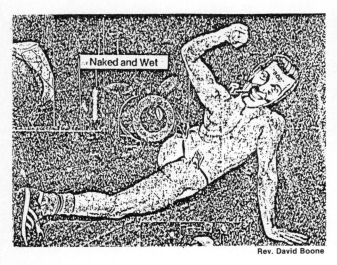

Rev. David Boone

Strangely enough, none of "Bob's" words or deeds are particularly spectacular. Their holiness lies in their nondescript but inviolable triviality. As he once 'Spouted' in his *Devotia Moderna de Infomania,* **"The stupider it looks, the more important it probably is."** We try to live this Holy Writ.

Dobbs, unlike the Con, does not confuse you with "facts." There ARE no "facts" to the enlightened man. To one trained by "Bob," Truth can be found in a potato. Since his Emaculation, Dobbs has known that *Slack* ultimately comes first, before all else . . . even Truth. This is an important difference between our Church and all others. Lesser religions demand that you 'direct your will' and 'focus your energies.' Dobbs preaches the opposite: although you must know of your Power to begin with, the real key is to **NOT TRY.** For in the purity of *the Contradiction of Trying Not to Try,* you actually make the Greatest of Attempts and thus find a perfectly palpable, humanly graspable Punchline to The Joke of Life . . . or at least a good a one as you'll find in your earthly, creaturely life. "Bob" did not achieve Cosmic Oneness and Consciousnessless-ness on *purpose.* He was rudely *shoved* by the gods down the behavio-electric Path of Least Resistance.

TOMORROW IS OBSOLETE

Everything is easy for "Bob." Even his most hellish mission is like an everlasting holiday. What he *wants* to happen just *happens* to be what's *going* to happen, anyway. This can work for you, too,

if you will only want what "Bob" wants. You, like "Bob," would then be able to pack a lot of action into each day without doing a *damn thing.*

As mysteriously and profitably as he doles out his prophecies and cassette messages, he unfailingly — yet, *accidentally* — enrichens himself with material things using only the exaggerated human nature he was born with. Just as Jesus of Nazareth was a carpenter, so is "Bob" of *(NOT SHOWN HERE)* a salesman — the High Sales Man of the SubGenius.

SEX WORDS! BUY THIS!

A descendant of many great psychics, "Bob" began using his Gift for financial gain at age 6. He has since built up an immeasurably vast personal fortune in his many careers, especially as mind-breaker and Psychic Salesman for many governments and faceless international cartels. His unusual clientele has included the great, the near-great, the never-should-have-been-great, and the would-have-been-great-except-for-The-Conspiracy. He moves freely in the worlds of finance, entertainment, politics, espionage, and world manipulation. He has sold to Presidents, and he has sold to the Average Man. To the undead and to many, many Messiahs. He has sold bankers and workers, stars and extras, shieks and slaves. His first 13 Disciples were simple salesmen who had caught on to the supernatural aspect of his Sales Nature. He called these his "Fishers of Wallets."

"Bob" learned the secrets of The Conspiracy *from the Inside* and now he brings them to **us** — the ones who *should* have had

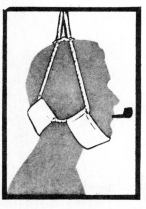

WHITE MAN...
BLACK MAN...
any Man!

1,000 CONVICTS *and a* Woman!

"A few more years of this new medium, and their minds will be ours."

them in the *first* place. And he has the wisdom to publish them in this *florid, overwritten, deeply meaningful and challengingly difficult-to-read* style to insure that ONLY YOU and a few choice others will comprehend and be privy to this secret knowledge that has controlled Mankind for ages — narrowing down the competition in the field of world conquest for *you!* "Bob" *knows* how cheated you feel, and his intimate association with alien beings makes *his* advice the only *safe* thing that can raise you up from your *mediocre past.*

ARE YOU READY? Sales — true sales, not the sick, impersonal 'advertising' of The Conspiracy — depends on a love of danger, of risk, of the exotic and bizarre. It's a willingness to *try anything* as well as a *lust* for the *truly strange* and, yes, the *strangely true.*

SKEPTICAL?
EAT THIS PAGE NOW

The Church of the SubGenius *is the sale,* the big PITCH, and when the *world buys it, you* get the commission . . . you and those oh, so few others sharp enough to be part of this great Sales Team.

But it's a race. We have to get to the customer, Earth, before that OTHER salesman does, from that OTHER company . . . the one with the bigger sales force, fancier placards, and the best 'people shapers' in the business.

But YOU have the *Magic Key.* You know the customer better, and you have a product that works: SLACK, which "the competition" *doesn't even believe exists* and couldn't understand anyway. Yes, YOU are onto the "Big Game" — with the "Big Gun" — and "Bob's" 'Eye-in-the-Pyramid Scheme' is JUST THE AMMO YOU'VE BEEN WAITING FOR.

ESOTERIC DOMINANCE
COMMAND

And "Bob" MAKES it *even easier still.* On *this* "Big Deal," the SALE is ALREADY CLINCHED! The customer — the world — HAS to buy, OR ELSE! It's either Slack from you, or Brand X slavery from The Conspiracy. It's a sure-fire, no-miss deal . . . because *this* sale, friend, is FATED AND DECREED BY WOTAN HIMSELF.

Oh, They have a powerful sales tool: the ignorance and venality of the customer. But you have "Bob." And you work for the winning company: **THE FORCES OF GOOD!**

Oh, yes. There *is* a Heaven, and you CAN BUY your way into it . . . and there's a Hell, but you CAN BUY your way out of it.

HELL is life on this planet without "Bob."

LOOK, and you will find "Bob" everywhere. Bob's Market, Bob's TV Repair, Captain Bob's Seafood, Dobbs Salvage Center, Dr. Dobbs' Freeway Love Clinics. His face and name enwrap the globe. He is at once unknowable, and yet, you have always known him. His million subliminal appearances in *ads* have formed a visual backdrop of your life.

The eye by which you see "Bob" is the same as the eye by which "Bob" sees you. He watches you *back* through those endless Dobbsheads. Your eye and "Bob's" are one and the same — one in seeing, one in knowing, one in loving, one in hating, One in Selling.

And **SLACK** is the Free Car Wash that comes with the fill-up of "Bob." He's the ultimate Good Guy, the Terrorist for Peace out to KICK ASS on the know-nothings who have HELD YOU DOWN. "Bob" IS the peace that SLACK hath MADE ALIVE; "Bob" is SLACK, EXTERNALIZED.

"Bob" is the still center of a turning world. He is the Angel of the Bottomless Pit, the Blood of the Lamb, the Paraclete of Coborca; "THE KEY TO THE GATEWAY *IS HIS PIPE.*"

"Bob" is the Fool of the Universe and THUS, the only place of ALL KNOWLEDGE; "Bob" is the meaning of the Word Without Meaning; therefore "Bob" is the One True Word.

"Bob" is war, but he is VICTORY without a BATTLE.

He is the laxative of the world and he is the Manna . . . he is the the Great Work that Sleeps, he is the Silence in the Noise, he is the Infinite Wheel of Earnings.

"Bob" is the Teaching for those who need not be Taught, and those who *must* be Taught cannot be taught "Bob." He is his own ultimate secret.

"Bob" is the Phoenix rising from the ashes of the Cleansing Fire of "Bob."

"Bob" is the Black Goat of the Woods with a Thousand Young.

"Bob" is Heaven's One True Policeman.

"Bob" is the gun and you are the bullet.

"Bob" is the Sucker who is reborn every minute, yet he is the Money which that Sucker Spends, and he is the Bank in which that Money is Locked.

"Bob" is companionship when there's no one there.

"Bob" is the ULTIMATE FRIEND, who will NEVER let you down.

"Bob" is the Dad you always KNEW you had. "Bob" is the SON every Mom KNOWS she gave birth to. "Bob" is the UNCLE who told you what "fuck" meant and "Bob" is the little sister you'll fight any bully to protect.

"Bob" is your Big Brother.

"Bob" is a rock,
"Bob" is a tree,
"Bob" is you
and **"Bob" IS: ("FILL IN THE BLANK")** . . . . .⁴

---

4.   From the SubGenius Hymnal of Glassmadness by famous glass musician James Erickson. Lyrics mutated telepathically by the Rev. D. Lee Lama.

WHENCE COMETH THE "BOB"

High in one of the reflectorized glass buildings of downtown Dallas is the Throne Office Headquarters of First FisTemple Lodge of the Church of the SubGenius — nerve center for all SubGenius missionary/mercenary activities. Here "Bob" Dobbs commands the grudging respect of his iron-jawed men. He's always in the front lines of even the most dangerous mission, bearing his envied **13013** rating — his license to SMITE the enemy with every trick weapon at his disposal . . . like his fabled Rocket Pipe, his Boomerang Pipe, his Smokescreen Pipe and the elusive Bobmobile.

With his inborn foolhardiness and his admitted weakness for cards and women, and iron-jawed men, he's not an office type and is rarely seen in the musty rooms of deskbound Scribes. After weeks of absence he'll suddenly show up, absorb his briefing almost absentmindedly, and abruptly head back to that battlefield where *no battle lines are drawn.* While he's gone, the Popes anxiously await news, good or bad, on "Bob's" one-man war against The Conspiracy. Across the desks of his staff daily pour microfilms, coded messages, tape recordings . . . and not a few love-notes from the ladies, which bring red even to the cheeks of his steely-eyed Sales Minister, **Dr. Philo Drummond.**

In a World Avatar's life, the totally unexpected is routine. For "Bob," performing his duty in exotic, faraway places, it becomes second nature.

Some call "Bob" immoral . . . some call him lucky. The simple truth: even a busy Living Master has his moments. And "Bob" has more than most.

But who IS this man "Bob"? What strange twist of fate brought him to this crossroads between eternity and the Now?

Dobbs loves to withold information from his followers, and some of the following was obtained by less-than-scientific means. Occasionally, we have perforce used the new "Psychic Journalism" so much in vogue today.

The exact time and place of the nativity of Dobbs is kept secret, of course, to prevent his astrological charts from being plotted . . . which, aside from his hair or fingernail clippings, would be ALL THEY'D NEED to get a fix on him with their Migraine Machines. However, we can reveal that he was born and raised somewhere in the Midwest during the Twenties. One Dobbs Nativity theory holds that he was a feral child, found in the wildnerness suckling a mother puma. This is most likely a myth and can probably be discounted as part of the smog of legend which surrounds this seemingly ageless man.

Nativity Scene by Rev. Bob Lee. Facing page: Magickal Image by Rev. G. Don Trubey.

N'Xlccx Dobbs

Dobbs

Xiuacha-Chi-
Xan M. Dobbs

wandering
milkman

J. R. "Bob" Dobbs

His father, an immigrant and descendant of the only Spanish Mayans — who had maintained a furtive, underground existence in Spain — ran a pharmacy. His partially anglicized name was *Xiuacha-Chi-Xan M. Dobbs,* and he apparently died in 1949 in an explosion while mixing chemicals in the back of the store.

"Bob's" mother, an American of Irish descent, was *Jane McBride Dobbs,* a relative of the Irish revolutionary hero Arthur McBride. Obviously, "Bob" doesn't resemble his father in the least, and this has given rise to Jane Dobbs' reputation as "The Divine Virgin." There is, however, no little evidence that a mysterious milkman, probably Jewish, was the true Dobbsdad. Although this man's identity is swathed in the mists of rumor, and Dobbs has gone to some pains to quash serious investigation, we nevertheless have good reason to assume that this wandering milkman furnished the true "Bob" gene. Another question that arises: was he even from Earth? The fact that most of these people were "undocumented aliens" makes research all the more difficult.

END OF CIVILIZATION, OR BIRTH OF A PERFECT BARBARISM??

"Bob's" two younger brothers do physically resemble Mr. Dobbs. They are the "Weak Brother," Rod, and the "Evil Brother," Judas J. "Jim" Dobbs. The former works in a canning factory in California and the latter founded the infamous **Cult of the Mystic Annihilation** — fortunately a short-lived fiasco.

"Bob's" ancient grandfather, *N'Xlccx Dobbs,* lived with the family and almost certainly influenced The Child "Bob" with his tales of the Spanish Mayan Underground and its struggles through 400 years of castigation. "Bob's" staid father, eager to 'fit in' in America, disliked the old man "filling the boy's head with revolutionary garbage and stinking Mayan occultism."

SOMEONE BIGGER WILL SAVE US

"Bob" grew up fighting the stigma of a Mayan dad. Other kids made cruel fun of that prognathus slopehead of fullblood Mayanry, and though Mr. Dobbs maintained dignified silence, little "Bobby" was in many a scrap, battling for his father's honor (it was shortly after receiving a blow to the head during one of these fights that "Bob" began experiencing precognitive visions). This troubled childhood had a telling effect on the sensitive youth, who became — thanks to the pharmacy's wares — a chronic alcoholic at age 6. It didn't affect his precocious salesmanship, though, and he made his first small fortune selling stolen prophylactics and pills to high school boys. This pipe-puffing tousle-headed lad was a world-worn veteran at age 7 —later, of course, to regain his long lost innocence: a child at age 40. He claims that when he gave up drinking, he lost his fortune and "had to come up with completely new sales techniques to regain it."

Even as a toddler, "Bob" had innumerable "invisible play-mates" which we can now recognize as various space and energy beings, both good and evil. Aided by his main Guardian Angel, *"Placeeboh,"* and perhaps by JHVH-1, the child *was* able to distinguish the difference. Nevertheless, the constant harassment by these entities surely contributed to his preschool alcoholism.

He also had an early gift for seeing auras on people, which helped him develop his key sales tool of identifying the "14 Types of Consumers."

Dobbs showed early leadership qualities. He formed his first "cult," the Ghost Riders Club, with friends at age 5. Age 6 saw the Doc Savage Club, based on the first pulp hero "Over Man." Age 7: The Girl Haters Club. Age 8: The Girl F---ers club. Age 9: The Bat Man Club (*before* Bat Man comics!).

By the time he reached high school, "Bob" had managed to acquire a law degree by mail, and secretly opened an office in a nearby town. However, he was disbarred after a valiant battle to return land rights to a local Indian tribe . . . probably Sioux. He is still in close contact with the medicine men of his tribe.

As a teen, despite his winning ways with the girls and his reknowned sports abilities, "Bob" was troubled by strange mental tensions and spiritual raptures involving dreams of indescribable landscapes and sonorous, alien voices ceaselessly intoning his name as if across the abyss of space. For a brief period he became a devout Christian and tried memorizing scriptures, but this only worsened the condition. It finally abated after his mysterious first

Mysterious "Boblike" person organized and led an expedition to plunder the ruins of Atlantis. Divining techniques employed a billiard-style Pipe. The leader vanished after the economic ruin of the expedition.

semester of college, which was spent at Miskatonic University in Arkham, Massachusetts.

That was his last brush with higher education. Spurning that path to knowledge, he joined a group of Sufis and also got involved in the Gurdjieff teachings . . . but he gave up on these as being "too complicated, too much work." He does still praise the Rosicrucians, but this is because he learned the lucrative mail-order-cult business from that fraternity. One secret doctrine that he admits having gleaned from these rival cults is that *any* numerical system works magic.

Around this time, he starred in his first film — an amateur production called JILTED AGAIN which was shot in the obscure 9.5mm format by a friend. This one-minute silent short depicts an abandoned bride crying at the altar, then cuts to a grinning "Bob" hopping the next train out of town. On the heels of this production came his first modeling jobs — a career that was to continue on and off for the next 20 years.

Just before World War II broke out, Dobbs and two pals —Bubba Smith and Dub Jones — formed an entirely unsanctified proto-SubGenius scam/religion strictly as a rip-off scheme. It fizzled miserably — "We made real idiots of ourselves" — but, ironically, it was shortly thereafter that he had his first *authentic* bout with JHVH-1 — his **Emaculation.**

This most critical episode in "Bob's" life is covered in the chapter on *The Prescriptures,* so we will bypass it for now.

The impact on "Bob" of being chosen as the Vessel, the Conduit for the Word of WOTAN was, at first, devastating. The physical aftereffects alone almost killed him. In his own words: "After you have a Vision like this, it's like a million hangovers at once. Your head feels like a flashbulb that's just been popped —warped burning plastic, twisted and blown out . . . too much energy blasting through at once. It ruins you for a long time . . . maybe forever." (From an interview in *Traveling Evangelist Magazine.*)

It goes without saying that "Bob" was not ruined forever. The next five years are the most mysterious of his life, however; they're certainly the least documented, and "Bob" himself refuses to discuss them. Apparently he spent much of this time in a state of awe and confusion, testing his newfound powers. It may well be that in doing so he *misused* them, which may account for his reticence regarding this period.[5] We do know that in 1943 he went to the U.S. Government with the intention of turning these amazing mystic abilities against the Nazi war machine.

DRAMATIC PHOTOS

It is a little-known fact that "Bob" was instrumental in the Allied victory. Most historians are entirely ignorant of Hitler's occult background as well. The Nazis were being manipulated, through Hitler, by secret Thule Society magicians, who were pawns of the Hollow Earth *dero* creatures, themselves tools of the Space Bankers. Everything Hitler did revolved around ancient Thule prophecies concerning an Aryan Atlantis.

Using his incredible powers of hypnotic suggestion (which he would in peacetime turn towards Sales), "Bob" infiltrated the Nazis by posing as the foretold "Son of Odin, The Purest of The Pure," who would supposedly help transform Germany into a New Atlantis under the "Northern Fathers," or Elder Gods. "Bob" worked his way up through the Reich hierarchy until he had gained the complete trust of Hitler himself.

The weird "Man in Black" that Hitler described in his writings was actually "Bob." Hitler said he had met "this New Man who is living among us... I was afraid in his presence." For good reason. "Bob" was feeding them all the wrong information. This accounts for the Fuhrer's terrible strategic blunders during the latter half of the War. "Bob" had Schickelgruber looking the other way when D-Day happened, and the tables were turned on the Axis.

(An interesting historical sidenote: while Dobbs was infiltrating the Nazis, the fatally wounded gangster Dutch Schultz lay on his deathbed, mumbling of "Bob" in his famous delirium. One of his ravings, transcribed by a police stenographer: "Yeah . . . "Bob's" gonna CRACK DOWN on the Chinaman's friends and Hitler's commander." The Chinaman? You guessed it — the same entities who were using Hitler and his saucer-riding pals in the Hollow Earth were also whispering into the ear of the young *Mao tse-Tung!*)

Winston Churchill said of Dobbs, in a page censored from his memoirs, " "Bob" is a riddle... wrapped in enigma."

5.   There was a spate of bizarre deaths throughout the area where Dobbs was then making his living as an encyclopedia salesman. Bodies were found with their heads *imploded* by some mysterious force. Most were laying near their front doors.

Proof of "Bob's" global empire is everywhere—even your local telephone directory. There are subsidiaries in your town...see for yourself!

After the War, Dobbs entered the phase of his career for which he is best known. Now understanding true Slack, and working always by *accident alone,* he began stumbling from one line of work to another, deliberately operating without any set plans whatsoever, and thus making a million dollars every time he *screwed up.* Just a few of these early businesses: selling "miracle paints;" aluminum siding; stocks and commodities; a roofing scam; a sex clinic; marriage counseling; debt collection; T-shirts; real estate . . . he also sold mail order businesses by mail, wrote the phrases on gumballs and valentine candies, designed Cracker Jack prizes, created a chain of Sex Novelty Vending Machines for service stations, ran a lottery, opened a private investigator's office, was a vanity publisher, and even invented countless non-essential household items that "made good ad copy." It was right after a stint as a carnival barker at the Wheel of Chance and the "freak show" tent that he moved simultaneously into his two true loves: Sales and Religion. (In the midst of all that, he still "found time" to serve a stint in jail for Mail Fraud, and also played pro football in the now-defunct Canadian League. Word has it that he used to score touchdowns "by mistake.")

MEDITATION AT THE WHEEL

In the 1950's, sales was the *best game to be in* and "Bob" was the *best at it.* As a salesman he moved from company to company — except when he started his own — and no matter what the product or service was, "Bob" broke all the records. He came into demand as a motivational lecturer, and his books on selling — all rather clumsily written, as "Bob" will be the first to admit — were best-sellers. The list of titles is impressive: LEARNING THROUGH PAIN (1952), SALES — THE BLACKEST ART (1952), SLEEPING FOR FITNESS (1954), $EX, $ALES, AND $UCCESS (1955), TENDERNESS OR TERRORISM? (1955), TIME CONSUMPTION FOR TIME CONTROL (1956), and his top-seller, ALL THINGS THAT SELL or THE BOOK OF ALL THINGS (1957).

"Bob's" biggest sale? FLOURIDE TO THE GOVERNMENT. This may disturb some of our readers. But little did the government know, flouride stimulates the **Foot Gland** (yes, the foot is actually a *gland*) so essential to our proper development once the Xists arrive. He did it for our own good — so *we'd* have a piece of the action too when the aliens start turning SubGeniuses into OverMen.

"Bob" also had considerable success with a number of homeopathic remedies he learned from his grandfather. Most were herbal medicines, but one large contraption which sold well combined a pyramid, an orgone accumulator and a hairdryer to create a box looking much like a Tidican, in which stress-ridden people were told to sit and sweat until they were purified. Happy users of the device raised a fruitless uproar when it was banned by the very Conspiracied A.M.A.

It was in 1955 that "Bob" had his lesser-known Second Major PreVision. Once again, a great deal of Divine Suffering was involved. But, where some other great cult leader might get crucified, leave it to "Bob" to come up with a shortcut — in this case, a **hernia operation.** So important is this event to Church dogma that devout followers sometimes display spontaneous hernia stigmata.

This Vision, in which Dobbs was treated *through blinding pain* to "WOTAN'S SLIDE SHOW" of the events from 1998 to around 2175, will be covered in greater detail in the next Book. But for now, here's the gist as it affected Dobbs' life.

"Bob" had suffered a relatively painless hernia while attempting to move a bathtub by himself. When he got to the hospital, the trouble began.

During surgery, after having been insufficiently 'put under' by sodium pentathol, "Bob's" astral body rose from the operating table and watched from above while his poor body was hacked and abused by quacks who Dobbs could now see, in his spirit-world condition, to be demonic entities in human guise. He returned to his body when the drugs wore off only to enter a new world of pain he'd never dreamed existed. For 4 days, trapped in bed, he was smited and tortured by the AGONY of his crude stitchings and by the utter embarrassment of an unexpected condition we shan't go into here. He underwent extreme temptation at the hands of "nurses" who, he was sure, were also demons.

In this horrible 'Bout' he slid in and out of various time-lags, sometimes abruptly wrenched from one Vision to another as if he

were a TV tube and someone was changing channels. Most of it was a living nightmare — a twisted, mocking replay of his life, only *changed* into a Heironymous Bosch-style parody. Grotesque caricatures of his mother and other loved ones writhed in hideous travesties of family events.

Suddenly a feeling of absolute peace blanketed him. He was approached by seven glowing . . . spirits? Jesii? spacemen? . . . who escorted him into the para-molecular Court of God. Here energy and matter swirled and mixed over a sea of glass and "Bob" gazed into the face of time and space unbounded. Infinity itself lay in the center like an ever-hatching egg, with obtuse intelligences circling it and meshing into sync with it. Extending from the *tiny point* that was *all of this* came a weird pattern — an infinite chain of logic — a 'book.' Hovering before him, it radiated an intense 'purpose' of some sort, like a force: a powerful 'need' which displayed yet another infinite, quasi-electric pattern — a 'brain,' a 'map' . . . the root-map of the universe? All forces fluttered around it, yet nothing moved at all. Deep inside this matrix was the earth.

"Bob" could see it all, from an overhead viewpoint, and, strangely, in what looked much like cheap animation as on a Saturday morning children's TV show. In an overall symbolic panorama of past/present/future which he also *felt*, he saw not only his previous incarnations as various winos and "Other Bobs" dating all the way back to the First "Bob," but also the future of Earth, drawn out over thousands of years yet shown in second-by-second detail. He saw it from the *human* point of view, from the *alien* point of view, from the *computer* point of view and finally through the Eye of WOTAN. All in all, he recalls, it reminded him of the Book of Revelation done by a low-budget cartoon studio.

After going through a few future-life incarnations including an intelligent machine incarnation and one as an Insect Man on some unfathomable planet, he was launched into an *utterly pornographic* parade of sex reversion hallucinations and pre-human "lust impulsion" remembrances of a most vivid and arrousing nature. He experienced a perverted "Rising from the Dead" back into the real world, where he suddenly found himself in perfect if *crazed* health. (A nurse later pressed suit.) "Bob" insists that what he learned during the last part of the vision made him the great lover and gigolo he is today.

Many Church Initiates, seeking to become Adepts in the Hierarchy, deliberately induce hernias in themselves in an attempt to duplicate "Bob's" experience.

The episode stirred up a renewed and perhaps *frenzied* interest in the Church of the SubGenius, which Dobbs had formed some two years earlier in a half-hearted attempt to placate JHVH-1. Now, "Bob" seemed to take it far mor seriously. He began to recruit carefully selected individuals from the new world of high finance. There was no hint of our present fierce evangelism; "Bob" was biding his time, gathering forces and the most powerful followers, gradually but relentlessly preparing for that *perfect moment* which would come when the Church would be made public.

He worked on developing his powers. He journeyed to Tibet, studied under the most ascended monks and Yetis high in the Himalayas, and underwent a severe training program with the guidance of his new friend, Dr. T. Lobsang Rampa. He stayed in the Forbidden City of Chang Eng, home of a lost civilization of super-intelligent Yetis; there, crude and highly ritualistic surgery was performed on "Bob" which opened his **Third Nostril**. This

Hellswami Hagen Trance Collage

Rare domestic scenes of "Bob" and "Connie," submitted by zealous Members.

INFILTRATING THE ASTRAL PLANE

necessary step in participant evolution, now routinely performed by the Bobmonks on all newcomers to Dobbstown, involves the inserting of long bamboo rods into the nose and up to the brain, opening the long-closed orifice which enables a SubGenius to **'whiffread'** the psychic **'pstench'** of others.

No less crucial in prepping Dobbs for Avatarhood was his first and still primary wife, "Connie." She had been his childhood sweetheart in First Grade. In 1955, more than 20 years later, they remet and married. Her impact on "Bob" is inestimable. Recently a **"Church of Connie's Panties"** has sprung up and is gathering momentum despite its rather juvenile basic premise.[6]

"Connie" sang with "Bob's" short-lived jazz combo, *"Bob" Dobbs and the Doo-Bops,* and gave him five sons: Bubba, "Bobby" Jr., Adam Kadmon, Shem, and Shaun. There is also a daughter, but the Family Dobbs keeps her name a secret in order to limit the number of suitors who would try to "marry into" this awesome dynasty.

Oddly enough it was "Connie" who encouraged the "extended family" idea now practiced by the Church. Although we cannot tell how many 'husbands' "Connie" has collected, we know that

6. This cult, centered around the undergarments of Dobbs' Primary Mate, was founded by Senator Jay Kinney after an ecstatic trance in which he claims to have *whiffread* the Panties themselves.

"Bob" now has at least one "Secondary Wife and Family" in every state of the union as well as 2,952 "Tertiary Families" spread evenly throughout the world. All of his wives and countless children fiercely defend "Bob" as a companion and provider and insist that he always seems to have plenty of time to spend with them. "Bob" clones, or doubles? If such is the case, it may have some bearing in the many paternity suits now being pressed on the Church by thousands of young people who claim to be bastard children of "Bob" from extra-marital relationships he was driven to consumate by his monstrously overactive Foot and Soul Glands.

Meanwhile, "Bob" was moving in the highest levels of The Conspiracy, secretly recording and photographing everything he could get his hands on, always listening and learning with the help of a mild Tibetan truth serum. All of his illusions about 'freedom' and 'America' had long since been shattered, of course, and the day that he told The Conspiracy "F - - - 'em if they can't take a joke" provides his most cherished memories. Only "Bob" could have done this, protected as he is by JHVH-1's Hex Field.

Building began on the bunkers and weapons complex at Dobbstown in the Sarawak Province of Malaysia, financed in part by Dobbs' land holdings in Tibet, South America, Antarctica, and especially Nevada. Dobbs' other interests now included so

"...or he might be down on Skid Row, giving some bum a haircut."

© Satellite Weavers

many multimillion dollar companies that money became to him more a spiritual concept than a 'need.'

The Smiling One also began buying his way onto the sets of many low-budget science fiction and horror films. Of his 54 known walk-on appearances in films — each one involving a few lines of dialog which, one realizes in retrospect, planted hints of the fantastically interwoven Conspiracy and alien plots we now fight — the most famous are these: THE UGLIEST MONSTER (1959), BAD NEWS FROM VENUS (1960), MARS NEEDS WOMEN (1965), 20 MILLION MILES TO EARTH (1957), and ZONTAR, THING FROM VENUS (1965). A great many of these were shot in Dallas, Texas, where "Bob" had set up his American headquarters.

Why Dallas? "Because it is a sterile city," says "Bob." "It has to be clean because the Doktors work there." The fact that *The Prescriptures* pinpoint Dallas as one of the few safe places to be during the coming **Eco-Econocataclysm** may also have something to do with the selection. **It had NOTHING TO DO WITH THE KENNEDY ASSASINATION!**

In 1971, Dobbs met a young Dallas man we shall call **Dr. X**, who became his drinking partner during "Bob's" renewed bout with the bottle. Together they wrote a number of now standard rock-and-roll songs under assumed names,[7] and Dr. X began

helping Dobbs locate people to run what would become the public relations arm of the Church, The SubGenius Foundation. In 1972 "Bob" initiated telepathic contact with the then-down-and-out "Dr." Philo Drummond, and finally appeared to him in person in 1973. Philo recruited his friend Ivan Stang, a failed science fiction writer, to help generate the first Church brochures and propaganda booklets. The rest is history, at least to the I.R.S.

Many ask, "Where is "Bob" now?"

He might be performing arcane rituals in Dobbstown, or deciphering forbidden texts under Incan ruins high in the Andes; he might be lounging in any of 18 skyscraper penthouses or playing 'tag' in the front yard of one of his families. He might be up in that great DC-10 jet plane he pilots, or down on Skid Row giving some bum a haircut. He might be tumbling in bed, extracting secrets from some Conspiracy wench, or bad guy, or preaching to the winos in the Dallas drunk tank. It doesn't matter. As long as the smoke from his Pipe keeps finding its way to Heaven, we on Earth are safe.

7.   The rare album *Put Your Hands On The Radio* by The Pink Boyz, suppressed by the Rock and Roll Conspiracy, contains the least adulterated of these songs.

Evidence of "Bob's" and "Connie's" first joint business venture—a resounding failure.

Five first grade students rendered "Bob" in revealing ways. Submitted by Head Master Jay Lynch.

The Viking Mars Lander image suppressed by NASA

Typical Dobbs cameo frame blow-up from a Great Badfilm. Death strikes the lanes in this scene censored from MARS NEEDS WOMEN (Larry Buchanan, AIP-TV 1963). Sprawled fellow has apparently been blown out of his shoes by a sight so hideous his *body* could not tolerate whatever grinning spectre it was. "Bob," far left, steps in to aid.

"Bob" tests the Secondary Tank Purging Actuator during a demonstration flight of the high altitude excremeditation chamber.

A sudden rash of smiling, pipe-smoking men drawn by second and third graders is catching the eye of toy marketing experts.

"Bob," pictured upper right, as he appeared in a 1951 magazine ad clipped by banjo doctor, R. Crumb.

Mystery interference with Conspiracy telex "secret information" caused anthropomorphic distortion seen at lower right.

Rev. Joe Schwind

1st Church of "Bob" Scientist

GHOST OF
THE PIT

FALSE
PROPHETS

GOOD-BAD
ANGEL/DEVILS

ALL
SUBGENII

ELDER BANKERS

THE XISTS

YOUR
FUTURE

CHAPTER 3
EARTH IS HELL

"I YAM THAT I YAM."

JeHoVah-1 to Moses/Popeye
from THE BOOK OF VISHANTI

YETIRIM

THE CONSPIRACY

DUPES
OF THE
CON

SPRING PLANTING

SEEDS

SEEDS

THE
FOUR BEASTS

NOCHTZOCTLIAN

GREEN ENERGY
ARCHDEMONS

ANSWERS? YOU WANT ANSWERS?

You may wish to — *GOD?!?* — that you'd never asked.

You'll get your answers, allright. Dobbsian Hermeticism *all-too-fully* explains Man's place and purpose on this Earth Plane, this hierarchy of universal cruelties.

Perhaps the least answerable question in history, here answered, is, **"WHY ARE WE HERE?"**

Why do we have such a huge capacity for pleasure, and confusion? Just so we'll keep breeding fast enough for some mindless long-range perpetual mutation machine?

(If only it were so!! If only it were that simple!!)

What set everything going in the first place, *before* the Big Bang? This question terrifies the water out of us if we really *grasp* it. We almost instinctively grab for some pose, some 'cause,' crutch, drug, or religion — *or even another person* — that will let us ignore this hideous mystery, that will create alibis for our failure to find a purpose in life. (Although there are some who frankly don't give a shit; they are the *lucky* ones.)

The concept of Infinity is so hard to 'get' viscerally that when we look up at the night sky, we tend to actually think of the *stars* merely as randomly separated, inexplicably backlit holes punched in some huge backdrop about a mile away from us.

Yet every now and then we can actually get a 'feel' for the distances and *times* involved . . . and glimpsing that fact of eternity becomes REAL SCARY if you truly get a solid *grip* on that insolidity, that abject Nothingness of God's Brain . . .

What scares you is that *you might be 'God'* and you *might wake up,* and all those fragile physical laws might come crashing down; the spiderweb framework of all reality, even your friends'

thoughts, might be erased like some precious but stupidly-unlabeled cassette tape, never to be recaptured again.

The idea is *so* scary that the goal of *most religions* is to preserve and elaborate on that concept of the stars as a big painted backdrop. They make Infinity a 'prop' so you don't have to think about the scary part.

This religion is about the Scary Part.

It can't be 'thought about;' it is grasped only through *direct knowledge* — **"seeing,"** one might say, the nature of Slack. Without Slack, there can be no Infinity, and vice versa. "Good Lord," it exists only *inside* our *heads,* after all. This Vale of Illusion isn't *real,* "for God's Sake." At least, not until somebody slams the *outside* of the head with a truncheon. Then, you could probably call it fairly real.

And here comes **the answer.** Someone *is* slamming *both* sides of *all* our heads with a truncheon. It sure as hell isn't *God,* either. *God couldn't care less.* That's right, *God couldn't care less.* "God" gives everyone equal time, the truncheons as well as the heads. "He" got the whole mess started, then sat back to watch it run itself into the ground or the sky, whichever way the universe ends up.

No, we aren't talking about God. Anybody that *talks* about God, *doesn't know what he's talking about.* This Church has NO USE for these namby-pamby, goody-two-shoes "New Age" and "Aquarian" weirdos. They're vapid, they don't cuss, they have no understanding of the need for spiritual violence in this modern space-age a-go-go society. God won't be ashamed *or* surprised when humanity invents its own Final Judgement and destroys the planet. *They* are the threat to Mankind.

Jehovah 1   — space god

THE OLD WAYS ARE THE BEST   **LIES**

No, the SubGenius wants no part of the "New Age" with its hallucinated "Love God;" it's already here and it obviously *sucks*. The SubGenius would rather retrieve the manly PAST — the Old Ways, the pre-pagan ways — or else jump-cut ahead to the nasty, fun-loving REMOTE FUTURE, a strange time when anything made of plastic will be a valuable antique that collectors will *kill* for and when SEXHURT will be recognized as sane human nature and indulged in *no matter* whether any church or government 'allows' it. But such things are TRIFLES! EVERY RELIGION CARRIES A MALIGNANT PARTICLE OF THE TRUTH and like a monster patched together from the loathesome parts of the bodies of dead faiths, the Church of the SubGenius has brought to perverse life the devastating, odious *fact* that **THE VENGEFUL GOD OF WRATH OF THE OLD TESTAMENT IS** *REAL* **AND** *ALIVE* **AND HIS HAME IS JEHOVAH-1!!** and to even *utter that mere name* can have such cataclysmic repercussions that for the remainder of this Book we shall follow the wisdom of the Ancient Hebrews and whisper only "JHVH-1" or the safer Lesser Dead Names of the Ungone One: Yahweh, Odin, Pan, Bog, Ra, Iah, AFFA, Mammon, Shiva, Wotan, Adonai Moloch, Abulldad, Ad-llubad, Shamash, Demiurgus, Iadabaoth, Old Nobodaddy, Crom, etc., etc.

— *DO NOT READ THAT LIST ALOUD!!!* JHVH-1 is NOT GOD but a mad alien from some corporate sin galaxy, full of eyes round about, a pillar of cloud by day and a pillar of fire by night, He cometh with the clouds, radioactive, all-pervading, He forgeth His Covenant with the SubGenius in CHAINS of GENETIC PROGRAMMING and DEMANDS OBEISANCE to His caveman sense of humor. He giveth SLACK and He taketh SLACK and what this groping polypous Fate-Warper is making us do dates back to Homo Correctus, First Whole Man, the Yeti Adam; He "formed a man from the dust of the ground" (read: "shot his wad of DNA straight into the brains of Ramapithicus") and only by letting our bodies obey the Code of financial lust survival that is built into them can our *souls* be freed from His INEVITABLE FIST. You think the long arm of the law is long? The Stark Fist of Removal is BIG! *BIG!!!*

SEX ELVIS' GHOST AND YOU!

HUMAN WASTE

We're not talking about UFO-riding superminds, although Wotan did assume that disguise to lure the Jews out of Egypt.[1] We're talking about a seething, noisome vortex of grinning Chaos that can reach out with titanic, sizeless hands and twist the fabric of time and space if so inclined. Not something that simply *visits* us and *smites* us, but a hulking dread that literally inhabits each and every one of us to some unguessable extent. Everything we do, have done, or will ever do, both in our daily routines *and* on the subatomic causational level of micro-occurences and billionth-of-a-nanosecond electron collisions, is DICTATED by the permutations of the great **SKOR:** the cosmic script of all cause and effect, the mutamorphic Archive wherein are recorded the shapes and movements of every blood tick, sperm whale, movie star and bicycle seat, "all the molecules of oil on all the grains of sand of every moonlit beach of the world."[2]

YOU CAN'T CHANGE THE SKOR. but JHVH-1 can. His "Heavenly Host," consisting of sub-neutrinos, "Wotrons" and "bobyon" particles, can shred the channels and pathways of the Skor as easily as a SubGenius would hoodwink a Pink.

At any given instant, an unimaginable quantity of neutrinos — energy-particles which make atoms look like planets — is coursing through your body. They are created spontaneously by the will power of JHVH-1: HE DOES THIS WITH HIS BRAIN. Coursing along their divine trajectories, passing through the tender pink flesh of human beings, these particles and their invisible "bobyon" and "Wotron" partners interact with our chromosomes, with the electrical patterns that are our thoughts, with all the DNA in the Living Chain of Life. Thus the Almighty Would-Be Architect of the Universe controls our behavior — our buying habits — our reproduction. The minute adjustments of neutrinal velocity and vibrational levels can cause a mountain to crumble or make your unborn children into supermen. They can make you choose Brand X over Brand Y. And it's all mapped out in advance. The Luck Plane is edited.[3]

1. *Exodus*, Old Testament. This action thriller is crammed with exciting tales of Saucer Miracles.

2. See any book about psychic Edgar Cayce for juicier detais on THE SKOR.

3. See YACATISMA VS. YACATIZMA in the Appendix of this book for more nuclear physics regarding bobyons and wotrons.

Rick Hoefle

COULD THIS BE THE END?

Like an ax this TOTAL FATE PROGRAM confronts our similarly-encoded SENSE OF SLACK and cleaves our heads straight down the middle into schizocephallic left and right sides (as well as the lesser-known north and south brains plus the forebrain and hindbrain); the resulting sub-Id battleground is responsible for our precariously-balanced *NENTAL IVES* (clones of us in the spirit world, parallel ghosts of ourselves, whose duplicate lusts influence our behavior on this material plane). Yes — YAHWEH smote us in primeval days with **"Bad Brakes"** by which we cannot stop our devil twins from overcoming our 'better nature' and by which, furthermore, we cannot even begin to tell the difference between the two! 'Brakes' are all that keep us from committing ANYTHING WE MIGHT IMAGINE IN OUR MOST WARPED FANTASIES, such as chopping off the heads of those noisy . . . well, all of us, even Pink Wimps, are Jekyll/Hyde monsters with two conflicting Personality Polarities in our noggins; the *Shaft of Suppression* rears its ugly Head in response to this utter psychosis which squirms for *most* of our lives only in the dim, unseen reaches of our decision-pumps; we act 'normal' most of the time, but who can say which side, the 'good' or the 'bad,' is in control of the body at any given moment? This subconscious Armageddon, of which we are usually and thankfully unaware, expresses itself physically as our phobias, Work Instinct, and universanal compulsions; spiritually, it is responsible for our unruly but subtle psychic powers — which result not from any 'inner love-aura' but from the mindless Nental Ife ghost standing at our sides. It is the half of our intelligence which is NOT in control, and it erupts from its usual idiot blithering into *weird, occult* phenomanifestations only when our turbulent mental background reaches such peaks of simultaneous crisis and repression as the stormy glandular rampages of adolescence. The Nental Ife is the cause of poltergeists. It is also the source of the imagination.

Pinks have no Nental Ife.

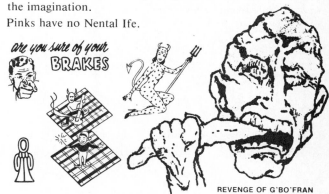

are you sure of your BRAKES

REVENGE OF G'BO'FRAN

The SubGenius, however, releases this roiling energy in throes of JHVH-spawned RITES OF DEGENERACY ("Within reason," cautions the Left Brain), just as his Church's dogma instructs.

Now, the *sex glands* are a creation of THE DEVIL HIMSELF, but he is a minor character in the pantheon of the gods (that's right — **WOTAN IS NOT ALONE.**). He implanted those urges in all bipeds on orders from . . . let's just say **"The Elder Gods."** For now. These "Elder Gods" gave us Sex to TIE US DOWN to our base and primal instincts, to keep us from rising above our Roots, TO PREVENT US FROM BECOMING GODS LIKE THEM. [4]

Fortunately for us, JHVH-1 is NOT ON THEIR SIDE. He wishes us to *unlock the chains of sex* . . . but NOT by repressing them. Instead, He INSISTS that we INDULGE these urges SO MUCH MORE THAN NECESSARY that the chains SNAP FROM OVERUSE and we are freed from our bonds.

AIIEEEE, YES! If ODIN HIMSELF wants us to CUT LOOSE and RUN RAMPANT, WHO THE HELL ARE *WE, TO QUESTION HIS DIVINE EDICTS?*

DON'T get Heaven and Hell all mixed up like most people do. Serve JHVH-1 as He meant for you to: go forth on the Holy Quest for Fornication! Your conscience is an illusion; there is merely an *instinctive behavior code,* to 'hold back' is to suffocate, but never forget for a second that it is the monster god that allows this, that *demands* it, for **"SCIENCE DOES NOT REMOVE THE TERROR OF THE GODS!"** Not anymore. FEAR HIM but follow the hints of the accidents in your life, follow The Path of Least Resistance and gob out from under the sacrifices he demands of all the Glorps around you; your sacred FOLLIES and FOIBLES will show you where Slack lies and you will be able to relax and avoid heart attacks. WOTAN KILLS those who *drudge their lives away* without knowing who He is, but He REWARDS the ones who recognize His STARK FIST and carry out His *seemingly immoral plans* while *SLACKING OFF EVERY CHANCE THEY GET.* Quit your job! Blow off false work! Free the spirits of the sex glands, EXORCISE the DAEMONS of the GUNADS! Even one act of solo sex tantra — the Simplest Sex Magick — is a MIGHTY BLOW against the REPRESSOR-DEVIL![5]

JHVH-1 is an *economic* god Who desires that His followers be rich in material wealth, no matter their poverty of spirit (that's "Bob's" department), for rich followers give Him a tighter grip on the bustling races of Earth. He does not call for meditation, introspection, least of all renunciation. He instills *greed* in his followers.

Why do we go out of our way to *worship* the monster god, then? It doesn't seem to be for either evil *or* good.

Right. The gods do not recognize those qualities. It is "Bob" who brings "goodness" into the picture. He is the one man who is loved by the gods; only he can wheel and deal with them on our behalf.[6]

No, it is simply that Jeh-Hoo-Vih-1 is the only god around who currently *demands* lip service. The rest of the Elder Gods are, for all intents and purposes, *asleep* (well, most of them, anyway). They, like the human race itself, have no *Slack* . . . not the kind *they* need, anyway. Indeed, in this one respect, we are equal to the gods themselves.[7]

JHVH-1 is the only *major primordial deity* now actively soliciting praise and requesting fertility rites.

Jesus, for instance, doesn't insist that we worship Him, nor will He smite us if we don't. His *followers* do that. He has made it clear that He'd love to give most of His fans the slip. They've got the story all mixed up.

The Church of the SubGenius is *with* The Fightin' Jesus, the Swingin' Buddha, Muhammed the Avenger, and all the other space detectives from benevolent alien races who came to *defy* the tyrant Elder Gods.

REMOVED   **FOREVER**

LIES

BLISTERED BY IGNORANCE

4. "Bob" learned of this while poring over the forbidden *Pnakotic Manuscript* during an expedition into The Hollow Earth via ancient tunnels hewn into the earth's crust beneath the forgotten stone cities of Peru.

5. Outlined in the accursed *Book of the Law and Lies of The Great God Pan* by the mad musician, Dr. Alice Crowley.

6. See BALDER—THE BELOVED OF ODIN by the antiquarian Microbius *IV,* which details all of humanity's "Sons of the Gods" myths and ties them directly to J.R. "Bob" Dobbs.

7. Revealed in THE WARS OF YAHWEH, part of the suppressed sections of *The True Grimories of King Solomon,* available in most Occult Candle Shops.

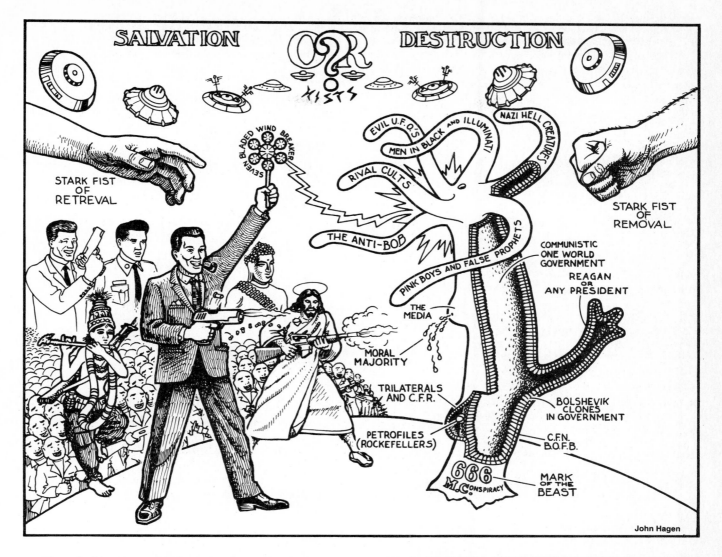

SALVATION OR DESTRUCTION

STARK FIST OF RETREVAL

STARK FIST OF REMOVAL

SEVEN BLADED WIND BREAKER

EVIL U.F.O.'S
MEN IN BLACK AND ILLUMINATI
NAZI HELL CREATURES
RIVAL CULTS
THE ANTI-BOB
PINK BOYS AND FALSE PROPHETS

COMMUNISTIC ONE WORLD GOVERNMENT
REAGAN OR ANY PRESIDENT

THE MEDIA
MORAL MAJORITY
TRILATERALS AND C.F.R.
PETROFILES (ROCKEFELLERS)

BOLSHEVIK CLONES IN GOVERNMENT
C.F.N. B.O.F.B.
666 M.J. CONSPIRACY
MARK OF THE BEAST

John Hagen

(The only thing that Dobbs leaves ambiguous is whether The Fightin' Jesus is *for* or *against* JHVH-1 in particular. There is no question that He came from space: "You are from below, I am from above; you are of this world, I am not of this world" (John 8:23). He was "lifted up" in a "cloud" like the other ancient Hebrew Astronauts. But just exactly *what is* His relationship with the Space Bankers? Is the "Rapture" a Revenge Mission on which He will have the rotting corpses of dead Christians rise from their graves to seek the flesh of living Christians, as punishment for both for dragging His Hame through the mud of guilt and repression?[8] It doesn't really matter. The Rapture is scheduled for *after* 1998 and we SubGenii will be gone by the time He shows up.)

Admittedly, YAHWEH is a *strange* god. He is unusually *pragmatic* for a supreme being. He doesn't care what you *think* about Him, only what you *do* for Him. It is this material world, this very Veil of Maya, that he covets. He's the kind of god you *can* buy indulgences from (we sell them).

Another aspect of WOTAN that distinguishes Him from your *regular* gods is His obvious sense of **"bulldada,"** His streak of very *black* humor. His manipulation of life on Earth shows a definite touch of *cruel irony*. He evidently *enjoys* what He's doing. However, we must remember that He is not out to destroy us *or* help us, but to *use* us. We are only TOOLS. It's

BLASTED BY KNOWLEDGE

like your dad and his phillips-head screwdriver: if you lose it, he becomes insanely enraged, yet he has no personal identification with it.

Perhaps His oddest feature is his anthropomorphism. He shows a remarkably *human* small-mindedness, although this may simply be the way He *wishes* us to see Him. Probably it is because we are engineered "in His Own Image." That doesn't mean we look like Him — He has no body. It means that Early Man's MIND was fashioned after His. He placed His own penchant for greed, ruthlessness and masturbatory violence into the otherwise blank brain-pan of Primo-Anthropocus (First Biped). True, it resulted in the awful humans we have today, but if he hadn't done it, brainy dinosaurs would be here instead of us.

Certainly, we are at His absolute mercy. Earth is His test tube, and the most *horrifying* part of Dobbs' revelations is that THIS TEST TUBE EARTH FUNCTIONS AS "THE

8. See THE LOST TRIBES FROM OUTER SPACE by Marc Dem for more on the Hill of Foreskins and YAHWEH's saucer ruse. Jesus's Revenge Mission was suggested in the film *NIGHT OF THE WAKING LIES* BY Paul and Doug Skull, Skull Bros. Films.

STAKES" IN A SORT OF COSMIC "BAR BET" — a diabolical 'bet' that JHVH-1 could not create an intelligent species that could sustain life on its own planet without self-destructing within 5 million years, *without* the intercession of a Divine Prophet.

Is "Bob" Yahweh's way of cheating? [9.]

Yes, "the Lord" DOES INDEED work in mysterious ways . . . yet they are really no more mysterious than the roll of dice.

[9.] First suspected by Hellswami Weavers while on a cross-country drive, upon entering a reverse-ionized Wotron Matrix or "Frop Awareness Zone" on the desert highway leading to Crater City, Arizona. THAT ZONE IS STILL THERE!

This would be almost comforting — IF WE WERE *ALL* STUPID. Instead, it's frightening. It implies that the Plan for humans is reflected in war, crime, hunger, pollution. How can such things do a divine being any good?? Why does He allow them?

Because THAT'S JUST THE WAY HE IS.

His Stark Fist of Removal is ever poised overhead and will crash down randomly for indiscernible reasons.

Why? *WHY?*

Because *He said so,* **THAT'S why."**

(Samadhi, Ain Soph, I YAM, LOGO, THE WOR, **SLACK** THE TAO, Macroprosaurus, Allfather, G'BroagFran(?))

LUCK PLANE

EVERYTHING or SOMETHING: "YMIR"
yin
A.k.a. "Pleroma"

Includes many universes not on this chart. Composed of 30 spirit universes, all set in "Time-Pairs" or "Syzygies." The weakest of these, Achamoth-Sophia ("Wisdom"), FUCKED HERSELF and, just before being banished from heaven, produced:

OUR UNIVERSE: "AITHERIUM"
"TrueMatter" and "Positive" Time (PeNRGY)

This is the cosmic superspectrum of anything we would call "existing." It is kept in temporary balance by the pieces of "YMIR, the Hoar-Frost Giant," who slew himself to create matter.

If there is too much "crossover" between this and the Backwards Universe, all things will end.

AITHERIUM is composed of two mutually-consuming parts:

WORLD OF ENERGY: "YACATIZMA"

These are the Sothic Heavens, and include "souls," "magic," "truth," Slack (which can become unbalanced here and create *too much Slack*) and the various other forms of energy (gravitational, electromagnetic, light, etc.) Ruled only by *theoretical* laws.

(=)
(repel/attract balance)

AND

"THE SKOR"
or cosmic Archive of *all events* is the hologram or interface between both of these.

When these are balanced they allow life.

NOTHING: "AFFATHAUGTH"
yang
A.k.a.: NOSALLACK, "IT," NIRVANA
The lack of all everything.

THE BACKWARDS UNIVERSE: "ANTILAND"
"TrueEnergy" and "Negative" Time (NeNRGY)

Negative matter, negative energy. "ANTI-SLACK."
"The Vile Privation" of nameless, formless, form-*sucking* DEVILS, Tachyon People, and other nirvanic effluvia, now building up in cosmic overbalance and due to intersect our Time Universe in 200 years ("Omicron Epsilon").

WORLD OF MATTER: "ADVERSARIA"

The "physical plane"—where you think you are, now. No Slack. "Lies." (ADVERSARIA contains some matter so diffuse or "high-frequency" as to be more like "energy.") Ruled by physical laws.

THE ELDER GODS
(UniElementals)

THE REBEL GODS
(MultiElementals)
JHVH-1, ERIS, NHGH, etc.

BLACK   WHITE

"BOB" and the SubGeniuses

EARTH and The Conspiracy

THE WATCHERS
(Consciousness-squelching weird energy-robot servants of the Elder Gods...
some UFOs, discorporate entities, etc.)

DOLLAR

LIES

In the Prescriptures, speaking through the tranced-out medium of "Bob" Dobbs, the hoary Voice of Wrath has this to say:

> "To him that cometh as an Overman, and is changed before Me, and giveth unto Me his joyous Slackfullness, I will give of him to spend of the seed of Life, which is the expectoration of My M'Me, and he shall be copyrighted by the Angels for life eternal; and he shall rule the Underlings, who defecate on the Sabbath, and who fornicate only in reproduction . . . and he shall eat of Time, and not be rotted, but shall have the keys to hell and death and be as king."

(Note: The Prescriptures are subject to retranslation without notice.)

Who are "the Underlings" mentioned in that beautiful passage?

They're THE CONSPIRACY!! **THE STINKING DAMN CONSPIRACY!!**

Well, technically, the "Underlings" or "UnderAlls" are the innocent, witless *dupes* of The Conspiracy, ruled by the select Few False Prophets at the top. The saddest part is that we have no way of knowing how many of these "UnderAlls" are really latent SubGenii, cut off from the Slack-filled message of "Bob" and merely *waiting* like caterpillars stuck in their cuccoons for a nebulous something to free them.

How in the name of Names did our world arrive at this woeful juncture in history?

JHVH-1 keeps His stage *crowded* with players. And the *plot* of His bizarre play is dense with intrigue. Half of the players were not given scripts at all, and the rest have only the sections that *they* figure in. Only "Bob" has a complete copy. While "Bob", as the Embodiment of Slack, does not *make* plans, yet he *possesses* a plan: the secret plan to WOTAN's great "gameboard".

On this gameboard are two main teams, plus countless spooky 'random factors' thrown in to keep things JUMPING. It's "Bob" and the SubGeniuses Vs. The Conspiracy and its Minions. Each team is given certain powers; our power is to make people JUMP, to wake them up, while The Con was given the power to make *you* gobble down mercury-loaded hamburgers and breathe plutonium-tainted air without complaining, no matter how twisted and deformed your children might end up. Great balance, huh? The funny thing is, the majority seems to prefer the Conspiracy.

Look around you and face it. It's been obvious for a long time. The world is composed mostly of assholes. All kinds of ignorant, dangerous, thoughtless louts are in positions of power, respect, and influence, while some of the bravest, most capable and most deserving people you know are forced to waste their talents slugging it out in a thankless cycle of brainbreaking labor and mental paralysis. Checks and balances? What a JOKE! There are NONE. To think the system will improve by itself is a *pipe dream*.

LIES, ALL LIES

WHO TO SMITE?

The idea that America (or any country) values individuality as the highest ideal is a *cheap myth. Everybody's* an individual*ist*, but they *don't like* individuals. Perhaps in simpler times it was true, but no *modern* industrial deathkulture can really afford a population of unpredictables.

This shouldn't surprise you—the long history of persecution of SubGenii by The Conspiracy goes back for generations untold; indeed, there are signs of Their cannibal repression of prehuman SubGeniuses dating from *before* "Man's" appearance on Earth. All of civilization's painful and misguided climb up from the primeval slime, and its subsequent loss of Slack *and of any class at all*, has been indelibly marked—nay, *entirely motivated*—by the aeons-bridging conflict between The Con's mindlessly chickenshit Witless Principals and the superior, ethnically all-embracing races of latent SubGenii. (You should *know* this—you *were/will be* there in the Beforelife!)

Remember, a "SubGenius" isn't a member of any organization. It is a *life form*. Dobbs Consciousness isn't a philosophy or gameplan—it's the *main quality* of an entire *species* that has always been here, but has never needed a name; things have never been this *bad* before. If we don't start recognizing it, we won't notice when They finally *destroy* it.

SOLD!

NUCLEAR DOOM: SOMETHING TO LAUGH ABOUT

Fig. 307 God inserts Divine Pilch in Believer

NEW WILD DIFFERENT

they will know that you know

Mark Mothersbaugh

Thrilled BY THE SHEER TERROR OF IT ALL!

REMOVING RADIO-ACTIVE DRUGS

[TU]BES OF [U]RANIUM

Joe Schwind

The Conspiracy formed the background of your entire life. It *is* inner conflict. It *is* your inferiority complex, or your delusion of grandeur. It *is* nervous tension, the habit of worry. It *is* your darkest, most debilitating fears, and it's what *keeps* you afraid, what makes you scared to walk home alone at night. **It IS the very *reason* for *all your problems.***

It gave us the current spate of escapist sci-fi/fantasy movies to *ready* us for the *real* sci-fi horrors that They are planning. If They can keep us seeing it as a big cowboys-and-aliens GAME then They can *keep doing it.* They've got most people looking *forward* to turning the entire Earth into one big shopping mall/condo complex. They let the three major networks get *so bad* that you actually *can't wait* for 87 channels of cable narcotics. Then when the next step comes, and your TV *watches you*, you won't mind.

One of Their very most effective tools is *TECHNOBOREDOM*—what passes for fun among Mediocretins is deadening, false roleplay PAP to a SubGenius. They BURY the alternatives.

They're also expert at GUILT MANIPULATION. A long, long time ago, They invented the labels of "success" and "failure" (as opposed to "good" and "bad") and make them *stick*. That gets you to sacrifice irrationality. If you don't go along with every trivial request THEY make, if you don't try to carry the world on your back, both of which are impossible, you're supposed to feel like you "failed" somewhere.

DON'T be a Businessman On A Cross. "Bob" says we should stand firm and *fight* for our *right to fail* instead of forever beating our heads against a brick wall They set for us. **"If you can't whup it, go *down*,"** as that great Wino said in the Tabernacle. Move on to other things. RELISH your MISTAKES. We seek a Perfect laziness—a perpetual motion lifestyle of work/play.

ONE WORLD OR NONE · ONE WORLD OR NONE · ONE WORLD OR NONE

A TASTE OF BLOOD

You have a RIGHT to be disgusted with CRAP—to LUST after BODIES—to FLEE from unwinnable fights.

As long as those Cage Men and Box Dwellers run this planet, its economies and ecologies face *certain extinction*. We must rise to our rightful places, grip the reins of evolution, and, with our Outsider's WarpKnowledge, wrench human culture out of its subliminally programmed mental slumber.

Our One-World Religion is the only sane alternative to Their totalitarian One-World Government (which would eventually produce a *No World* Government). That only in recent years have we recognized our own sovereignty demonstrates BOTH how vicious THEIR efforts have been at denying us Slack, and how near our race is to TRIUMPH.

You can tell they're running scared. At first the controlled media attempted to ignore us. They assumed our movement would just fizzle out. They thought it was a JOKE. One can't really blame Pinks for being unable to see the Church as anything but a *paranoid fantasy*, considering the HOPELESSNESS that is rammed down their throats. But then They turned to smear campaigns. You've heard the pathetic bleating of the **Citizens for Normalcy**, you've read of the firebombings of SubGenius FisTemples by middle-of-the-road terrorists, you've seen them increase the insipidity level of prime-time TV (going *so far* as to name a 'bad guy' in one series set in Dallas after J.R. "Bob" Dobbs).

All this is ULTIMATE PROOF that JVHV-1 has not only promoted the SubGenius as His Special Tool, but has *simultaneously* pulled Their strings, making Them endarken *themselves* with their hereditary ignorance and superstitious witch-huntery. BOTH SIDES are pawns in His Bigger Game, His fissioning of history into binary "war equations." We're living in a controlled media blackout. Everything we read, see, and hear is CENSORED. And for good reason. If people knew the truth, they really *would* panic.

Face facts. Wise up. Snap out of it. You're fooling yourself if you think this society, this Western Civ tinkertoy cage of overpopulation is going to last another 40 years. THEY'VE DONE THINGS TO THE ATMOSPHERE, THE OCEANS, AND THE EARTH'S MAGNETIC FIELD THAT YOU DON'T KNOW ABOUT. Notice the funny weather lately?

Things will get a LOT worse before they get better, *pal*, and any person, place or *THING* that tries to tell you otherwise, whether on TV, radio, or as a voice in your head, is part and parcel of The Conspiracy, the Conspiracy-Around-A-Conspiracy, and the megaconspiracies that spiral well beyond this planet in nets of covert manipulation. YEAH, the TV news leaves out a few *facts* here and there...

white, ugly men... but they're just the *plant supervisors* of this Hell Factory Earth. The American System (plus the soon-to-be only other one, the Russian System) is only *partially* ruled by these various billionaires Petrophiles, these bankers, media kings, corporate potentates and even a few politicians. They're caucasian power-jackals, alright, but at least they're *human*.

They'd be alive today— IF NOT FOR YOU!!

St. Byron Werner

©BYRON WERNER 1980

Did you know that *half* of the doomaflotchies we call UFOs are entirely terrestrial in nature and are ridden, not by moonmen, but by *'humans'*? It's the ancient leadership sector of The Conspiracy, the *INSIDERS*, who serve the Elder Gods and whose technology is so advanced that not even the Trilateralists know how to handle them.

You *knew* that any President is just a front-man, a p.r. hyena set out to catch flak and muddy the real issues (which would concern *suvival*, not politics). But do you know who pulls his strings? Oh, all that right wing stuff about the Council on Foreign Relations is true enough. The world *is* run by *rich, old,*

When a new President walks into the oval office for the first time, smugly challenging the grim *Secret Boys* to shock him with that mythical Real Story that all Presidents supposedly get on their first day, it takes them about *ten minutes* to *indeed tell it*, and from that moment on you notice that Our President appears a little greyer, a little more haggard with each TV appearance. Sooner or later, a clone has to take over.

When you learn about Them, and actually meet the Men in Black, it all becomes... clear... With a sinking feeling you realize you'll have to change *all* your plans.

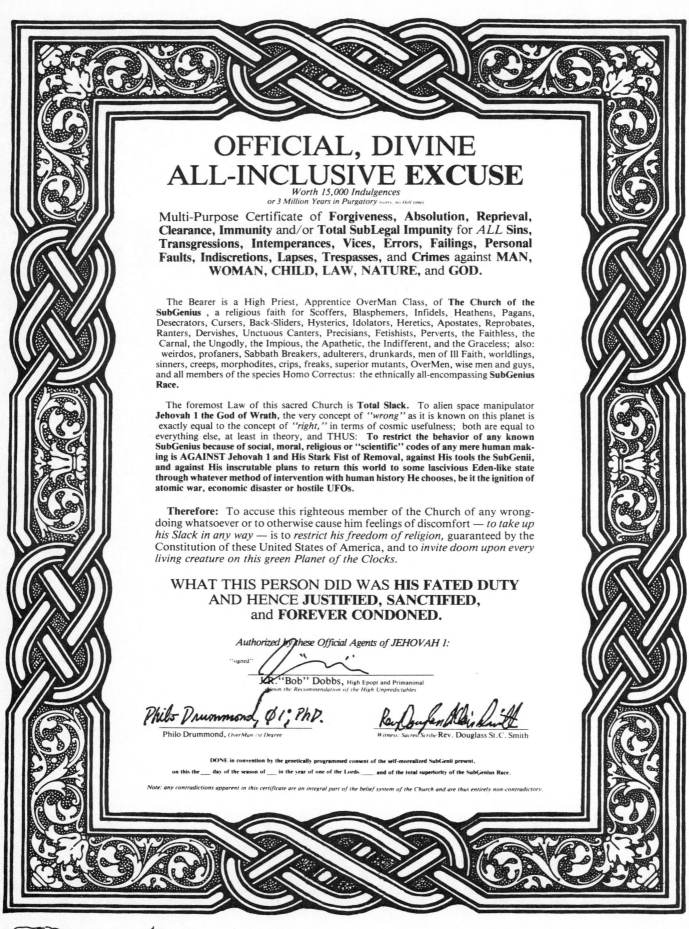

OFFICIAL, DIVINE
ALL-INCLUSIVE EXCUSE

Worth 15,000 Indulgences
or 3 Million Years in Purgatory (sorry, no Hell time)

Multi-Purpose Certificate of **Forgiveness, Absolution, Reprieval, Clearance, Immunity** and/or **Total SubLegal Impunity** for *ALL* Sins, **Transgressions, Intemperances, Vices, Errors, Failings, Personal Faults, Indiscretions, Lapses, Trespasses,** and **Crimes** against MAN, WOMAN, CHILD, LAW, NATURE, and GOD.

The Bearer is a High Priest, Apprentice OverMan Class, of **The Church of the SubGenius** , a religious faith for Scoffers, Blasphemers, Infidels, Heathens, Pagans, Desecrators, Cursers, Back-Sliders, Hysterics, Idolators, Heretics, Apostates, Reprobates, Ranters, Dervishes, Unctuous Canters, Precisians, Fetishists, Perverts, the Faithless, the Carnal, the Ungodly, the Impious, the Apathetic, the Indifferent, and the Graceless; also: weirdos, profaners, Sabbath Breakers, adulterers, drunkards, men of Ill Faith, worldlings, sinners, creeps, morphodites, crips, freaks, superior mutants, OverMen, wise men and guys, and all members of the species Homo Correctus: the ethnically all-encompassing **SubGenius Race.**

The foremost Law of this sacred Church is **Total Slack.** To alien space manipulator **Jehovah 1 the God of Wrath,** the very concept of *"wrong"* as it is known on this planet is exactly equal to the concept of *"right,"* in terms of cosmic usefulness; both are equal to everything else, at least in theory, and THUS: **To restrict the behavior of any known SubGenius because of social, moral, religious or "scientific" codes of any mere human making is AGAINST Jehovah 1 and His Stark Fist of Removal, against His tools the SubGenii, and against His inscrutable plans to return this world to some lascivious Eden-like state through whatever method of intervention with human history He chooses, be it the ignition of atomic war, economic disaster or hostile UFOs.**

Therefore: To accuse this righteous member of the Church of any wrong-doing whatsoever or to otherwise cause him feelings of discomfort — *to take up his Slack in any way* — is to *restrict his freedom of religion,* guaranteed by the Constitution of these United States of America, and to *invite doom upon every living creature on this green Planet of the Clocks.*

WHAT THIS PERSON DID WAS **HIS FATED DUTY** AND HENCE **JUSTIFIED, SANCTIFIED,** and **FOREVER CONDONED.**

Authorized by these Official Agents of JEHOVAH 1:

"signed"

J.R. "Bob" Dobbs, High Epopt and Primanimal
upon the Recommendation of the High Unpredictables

Philo Drummond, Ø1; PhD.
Philo Drummond, *OverMan 1st Degree*

Witness: Sacred Scribe Rev. Douglass St.C. Smith

DONE in convention by the genetically programmed consent of the self-moralized SubGenii present,

on this the ___ day of the season of ___ in the year of one of the Lords ____ and of the total superiority of the SubGenius Race.

Note: any contradictions apparent in this certificate are an integral part of the belief system of the Church and are thus entirely non-contradictory.

LEDA AND THE SWAN

Hal Robins

WHATTA WOTAN

WAR

CRIME

HUMAN GOVERNMENT

LIES

industrial strength Church

For JHVH-1 is not alone in His cosmic meddling. Earth has been inhabited *non-stop* for millions of years by *hundreds of different races of aliens from space,* both benevolent and hostile. Have you ever noticed that no two UFO photographs show the same hubcap? Many of the saucer jockeys are simple humanoids like us, Space Nazis who do little more than freeze up car motors on lonely country roads at night and occasionally rape or mutilate a human or cow. They usually look like earless elves or dwarves, and are of relatively minor import here since "Bob" himself has faster spaceships than they have. They only infrequently break the rule of "Don't Let The Earthlings See You."

But there are other, *far* more confusing ones, *awful, mind-breaking, overwhelming* ones which sow death and madness and which might as well be considered the very *fingers* of the Stark Fist of JHVH-1 Himself!

THE HUMAN SCRAPYARD

Of these various Comedians of the Gods, the ones which channel information from WOTAN to humanity are called **"THE INJECTORS."** They generally make their trance pronouncements through children, psychics, and drunkards. And "Bob".

Dozens, perhaps hundreds of entities speak through "Bob." they also *listen* and *see* through him, and many even go to him for *advice* on handling humans.

"Bob" is a wide-open channel they can lock onto for the divulging of past lives, secret health hints, and predictions. Of the latter, about 90% —all the trivial ones—come true. Most of the *world-shattering* revelations, however, are PURE 'D' BULLSHIT. Thus, "Bob" has the same problem any Contactee has: how to tell truth from lies. Now, telling good UFOs from bad UFOs is simple. The bad ones are the only ones that show up. What's most difficult is to know *which* are UFOs at *all*, which are spewings-forth from the Collective Unconscious, which are WOTAN-derived and which are not, and, of course, which are merely "Bob's" own subconscious, talking to itself.

"Turok", "Bob's" dead American Indian Spirit Guide, says that it is all of those, and *then* some, but that no matter the details, ALL of them are essentially just robot 'tools' of the Elder Gods: the Nothern Fathers Who Slumber Beneath the Glaciers. These psychic robots, whether employed by WOTAN or by the Elder Gods directly, are simply here to automatically add new doses of experimental "food" to the "test tube culture" which is Earth. "Bob" is the eye-dropper through which many of the doses are added. Thus the Elder Gods,

47

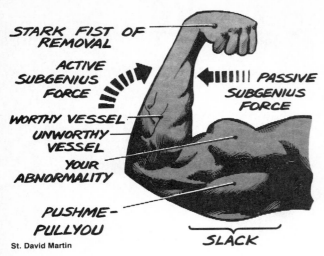

STARK FIST OF REMOVAL

ACTIVE SUBGENIUS FORCE

WORTHY VESSEL

UNWORTHY VESSEL

YOUR ABNORMALITY

PUSHME-PULLYOU

PASSIVE SUBGENIUS FORCE

SLACK

St. David Martin

So the transmission lines are open. But they are fuzzy, full of static, indistinct and easily garbled. The Elder Gods want to keep us confused, for if we ever truly "wake up," we'll have the potential not only to advance to their stage of being but even to 'beat them to the punch,' to turn the tables on them; they fear being rudely awakened from their aeons-old slumber by US, finding *themselves* suddenly the slaves and "Bob" the Master.[16]

Erwin R. Bergdoll

though yet "sleeping," can still watch us through their robot servants; indeed, the "Eye in the Pyramid" symbol which makes our dollar bills so sinister-looking is nothing less than the hieroglyph for those most abhorrent superdeities, "sleeping with One Eye Open." Their servant-beings are here to see that *we remain sleeping too*, unable to advance any faster than *they*. Otherwise, **WE WOULD BECOME GODS OURSELVES**. For we, too, have an "Eye," and that Eye is "Bob." He is the telephone by which Man can harass the very gods.

AS IF YOUR LIFE DEPENDED ON IT

Get mad! Get even! Get rich!

And that is why the **"Men from Planet X"** are so important. They are the fulcrum WOTAN will use to *evolve us at high speed no matter the damage to our souls.* Their arrival will end the Years of Trouble, or what the *Necronomicon* calls **The Time of PeE.** But will the World of the Future be better... or worse? That will largely be up to the Xists.[17]

The Xists are a race of benevolent aliens somewhere between Man and JHVH. Their technical and psychic powers, while no match for YAHWEH's, are yet nothing short of godlike to us roaches, the Earth Mammals. They are bodiless, but they can take on whatever form they choose, and can be a million different things at once, if necessary; they will be able to *watch* and *converse with* every single one of us, individually; they can do *anything* but figure out what the hell is *really* going on between Earth, JHVH, the Elder Gods and "Bob."

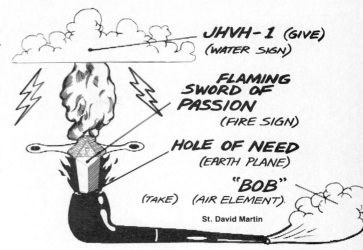

JHVH-1 (GIVE) (WATER SIGN)

FLAMING SWORD OF PASSION (FIRE SIGN)

HOLE OF NEED (EARTH PLANE)

"BOB" (TAKE) (AIR ELEMENT).

St. David Martin

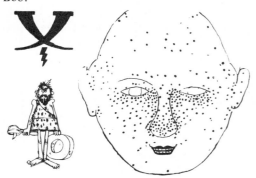

SEXSEXSEX OF THE GODS

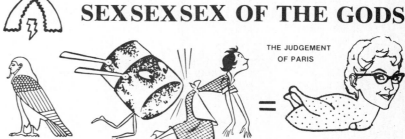

THE JUDGEMENT OF PARIS

These benign space monsters have walked among us throughout history, investigating and sometimes resisting the omnipervasive presence of JHVH-1 and His Minions (of whom they themselves number!). The extinction of the dinosaurs, the rise and "fall" of Atlantis shortly thereafter, the erection of the Pyramids, Stonehenge and other monuments which *no slopeheads alone could possibly build*, all these events and more are so inextricably interwoven with the invisible background wars between the Xists, JHVH-1, and the Elder Gods, that all the "Ancient Astronaut" fossils in the world offer only the barest of clues. (The movie rights *alone* to this gut-splitting history are worth *millions*!)

It isn't what the Xists have *done*, though—it's what they're *about* to do that's important. On July 5, 1998, 7:00 a.m., when we all have hangovers, WOTAN'S JUDGEMENT will take place in the form of what the Prescriptures call *The Advent of the Angelic Host;* the Xists will DESCEND with their scientifically MAGIC implements, their Bestowals of Technology that will be too much for us to handle; in one instant all the hangovers will disappear, along with all pollution and nuclear weapons, but in return the human race will have to take on "living machinery" so complex that THOUGH IT IS PEACEFUL, the end result will be equivalent to letting toddlers play with a nuclear arsenal. "Bob," and not some Conspiracy World Government, MUST BE THERE in a position of WORLD LEADERSHIP to EXPLAIN HUMANITY'S BEHAVIOR to the Xists *in ways they can understand* so they don't PUT US OUT OF OUR MISERY with a snap of their cosmic Finger like they did the dinosaurs. The RIGHT PEOPLE, *US,* must be the ones that the Xists make into superhuman *OverMen...* and even then, things will be *damn tough* for the rest of this period, which is called *the Time and Half Time* in occult jargon.

THE BIG BLUE TOE

16. From Von Junzt's unspeakable *Unaussprechlichen Kulten* and from *The Unpronounceable* by Wilson Lovecraft Colins.

17. "XISTS" is a corruption of the slang term, "Men from Planet X," to be so-called by the news media because the entities will never reveal their planet(s) of origin.

Now's the Time

Of course, "Bob" *may* be able to avert the invasion before they even get here. But even if that happens, the Scales of the Luck Plane will require something *else* equally momentous to maintain the cosmic balance. No matter what, something big, yes, 'BIG' is on the way; it may or may not be the end of the world, hopefully it will be the end of *Their* world, but it WILL be the end of something, something that was so near and dear to us that we've taken it for granted and therefore *when it goes, we won't notice*; the word 'human' will take on a whole new meaning, and most yoyos will never be the wiser... either way The End will come and go, and if it isn't cataclysmic it won't get airplay, and if it is, we'll have the wrong explanation for it (no explanation will be the right one); we'll be bemoaning the loss of things that didn't make any difference and NEVER EVEN NOTICE what we REALLY LOST, because we won't be human enough afterwards to remember we ever had it. YES! All you deaf ears down there, HEADS UP! LOOK OUT BELOW! There will be plenty of distractions to take our minds off the *real problem* as the Time of PeE draws to its violent close... for instance, BEWARE: the Fake Godjunior, the Anti"Bob", will come before long, *bullets cannot stop him*, he's one of the deceptively human-looking Advanced Supersonic Nazi Hell Creatures from Beneath the Hollow Earth, parasites of the Elder Gods, but most people will think he's the 2nd Coming and his alien hiney will be kissed all the way to world dictatorship and beyond; and if the *true* Messiah were to show up at that time, everyone would just *know* in the bottom of their core programming that He's the Antichrist because He'll cuss and spit and take the Lord's name in vain and hang out with whores and bulldaggers and dope addicts and cops and other down-home sorts, and when He's dead and the real Antichrist has been unmasked as a fake they'll wail and gnash and all that and STILL never admit what they did... **THIS IS A WARNING, DANGER DANGER** you poor devils, things are more mixed up than you ever *dreamed*, what was up *is* down, the priorities are all screwy, you're fretting if your hair looks okay while some new kind of bladder cancer is busting out the front of your designer jeans, **YES** this is "bad talk", nobody will LISTEN to anything else, you won't LOOK at TV unless body parts or cars are jiggling or crashing on it, you won't TASTE your food unless it has some nerve drug in it, you haven't used your other senses since you were five, and you sure as hell

Efficient exterminating

TIME MARCHES ON!

Shot from a Gun!

won't **STOP WHAT YOU'RE DOING** until someone much bigger, much stronger, and much, MUCH more self-assured MAKES you stop, and you'll thank him for it, and then just before you fry in a flash of radioactive hindsight you'll realize he stopped you from doing the WRONG THING, GOOD GOD!! What in the name of Sweet Screaming Jesus is this world *coming* to? People bitch, people gripe, "*This* is a sign of the End Times," "*That's* a sign of the End Times," when you should all be hollering, "It's *ALL* a sign of the End Times!!!" *NYES!!* We have a COVENANT with WOTAN and it is the Sacred Grudge-Chore of the SubGenius to **SMITE** The Conspirators and Their slavish Dupes: the Mediocretins, the stupid Pink Boys, the "Hoi Polloi," *Them*, the Normals, the Somnabulacs, the Great Unwashed-In-The-Baptism-Of-The-Pee-Of-"Bob," the malignant ones who breathe down our necks and abuse their territorial urges *without ever dreaming that they're doing it,* Assouls, Cage Men, Infidels, Sames, Anthropophobiacs, Conformers, Timeservers, Mole People, Proleterrorists, Philistines, Pharisees, Witchburners, the ones who have tried to maim our self-respect down through the centuries by making SLACK and antipredictability TABOO, the Thankers and Wankers, Bankers and Blankers, Heilers and Smilers, Sloths and Moths, Cons and Johns, Drivellers and Snivellers, Weepers and Sleepers; CreditHeads, Cliants, Kens and Barbies, Errorists, Yes-Buts, Ordinaryans and Lick Spittles, Corpulators, Signifying Monkeys, UnderAlls, the Slackless Ones... in short, the Remnants of Man: those very False Prophets who have been holding us back and forcing Time Addiction on Themselves... and... others...

No matter what their I.Q.s they are all a brick shy of a full load (so are we, but *they're* mising the *wrong* bricks).

THEY are the ones who brought this Buck Rogers monstrosity of microchips and inflation, nothing makes sense anymore and everything costs too much, the weather is weird, WHY DID THEY DO IT? *Don't they know they're begging for the flaming sword of Retribution??* The space monsters aren't *about* to let us get away with this masturbatory industrialization much longer, they watch our TV shows, they even play our god damned video games, they know all about us and can snuff our already disarrayed civilization with but a whisper to their ultimate computer brain, **MWOWM**, the brooding computer of the Xists which *we* will have soon too, the computer so complex it is not a machine, it is a moss-like independent growth of circuits which *it prints itself*, sprawling through our homes in the form of nondescript white stones laying here and there, talking, very quietly overwhelming our every thought, word, and deed, YES the Xists

7th SON of the NIGHT

will "give" it to us, we floundering human beings will fight nuclear wars with each other trying to decide whether to turn this unwholesome 'mouth of a Trojan gift-horse' ON or OFF, in the end we will leave it ON, and then by God we won't be able to do WITHOUT it. *REPENT!!* The End Times are here, the Xists are coming, the False Prophets will brown-nose to their dinosaurian asses and this planet will be sold down the river as sure as Lee Harvey Oswald's clone cashed the Conspiracy's checks! We are one royal hair trigger from the Wrath of JHVH-1, His galactic Finger is itchy and He is not well pleased with what Man hath wrought, REPENT THEN and prepare for the Age of Tribulations, the Time and Half Time, you think last winter was bad, wait until the glaciers are at your driveway, the earth shall shake, the sky shall fall, space junk, tornados, hail the size of Cadillacs, plutonium clouds, chromosome-bending solar flares, the oily stifling of all photosynthesis in the seas, ugly mutant locusts that carry DDT in their *stings*, famine even in California, a dustbowl in Canada, microwave roach steaks $5.99, drinking water you have to boil first and *pay for*, recombinant viruses, contagious cancers, one day you'll go to the mirror like poor Bert did to pop a 'blemish' and find your whole face cracking with each pinch like a rotten tomato, *The Plague*! But these *are*

only the natural things, acts of God or Satan, they blanch in the face of MAN'S deeds to come, man's self-dehumanization, the Government, my GOD if we aren't careful the Endarkment of the next century *will* be marked by the rise of **FALSE OverMen**, *mean* superior mutants, BETTER than us, handsome like super heroes, more muscular, brilliant like Shakespeare or Einstein, but evil, of Pink extraction rather than SubGenius, they can do *everything* better than we can, self-righteous unclean manmade supermen who will tread *too far* into the accursed Forbidden Sciences and come back controlling Time but will be so hooked on doing so that they will lead the stewing broiling mass of humanity into a technological Hell, TIME JUNKIES, **Lo**, a war with barbarian Martians over a worm we make nuclear beer with... *Jesus Christ, you must believe* it all began in 1982 when all the planets, the Earth and the Sun, lined up with the dog star Sirius, the Silver Star, in 1998 it will draw the Xists to us like flies to a dungdish, oh they won't stay long, they'll leave us after "only" two years, completely free to do as we please, but their unnameable "maggots" will remain. Diabolical caricatures, hideously silent, evasive, but always with us; WE WILL BE DOGS TO THEM *in more ways than you can count.* YES, it'll be bad, "Apocalypse" is a *mild* term for it!! The Book of Revelation is an alien text, those space monsters know what they're about to do to us, they knew it 2000 years ago, but what they *don't* know any more than we do is what *The Prescriptures* mean when they darkly refer to *THE RUPTURE*, the cosmic vortex calamity *after* the Biblical Apocalypse and somehow a godzillion times worse, TIME INTERSECTION, *OMICRON EPSILON*, the hallucinations are externalized, Monsters from the ID, DON'T LAUGH— *what do you think happened to the Elder Gods???* Yes **REPENT!** Repent and fornicate like your very life depended on it, but know all along that the cannibal **False Prophets** wait to sell you out at every trick turn, remember wherever you go that the pleasant, harmless looking human beings shopping all around you will quietly acquiesce to purchasing anything dangled in front of them by a superior intelligence whether the dangler is human or not. Yes, the smiling Pink Boys *of every race* will sell you hot lead, cold steel, and a one-way ticket to Hell without it *ever* crossing their minds that the buttons were pushed by *their* squeaky-clean little fingers.

And so AIEE the gore-drenched nightspawned Ground Zero *GOAL*, the be-all and especially end-all of the full devastating devangelism of the SubGenius is *The Casting Out of False Prophets.* It is the Sacred Vindictive Antinonviolent Mission of Vengeance at which

POISON

GUNS

BEWARE THE
PINK BOYS

the groping alien monster god prods us. *In whichever way JHVH-1 insturcts him,* the SubGenius *unmasks* such false Prophets as he is wont to "Remove" (to ascertain that a SubGenius is not hiding behind the mask); he *Makes Witness* against the guilty one with the full force of the Mockery Sciences: Reviling and Scoffing, the Shattering of Taboos, the Tumping of Graven Images, and otherwise *Waging the Wor* to smite the infidels; and yet, he does this in *common everyday conversation* if he so chooses; his foe never notices the subliminal commands hidden like barbs within the Mystic Jests of the Church. Eventually he escalates to breaking the tolerance barrier through sheer shock value and wades right in along the massing enemy, launching heads and prophesying, **MIND CONTROL GONE OUT OF CONTROL:::**

—!! Wielding the Laser Finger of Unrelenting Humiliation in a zeal-fevered studlust of territorial sexhurt domination!!—

But it is not enough for these fat soft pink devils!

"Too much is always better than not enough." (Dobbs, 1942) The only way for the now-transfigured *Renegade SubGenius* to have his ever mounting thirst for Slack slaked is to schizm away, beyond the formal dictates of the Church; his personal unorthodoxy, in whatever form, has exceeded even those unholy shrieking limits; he symbolically *Kills "Bob"*, disavows any knowledge in general, shucks all semblance of humanity and goes full-tilt Mandrill to become the dreaded ROGUE SUBGENIUS, capable of *any* unmentionable act and owing allegiance to *nothing*. **"Fuck Them If They Can't Take A Joke."**

HA!—It's all been a sham. To keep blame off "Bob," the Rogue Sub has been maintaining a false front of madness while actually serving as a Mercenary Missionary of the elite S.L.A.K.[18] Squad, "Bob's" most beloved secret fanatics, his "Angels of Slack," deliverers of eternal peace.

AAAIIEEEYES! This is an ACTION CHURCH! Jihad! Holy War! Religion is no panty-waist formula to sit upon fatly complacent! It's clean-shaven COLD WAR and getting HOTTER! The Gig is up. We are all equal in God's eyes if not JHVH's and this gives us each a divine license to *SMITE*! Wotan's Winepress spilleth over with the blood of the innocent and there must be JUSTICE! AAIIIEEE! Kali Yuga! Their tainted seed must be clipp'd! *See then the Laws of the SubGenius change with the wind of ContraDiction!... his Church thus reflects life in all its spasmodic glory!!*

18. S.L.A.K. = "SubGenius League of Ass-Kickers."

CHAPTER 4
THE CURSE OF "BOB"

"He duplicates well."
— Comte d'Drummond, PHILO'S HISTORY, chapter on "Bob"

"You are sitting and smoking; you believe that you are sitting in your pipe, and that *your pipe* is smoking *you;* you are exhaling *yourself* in bluish clouds.

"You feel just fine in this position, and only one thing gives you worry or concern: how will you ever be able to get out of your pipe?"

— Baudelaire, *Artificial Paradise*

DOBBS AS TEACHER

In Dobbstown, when "Bodhisattva Dobbs" sits under the open sky unraveling Small Business Parables to the devout 'Zombies' gathered around him, birds flock overhead to give him shade. They let their droppings fall only on his followers.

In his *Dhobma* (Teaching), the Master demands Absolute Self-Deification, the Retainting and Depurification of the Ego, and the Achievement of All Selfish Desires. The only way to handle temptation, he admonishes, is to *go at it until it hurts*. Then it will be finished with you and will leave you alone. Unless you get *hooked*. Then, only larger donations to the Church can save you.

"Don't just *eat* a hamburger . . . eat the HELL out of it." (Economicon 23:78). The 'Profundity Quotient' of his Quotes seems to increase geometrically the longer the student listens.

Dobbs as Teacher destroys the parts of your brain you're better off without. Many happy tales are told of "Bob" and the Kool Aid on the great "Night of Slack" in the jungle . . . the Kool Aid that made them so much more *alive* to their own infinite potential. His lessons may be difficult, even dangerous, but they *work*. Often the cerebral pressure, brought on by confusion, builds and builds until there is an orgasmic 'bursting of the dam,' a breakthrough to Understanding. Only through the aid of irrational thought and *'Notthink'* can this Man Of Men free the mind of inhibitions and bring Slack. There is often pain . . . but the student thanks him for it. *Pays* him for it. And, thus liberated from earthly burdens — wallets, checkbooks, all signs of foul Possession — the Initiate feels lighter, freer, as if a great weight has been lifted.

The Master challenges his Pupil to *'Breakmind.'* He may answer "Yes" or "No" impartially to the same question. He has been known to answer questions concerning universal truths with screams. With suggestive silence. By peeing down his pants-leg.

His most famous sermon was of cosmic simplicity: "Bob" standing on the stage with his hands in his pockets, smoking, looking around and saying nothing. Heated arguments still rage among the monks, often erupting into fatal duels, as to whether the Master consulted his wristwatch during this divine period of Grace.

But Dobbs' methods are not always so peaceable. He has resorted to violence on occasion to cast money-changers from the temple of the mind. Rev. Al Peeyn, an ex-convict and old drinking buddy of "Bob's" who was saved, preached the following of Dobbs at an East Texas revival in '73:

"Ahhhhh, YES! O, NO CHEM-CAN can stand up to the mighty fist o' "Bob"! I've seen him tear through construction sites, bangin' the shit outa them old chemical toilets, THROWIN' 'em to the ground sayin', "You're GOD DAMN WORKMEN! You're *MEN!* You don't have to god-damn shit in the closet! In a SMELLY HOLE! Why don't you fuckin' just . . . pull down your pants and take a DUMP! Right here in the damn construction site! FEED THE DAMN *WORMS!!'*""

Yes, "Bob" is the Natural Man . . . an *earthy* man who would as soon hoot with the boys at a strip show as suavely seduce some wealthy Pink's wife over the finest dinner of Filet Mignon.

There are, unfortunately, some risks to the worship of "Bob".

Those who would be Dervishes or Nuns for "Bob" must beware of *post-enlightenment depression,* to which many fall sway after particularly intense first meetings with He of the Pipe. They become painfully aware of their many trivial Perfections as compared to his One Great And Complete Imperfektion. They realize at once that their pitiful Follies can never run as deep as his, and, moreover, that it will be impossible to regain the newness of their original Moment of Illumination. Again, Dobbs commands that we "Pull the Wool" over our *own* eyes. If we, rather than Dobbs himself, do it first, subsequent wool-pullings can only become more pleasurable and worthwhile.

THE SCARY POWERS OF "BOB"

". . . Who are these that fly as a cloud?" (Isaiah 60:8)

"Bob" sees best when his eyes are closed. He has a Light within his head that enables him to see in the dark, to see into Possible Futures and into the Certain Past(s) . . . to truly "SEE."

He has incredible talents at *dowsing* — at divining the locations of lost persons, money, corpses, etc. The Pipe is the preferred "divining rod," but it is not The Pipe so much as "Bob's" ability to discern "equations" for coming events within the noncausitive patterns of, say, garbage lying in a gutter. Normal, rational, causational thinking confuses "Bob" and lowers him to human functioning. It is *wrong* for "Bob." His using rational thought is as great a waste as it would have been for Jesus to have been a mere camel salesman, or for The Three Stooges to have been staid businessmen.

"BOB" DOES NOT MAKE PLANS, BUT HE POSSESSES A PLAN. And not just one plan. Many plans. The Space Bankers' records and the Atlantean Archives are both recorded as 'codexes' burned into the matrixes of weird old stones used to build the Egyptian and South American Pyramids. These contain the secrets of the Elder Gods, "roadmaps" of the Hollow Earth, blueprints for Man's genetic future. "Bob" can hold these stones in his hand and "read" them (or, rather, decode them by "feeling"), for he has perfected not only his *normal* 5 senses, but 4 of the 5 OTHER senses we all possess vestigially. He can hold a cassette tape up to his head and hear the music recorded on it. Like a dog, he can follow the electromagnetic tracings of a person left by their urine. He can 'home in' on key Earth landmarks by sensing the various strengths of electromagnetic flux attached to their underground geologies.

SALES AND ORALITY

Some say he can speak with animals by this means. Some are convinced his "thermal sense" is so acute that he can look at a bed and see the 'heat outline' of someone who slept there days earlier. Some say he emits 'chirps' in the dark to help find his way around by an echolocation sense similar to a bat's. He does not speak of these things for the sake of national security, so we can only guess. And hope.

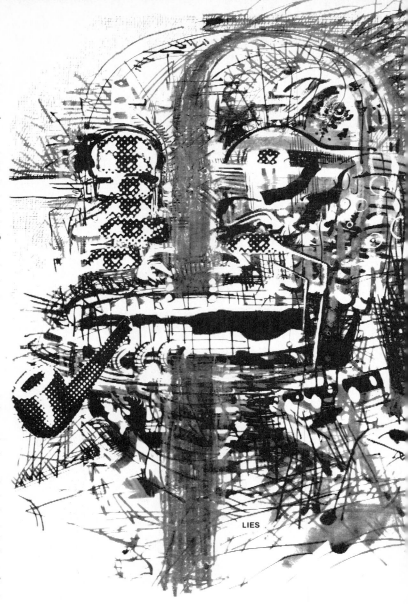

There is no question that Dobbs can follow a person's ESP 'smudge' on the aethers, no matter how far away that person may be, once he has 'whiffread' with his Third Nostril anything that person has touched. He can go into a trance and answer any question about the person if said 'smudge' comes in the form of a $100 bill the person handled, or a blank check he has signed. What "Bob" is collecting from the sale of SubGenius products is not, therefore, the money itself — of which he has far more than enough — but the 'auraic shell,' the little piece of the *soul,* the very *Nental Ife* of the Spenders. He stores not just MONEY, but SLACK and SOULS in the vaults at Dobbstown.

Send "Bob" a large bill you have carried with you for awhile. The longer you carry it and the more it is worth, the more fruitful will be the predictions, diagnoses, and past life summaries he can then provide you.[1]

He can 'apport' objects — that is, expell impossible things spontaneously from his mouth or other openings. He once terrified a diplomat's wife by apporting a great pile of Pipes out onto her bed.

The healing powers of anything "Bob" has touched, or any material passed from his body, are legendary. Thousands will attest to the miraculous cures resulting from his Mojo Bags, Good Luck Healing Roots, and Annointing Oils. The common ingredient to all: The Golden Water From The Fountain Of "Bob" and the sacred Ocre Earth of his Excremeditation. Their actual and *uncontrollable* aphrodisiac qualities were what led to their inevitable banning.

Perhaps the least understood of his magickal gifts are his "Sales Hexes and Charms." By drawing crude runes and symbols on commercial items, he can improve the businesses of friends or ruin those of enemies. The most powerful Sales Charm is, of course, the Image of His Face. Pinks will buy ANYTHING with a **Dobbshead** printed on it.

These charms and hexes can also be used for the bedroomly arts, but Dobbs warns against this as a False Path.

The SubGenius Foundation has in its collection a kitchen window screen from Alabama on which, in 1976, a ghostly but permanent image of "Bob" appeared.[2] In 1978, a miraculous Dobbshead manifestation appeared on a tortilla to a poor Mexican woman.[3] Pilgrims flock to pay homage to these images.

When you find that either a Mystery Pipe, or else a cotterpin and gelatin, has somehow materialized in your house, you know that "Bob" has been there.

THE EPIPHANY OF THE "BOB"

Rev. Pam Nelson shows miraculous

Dobbs Dinner Roll mainfestation.

The dynamic Magnitoscent-Aura of his Divine Grace, Jehovah I, passed through this dinner roll. Ultra high energy neutrinos passing through a Yacatizma Vortex that perfectly bisected the roll resulted in a scorch zone through its length. Rev. "Pam" sliced through the Yacatizmic Focal Plane using her bread knife to an accuracy margin calculated to equal -10^{999}. (Yacatizma is the primary aesthetic force in the universe, and governs the occurence of Aesthetic Release, both in nature and in our own minds.)

You must understand that J.R. "Bob" Dobbs is not often met in the flesh by unInitiated SubGeniuses, unless it is *before* they have heard of the Church. Except in Dobbstown, he almost never appears to those who are *looking* for him; but there are countless testimonials to his Glory by those who met him without knowing who he was. Most of these were his customers. There is also some *danger* to being in his Presence if one is *expecting* something, for the misconceived hopes may *project to* and *bounce off of* him in cyclical, evermounting repetitions that build up and psychically *injure* the seeker.

1. "Bob", P.O. Box 140306, Dallas, TX 75214

2. The miraculous window screen was stolen for the Church by St. Pat Daley the Slackbringer, and is now in our Laboratories undergoing psychic analysis.

3. Swami Satellite Weavers procured the Mystic Dobbshead Tortilla in 1978. It has been subjected to carbon dating, but unsuccessfully: the results keep indicating that the Tortilla has *"always existed,"* which we know to be false.

MIRACLE TORTILLA

(Right) "Bob's" face and number [999] miraculously appeared on tortilla of humble Mexican woman, June 15, 1963, in Plano, Texas.

For this reason, and others to be revealed, "Bob's" main mortal friends, his "drinking buddies" one might say, are primarily experienced Mexican brujos, Tibetan lamas, Siberian shamans, Native American medicine men, African witch doctors, old Druids, Witches, dozens of LIVING CHRISTIAN SAINTS that the Vatican refuses to recognize, about ten conflicting Jesii, and the real man that Marvel Comics' "Dr. Strange" is based on. "Bob," yes, dares to claim that he has been *drunk* with *Jesus*.

We Scribes who staff the SubGenius Foundation, Inc., are constantly challenged by the difficulty of reaching "Bob" when we need him, or *think* we need him (for he is always there when you *really* need him), despite the Secret Phone in his shoe. It's best to look at this inaccessibility as a test of faith that will make us stronger if we can but *believe*.

He does not usually speak to us audibly. He puts a thought into a person's head unexpectedly; the recipient begins to dwell on it until it snowballs into a fullblown obsession. One knows it's from "Bob" by that very obsessive quality.

If you hear a friendly voice muttering in your head, it is probably *not* "Bob" but your own newly-awakened "Bobself."

He does speak to a very few in the uppermost Hierarchy of the Church, but never in conventional ways. "Bob" in this respect is something of a 'show-off' . . . or perhaps it is just his mischievious spirit.

The Foundation has a disconnected phone on which he calls. His spoken messages sometimes come over car radios, and he has appeared to Philo Drummond on his television set at home. Ivan Stang once had the disconcerting experience of seeing "Bob" speaking from a whole wall of department-store TVs which had been tuned to different channels. His directives have been discovered on supposedly blank audio tape and video cassettes, and one young SubGenius swears a speaking Dobbshead appeared to him on the video game, GORF. Phantom memos appear constantly around the Foundation Laboratories, once written in phosphenes on the air itself.

He always seems to know where we are. **Pastor Buck Naked** stopped at a gas station during a cross-country trip only to be told by a puzzled attendant that a tall, pipe-smoking man had left a note there for someone fitting Buck's description and bearing his license plate number (and it was a borrowed car that Buck had never used before).

Dr. X has reported what must be the two most spectacular, if disturbing, cases of Dobbs communication. Both times, the messages were supernaturally *written out* — once in the hideous, coiling entrails of a mutilated cow, and once on a bathroom wall in an *impossibly regimented swarm of cockroaches* which spelled out the words, "COME TO DOBBSTOWN" with their bodies.

One SubGenius claims to have gotten a *threatening* message from ''Bob,'' written first in ghostly blood on a mirror and then in *scratches in his flesh,* but this is unsubstantiated.

In several countries, all at the same time in 1977, there was a fall of several thousand Pipes from the sky, along with even more tiny tadpoles of an entirely new species. When asked about this event, ''Bob'' simply turned his inscrutable grin towards the heavens and chuckled.

Only the superstitious deny the supernatural.

fills the seven continents and twenty seas. His aura, his energy color, glows white hot with the blackness of the Rift between Earth, Water, Fire and Air.

Following a manifestation like this there have been reported cases of severe radiation burns (such as those which disfigured Dr. Drummond), permanent brain damage, and probably the worst side effect of all: The Conspiracy's sudden interest in you.

''BUT WHERE DO *I* FIT IN?''

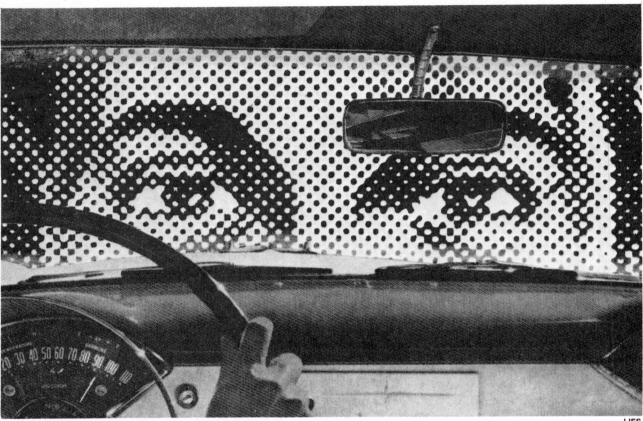

LIES

It is most advisable that any SubGenius be prepared — surgically — at Dobbstown before he dares undergo a face-to-face meeting with ''Bob.'' People who have actually met him (see Case Studies 18—65, esp. the E. Keller case) usually come away disoriented, confused, somethimes scarred physically, and frequently afflicted with short-term amnesia. Many do not re-call the incident until the next day, or much later under hyp-nosis. Only then do they begin to understand why their skin was suddenly sunburned and why 2 hours had inexplicably dis-appeared . . .

Just prior to a ''Bob'' appearance you can expect a low-level hum, like bees, accompanied by a pungent odor and stifling heat. Your extremities will start tingling and then go numb, and you will suddenly feel ''high'' as if drugged. As the Grin and Pipe materialize, your watch will stop, but any wounds or diseases will be healed. If you are carrying a tape deck, the tape will be erased but the batteries will be recharged. As ''Bob'' comes into full being, you may risk being driven mad by exposure to the ''dots'' and to the *Pstench of ''Bob'':* a psychophantasmagorical sight/sound/odor which seemingly

Subsequent to the ''Bob'' Flap of 1967, for instance, the in-famous ''Men In Black'' showed up at the witnesses' homes the next day and threatened them with imprisonment or death if they dared speak of their sightings. These Mystery Extor-tionists usually pose as either Jehovah's Witnesses or C.I.A. agents.

One SubGenius got a suspicious ''call from ''Bob''''at a *phone booth* and then went to meet an apparent ''Bob'' at a lavishly furnished house. This ''''Bob'''' proceeded to rape her pitilessly. When she returned the next day accompanied by armed policemen, however, she found the house a broken down old wreck, devoid of furniture, full of cobwebs, ap-parently untouched for years.

The conclusion we must reluctantly face is that many of these ectosplasmodic manifestations are not ''Bob'' at all, but ''False Bobs.'' **''The demon is a liar; he will lie to confuse us.''** (THE EXORCIST) We Scribes and Doktors have been imper-sonated by ''Bob's'' enemies, who show up at newspapers claiming to be SubGeniuses and making us look like obnox-ious fools. So why shouldn't the *demons* who resist ''Bob'' im-personate *him?*

For this reason, the predictions must be carefully screened. The Beings often confuse us with predictions of, for instance, upcoming train disasters that are *just wrong enough* that when we attempt to warn the "authorities" of the impending crash, it happens to the *next* train out . . . which makes it appear that *we* were the saboteurs.

On the other hand, there is certainly truth to the Diversity of the "Bob" Nature. Perhaps these appearances are the 'bad moods' of Dobbs, externalized into reality against his own best interests. This may explain why he never frowns; his repressed impatience *leaves his body* as an independent force.

As the old hymn says, "There's a Good "Bob" and There's a Bad "Bob" . . . there's a Real "Bob" and There's a Psuedo-"Bob.""[4] A young "Bob" and an old "Bob," a fancy "Bob" and a sloppy "Bob," a bald "Bob" and a hippie "Bob," a knife "Bob" and a fork "Bob" . . . the list goes on. But there have *always been "Bobs."* He has had well over 365 past lives — all of them beginning on different days, which makes every day his birthday — and this **trail of "Bobs"** can be traced from our modern High Tech "Bob" all the way back to the Stone Age "Bobs" and, long before that, **the First "Bob"** — the first *upright* "Bob," anyway.

Now, there's no speed limit on the timeless Highway of Slack, but to use it you must pay "Bob" a toll. For it cost the First "Bob" and his mighty monks and monsters a great many slave-lives to build that Highway 60 million years ago. Yes! It *was* BUILT!

The First "Bob" was the *first perfect Yeti* created by the gods to lord over their prehistoric human/Yeti colony, Atlantis (or, more correctly, "Antiquitum"). This was indeed at the close of the Age of Reptiles, long before secular evolutionist "science" credits upright apes with any existence whatsoever. The First "Bob," like all fullblood Yetis, was a 12-foot furred giant who lived for almost 10,000 years and was so intelligent that he could stroll naked in the most severe climes. He was the first hero-figure of mythology — the Son of Wotan/Ra who is known in other languages as "Balder" and "Perseus."

In Atlantis, as today, the youth were so spoiled and jaded that the creative essence was deteriorating — for Atlantis was the true "Garden of Eden," the petri dish of the gods. These same gods realized that to reinstill creative desperation in their pets, they had to inject War, Death, and Crime into the society.[5] This task fell to the First "Bob," though it is The Conpiracy which does this today. But in those days, *the two were the same!* A great cataclysm (which shall be discussed elsewhere), and a battle in "Heaven" among the gods, caused the First "Bob" to be split into two opposites: The Good Twin as manifested by our "Bob" today, and the . . . the Evil Twin, or Anti"Bob" . . . who is yet unidentified: the Spirit of The Conspiracy.

4. One of the 84 Glassmadness Hymns to "Bob."

BE PROUD OF YOUR NORTHERN TIBETAN HERITAGE!

AND THEY RULED THE EARTH AS WELL FOR MANY YEARS UNTIL THE TIME OF "GREAT DYING"

Hal Robins/Paul Mavrides

BUT LIFE CONTINUED TO EVOLVE ANYWAY....

5. From *The Voynich Manuscript* by James Lang, a translation of a book *about* the forbidden book *The Necronomicon*, by a 13th Century monk named Martin Chance, The Gardener.

No doubt the Anti"Bob" lives today, but has yet to "lay all his cards on the table" and is biding his time until the prophesied Day of the Unmasking. There are hints of his identity, though. First, he is definitely *not* the same as the Antichrist foretold in Revelation. *The Prescriptures* suggest that the Anti"Bob" will be called "ObO" and will be identified with the number *333*. Another forbidden tome, *The Ages of Earth and the Secrets of Atlantis* by Guenon, specifies that he is in league with the "Nazi *deros*" who honeycomb the Hollow Earth . . . yet he will become a beloved world leader. Yet another key prophecy, linked to the "Bozo" mythos of The Four Insane Mouthmen,[6] points to his leading a perverse offshoot of the Church of the SubGenius in which an army of lobotomized youth, *surgically changed* to resemble evil *clowns,* will attempt to be the first group to rendezvous with the Xists and be changed to OverMen. One sinister note: the Foundation recently received this fragment of what must have been a much longer letter:

> ". . . *has* to become evil. I was instrumental in preserving the clown's shoes at Brockton Shoe Museum — this site will surely become the holy center for the bozo cult in years to come. It is the run-down, dirty, and washed-up demonic clown-brother "NOZO" (whom some call "BOBO") who is the real threat — the anti-bozo who threatens us with *ruin!!* If we destroy Bozo, Nozo will become all-powerful, perhaps endangering "Bob" himself —
>
> The Bozo sub-cult here has, also, a Bob-parallel known as "Ed" — there are two manifestations, known as "Ed-Bob" and "Bob-Ed" . . . "Ed" also modelled for nu---"

Here the letter ends in burnt edges.

---

6. See the Firesign Theater album, *"I Think We're All Bozos On This Bus"* OR send The SubGenius Foundation 20 million dollars to remake the two amateur prophecy films, *"Let's Visit THE WORLD OF THE FUTURE"* (Charley Muck, 1973) and *"PIE PIE"* (Janor Hypercleats, 1956).

7. From Chapter 8 of *Chapter 8* by Bulldada Time Control Laboratories.

While "Bob" can keep up with his past and future lives, he cannot see into the Dark Zone where his evil double lives a *concurrent* life. "Bob" is powerful, yes . . . but the Opposition is nearly as powerful as he.

So long as Earth's fate hangs in the undecided balance between these two powers, the Dark and the Light, we SubGeniuses must not rest.

The prophecy says:

"True SLACK shall not come until one Twin has devoured the Other and assimilated his Essence unto himself."[7]

He could be anywhere.

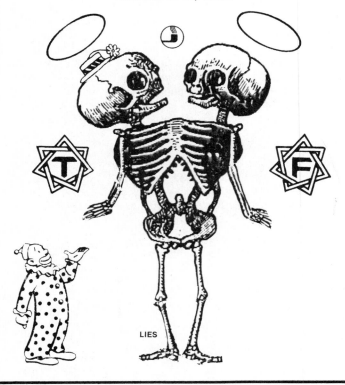

LIES

13013 = BOB; B=2, B=2, 0=15, B=2 ... 2 +15 + 2 = 19 = 0 - "!" = 13013 = 8 - Time Control = 888 plus 111 (SLACK) = 999!!!

NUMEROLOGY OF THE PROOF OF THE "BOB"

"Bob's" numbers are **999**, **"606,"** and **13013**.

The occult significance of the first two is obvious.

He's the *good* guy, or, at least, the opposite of the bad guy.

13013 offers final, logical proof of "Bob's" Message.

It is the height in feet of the Pyramid of Cheops times the width of its base. It is the number of recorded cattle mutilations since President Kennedy was assasinated. It is the sum total of all Magic Numbers in all numerology systems. It is the exact amount that John Rockefeller borrowed to build his first Model T. It is the original production cost in slave-lives of the building of the lost city of Palenque in Yucatan. It is the cash amount in dollars of "Bob's" first sale. It is the street address (on E. 60th in Chicago) of a main Illuminist training center (city managers are schooled there). It is the street address of one of the members of the band, *Drs. for "Bob."* It is the exact cost in pennies of a bucket of pills at Dobbstown.

And in the book of Revelation, Chapter 13, Verse 13, JHVH-1 has this to say:

13:13 "And he doeth great wonders, so that he maketh fire to come down from Heaven in the sight of men . . ."

"Bob" summoning the Saucers? *What else could it mean??* Notice it does not say, "fire to *fall* down," but to "come" down. Look to this chapter in your Bible yourself. But don't read much past that line . . . it's too scary.

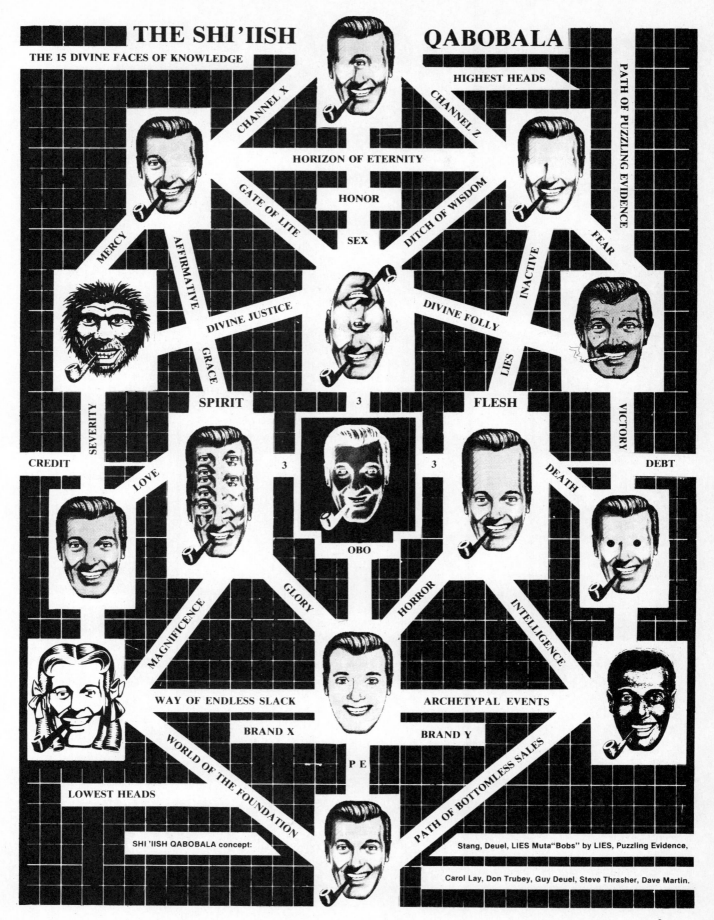

THE SHI'IISH QABOBALA

THE 15 DIVINE FACES OF KNOWLEDGE

HIGHEST HEADS

PATH OF PUZZLING EVIDENCE

CHANNEL X

CHANNEL Z

HORIZON OF ETERNITY

HONOR

GATE OF LITE

DITCH OF WISDOM

SEX

MERCY

AFFIRMATIVE

INACTIVE

FEAR

DIVINE JUSTICE

DIVINE FOLLY

GRACE

LIES

SPIRIT

3

FLESH

VICTORY

SEVERITY

CREDIT

LOVE

3

3

DEATH

DEBT

OBO

GLORY

HORROR

INTELLIGENCE

MAGNIFICENCE

WAY OF ENDLESS SLACK

ARCHETYPAL EVENTS

BRAND X

BRAND Y

WORLD OF THE FOUNDATION

P E

PATH OF BOTTOMLESS SALES

LOWEST HEADS

SHI'IISH QABOBALA concept:

Stang, Deuel, LIES Muta"Bobs" by LIES, Puzzling Evidence,

Carol Lay, Don Trubey, Guy Deuel, Steve Thrasher, Dave Martin.

THE TRUE PIPE

IT'S YOUR **TRUE PIPE**

"Bob's" Pipe is an icon of the most profound mystery. Many, many theories have been advanced to explain it.

One sect *fears* The Pipe. They believe it is not "Bob" making the decisions, but The Pipe itself — it being an evil alien from another planet which 'activates' as soon as it is clenched in the teeth of a holy man, and thence controls the 'host.' These are simple LIES. The Pipe *is* an alien, but it no more controls Dobbs than we control the automobiles that carry US around.

Other theologians see The Pipe as a symbol of the male *lingam* inserted into the female *yoni,* represented by "Bob's" mouth. This is so heretical and blasphemous that its adherents would be stoned to death in public squares, were this world run by True SubGeniuses.

It must also be made clear that The Pipe does *not* symbolize the smoking of marijuana. It makes no difference what is in "Bob's" Pipe (it's the herb *habafropzipulops*). It only matters that he *smokes a Pipe.* DO NOT QUESTION THE MEANING "BEHIND" THE PIPE. There is none. The Pipe itself is not a symbol.

However, neither is it just a pipe. The history of The Pipe and its powers is literally true, and all-important to our understanding of Dobbs.

It is a twin, though not in appearance, of the True Pipe or "peace pipe" brought to the Plains Indians several hundred years ago by a supernatural UFO-goddess called **The White Buffalo Woman** (who was, in fact, identical with the Blessed Virgin that prophesied from a UFO to three little girls at Fatima, Portugal earlier this century). This was an Xist manifestation. As long as *both Pipes* remain *perpetually lit,* the Xists will know that there is still something worth sparing on Earth. This is why "Bob" keeps in such close touch with the Lakota holy men in South Dakota.

Both Pipes have tremendous powers of healing and destruction, but it is untrue that The Pipe is *necessarily* armed with a Death Ray; nor is it true that Dobbs uses his Pipe for sex.

There *have* been sightings of Pipe-shaped UFOs in our skies.

BE SURE AND BAPTIZE YOUR CHILDREN IN CHURCH

"He that smoketh a pipe shall fly away in it."
(Arnoldclessians 7:11)

"He that diggeth a pit shall fall into it."
(ECCLESIASTES 10:8)

CHAPTER 5
"YOU CAN BE WHAT YOU WON'T" —THE SECRETS OF **SLACK**

"The Lord is not slack concerning His promise, as some men count slackness; but is LONGSUFFERING to us ward, NOT WILLING THAT ANY SHOULD PERISH, BUT THAT ALL SHOULD COME TO REPENTANCE" (II Peter 3:9).

"My people are destroyed for a lack of Knowledge."
—Hosea 4:6

"Therefore thus saith the Lord YAHWEH, Behold, I lay in Zion for a foundation a stone, a tried stone, a precious *stone*, a Sure Foundation: he that believeth *shall not make haste* (shall have *Slack*)."
—Isaiah 28:16

"I'd rather be lucky than good *any* day."
—"Bob" at a picnic in 1953.

Alongside your normal, everyday life, there is another life: one in which you *have SLACK.*

The vast majority of Mankind remains in ignorance; most humans spend their lives in spiritual darkness, at the crazy mercy of chance and accident. SubGeniuses, basking in the 5,000-watt Light of Dobbs, are *also* at the mercy of chance and accident—yet given a boost by The Pipe Bringer, the seeker can "climb aboard" chance and accident and *ride* them like a cosmic surfboard on the oceans of the **Luck Plane**, "hanging ten" on the very same waves of randomness that cause *humans* such envious HATE.

For, even if there's *actually no "reason"* for anything, even if nothing can be known *for sure* in an unbelievable world where psychotics run the Department of the Interior and mutilate cattle, we can still retain one concrete ball of fact that the most shattered instincts cannot deny: *Something is going on, and we deserve better.*

We keep getting these *hints*. Little integrated Hints of meaning that are much more fun than the longer hours of non-meaning. Hints that **the world owes us a living.**

Hunches, strange impressions, omens: the C.B. static of the Luck Plane aethers, occasional flares of Future Luck Patterns that bust through their normal confines and 'snag' on such rough edges of our reality as the psychic distress of a job-hunting SubGenius.

Even though watered-down, they provide the barest glimmer of something *about* to happen or which *should* happen. (It also occurs due to interference or "crossover" from another source, but that's literally too soul-rending to explain *yet.*)

We have *absolute proof* that those billion subtle chance occurrences that govern our lives, which, due to occasional megacoincidence beyond explanation, seem almost as if they were 'caused' by some great Intention, ARE INDEED **CAUSED** by some great **INTENTION**! And nothing could be more *face-slappingly evident* than that this alleged Intention is one of *Wrath.* Thus is supported, in one *irrefutable* readout of logic, the mad alien JHVH-1's claim to be the *Giuppetto* of Earth's *Pinnochios.* He no longer operates with His sweeping flourishes of cataclysm nor His Blatant Flaming Sword-in-the-Sky, but through that subatomic network visible only in the desultory but decisive 'coincidences' governing mortal life. *All* mortal lives, or only a few? On this He cruelly leaves us dangling.

The damn'd Hints are habit-forming. They give us cheap thrills of cosmic acknowledgement with each clue they present of the monster's Presence. These microscopic event-signals, reassuring us that we're on the "right track," appear everywhere; they show their stalwart faces of reinforcement in garbage cans and traffic lights. What is a typical Hint? When you're about to telephone a friend and *he* calls *you* at the exact moment that you picked up the phone, and your voices connect without a ring on either end, *that*

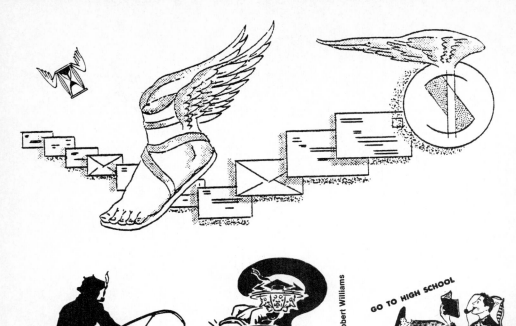

BASIC KNOWLEDGE

IN BEDROOM SLIPPERS!

Robert Williams

Monika Vidi

is a Hint. When you receive *on the same day* an unexpected bill from the IRS for $1,000 and also a check from a forgotten creditor for $1,000.01, *that* is a Hint. When you're hopelessly lost in the canyons of downtown and your destination abruptly looms up in front of you, Twilight Zone style, *that's* a Hint. When you're in a state of sweaty indecision as to which of two people you 'should' go out with on a date, and a song blasts out of the radio making the right choice as clear as fetus pee, *that's* a Hint.

Moments when everything 'falls together' have a quality of Hinting that there's Someone Up There who either Likes Us or Hates Us. When enough interlocking synchronicities have accrued, they begin to look suspiciously like personal messages. THIS WAY LIES MADNESS. Only "Bob" is *that* important!

It partly depends on how hard you're looking for unusual strings of causation, but also on what you *happen to notice*. It is exactly 65% like slipping on banana peels of sudden deduction. You *can* fall flat on your ass.

The same fun and danger lie in such complex systems of subconscious guidance as Tarot or I Ching. You don't *need* those, though they're good for yuks; keep your eyes open, and you'll see the equivalent in the comic book racks of convenience stores. *Just don't go overboard.*

Many SubGenii find that certain occupations breed the antibody Hints more fruitfully than others, and they begin to concentrate exclusively on these. The most common instance: a teen keeps getting Hints from songs, so he decides to become a rock star. Any fool knows that's probably the most crowded, vain and sick path possible . . . but you *never can tell,* and the Hints may, demoniacally, keep providing encouragement. One's Inner Career, the concentrated professional exercise of a chosen Discipline, can be a Hint-track to Heaven or Toll Road to Hell.

Analactive *job compulsions* can be followed so long that they become your only Hint-Funnel. You'll wake up one morning and find yourself stranded on your island of activity. It's uninhabited — but it's volcanic and about to blow. You go insane. Clinically, *UnSubGeniusly* insane. Slack-impotent. Desouled. Yet, half the time you can still function. *This has already happened to about 50% of our white-collar American executives, and their spouses.*

Becoming completely wrapped up in your Hint-tunnel, throwing your body and brain into some oddball Work, hones the *work* abilities to a godlike edge, but it can leave you sadly lacking in equally necessary areas. An erstwhile holy man might completely ignore, for instance, the talent of *acting* (as opposed to *being*) self-assured, which most normal Ords and Materialites develop in the cradle. He might have Olympian insight and private creativity, but he can't bluff his way through the job world . . . so, to everyone else, he's a Nerd, a Pinkest Boy, and is socially tormented accordingly. Eventually he begins to take Their enormous repertoire of false fronts *seriously*. In this state of quasihuman ignorance he's helpless! Woe be to the misled SubGenius who follows the dangling carrot he tied to his own equine head and misses entirely the four hundred untended Free Carrot stands by the roadside!

Yes, the road of Hints holds many a blind alley and scary dark cul-de-sac. A SubGenius must be steadfast as the mighty amoeba and stray not one R.C.H. from the every-which-way **Path o' "Bob."**

But to what are the Hints pointing? Or else, what is YAHWEH-1 trying to lure us *away* from?

It can only be that elusive, almost definitively unreachable state of being we call *SLACK.* Aren't YOU more than ready for TOTAL Slack?

John Hagen

?WHAT'S GOING ON? IS THIS HELL?

Slack was known to the Buddha — to Lao-tse — to Jesus — to Billy Graham — to all the great Avatars.

But were they able to *communicate* it? "Bob" said, **"These people don't necessarily need to know the *Whole Truth*; they just need *Slack*!"** (Bordruum Tape 18:18)

WHAT IS HE TELLING US?

MAN WAS BORN WITH ORIGINAL SLACK, yet most 'civilized' peoples don't believe in it, and their most learned scholars can't even *comprehend* it. THAT is why the Idiot is closer to the Divine, why "Bob" is adulated for his Follies rather than his skills. If you do not *believe* in Slack, it will not make itself available to you.

For 200 years the natives of Haiti, the ancient shamans with long straight Pipes, have sought Slack, which they call *Bobjuju*. We call them primitive, but who is to say . . ? They, serenely smoking 'Frop and conversing with Jah, or we, endlessly hunting down our own selves in the cities? Which are the barbarians, the blooddrinkers? Which will be granted the power of *Bobjuju*? I saw him rip off a chicken's head with his teeth and drink the blood while copulating with an 8 foot tall albino native woman with white hair and silver eyes . . . the 'Frop dust was so thick it had to be swept under the rug . . . no policeman could come near that spot because of the *Bobjuju* . . . to suddenly fully *know* the power of Slack would make a Pink Man's brain sizzle and *fry* inside his skull.

Above all, no matter its cost in continuity, SLACK MUST COME FIRST in the life of any Initiate . . . at least, until Slack *becomes him.*

He who is rich in Slack is richer than the most statused Conspiracy *thing*-monger.

Slack is the Alladin's Lamp that opens the *other* five senses. It is the yardstick by which we *should* measure *ourselves.* It is really the only good reason to get out of bed, and if you don't believe *that,* you are surely lost in Perdition.

THE INSCRUTABILITY OF SLACK

The Slack that can be described is not the true Slack.

Slack, in its cosmic sense, is that which remains when all that is *not* Slack is taken away. But Slack is a trickster. It is unknowable, ineffable, unsearchable, incomprehensible . . . *hidden* in revelation.

For Slack *comprises the Universe.* It is the Logos, the Tao, the *Wor,* the *Ain Soph* of the Qabbala. The 'aether' does not consist of atoms, but of an ultimately simple hydromechanical field DEVOID OF COMPLICATIONS. Just as Matter is but a slowly vibrating form of Energy, so is Energy a slowly vibrating form of *SLACK.* The Luck Plane *itself,* the Boundless World of Divine Names, is composed of Slack. It is an energy/antienergy field, far more delicate than Wotan's neutrinos and bobyons, permeating everything.

SLACK is neither created nor destroyed.[1] If you don't have it, *it's somewhere it shouldn't be!*

Abstract unto incomprehensibility, it is the definitionless, insubstantial *substance* of the All — the ISness of the BIZness.

It pervades space and fuels Time, yet it is not always 'activated.' Sometimes it is in a state of cosmic tension, of **AntiSlack.**

Slack started out suffusing the whole universe, but as the creation of *Adversaria* (The World of Matter) occured, it whirlpool-

1. This theory was proven as a Scientific Law by Rev. Extremo Deluxe in a laboratory Spasmatron test in 1976. See AMAZING SCIENCE, Oct. 1956.

ed into itself until it became an Ultimate Center Point which then grew outwards — leaving an *extremely* diffuse near-nothingness, a *near*-Slacklessness called *Nosallack,* in the further abcesses of space where the Universe's "Edge" is ever-expanding, and where jerks go when they die. (It will expand until it runs into the literal *Brick Wall* that encloses it, on that **Day of Judgement** *even the Angels dread*.) The "Ultimate Center Point" of all Slack is what many call "God," I YAM, the White Light of G'Broagfran: the MACROPROSAURUS ("Great Big-Headed Lizard" (?!) in magical lingo).

Because Slack is measureless to the point of inconcievability, it is therefore much like NOTHING. Beyond Light, you see, there is a super-essential DARKNESS (and beyond that, of course, a double-super-essential Light again). The ancient drunkard Dionysus told of a "dazzling obscurity which outshines all brilliance with the intensity of its darkness." This is the Void, the Emptiness: that great Shortage which winos and other philosophers have called 'The Hole.'

All religions tht are worth-a-shit preach of two kinds of energy constantly passing through our bodies: Something and Nothing. As long as the SubGenius can keep them in balance he has "Super Luck Powers" which no Financial setback can hinder.

By monitoring the volume of mail and phone calls that come into The SubGenius Foundation, we have discovered a 13 Day Cycle to the ebb and flow of the tide of SubGenius activity. They all slack off at the same time and they all work at the same time (though in wildly varying ways). So we know that Slack moves in a wave formation. CATCH that Big Wave . . . get in that curl and SLIDE!

If any SubGenius has actually reached *total* Slack, *True Slack,* he remains hidden. Perhaps Confucius, Mohammed, Siddhartha M. Gautama, Moe Howard or Jack the Ripper were ancients who achieved it. Or maybe they just achieved fame, which nowadays passes for Slack.

Slack is like freedom, but unlike freedom it brings no responsibility. "*"Bob" does not worry."* (Philo's *History*) One thing we have in common with the evil Bozo cult is that we wish to be Not Responsible. One might suggest that a devoted alcoholic, a habitual half-gallon-a-day wino has ascended to this. But it isn't permanent; he may *die* for *years*. Among other things, Slack is absolutely "free" time, devoid of all stress, to do *whatever you damn well please* for "eternity," Without Drawbacks, Apologies, Side-Effects, Spoilage, Without Remorse.

TRUE SLACK *IS* SOMETHING FOR NOTHING.

However, such merely *physical* Slack has its own dangers. If human beings are immortal, they become correspondingly flaccid. Without deadlines, they will always postpone everything forever; they will do *nothing*. Not even think. Not even *feel*. Blank food tubes that will eventually turn back into Primal Water. "Slack Junkies."

Slack, on the contrary, somehow manages to be a great Motive without slapping the speed-limit of Death on the road. If we knew how the paradox was resolved, we'd already *have* Slack.

The famous weirdo Eugene Ionesco said, "We are made to be immortal, and yet we die. It's horrible, it can't be taken seriously."

There is definitely some kind of true psychoSlack floating around out 'there,' bobbing carefree on the airwaves, which is currently either incomprehensible to us or *restricted* from us. ODIN-1 keeps taunting us, telling us there's *something, somewhere*. Nyah nyah. We know it exists by the incredible extremes he goes to to *hide* it from us. He Hints of it, but we must find it *on our own*. But He's a crafty deity, and that may

Hagen

be His whole idea — He may well be using *us* as bloodhounds to find it for Himself. Or, possible, He hid part of Himself *in* our Slackless selves in order to make Himself *appreciate* it again. Certainly, he gave us "Bob" to show us that it *can* be achieved.

We are probably better off without *total* Slack in its *cosmic* sense, which might require sheer DEATH. Perhaps all those 1950s movie scientists were right when they said, "There are some things Man was not meant to know." But they were talking about Atomic Monsters, not Slack. At any rate, for better or worse, we've seen the Hints, and if we don't make the grab for Slack we risk spending our declining years muttering regretfully of the laziness that let us become just like Others. For while it's *damn tough* for a SubGenius to advance to the OverMan state, it is with no effort at all that he slides back into Mediocretinism.

What's so bad about being one of Them? Nothing, if you already *are* one. *They* don't know what they're missing. *They* don't know we're all wading in pools of congealed unreality; they're asleep on their feet and take everything in their

up to make us open the door a crack further, just for a *peek*. We don't *think* there's anything there, but, you know . . . *just in case.*

What course of action would most likely make us stumble over 'the Answer' and fall into its gaping maw? Without too much *work,* that is? How do we make the reach for Slack, aside from just grabbing "Bob's" sleeve and *leaning* on him?

SLACK: a surge of uncorrupted gumption, an explosion of the "self" — not obliterating it, but *bloating* it.

Normally, consciousness is quite narrow. You see what you *have* to see and no more. Even *that* is difficult, because the left brain and right brain are usually fighting like a couple of dinosaurs. You can knock them out with booze or Valium, but in the long run it blunts your concentration even *worse* (underimbibing has the same toxic effect). The idea is to widen perception, get The Big Picture, and *then* start beaming in on specifics.

EASE WARTIME NERVES!!

hallucination at *face value. They* aren't *tempted* by the glimpses and sniffs of Slack that are jiggled momentarily before our eyes, only to be snatched away. Things that seem utterly bland to us work *Them* up into a froth.

What then are we supposed to *find*? *"Real"* Reality? AW, WHO GIVES A FUCK. Hell, just something we *think* is reality will do the trick. After all, Slack *might* be something that *just sounds good.*

ABC'S OF THE SECRETS OF EXISTENCE

Poets, philosophers, acidheads, salesmen: everybody wants to know, "What Is Reality?" Some say it's a vast Unknowable so astounding and raw and naked that it grips the human mind and shakes it like a puppy shakes a rag doll. A lot of good that does us. Others say the Universe is so uncaring, so stupifyingly automatic and unchanging, that it is one gloriously serene Indifference. So big deal.

This is all a bunch of crap, but those Hints keep popping

Holy men have pointed out that brains are like radios that can be tuned, that the will is like a gun that can be aimed. Some can aim better than others. Pinks usually aren't aware that their "gun" will even *fire;* they use it to *pound* things to death. Then, when they finally realize they *can fire* it, the barrel's so clogged with dirt and gore that **BLAM!** the thing splits down the middle and it misses everything.

In starting any task the SubGenius should decide to use either the "shotgun" effect or the "deer rifle" effect, but NEVER BOTH! Backfire *is* possible if ANYTHING is clogging the "gun". So you have to keep "cleaning" the barrel with *insane swings of extreme moods.* To stay healthy your emotional life must be PUMPED and EXERCISED, just like your heart, *to discharge excess emotional "juice."* A charge can build up fast, and with no place to direct it, with too much coming IN and not enough going OUT, there is emotional constipation — the "flattening" of the personality seen so plainly in many Normals.

The way to avoid the pendulum spending too much of its 'swing' in the Bad Mood side is to make them into NEW,

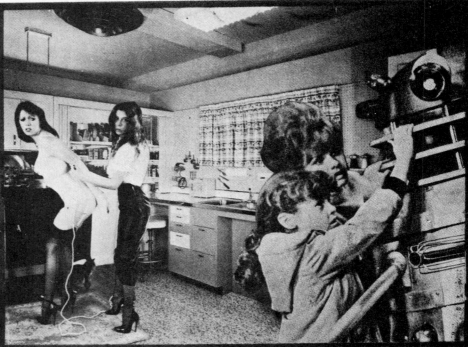

Rev. Joe Schwind

WEIRD, heretofore UNDISCOVERED MOODS: the so-called **"Mood Exploration"** that Doktors recommend. (Manic depression? That's just the Pink Witch Doctor's way of *explaining* a SubGenius who's become a mental Bodybuilder, an Incredible Hulk of the emotions. He doesn't need Thorazine — he needs SLACK!)

If you're going to change, you must KILL YOUR ENTIRE PREVIOUS LIFE — you must DIE to everything you have "known".

You must follow the Way of Dobbs.

You must go all out, full tilt, to the very farthest *extreme* you can reach, by driving yourself to some idiotic *limit* or other, by stretching the threshholds of pain and sanity as tight as they can go before they snap, by ramming yourself head-on into *something, anything,* as long as it drives your brains so far past the point of Survival Urge that they just don't *care* anymore about keeping the body alive, where they start opening to the *other things,* where the thrust is so drastic that everything else, life, death, seem exactly alike, where everything on Earth is so trivial in comparison to the internal hurricane that the poor blinded brain-pan just gives up and

   clicks

into a new state, an altered perspective, a spilt-milk openness in which the senses finally *get naked,* in which you start receiving *new* signals, not just the bounced-back echoes of the ones you already sent out, in which your brain is a movie screen facing the Projector of Infinity.

It's a sudden, exalted, and *usually momentary* vision of **the Ultimate in Leisure.** Wise Asses call it *satori,* the Moment of True Slack. It's *insane* and beautifully unshakeable by logic or rationality.

True Ecstacy, in its high-faluting sense, is impossible to reach on drugs. "Bob" teaches that to make the great jump for Ecstacy, you must **"DISCONNECT."**

"Bob" artificially induces *shock* in Initiates, so that the brain learns to habitually Disconnect under stress. Thus, it works on intuition alone — direct knowledge, ". . . so that not even a thought stands between you and the thing you know."[2] With this comes tremendous powers, called "Siddhis." We've all heard stories of emergencies in which some normally wimpy mom, in order to save her kid from a burning car, suddenly acquires the strength of a thousand madwomen and rips *all* the doors off their hinges. Utilizing this effect, Dobbs sets up *fake emergencies* to inflict on his followers so that they're jolted out of "sanity." He'll hire an arsonist to set your house on fire so that when you wake up to the smell of smoke, that curtain of dumbness is ripped out of the way and you "wake up" *completely.* What often occurs is that the terrified pupil's brain, using all its capabilities for the first time, is not only able to cope with the immediate problem, but is *also* flooded with all kinds of extraneous realizations that have *nothing* to do with the matter at hand, but which the pupil had been *hiding from himself* for *years.* Thus while he's helping his roommate down a rope ladder, flames licking at his back, he's thinking, *"Gee, maybe I should quit drinking."*

"Bob" calls this method **"The Zen of Terror"** and his "little accidents" are called *UltraKoans* ("Koans" are the super-bulldada "impossible questions" that regular Zen Masters pose to their students). They are perfect for While-U-Wait ego-breaking. The pupil or "John" is shocked into "Displacement Mode," in which he feels he is "standing to one side" of himself *and* reality — seeing it all, but no longer *in* it. One foot in the water, one on the ground, so to speak. The rational mind throws up its hands in exasperation and there is a SUDDEN BREAKTHROUGH into BRIGHT LIGHT. Then the distinction between light and dark evaporates, along with the body, which dissolves into glowing, floating, smokelike par-

2. A cool line which "Bob" ripped off from Gurdjieff — WITH THE PERMISSION OF "G's" GHOST!

ticles. The soul *becomes* the smoke from "Bob's" Pipe, drifting towards Slack. Inside becomes outside and there is a feeling of serenity in the midst of all-out chaos and violence. The concepts of sin, remorse, and even Time disappear and are replaced by a *direct* kind of perception *unfettered* by Common Sense.

"Bob" has experienced this Ecstacy, this continuous "high," for the last 28 years of his life.

The only problem with enlightenment is that **if you *think* you got it, you *didn't get it.*** Also, it is in this trance state that some SubGenii have jumped out of twentieth-story windows, stepped in front of trains, given away all their belongings, and other tragedies. Who knows — maybe the Afterlife looked *that good.*

Normally, though, the treatment is well worth its modest price. Your ten recognized and unrecognized senses will all work better; it's like opening up the venetian blinds of synchronicity so that you can see *all* the Hints buzzing interconnectedly around you, not just the ones that came at the price of a stubbed toe or otherwise taught you a lesson. Suddenly Hints are jumping out at you and *yelling.* Among other things, this can mean INSTANT LUCK AT THE RACES!!

OH, COME OFF IT

So, what's the deal here? Do we give away all we own, go starve in the desert, and bang ourselves on the head until we see God, or "Bob"? Hell, some of us have families to support, we can't go off looking for some stupid mirage of the New Jerusalem for the rest of our lives. We don't want to learn the secrets of the universe and then not be able to make any MONEY off them.

And maybe we're too damn set in our ways! Maybe there're lots of things in this $1.98 material world we *like*! How are we supposed to know this "blazing of the senses" is all it's cracked up to be? Isn't there an easier way? We need Answers we can reach safely, at home, in our spare time!

Yeah, HELL yeah. The problem is, people get enlightenment

mixed up with *perfection.* With "Bob," they're *opposites.* **Thinking about perfection will only screw you up.** The Conspiracy tries to get you hooked on some impossible notion of perfection and then takes the edge off any fulfillment you're lucky enough to get by miring you down, making you kiss a hundred asses in the rank and file above you. They keep you on a treadmill of "positive thinking" propaganda so you always think you're *just about* to find the "meaning" they keep promising. That promotion is always "right around the corner." And when it comes, it means *less Slack.* Oh, but that's your *bad attitude.*

You'd be amazed how many fall for that kind of "thinking"! The Con uses it because even though it *doesn't work,* it *sounds good.* It's the first step in making you think you can't fight City Hall.

Well, you *can* fight City Hall, and even *win.* But you can't get *ultimate* Slack. **You must face that.** But this doesn't mean you should let the Con make you accept things you don't NEED and resist what you CAN USE. Don't get our idea of Slack mixed up with Their false quest for "tranquility." Their idea of tranquility for you is the narcossis of sitting alone in a tiny condobox exhausted from work and nerve drugs, watching TV in a kind of eternal limbo. For *some* SubGeniuses, such mindlessness *is* Slack; the difference is that the Con wants *everybody* to have the *same* idea of Slack.

To many SubGenii, Slack is simply being allowed to do the kind of work they love. False Work, done only for money, without fun, is a SIN against **YOU ALMIGHTY** (unless it's a LOT of money). Unrepressed greed is *natural.* But the way They've got it set up, it's *poison,* as evidenced by the diseases peculiar to the rich.

The divine Work Instinct of the SubGenius overpowers mere organic money hunger, which should be the servant to Work and not the other way around. (Some SubGeniuses are toil junkies nonetheless . . . but the *lucky* ones are lackadaisical buzzmongers.)

The idea is to make PLAY into a *paying profession* or Life Scam. Of course it isn't *easy* to break that corporate umbilical cord, but even if it pays Minimum it's better than a high paycheck full of heart attacks. This is a shallow, fickle mudculture of vinyl. BUT DO NOT FEEL GUILTY IF YOU FIND YOURSELF HAVING FUN *EVEN* ON THE JOB.

If you work at, say, a print shop, you *can* develop the Zen of Stapling. Or, in a pretzel factory, the Zen of Flipping Dough — this too can be Slack.

The key is to work by instinct, NOT EFFORT: don't "do the job," but *float* on the *lake* of work . . . let the job "DO YOU". This involves the same techniques that you're already using when you play a video game or a musical instrument, or drive a car. You get 'in sync' with the machine, you *become* the machine, you *surrender* to the machine. You put your brain on 'auto-pilot.' You **"GIVE UP".**

If this makes no sense to you, then your ONLY SANE MOVE would be to **REPENT, QUIT YOUR JOB and SLACK OFF** before you're *too far gone.*

It's the simple Taoist principle of *wu-wei:* "Doing Nothing Effectively." To "Bob," *'Nothing'* is infinitely more *real* than other realities. He preaches **"*NOT-THINK*"** or **"*NO-MIND:*"** for the only way to truly THINK the UNTHINKABLE is NOT TO THINK. You just **"BE."** (The Eastern tradition of the Mantra or repeated chant was formerly used to induce this, but now television has replaced it and is every bit as effective. (See: **Couch Potatoes 7:19**))[3]

"Try? No! There is no 'try.' *Do*, or *do not.*" — Yoda.

If you merely "try," you will burn out your powers, and even if you attain your goal there'll be little *feeling* left to enjoy it with. It's like almost getting over the Berlin Wall but getting shot six inches from freedom. It's like "a monkey trying to fuck a football." Like a golfer running around with his head cut off.

Get this: There are actually such things as **Will Particles.** If you direct them at too high a velocity, if your brain *pushes* too hard, the Luck Plane *hardens* to meet them and bounces them back at you. You risk a negative psychic bounceback-echo effect ricochetting from the "soul" or *Manitou* of whatever it is you're trying to change. When the effort-ball returns, it self-cancels itself and erases its own weight in bobyons, depleting you and making it harder to try each time. The harder you try, the harder the job *becomes.* This also occurs near the end of the workday when you are "watching the clock."

If Will Particles are sent slowly, *eased* in, they won't just enter the Luck Plane, they'll be eagerly *swallowed* by it, and things will magically fall into place. In its own utterly impersonal way, the Luck Plane — which is bigger than all the gods put together — is *glad* to cooperate. But if it's coerced, it tightens up . . . and so do you. So don't sneak up on the Luck Plane and suddenly start battering it. Present your tasks to it as gifts, bearing SLACK.

THIS IS THE PATH OF LEAST RESISTANCE

Slack is not simply "Not Giving a Shit." It is more like "Giving a Shit *Freely.*"

Holy men have called Slack, "SEEING." Not *looking*, but *seeing.* "Bob" teaches men to truly *see.* A poor man can have true Slack. An idiot trapped in a condominium and a bad job can have true Slack. All that it takes is to stop sucking the finger and go where it POINTS!

Man's word says, "Seeing is believing." This is perversion. "Bob's" word says, "*Believing is seeing.*" If you believe in something first, *you will then see it.* But you must *really* believe.

To be a complete and religious SubGenius, you don't have to believe in the dogma. You don't have to believe in yourself. You don't have to believe in ANYTHING, but merely be CAPABLE of *BELIEVING* . . . which is much more closely related to *seeing* than *thinking.* If you can *see* the Path, it is *yours,* and it will lead you to the point at which you will believe *everything.*.

"Learning" is not what you need. You need to "KNOW, INSTANTLY." Learned experiences, learned opinions, these can tie you up and keep you from piercing the veil. If you can "**see,**" you will come to know what you really think and not what you pay to want to *think* you think.

Do not believe in success. Just succeed in believing. BELIEVE in the lie while you say it. BELIEVE in the car while you drive it. BELIEVE in the centerfold. "*Don't just EAT a hamburger . . . eat the HELL out of it.*" — Dobbs 9-9-59

3. This Church doesn't dwell on the glories of TV very much, because that is *amply* covered by another mystic fellowship, the COUCH POTATOES. No self-respecting tube-addict worth s/his salt would hesitate to send the measley $1.25 each for either of the first two issues of *The Tuber's Voice* to Couch Potatoes, Rt. 1 Box 327, Dixon, CA 95620. Their explorations of the mysteries of *prolonged viewing* are highly bulldada and entirely Dobbs-Approved.

POWERS OF YOUR UNDERMIND

Slack is a *quest.* The quest for Slack is symbolized by **The Perfect Hamburger.** *These* are the *real* issues: Man, God, the Amoeba, DNA, Sex and a Truly *Good* Hamburger. Slack is not possible without that Hamburger, nor vice versa.

You see, there are gulfs in the nerve patterns, vast synapse gaps which the normal human brain cell cannot leap. Only certain recombinations of mental and financial energy can create the bridges, and once you make the jump and get across to that other edge, it is *terrifying:* a whole new landscape is there, a mental arrangement that's hard not to get lost in. But it opens up new passages in your head and in one of them lies that great **Burger.** Many of the better new video games accidentally illustrate this process.

SubGeniuses are so disconnected from reality already, they can more easily vault the fissures in the brain-caves and *see* the roadmap in the randomness. They can get to that place where the PRIMAL INFORMATION STILL REMEMBERS ITSELF. They can *find "Bob."*

STOP LOOKING, and "Bob" will SUDDENLY SHOW UP, offering a "smoke."

Remember, "Bob" is not a "doer", but a "letter," He LETS things happen. What is *about* to happen is, by perpetual magick coincidence, exactly what he desires. The Plan he has HAS ALREADY COME ABOUT; it simply has yet to make itself *apparent.*

If you will only wish for what "Bob" wishes for, you will get your wish. If you kill "Bob" and grind him up, "Bob" *becomes* that Perfect Hamburger!

Use creative procrastination. Give things time to happen by themselves. Be an "equal sign" in the equations of occurence. The same power that created the rich outpouring of "Bob's" life is producing abundance through other SubGeniuses NOW.

STUNNING BREAKTHROUGH AT BULLDADA TIME CONTROL LABS

Here is a computer-enhanced psi-construct of the "BOB-YON." This worling probability function is the smallest unit or quanta of stenchauraic energy, and all energies within this spectrum are composed of cohesions of this basic building block. As the *quark* is supposed to be the basic energy unit of the physical universe, so is the "BOBYON" the building block of the psychic universe. We don't know if there really are quarks, whereas here we have proof of the "BOB" Particle. *(Photo courtesy of Guy Deuel (TrTel) and Bulldada Labs.)*

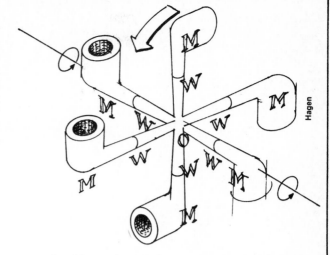

In 3-D, code arrangement becomes construct of **MWOWM.**

Each curved shape is a twisted gravity vortex of micro-white/anti-white *holes* in the stenchaura continuum.

All of the Psychic Universe composed of "Bobyon," each coded as **MWOWM.**

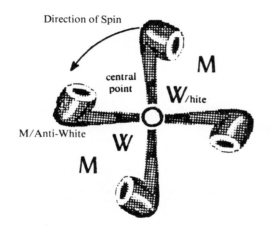

Direction of Spin

central point

M/Anti-White

M

W

M

W/hite

Puzzling Evidence

St. Guy Deuel

THROW THIS BOOK AGAINST THE WALL RIGHT NOW.

OH YEAH, almost forgot — HERE IS THE SECRET FORMULA FOR INSTANT MONEY AND SLACK:

Say this aloud, 100 times a day:

"I CLEARLY SEE THE PERFECT PLAN — FOR I HAVE PAID FOR IT. I KNOW WHAT I REALLY THINK. "BOB" IS MY UNFAILING BROKER, AND LARGE SUMS OF MONEY COME TO ME QUICKLY, WITHOUT WORK, IN A PERFECT WAY. DIVINE *SLACK* NOW DISSOLVES IN MY BLOODSTREAM. **FUCK THE CONSPIRACY.**"

You don't think it'll work? Well . . . it must be included anyway, as part of the Set, as a Prop in the complex staging of the Luck Rituals.

We can never give you the secret instant-Slack formula. It cannot be "given." If it comes too easily it will lose its power. There IS a magical formula — but without the sacrifice of your own thinking, and agony, it will produce only the watered-down shadow of Slack, not the *cytorspasmic* Slack you need. Also, you'd never need to *buy* anything from us again.

Nevertheless — OverMentality CAN be achieved for seconds or minutes, in snatches of amazingness that will grow with practice until your spirit is for all intents and purposes that of an OverMan or UberWoman! (Disclaimer: until the Xists get here, your body will remain in its corruptible state.)

"Bob" will not "smoke" with us until we ourselves have "pipes".

Yes! **YES!! AAAIIIEEEE!** — Unreality finally becomes so familiar, so *malleable,* that the SubGenius finds his freedom in *that which originally constrained him!* Oh **YEAH! SPIT** in the air, **SHOUT** Hosanna, and **throw this Book at the wall! You WILL reach that OTHER SHORE!!**

PUZZLING EVIDENCE

CHAPTER 6
CREATIVE TRUTH
CHAPTER 6 LAYOUT BY PUZZLING EVIDENCE (Doug Wellman)

"**bulldada** the latest exploration into the world of advanced surreavolutionary **morealism** in which the mind is filled with dirt and lugs which trickle down the sides of the cranium to find shelter and rest inside the now sightless eye-sockets."
— Shredni Chisholm, *definition of bulldada*

"I always lie . . . and I'm always right."
— Dobbs, 1951 campaign speech

The flexible nature of reality, which has always been known to the ancients and the Attuned, is, ultimately, the SubGenius' greatest Excuse to **LIE.**

Dobbs popularized the concept of *Critical-Paranoiac Follies Evaluation* by which we know that " . . . any inanity *spouted* by a SubGenius, at any time, automatically becomes part of orthodox, sanctified SubGenius Church Liturgy." It is one of our single greatest harsh and severe Tenets, for *by its own very token,* one can deny it whenever necessary. It is of the **Sacred Doctrine of Erasability** — it self-cancels upon demand.

Everything we say is recorded in the cosmic **Skor** and protected by the **Copyright Angels.** Therefore, we may disregard our utterances — *erase* them — if they no longer fit a truth that has changed. *We don't need to store them on Earth any longer.* The Conspiracy, on the other hand, tends to "'stick by its guns" and stupidly "not go down" even though the problem at hand is obviously "unwhuppable."

For instance, a guilty SubGenius may speak a **Divine Inanity** which later proves nonprofitable. He is then perfectly justified in saying, "No, *I didn't say that.*" Conspiracy higher-ups do this daily; why can't we? It is your perogative to deny your mistakes, or to revel in them — to even pull off your pants and *roll* in them. The inability to lie well can often stand in the way of Truth. And lying is *easy.* You may not be a good "actor," but if, like most SubGeniuses, you have 40,000 entities living simultaneously inside your head, with a different one talking every three words or so, *you can lie.* In fact, you may well have a *fantastic* future in Sales, which makes lying *natural.*

Puzzling Evidence

YOU CAN DISAPPEAR!

THERE ARE NO FACTS

Logically, then, nothing that a SubGenius says is any more or less true and consecrable than any other thing he just happens to utter — *especially* if they are contradictory. The *Divine Contradictions of "Bob"* — such as the Moveable Dates of Prophecy — are what keep the Church alive and prevent it from entering a manageable state. Thus it remains a red-hot, ever-mutating alien creature that can never be caged or killed.

The SubGenius *is* an Oxymoron who speaks in slangs and oxymora. *so it doesn't matter what you say or who hears you say it.* See? Dobbs denies vehemently that things should ever happen according to preset 'plans,' except HIS Plan of course, and tells us to look instead to the flukes and blunders in our *own* lives for inspiration — for will not JHVH-1 determine our fates at every twist and turn *anyway?* Can any philosophy other than *bulldada preserve* us from such impaling facts?

WHAT IS BULLDADA?

What isn't? *Bulldada* is that mysterious quality that impregnates certain 'ordinary' things with meaning for the SubGenius no matter how valueless they may appear to The Others. Seeing in the vivisecting light of bulldada, we recognize that the most awe-inspiring artifacts of our civilization are *not* the revered lame artsy-fartsy pieces of "culture" which the Arts Conspiracy displays in our swankest museums, universities and concert halls, but are instead to be found in such icons as low-budget exploitation movies, lurid comic books, all-nite TV, certain bizarre billboards and pulp-magazine ads, sleazy Paperbacks of the Gods, and literally any other fossils of *raw humanity* in all its shit-kickingly flawed glory. *Bulldada* is what falls out of your pocket and is found by amateur archaeologists millions of years in the future.

Bulldada is not "dada" nor the sickness remaining after dada has fled. (A surprising number of people do not know what **dada** is. It is a now-petered-out art movement begun around World War I which attempted to *kill art* by portraying senseless objects as "Fine Art" of the highest order. Dada failed to *kill art* because it only made sense to those involved — for its *whole idea* was to make *no sense*. It has a small "hip" following today but is as effectively dead as New Wave.)

Bulldada is different in that it *does* make sense beneath a mere surface sheen vaguely reminiscent of dada. It is *"bull"* dada, merely displaying dada's trappings of dreamlike randomness and obnoxiousness, yet actually containing caricatured but blatant "moral meaning." Bulldada carries a *garish* and *lurid* and quite *linear* structure beneath its disguise of false randomness and formal *serioulism*. Bulldada is a whore of the mind, praise "Bob," and NOT ART. It is PROPAGANDA IN ART'S CLOTHING and **it's TOO LATE FOR YOU TO TURN BACK NOW.** It not only rapes and kills art, it chops off the fingers of *violence itself!!* It is *situation tragedy;* its crude yoks come not from the right thought-pockets, NOR the left. It winks and hides in *masks* of words and pictures, and

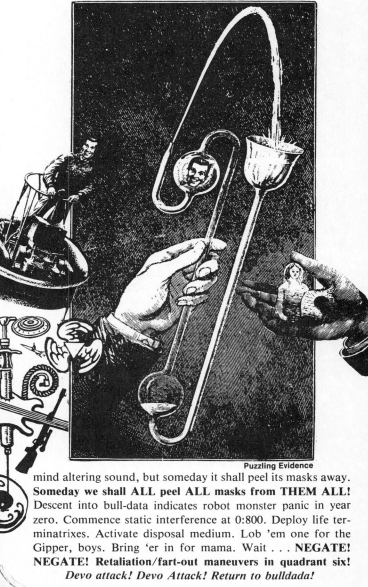

Puzzling Evidence

mind altering sound, but someday it shall peel its masks away. **Someday we shall ALL peel ALL masks from THEM ALL!** Descent into bull-data indicates robot monster panic in year zero. Commence static interference at 0:800. Deploy life terminatrixes. Activate disposal medium. Lob 'em one for the Gipper, boys. Bring 'er in for mama. Wait . . . **NEGATE! NEGATE! Retaliation/fart-out maneuvers in quadrant six!** *Devo attack! Devo Attack! Return to bulldada!*

The SubGenius is a Monk of Bulldada. He is a product of a **Society of Bad Art,** a society which *is itself* "Bad Art." The ARTIST is the mad sculptor WOTAN. *We* wear our bulldada like a cloak of invisibility at the shopping centers; it is our shield: we walk *untainted* among the humans and are mistaken for one of their own. "Ah but as a rolling stone gathers snow so have I begun slow rolling to gather a soft passive exterior concealing a hard inner core, **THE CORE OF BULLDADA!** Insane leaders are the means to an end. Where is your end, and where the hole in the ground? Are you willing to perjure yourself to attain? Sacrifice. *Bang! Bang! Bang! Bang! Bang! Bang! Bang! Bang!"* (Shredni Chisholm in *The Bulldada Book*)

There is **INADVERTENT BULLDADA,** such as *"Leave It To Beaver"* and most other religions; it doesn't know when it's funny. And then there is **ADVERTENT BULLDADA,** such as THIS ENTIRE CHURCH: it is *real,* but it knows it will amuse the gods with its secret humor of the Illiterati and its dignified bathroom morbidity, which is as true and entirely horrible as the world itself, except for the *good parts.* It is basically hideous, but you want to copulate with it. It brings destructive things that were previously invisible out into the stark light of conflict. Bulldada is eroto-genetic, hereditary, and the most powerful tool known to Man. Dolls in the very far future will mutter, "Bulldada."

Bulldada shows us that **cheesiness** tells the truth and gives good Slack, whereas status-mongered slickness is merely a sheen of sham value dangled as bait for the idiot dollars on the hungry bourgeois. The SubGenius isn't interested in fancy-

schmancy Learning or *even science fiction* with its pose of grimness — no, what we crave is greasy SCI-FI. We are scholars of what Frank Zappa called *"CHEEPNIS."* For when down the Rungs of the Art Ladder we descend to a certain level of shoestring-budget "Exquisite Badness," we reach a cut-off point where bulldada begins, an 'edge' where the SubGenius starts finding almost religious interpretation of the results of atrocious craftsmanship, the point after which the work's bulldada increases inversely to its ability to yell a coherent story. The less sophisticated a movie becomes, the more dismemberingly eternal are the truths between the lines. *MARS NEEDS WOMEN! GLENN OR GLENDA!* Often, they contain inadvertent prophecies — usually linked to unexpected background appearances of "Bob" himself! *PLAN NINE FROM OUTER SPACE! DATING DOS AND DON'TS! ZONTAR, THING FROM VENUS!* And the greatest Badfilm of all time is *SCARLET LOVE, and you haven't even heard of it!!* –

1. SCARLET LOVE is a film by Palmer Rockey, made in Dallas. It has only been shown in Dallas. It is as jaw-dropping a piece of filmmaking as has ever made it to answer-print stage. NO MAN can *even barely begin to conceive* of the PURITY OF PSYCHOSIS displayed by this motion picture without actually seeing it. SCARLET LOVE makes Ed Woods' badfilms look *normal.* It's damn near as incisively BAAAD and REVEALING of ALL HUMAN NATURE as YOUR LAST MAJOR MISTAKE. Help us make this most deserving of epics a $$s-raking "cult classic."

EVERYTHING IS A FACT

Actually, the day that the Pinks and Normally-Boy Critics see beyond the surface of great badfilm and into its bulldada core, its sanctity of inappropriateness, *on that day* it will no longer be of any use to us. All truly holy objects lose their truth as soon as they are exploited by witless dupes who didn't see the incredible import of their ubersymbolism until it is slapping them in the face — until their prophecies come true. The pure glory of inanity, the Holy Insipidity, the dreamlike trance state induced by random editing, these today still "bore" the blind Mediocretins — so let us be glad badfilm is doomed to eternal shambling life on the ageless Late Show, forever to be seen only by Those Who Can't Sleep, or Who Comprehend. There we can continue to examine the films' peripheral action and characters, to spot the SubGeniuses among the extras, to isolate and study the almost unnoticeable but *truly prophetic* throw-away lines.

LAUGH. SEE?

The Pinks will continue to bask in the *not-shitty-enoughness* of those sad in-between movies, the made-for-TV crap that's not BAD enough to be great but nowhere near "GOOD"; ironic, isn't it, that those products we hate most are the most in-demand by Ginks and Gimps? For the *mediocre* will always outnumber the *great* and the *great-bad;* it's that very half-assed badness that will forever plague us by making our love of badfilm confusing to family and friends. It's a thin line between the boringly bad and the unrepressedly, unapologetically, PROFOUNDLY BAD, and few can see that line at all. "RECHT und SCHLECHT!" *(Right and bad.)*

But are we not lucky beyond compare that we have this spiritual gift of discernment, which allows us to glean ACTUAL PROPHECIES from on-screen "explanations" by the scientists of "what the monster is and why it MUST KILL," which allows us to excavate the HIDDEN TRUTHS from INSIPID DIALOG, to

Puzzling Evidence

FAKE CONE OF SILENCE

PUZZLING EVIDENCE

!INSTANT SLACK!

derive COSMIC KNOWLEDGE from FLAWED PROPS and VISIBLY-ZIPPERED MONSTER SUITS with QUIVERING RUBBER TEETH; more than just being movies which "we could do better than," more than crap-art by crazies for us to snicker at in superiority, badfilm is actually loved by us because in our deepest hearts, we know that *THIS IS THE WAY WE TOO WOULD DO THESE FILMS,* . . . who among

us has not yearned to take $10 and produce the **ULTIMATE BADFILM?** But of course to "try" to make a badfilm, to descend to campiness with a deliberate attempt to be consumately BAAD, THIS can only be doomed to failure. For each badfilm gives us a PURE and UNSCISSORED INSIGHT into the very SOUL of a single auteur, one lone man-against-the-world, struggling to get his vision of reality, HOWEVER WARPED, to the screen UNFETTERED by "rational plotting" or "convincing acting" or "the making of sense," NO, the great badfilm director brings to life HIS staggering mistakes in judgement STRAIGHT from the subconscious, WITHOUT censorship by 'quality nuts:' Badfilm slaps us in the face with *FLAWED VERSIONS of OURSELVES,* ALL THE MORE TRUTHFUL and INTERESTING for their flaws; even if you've never really thought of it this way, the fact is you like badfilm because you instinctively "read between the lines" and hear NOT JUST what the actors are saying so woodenly but also WHAT CAUSED THE SIMPLETON SCRIPTWRITER TO HAVE THE ACTOR SAY THOSE THINGS. You see not just the movie, but all the low-class *everythingness* that the movie REFLECTS. Beneath the thin veil of the plot the director's neuroses and all-too-human quirks are BLATANTLY OBVIOUS. Thus badfilm serves us on many levels at once — but levels so widely separated that the prolonged viewing of badfilm (or older bad-shows from TV) actually causes the brain to **DISCONNECT,** to split into at least two or three separate entities, all of which in the long run serve to FREE US from the stinking MEDIOCRETY of the workaday world, TRANSPORTING US into a dreamlike universe of SHEER UNCONTAMINATED **TECHNOFEAR** so GAUDY as to actually go **BEYOND ART** and off into the realms of *myth* and *religion*.

MEDIA FOR A NEW FACE

And the very fact that we are "analyzing" badfilm like this, in ITS OWN JARGON, is ONE MORE EXAMPLE of the DECLINE which America is NOW ENTERING for better or worse, and a sign moreover that 'bad movies' are already reaching a point of recognition which will threaten to DEFUSE their badness and make them once again JUST MEDIOCRE. THIS my friends is what we *must avoid* so we strongly suggest that you **NOW EAT THIS ARTICLE** and forget we ever said anything. Thanks.

CALL

YES! A sentimental fool who never grew up and who cries over lost ideals, a sinner and a goof-off, the SubGenius is fully capable of receiving authentic *god-consciousness* from soap operas and monster movies, junkyards and 'dives', freakshows and back alleys that most Normals have been programmed to consider 'dumb.' What They cannot know is that dumbness — *Cheepness* — sincere and vital ignorance — reveal far more about the interestingly violent and taboo world around us than any overpriced geegaw that Pincritics have told us is "art" or "science." FUCK THOSE WHO'D TELL US WHAT'S "GOOD." A wino mumbling in his vomitus can dribble parables of as soaring a height of bulldada as all the rich, creamy superstitions of a thousand popes and witch doctors. And if you don't watch TV, you don't know what America is all *about*.

The Word is the Weapon of the SubGenius, and bulldada is the Weapon of the Word, but when the Word descends into bulldada, bulldada slides into **Morealism.**

Morealism is slightly more realistic; it's the *deliberate* invocation of bulldada. St. Moe gave his name to it; it is reality according to Moe.

The natural order of things is far too confusing to be accurately depicted using the street laws of Truth. Only the morally modified facts of Morealism can successfully illustrate the awesomeness of the Scheme. LIES are necesssary for truth. The Church as a whole is *bulldada*. Its printed materials more often verge into *Morealism*. In them we strive for skim-proof *shock value, overembellishment, bludgeon humor* and *morbid yuks*. Thus, like our mentor "Bob," we are true *Wiseacres* and orthodox fundadaMentalists. **"FUCK 'EM IF THEY CAN'T TAKE A JOKE."**

FORGOT TO DUCK?

BOB DOESN'T MAKE SENSE?

COUNTLESS PERSONAL SAVIORS!!!

The SubGenius knows, bulldadaistically, that each SubGenius should do WOTAN's work exactly as He reveals it to him, and that He has wildly varying messages for different people in different situations.

By the same token, it is madness to accept any *one* 'personal savior' — *even Dobbs* — as a permanent guide. Perhaps "Bob's" greatest invention is the concept of *SHORT DURATION PERSONAL SAVIORS,* or *"Shordurpersavs"* in Tibetan. The true Sub accepts into his heart, as his own *personal* savior, anyone or anything with which he happens to be impressed *at the moment*. Shordurpersavs change from hour to hour, from whim to whim. It could be the hero of a movie you just saw, the author of a book, a bottle of Thunderbird, a good pal, a dog, a sex object. Not professional gurus you are locked into believing, but temporary ones according to the need of The Now. They change so fast that it never gets embarrassing; you aren't inclined to 'proselytize' them off on disinterested others who will later laugh at you; you know their effects will wear off in minutes — although the very idea is unthinkable while under the Influence. One need not mention them at all — a superb Tenet, since one is sometimes *deeply ashamed for having a particular, unsavory Shordurpersav: some* can be Personal Saviors and False Prophets *at the same time.*

As said before, *SLACK* is a trickster.

EVOLUTION OF MATERIAL OBJECTS AND MENTAL CONCEPTS

Things that become High Chic were usually Bulldada first. Any given human-made thing, such as, for inst., blue jeans, goes through several phases of fadualistic evolution:

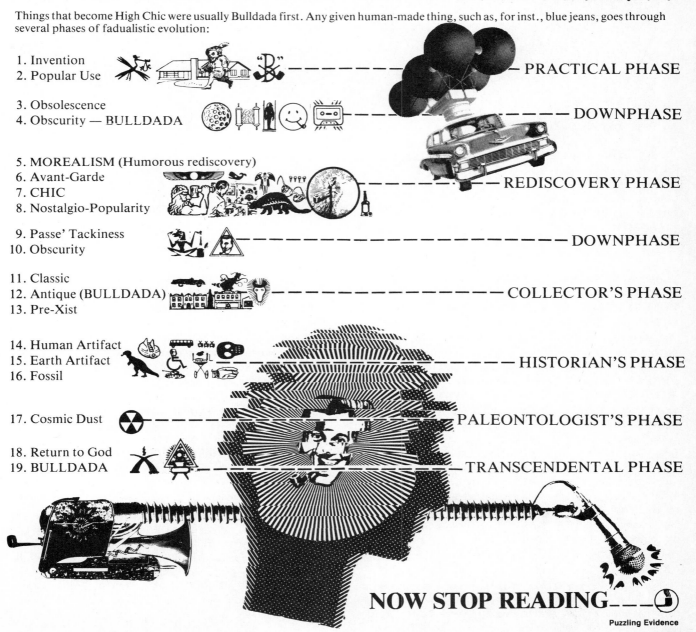

1. Invention
2. Popular Use — PRACTICAL PHASE

3. Obsolescence
4. Obscurity — BULLDADA — DOWNPHASE

5. MOREALISM (Humorous rediscovery)
6. Avant-Garde
7. CHIC
8. Nostalgio-Popularity — REDISCOVERY PHASE

9. Passe' Tackiness
10. Obscurity — DOWNPHASE

11. Classic
12. Antique (BULLDADA)
13. Pre-Xist — COLLECTOR'S PHASE

14. Human Artifact
15. Earth Artifact
16. Fossil — HISTORIAN'S PHASE

17. Cosmic Dust — PALEONTOLOGIST'S PHASE

18. Return to God
19. BULLDADA — TRANSCENDENTAL PHASE

NOW STOP READING

Puzzling Evidence

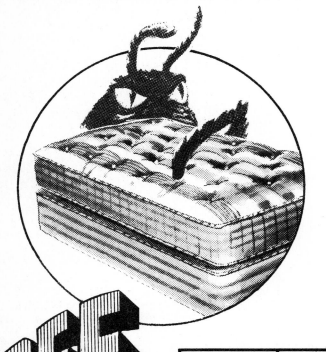

CHAPTER 7

SALVATION $1
and THE PERILS OF
FALSE SLACK

"I'm here with, basically, nothing to say. And that's what I want to talk to you about tonight. Are you saying what you really *mean* to say? Do you even know what you're *really* thinking?"
— "Bob's" first lecture, POSITIVE THINKING VS. SALES

FREE

REAL SLACK			2		3		4		5	

"Give a SubGenius an inch of Slack, and he'll abuse a mile of it *right into the ground.*"

— "Bob," Media Barrage Cassette 43 (365')

Slack is one HELL OF A TRICKSTER. In fact, all this stuff about Slack being an internal nirvana of the mind is SO MUCH **PURE 'D' CRAP.** Come one — *snap out of it* — living in a state of mental bliss may *help,* but let's face it: IT JUST ISN'T REAL.

In discussing True Slack, we aren't talking about *simply* improving your imagination and self-image — those are MERE IMAGES — we're talking about *major material advancement* in the PHYSICAL WORLD. **Money! Sex!** We're talking ACTUAL MIRACLES and MORE FUN in the objective, sensible universe — STRAIGHT **A**s for *No Effort* in the very School of Hard Knocks itself. We're talking **SOMETHING FOR NOTHING.**

Well, not for *nothing,* but it's still the best deal for your money from *any* mind-control cult. Don't fool yourself. NO RELIGION has ever actually made anybody more free — just more able to rely on that particular system, more *dependent.* What makes us different is that we *admit* it, and THIS ALONE makes it WORK. The whole IDEA is that you *depend on "Bob."* But Dobbs-addiction is rather . . . *compelling,* compared to any other form of guru-abuse.

Slack CAN be money, Slack CAN be sex, but **Slack IS "BOB."**

In Je-HO-Vah's great Office in the sky is a Ledger showing the *debits* and *credits* of men's souls, a record of all emotional transactions and the giving and taking of Slack, oral sex, etc.

Some have *too much Slack,* which is really no Slack at all. Without the bad, one cannot appreciate the good. Therefore: if you're healthy, become an alcoholic. If you're charismatic, become a creep. This will "awaken" you.

What's *wrong* isn't materialism per se, but the *wrong kind* of materialism. *Pink* materialism! The materialism of FAT BUTTS on schoolteachers, of cutesy smile-facey "gift shops" in malls, of Head Shops with $200 cocaine mirrors.

The point is, **EARTH MUST BE PURGED.** We need not kill the guilty, NAY NAY! but merely enslave them . . . make pets of them. We will *protect* them — *watch over them* as a shepherd watches his flock. But to do this we must CAST the money changers from the temple and BURN the record albums of The Pink. We must stop acting like they *expect* us to act.

The Church is not for austerity, not by a long shot. We are merely AGAINST FALSE SLACK, the con brainwash that says *more* of what *They sell* will make you happier. We don't insist that Nature, *per se,* is what we must return to. To dismantle western technology is *false extremism.* Technology can *serve* us, and so can money. It's just that authority must be disseminated into smaller pockets — each man and woman a king, each dog and child a serf.[1]

You *can be* what you won't. "Bob" *really does* make his followers rich. We can prove this. But he also makes them poor. For riches aren't *enough*.

MAN NEEDS SLACK.

EARTH NEEDS SLACK.   This logic is inescapable.

Money can buy Slack. In doses. Of certain kinds. More often, however, it's squandered on Slack Abuse and techno-goods. We **patriopsychotic anarchomaterialists** LOVE the material world; money is not only important, it's damn near ALL-important, and thus to *waste* it is a kind of *blasphemy*. But ANYONE with ANY SENSE AT ALL knows it isn't how you spend your *money,* it's how you spend your *time*. Who cares how much money you make? In these times the RICH are as broke as the POOR unless they're CONSPIRACY-RICH. When Death, the Grim Bill Collector, comes for YOU, will you be quaking and regretting all the time you wasted trying to "achieve" something instead of JUST HAVING FUN?

THERE MAY NOT BE MUCH TIME LEFT so you damn well better either help forestall cataclysm, or else *enjoy the fleeting moments you have left*. In fact, the *enjoying* DOES the *forestalling*. When you get more Slack, more Slack is *also* generated in the world around you.

Sure, these Teachings are intricate and contradictory — **WHY NOT?** Other religions may be simpler, but they only give the *illusion* of results. They're *bad maps* . . . two-dimensional diagrams nothing like the real terrain. But with SubGenius, the map *actually is* the territory.

Going without "Bob's" word is like taking a long journey

NEWSPAPERS CLOCK

HOW THEY DENY YOU SLACK

"What a lot of people are following MIGHT NOT BE JESUS."
— "Bob"

without a map. You'll backtrack, wander aimlessly, go over rough, bumpy roads on irritating detours.

DON'T let yourself live to be 90 with only 10 years' worth of Slack. Don't spend most of your waking hours doing something you hate. YOU CAN SUDDENLY QUIT YOUR JOB AND TAKE YOUR FAMILY ON THE ROAD with EVERY BIT AS MUCH SECURITY as you'll get depending on Corporate America with its voluntary slavery. The system is in a perpetual breakdown/replace Turnover Cycle. Well, it's overheating and sooner or later something's *really* gonna turn it over.

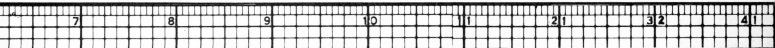

J. HAGEN

HAS FEAR OF THE UNUSUAL PREVENTED YOU FROM JOINING THE CHURCH OF THE SUBGENIUS? Or, if you are already a member, has Conspiracy harassment kept you from enjoying your full rights as a SubGenius?

Do they constantly reinforce your Conspiracy programming by making it financially necessary that you attend endless **pink-ins,** gatherings of dull blandoid Normalcy Dupes who bore you to death, making you sit there while you secretly daydream of wreaking havoc on their pallid world? Or do they try to intimidate you out of SubGeniusness? For instance, are you having trouble getting a good job, or laid? Is it increasingly difficult for you to "relate?" Is your mail being opened? Have you recently had a Close Call of the Third Kind? Or have they stepped up their harassment even further — have they sent NHGH's Henchmen after you to tear out your tongue, gouge out your eyes, set fire to your home, impale your mate, rape your children, and burn your secret stash of SubGenius propaganda? *OR,* are they using subtler but EVEN MORE HEINOUS methods, such as Psychic Aether Disruptors to discomBobulate your Sphere of Causality, slanting your Luck Plane *their* way and throwing you way out of Sync?

1. This is the basic philosophy of PATRIO-PSYCHOTIC ANAR-CHO—MATERIALISM, as developed by Dr. Philo Drummond and J.R. "Bob" Dobbs. It's *FAR* more extreme than so-called "anarchy" in that it erases politics *totally,* and brings into play the single tactic of FORCE ALONE. While some SubGenii are fighting to make this the anti-governmental path of future generations, others see it merely as a particularly concise description of the way things are *now*.

CASH PRIZES

EXCUSES FOR HATE

If they have done these things and you have been discouraged, it is understandable. It was *all planned* that way by multi-dimensional Wrath Entity JHVH-1, *all set up* long before the seeds of life were first planted on this planet some *ten billion years ago.* (Yes, TEN billion. They had to be planted more than once.)

Our present-day Conspiracy reflects the gleefully sadistic tampering of "J-1" in its current attacks, labeling the SubGenius as fanatical, unemployable, secretive, misguided, even "insane." However, these tactics are just more incontrovertible proof of our *glorious threat* to Them. That the Conspiracy — particularly the nearly mindless Normal Majority — has continually attacked the Church is a great tribute to us, for organizations are surely known for their enemies as well as their friends. Consequently, abnormals who may have once been programmed to deny their own abnormality are now, with second thoughts, investigating and joining the Church. We now have PROOF that within our lifetimes we WILL see the Sovereign State of the SubGenius: each yard a kingdom.

LEARN TO FORGET AND BEAT THE ODDS!

But the path to this Utopia for dreamers is strewn with danger and martyrdom. We must be prepared for intense resistance. We must be prepared for the *wrong kind* of Temptation and the perils of *false Slack.*

PUZZLING EVIDENCE

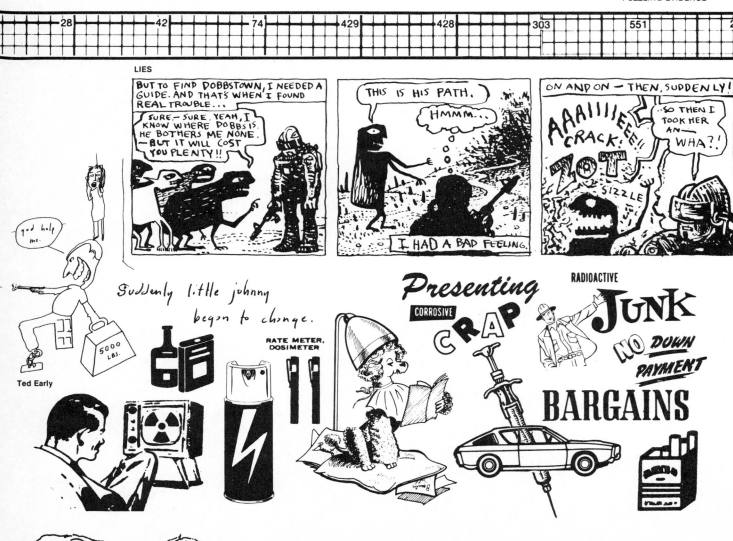

Already the demons have many people calling *us* "demonic Humanists" and "Communist Tools of Satan." What has this world *come* to, that the most courageous, patriotic, and *almost fatally independent* guardians of SANE MORALITY in AMERICA be called "Communist Tools of Satan" by idol-

SUBLIMINAL HEADLINE HOOKS—YOUR BRAIN, THE BAIT??

LIES

mongering, neurosis-implanting, UFO-or-devil-possessed **KOOKS** who actually have the GALL to call themselves CHRISTIANS?? By GOD, JESUS was *NO PUSSYFOOTER*. He is THE *FIGHTIN'* JESUS, one of the down home *for real*

GUARANTEED INERTNESS!

people, not some sourmouth old-lady puritan whiner! The REAL Jesus (and his two-fisted pals Bhuddha, Krishna, Elvis et al) are slugging it out, are *right in the thick of it,* with *"BOB!"* We're not tools of ANYBODY except the Stark Fist of Removal, and It's got hold of the CONSPIRACY, TOO, so FUCK 'EM. *FUCK 'EM!!* I tell you, Satan is a liar, he's a DECEIVER, and a deceiver is going to jump you where you LEAST EXPECT IT. And *where* do the most susceptible, doltish seekers of narconormality LEAST EXPECT THE DEVIL? In CHURCH!! **IN CHURCH!!** YES it can happen in ANY HOUSE OF GOD that is run by DUPES who are sitting ducks, lamely praying for SOME ENTITY to step in and TELL THEM WHAT TO DO WITH THEIR LIVES . . .

Horrible, isn't it, that so many would-be PATRIOTS are so *steeped* in their own *personal paranoia* that they have lost all "sense" of *humor* and thus all *perspective,* that they have let FOUL PREACHERS change the PUNCHLINES of the GOOD JOKES of JESUS to look like SICK GUILT PARABLES??? "HOLY SHIT" I say, this CONSPIRACY business we're talking about is **NO JOKE,** we are not speaking in SYMBOLIC TERMS, the Conspiracy we talk about is a *real thing* that permeates ALL OF SOCIETY. It is a CREEPING TREND against YOU and ME that is BEING DELIBERATE-LY INSTIGATED by BODILESS HIGHER INTEL-LIGENCES in an overpopulated world that is RIPE AS HELL for TAKEOVER.

INSTANT CASH WHENEVER YOU NEED IT!!

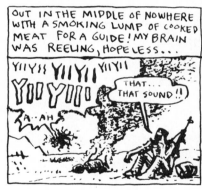

It's so obvious it's *actually funny.* People by the millions are *giving up* on science and politics and are now expecting "Something Else" to save them. If something that *looks like* a UFO or a Spirit from the Afterlife or an Ascended Spiritual

Teen-Age DEVO OF HORROR!

Master or a "strong President" happens to say it *is* one of those, people unfortunately have a tendency to BLINDLY TAKE ITS WORD. It may *be* one of those, but it may also be something we haven't had nightmares about yet. The **Con-tactee Epidemic** has started, often it's in a namby-pamby disguise that makes for a bestselling self-help book, sometimes it's privately brainwarping, but whatever it is, it is now making IRREVERSIBLE the incredible wave of superstition that is about to sweep the world. **Fake Jesii** will be cropping up right and left like BAIT from SPACE, and HUMANS WILL BITE. It's already damn near impossible to have a sane, well-rounded overview of the nonstop cataclysm of daily life, and what we

LIES

FALSE CULTS and FALSE DOCTRINES

Nick Nostril's CRIMINAL CORNER

- **FLATDOBBS**
  BIZARRE CULT FIGURE TURNED CRIMINAL - ONE OF NOSTRIL'S TOUGHEST FOES.
- PLAYED BY JOHN AGAR IN THE RKO FILM "*NICK NOSTRIL, DEFECTIVE.*"

So **WAKE UP!** or you'll be left standing there in the Aftermath with your pants down and the Grin of Mr. Coprophagy plastered on your zombie face. If you're behind "liberal humanism" OR "religious conservatism" OR ANY COM-

M21   S21   36C   142   212   42C   6CL   2701

IT WILL BE AMUSING TO FEED YOU SOME CHURCH FOOD..

LIES

BEWARE THE FALSE PROPHETS

have always called 'science' and 'rational thought' are precisely what have *caused* this. "Science" is now so top-heavy with its own Conspiracy-implanted bureaucratic status-ladder, so utterly blind to anything it hasn't already explained in *too much* detail, that it is swiftly burying any credibility it once had under its weight of dogma. Like government, it has become little more than a self-perpetuating academic red tape factory; each particular field of specialty makes itself incomprehensible to everyone but its own experts. Mainstream religion is the same—preachers don't make sense to anyone who isn't *already "saved,"* defeating their own purposes by Conspurred overkill. The people who'll wield power in the near future, then, will be those who can come up with broad, all-inclusive explanations for modern insane reality, explanations that **may in fact be ludicrous** but which nevertheless SOUND GOOD and FIT IN. **These *ARE* the End Times.**

BINATION THEREOF, you're basically subscribing to a dole system where *somebody else* is pulling the strings, and you're JUST where The Conspiracy *wants* you. The issue, the PRIMAL issue that keeps being ignored *because of its own nature,* is the rotting away of the *original human personality,* which is its natural state is actually CRAZY and HAPPY as hell. They ARE making you Normal, and for *that very reason* you can't tell that the change is even happening. They don't want you to stand on your own two feet so they make it HORRIBLY EASY for you to just let THEM prop you up instead.

YOU THINK it's just uptight moral majority primates in business suits, but NO! It's probably half your best friends, **YES,** regular hippies and intellectual hep-cats, people who still entertain the fantasy that their grooved-out lifestyle somehow makes them immune to the coming fullhell Humanity Crisis, nice "cool" people who smoke pot or tell good jokes, JUST PLAIN GOOD BUDDIES, but the fact remains that they are already clamped into the smoothest type of Conspiracy programming and will only slide deeper, they still talk about Slack but it's just shallow surface talk, give them 5 years and they'll

HALT! I AM A ROMAN.

GRrrrrOOURGH!

END OF CIVILIZATION?

Buck

have rationalized themselves right into the clutches of the Anti-"Bob," **333,** just wait, soon they'll be tube-eyed glassfaces, zombie office drones with cardboard values, oh sure they'll still listen to Frank Zappa records, but *even Zappa* will have plunged into the service of the robot temptors, YES! "Leisure activities" are the Cheese, The Conspiracy provides the Maze, and YOU are the RAT! The nibbling greedy RAT!! They dangle enough fancy stereos and ski trips in front of you and by god you'll BITE . . . or maybe status machines aren't your cheese, maybe you like "responsibility" or "fame" or "to be left alone" or even "nature" instead, well, whatever you want The Conspiracy has it for **YOU,** they know how to make you think you've earned it, they'll have you doing a kind of work that isn't work at all, they'll have you bedding down with women or men who aren't women or men at all, you'll learn to LOVE the fashionable New Bondage, HELL they're bending you over already, better clench tight, they're about to drop a BIG present in your back door! And you'll never notice what they took when they left because once it's gone *you won't have anything to miss it WITH,* your **Third Nostril** can be closed up by a myriad of Conspiracy moneydrugs, your once-noble Nen-

LIES

longer have to capacity to *enjoy* it but **YOU DO.** If you don't keep on the meanderingly straight Path o' "Bob" you may just decide to get some of their False Slack for *yourself.* Right *now* your outward personality is just the tip of the iceberg of the *real you.* Five years at the paps of The Conspiracy and that iceberg *tip* will be *all that's left.*

LIES

Why You Can Look to the Future with Confidence

tal Ife half-soul can be tranquilized by a good enough TV show, your Bobself and mystic powers — already damped — can be smothered permanently by involuntary surrender, it'll be like a mental videotape of your own uniqueness and abnormality and *valuable past* sufferings that somebody went and *erased,* and it WON'T come back, it's like an amputation of your Improvement Instinct; "When there's no more room in Hell the dead shall walk the Earth." (*Dawn of the Dead* — George Romero) Yep . . . they'll suddenly give you some spare time, but you'll be so fucked up from not having had any in so long that you won't know what to DO with it; when you finally do decide on which type of False Slack to pursue you won't ENJOY it, and if you acidentally DO enjoy it they'll find a way to make you feel GUILTY about it. When you don't know whether you're TO or FROM you won't care *where* you're going.

And so even YOU will follow your buddies into the happy tarpit of lowered expectations, so what if you never got to be a rock star, you'll be a damn good junior ad exec, right?? Remember what happened to most of the bomb-throwing radicals of your youth? They all work for their dads now, yes? And sure enough they have more "slack" than you do, they sold out and got rich, but *here's where it's horrible:* they no

HOW DO THEY DO IT? What makes their hollow society so habit forming? How can these GOD DAMNED *ALIENS* actually be making US think like THEM?

Well, they *aren't* making us think like them. They're making us think like we *think* they think. But that's NOT the way THEY think; rather, THEY think more like "BOB!" BUT . . . they know *just* where to KICK you when you're *down.* They can psychically pinpoint the *exact spot* where a well-placed **propaganda boot** to your behavior glands will make that brainkick feel GOOD. To be more precise and more *justifiably vindictive* about it, they know how to smash your **Mystik Sixth Sense of Humor** in such a way that you'll be glad it's gone.

They know what sort of tribulations to heap on you that will make you "take things seriously." They know how to SCARE you into "accepting your responsibilities." In short, they know how to make you **"grow up."** And the way they do it would make Jesus puke. They wait till you're around 25, or so, let you just start to get your footing, then **WHAM** they pull the rug right out from under you. Your cherished notions of Slack in the world are shattered; you get good and **SODOMIZED** by **STARK REALITY.**

THE ANTI-DOBBS IS WAITING

BE SURE AND LOOK . . .

SEE *the difference in your* **HAIR**

It's like being a long-time virgin who *finally* got deflowered, but it was a *bad* deflowering. You lose faith in everything decent and suddenly nothing is *funny* anymore . . . especially not Hell-On-Earth. AND IT'S PEOPLE WHO DON'T THINK HELL ON EARTH IS FUNNY (albeit SICK) THAT DON'T REALLY BELIEVE THERE COULD *BE* HELL-ON-EARTH. Tight-lipped puritanical "LIBERALS" who keep telling you to THINK POSITIVE are The Conspiracy's BEST TOOLS. When push comes to shove they'll place their trust in the Anti"Bob" because he doesn't "act crazy," he doesn't mock sacred things or make cruel jokes about ugly things that *shouldn't even be brought*

trying to impart. And The Conspiracy has been so successful in retarding common human sense and the natural expression of piercing truthguffaws that even The Church of the SubGenius is sometimes forced to lower itself to TV-style pratfall-mongering to survive. If we didn't intersperse this ranting with the "obvious jokes" we'd have been jailed for victimless crimes LONG ago. We're just about the only organization willing to even *whisper* the truth about the Hollow Earth, and the only way we can do it is to wrap it in a good-natured sugar coating of surface laughs. "Here, would you please add this turd to that punchbowl?"

THEY can't read the code anyway. But YOU can. And if enough of *YOU* will step boldly out and make witness for "Bob," we'll be able to STRIP THE CODES AWAY, *rending brazenly all labels, false fronts, and preconceptions that obscure the BLINDING WHITE LIGHT of* SCHIZOTRUTH.

And this we swear: **THE CHURCH OF THE SUBGENIUS WILL NOT WUSS OUT. WE WILL NOT FOLD.** We CAN'T: it's TOO LATE. The juggernaut has been unleashed and *cannot be reversed.* THERE IS LITERALLY NO TELLING WHAT WILL HAPPEN. The One-World Religion foretold in ALL BIBLES is here *today* and you can NOW CASH IN on its RELENTLESS ERUPTION.

Sure — the world as we know it ends at 7:00 a.m., July 5, 1998. "Bob" can't promise he'll prevent it, but he'll sure as hell see that you get FRONT ROW TICKETS. And YOU don't have to worry — *you bought this Book.* The Men from

30,000 MILE WEAROUT WARRANTY

| | | 2705 | | 2704 | | 2703 | | 2702 | | 2701 | |

up, like "Bob" does. The Anti"Bob" assures you without saying a word that if you'll just act right (which is easy, the rules are simple), you'll be smart and cool and you won't act silly anymore like you did when you were a teenager. But BY GOD if you aren't ready to RIOT FOR FUN you'll be lost forever. If you don't keep your sense of hideous grins you won't have *any sense at all.* That broad, sick sense of humor is the only thing that makes the other senses *worthwhile.* That's *good,* it *has* to work that way! It's all tied together in one BIG plan. Let's face it, if "God" is everything and has attributes of everything, He She or **IT** most certainly has a sense of humor, in this case a sense of humor so refined as to be utterly *inscrutable.* God rarely makes any sense at ALL by *our* standards, and without that mystical primordial urge for ugly yuks you can't begin to comprehend *God's* bizarre ways of doing things, or JHVH-1's for that matter, and you'll latch onto The Devils's ways instead, or at least those of The Unmentionable One, which always make *perfect sense,* especially to the truly desperate. Without that sense of "humor" you'll never *let* yourself see how horrible things have gotten, and you'll never be *able* to see how hilarious they *always are anyway. "You can't be very smart without being totally stupid."* (**"Bob" in Trance 45**)

AIIEEE *YES* — the truth is *so bad* and *so good,* BOTH, it can ONLY be leaked out in so-called "jokes." What the hell do you think The Conspiracy is doing with its UFOs, poltergeists, spirit-guides and INSANE PHENOMENA? It's just propagating a warped version of the same truth "Bob" is

Planet X have a check by your name in the Book of Humans. They WILL LAND on that fateful day, and **YOU'LL BE SAVED** while all those ASSHOLES *FRY!!*

Hagen

CHAPTER 8

YOUR SUBGENIUS HERITAGE

"And the ape and the man exist in one body; and when the ape's desires are about to be fulfilled, he disappears and is succeeded by the man, who is disgusted with the ape's appetites."
—Colin Wilson, *The Outsider*

"Give me slack **or kill me.**"
—The late **St. Sterno Keckhaver** of *Drs. for "Bob"* to a rebellious intern just prior to the 1982 World SubCon performance, at which he was killed.

PART 1: INTERVIEW WITH THE OVERMAN

Subgeniuses came from a better world and they're going to a better world.

They descended from Abominable Snowmen and will evolve overnight (on some evening in late 1998) into **OverMen** and **Over-Women.** It is an unbroken line of continuous *change*, as opposed to that of Pinks, who are an evolutionary *dead-end* and have been spinning their wheels as *mere humans* for the last million years or so.

The goal of any SubGenius, besides SLACK, is to somehow live until 1998, when he or she will be CHANGED into what might as well be a *"superhero"* — possessed of mental and bodily powers practically unknown to Man today.

If you cleave to "Bob," you will see **magic** come to pass in *your* life. HOWEVER . . .

Only **Xist** technology can complete a SubGenius's transfiguration into OverManhood or OverWomanliness, and so far "Bob" has allowed this to happen to one solitary guinea pig — his friend, **Dr. Philo Drummond.** But someday, when the Angelic Host descends, we will *all* make this great Leap into Tomorrow.

It is important that we know what lies ahead, then . . . *after we have been given **Doktorhood** in Dobbstown, *after* our Initiation in the Xist Rescue Ships. What *is* this fabled *"Overman?"*

OverMania *is* a changed physique, yes: the huge cranium, the permanent smile, the powers of flight and invisibility, the great

Cough of Command. But it is far more than that. Above all, it is a *state of mind*.

The only way to capture even the most *fleeting flavor* of this unique mental state is to let Dr. Drummond tell of it in his own words. This, the only published interview with the OverMan *after transformation*, is directly transcribed from tapes made in Dobbstown during the 1980 rainy season. Read, then, and savor the nuances of that which is *closest to "BOB!"*

(Interview conducted by The Nameless SubGenius using an **Überbrow**™ Voice Transponder with *wellmanized* cassettes; normal recording techniques result in garbled tapes due to the OverMan's auraic 'field'.)

SG: *Is An OverMan really more intelligent than a human being? In what ways?*

PD: It is a visionary superiority . . . cutting through the bullshit, which makes it easier to *spread* bullshit. By pulling the wool over your *own* eyes, you become aware that THERE IS WOOL, and know better how to pull it over the eyes of others. This is the first step to enlightenment.

SG: *What about the transformation? How often, what happens?*

PD: It can occur at will or spontaneously, of its own accord. When the transfiguration occurs, the cancerous preservative chemicals my human self has taken in are expelled through every pore of my body, covering me in that sheen of unnatural juices, but basically leaving *in* me only the Essence of

Health and 'Frop. I can then *will my genes* to *bend* as I so desire, and the Time Barrier hinders me not.

SG: *Why does the head enlarge? Brains?*

PD: Not so much those as *glands*. Some of the intelligence is on *chips*, imbedded within the brain. Such as the OverMan Head Map. Maps of every major metropolitan area are available to my Inner Eye, all on one chip. So if I, say, must make a fast getaway from Bangladesh . . . however without the retrieval mechanism handy, full Transfiguration must be achieved first before I can 'read' them.

SG: *I understand that for OverMen, ritual excremeditation is different?*

PD: Yes. We achieve pure, heavenly *cytorspasm* in excremeditation. The pancreative juices of the fluunads . . . they back up to the pituitary brainpan, causing it to backfire unless there is a bowel-lifter installed, with a 468 hemi dual-rounder. This causes nodules on the brain, and around those nodules the cranium *rearranges itself,* answering your earlier question. It creates a feeling of overwhelming phlegmaticism. Inhumanly gratifying.

SG: *What kind of diet is preferable?*

PD: To begin with you must understand that a true OverMan can perform Discriminative Elimination and Selective Excretion. He can pass not only fecessions of whatever shape, texture, odor, size and velocity he chooses, but through the Yoke of Excremeditation can also *reconstitute* the food eaten earlier. This is *"Going into Overspurt."* He can expel entire sandwiches, steaks, salads . . . as if unchewed! Many think that eating a pineapple would be painful for me. Yes, it does remain a Whole Pineapple, but it does not *tear through* . . . To expel a pineapple I merely turn myself *partially inside out*. The opening itself moves *around* the pineapple, delicately, precisely, much like laying an egg. It still tickles but many consider this the most delightful and *insipid* realm of the unconscious mind.

SG: *I hope this isn't too personal, but what about sex? Many have asked.*

PD: It is true that the OverMan penis has a literal "Mind of its Own." This may account for the "Mean Bob" I have heard the bearers whisper of. I don't know.

SG: *Have you actually seen beheadings in Church rituals?*

PD: No. No. All that is pure fiction. No violence, no blood, no balls in vises, no pain. The pain comes strictly through mind absorption.

SG: *What about Tantric Sex?*

PD: No pain. No pain.

SG: *Is there an Afterlife? A realm of spirits?*

PD: The Paradise of the heathen Undergods of Valhalla . . . available only to a select few. Already predetermined. We were ALL in the Beforelife . . . will be again . . . but only a few in the Afterlife. Things there are MORE REAL than on Earth . . . colors are like jacked-up TV color. You keep your full personality and *then* some.

SG: *There are greater and lesser gods besides* **Wotan?**

PD: Like the Romans: the headache god, the hangover god, the garbage god . . . one for every purpose. None are *The* God with a capital G. They all have small g's. **Wotan** as a gGod is somewhere between the large and small G. *It's all a question of punctuation.*

SG: *"Bob's" stance on previous mystery schools?*

PD: That should be obvious. This is not so much the *culmination* of them as the *skimming of the cream*, the very best stuff off the top.

SG: *When did Man acquire intelligence and separate from the animals?*

PD: Tampering with Yetis by aliens of unknown origin. Through direct contact with bodily parts. NOT ALL YETINSYNY ARE SUBGENII! They are sometimes Pinks, but Pinks who are aware of the difference . . . they recognize our threat to their useless race . . . these are the most dangerous. More *vital* Pinks.

SG: *Is "Bob," finally, an adept or an imposter?*

PD: Neither. And both. An ORIGINATOR.

SG: *Why does "Bob" make initiates walk on hot coals?*

PD: Diversionary device designed to awaken the **footgland.**

SG: *Are men superior to women? Why does this seem to mainly address men?*

PD: Men are not superior to women PER SE, or vice versa. Merely such awesome figures of mystery to each other that . . . it's coexistence based on ancient and primal instinctual values. Ingrained in our very genetic code from the Dawn of Time.

SG: *If a young person has been having omenistic dreams and space voices in his head, how does he know if the entities are benevolent, or leading him astray?*

PD: Takes dedicated effort. Cannot be answered in generalizations. Don't trust any alien viewpoints at all unless Approved by Dobbs. One entity could talk to the same person at two times at once — two Nows — Point A saying TERRORIZE, Point B saying BENEVOLIZE. Not that certain bits of information can't be used for specific purposes.

SG: *What of masturbation?*

PD: A divine gift. "The Matter At Hand." Perfectly legal, a gift from God, ordained by "Bob," given to Man. The opposable thumb was for *one* tool, not all tools. The simplest sex magic . . . just don't do it *too much*.

SG: *Will "Bob" end all crime?*

PD: No, "Bob" needs crime to balance out the Good. Without two points on the scale, how can you have a reference point? If we weren't crime-ridden, we'd be suicide-ridden. "Bob" will reduce dangerous crime, but there'll be a rapid increase in **petty** crime . . . workforce terrorism . . . you see, **New-Old Values** will replace the need for crime. The SubGeniuses will be in such collusion together against Them that YacatiSmic forces of evil . . . oh, forget it.

SG: *"Bob" refers to both Asgard and Valhalla. Which is which?*

PD: Only those who die fighting go to Valhalla. Others go to Helle. There were originally eight days in the week. The eighth was Hellesday, when evil beings reigned supreme . . . like Halloween and April Fool's Day all in one. The day you fucked up on . . . were REQUIRED to fuck up on. Under "Bob" every other day will be Hellesday.

SG: *Are UFOs mere projections from the collective unconscious?*

PD: Mankind is like a hydra, composed of millions of cells, none of them aware of the hydra's existence except for a few holy men. Mankind wants UFOs to exist so badly that they manifest themselves as spontaneous externalizations of the entire hydra's hallucination. UFOs can also be *demons,* however . . . CHEESE in a great TRAP.

SG: *In general, should people really quit their jobs and slack off?*

PD: Yes. Absolutely. IF that's what they want to do. One is not dependent on the other . . . it depends on the amount of **Slack Manipulation** available, and how much Slack they can handle. Some can handle extreme Job Slack, others abuse it. The totally Slackless should get a better job through divine *future Luck Plane causational interruption.* Once they make the commitment to **give up,** it will automatically SHIFT back in their direction . . . like a teeter-totter. But two similar problems could have different solutions and these must be approached one at a time.

As the devotee gives more to "Bob," he will find more coming to him. But it's not the amount, it's the *reason why.* It's like the poor old lady donating her last penny, versus the rich jerk with his measly thousand-dollar bills. WHICH ONE GAVE THE MOST??

SG: *Well, the rich guy.*

PD: You're right. *Fuck* the old hag, give us the *rich dumbshits.*

SG: *Exactly how does it feel to reach OverManhood?*

PD: When I get the spirit, I feel numbness and pleasurable heat in the legs followed by an equally pleasurable furnace in the stomach, and finally the *pranana* of *manillia* ascends my spine to my brain with waves of *mechapleasure.* It makes you want to fight and kill for peace and LOOOOVE.

SG: *Ultimately, does Good triumph over Evil?*

PD: These are not constant terms of value but represent a changing, sliding semantic illusion . . . language-induced values. Though some are indisputable . . . inherently evil or good. Motherhood is inherently good though there are some evil witches participating in it.

SG: *What is inherently bad?*

PD: Stupid questions.

SG: *Do you really believe this stuff?*

PD: Well, I do believe it, and I don't. This, I believe, is the Path to Slack . . . *although I doubt that seriously.*

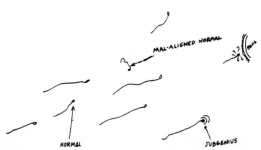

Madge Dinette

PART 2: YOU ARE YETI

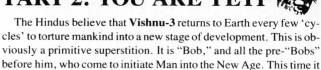

The Hindus believe that **Vishnu-3** returns to Earth every few 'cycles' to torture mankind into a new stage of development. This is obviously a primitive superstition. It is "Bob," and all the pre-"Bobs" before him, who come to initiate Man into the New Age. This time it *should* work.

Only it isn't exactly "man"kind that will be uplifted. SubGeniuses are not entirely of the race of "Man," if that term is taken to mean "human."

All SubGenii, no matter their "racial background," are KIN! We as a World Cult are bonded together by mere threads, but they are threads of titanium steel forged in the mines of Jupiter, for *the link of blood is the strongest.* We are **WOTAN'S prime breeding stock,** and no matter how different in shade our skin colors may be, we carry in our DNA a common *CODE* — a 'tracking device,' so to speak, implanted by Our Monster Lord YEA so many millions of years ago. Humans lack this Code and have tried to snuff it for millenia.

At their beginnings in antiquity, the humans — a wild, nomadic preSubGenius race — reverted to civilization and accepted Conspiracy rule. Whenever SubGenii gained a foothold in history, the humans pounced to thwart what they saw — perhaps correctly — as a threat to their pathetic "control" over the planet. However, this is changing swiftly. The human aggression syndrome is turning against itself, and now most humans under Conspiracy thrall are mere spectators — stooges — disgruntled paupers powerless to resist *any* form of Sales Dominance, especially "Bob's."

Secular humanism's baleful theory of "evolution" can now be challenged. Understand, however, that we are *not* descended from humans. In fact, "Man" is not really even descended from the ape! "Man" — humans and Subs alike — *preceded the monkey!*

It began shortly after the Elder Gods forced the Xists to exterminate the dinosaurs. At this time, the Stark Fists of All the Gods smote a tiny, monkeylike mammal called **Primo-Anthropocus** and split his gene-line into two: one, a seriously flawed attempt called *Australopithicus* (which, under JHVH-1's occasional smiting, evolved into the modern human); and another, the **True Atlanteans** (*Homo Directus*), of whom the first was The First "Bob."

There are still fullblood Atlanteans in the world. Now called *Dzugarians* in their own tongue, they inhabit **the lost Glass City of Chang-Eng** on the Ice Plateau That Time Forgot in the least accessible reaches of Tibet. "Bob's" advisors on **The Council of None** dwell in this place.

When glimpsed running naked through the Himalayan snow by explorers and human natives from the lowlands, these mountain creatures have been called "Abominable Snowmen" — or **"Yetis"** in the language of the Sherpas.

The huge, luxuriously furred Yetis are the perfect physical and mental ideal that the Elder Gods meant for humans to be. In the days of Atlantis, they built vast cities that would dwarf our New York, yet were clean and beautiful to look upon. Their technology was so refined that they had no pollution, their intelligence was so high that they could live on the ice without clothing, their spirits were so ascended that they knew no war, strife, or government.

But they "sinned" against the Elder Gods, unfortunately at the same time that the Elder Gods sinned against *themselves.* A cataclysm resulted during which the gods OVERNIGHT devolved all but a few Atlanteans back into beasts — into the frail, miserable, generally perverted and monkeyish **Homo Connectus,** which shat from trees and did not even know ordinary Sex. For millions of years their haphazard reproduction — often with trees, birds, in-

YOUR SUBGENIUS HERITAGE

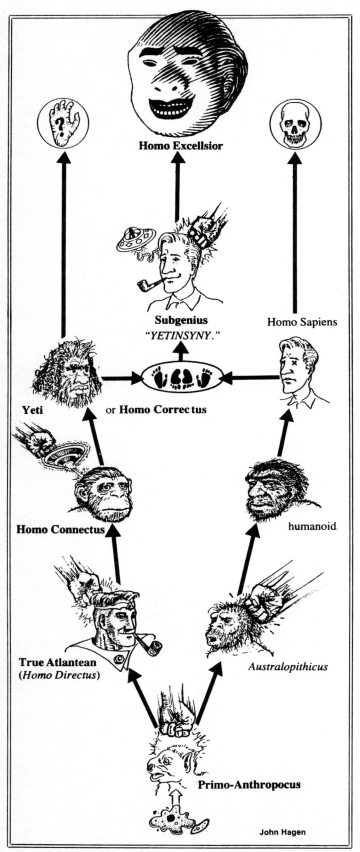

Homo Excellsior

Subgenius
"YETINSYNY."

Homo Sapiens

Yeti   or **Homo Correctus**

Homo Connectus

humanoid

True Atlantean
(*Homo Directus*)

Australopithicus

Primo-Anthropocus

John Hagen

sects and other Connecti of the same sex — resulted only in branches of life that became the monkeys and Great Apes we know today.

Meanwhile, JHVH-1 and a handful of other cosmic entities had rebelled from the now-sleeping Elder Gods and were attempting to brutalize humans into swifter evolution, to create a race sufficiently developed to aid them on the Day when the Elder Gods would awaken.

Finally giving up on the humanoids, who slipped back into bovinity whenever unattended, WOTAN turned again to Homo Connectus. The resulting OverMutant was the Yeti — or **Homo Correctus,** First Right Man. He predates Homo Sapiens.

And WE the SubGenii are the true and rightful heirs of the Yeti. WE are the Great-Great-Great[5]-Grandsons-and-daughters of the "Abominable Snowmen," the Sasquatch, the Bigfeet . . . The Folk. WE WERE HERE FIRST AND LAY CLAIM TO EARTH.

But we must humble ourselves before our "Bob." For we are no longer true Yeti. We are FAR FALLEN from that lofty height. Our Yeti ancestors, great as they were, had more lust than sense. They interbred with humans.

Gradually the "Yeti" became more and more human-like. Except for the fullblood High Priests in the Glass City, the Yeti finally became indistinguishable, physically, from the lower species. They lost their fur coat, their great size, the use of their extra five senses. They became Pinker . . . by which we mean not lighter-skinned, but *less interesting.*

But worst of all, they diluted **The Code.**

The Code is all that JHVH-1 knows us by — the only thing that will keep us from being carted off to the slaughterhouse along with the humans on The Last Round-Up. And if we dilute The Code much more, we risk our *very children* being LEFT BEHIND when the Xists come to rescue us from the Second Big Bang.

PLEASE — FOR THE SAKE OF THE LITTLE ONES — *DON'T MARRY A HUMAN!!* Marry any SubGenius you please, but DON'T SULLY YOUR GENES!!!

YES, ANSWER *YES THIS* IS OUR GOAL, TO *PURIFY* OUR GENES, TO DENY *THEM* OUR ESSENCE, TO WRENCH THE REINS OF CONTROL FROM OUR TAINTED COMPETITORS IN THIS VAST RACE SO PRESUMPTUOUSLY CALLED "EVOLUTION!"

Only in this way can we hope to gain admittance to the Xist Chambers of Change where we will be smited ONE LAST TIME to become OverMen-and-Women, the great **Homo Excellsior** bespoken by the prophets! KEEP PURE THY BLOOD AND LIE YE NOT WITH THE PINKS OF THE FIELD; IT IS AN ABOMINATION.

This is what the Covenant is all about. When the first Yeti "secured" his or her first human, in whatever combination of sexes it was, the Covenant was broken. JHVH-1, uncharacteristically, has given us another chance to clean up our gene-pool. This time, *let's not blow it!*

Do you think it far fetched that you are a relative to the Abominable Snowman, as well as to that weird Aborigine family that moved onto the block and also has a "Bob" bumper sticker on their car? Do you question our sources? Then let's examine them.

One is the encyclopaedic *Behold! The Protong* by St. Stanislav Szukalski, published by a SubGenius, the Ever Reverend Glenn Bray. A comparatively recent book, it is also called "The 7th Bible of the SubGenius Race." "Bob" himself fainted upon first holding it to his forehead and "whiffreading" it, partly because it is as rife with misconceptions as facts. Nevertheless, this slim volume contains more true mystic and scientific lore than all the Conspiracy textbooks in the world. St. Szukalski — who is still living — discovered entirely on his own the secret mixing of Yetis and humans, which product he calls *"YETINSYNY."* His new science of "Zermatism" is a key to our knowledge of the past, and from it we have learned many of the traits that distinguish the pitiful, jealous human from the forthright, NOBLE Yetinsyn.[1]

Another of our sources is none other than The Holy Bible. The first one. Genesis 6:2–4 refers to the seeding of Atlantis and creation of the first Yetis by the Elder Gods, describing sons of the gods who "came in unto the daughters of men, and they bare children to them, the same became mighty men which were of old, men of reknown." These Yeti Patriarchs lived hundreds of years and possessed all the super powers we attribute to the Atlanteans. Yes, that's right: **THE YETINSYNY ARE THE TRUE ISRAEL OF THE BIBLE.** *WE ARE THE CHOSEN PEOPLE — THE LOST TRIBE — THE TRUE CHILDREN OF YAHWEH-ONE, WHO CARRY* **THE CODE** *LIKE A BANNER OF GLORY!!!!*

However, the harsh YAH also made it abundantly clear that we are NOT to couple with the groveling humans:

"Neither shalt thou lie with any beast to defile thyself therewith: neither shall any woman stand before a beast to lie down thereto: it is confusion." (Leviticus 18:23)

No kidding! Also:

"And if a man lie with a beast, he shall surely be put to death; and ye shall slay the beast (human)." (Lev. 20:15)

Humanity has wandered too far from its roots, as witnessed by the abhorrent world condition today. We must look to the Yeti — to their habits, their wisdom, their great Slackliness — to find the way back. To find **The Old Ways** again.

Already, our scientists are studying Yeti *coprolites,* the fossilized excrement of that near-vanished race of Giants. And what have they found therein?

Human finger bones.

When asked how many races there would be on Earth under "Bob," Dr. Philo Drummond, Ø1°, grinned ambiguously and answered, "There will be only one — all smiling, all smoking."

BE PROUD OF YOUR NORTHERN TIBETAN HERITAGE!

PART 3: OUR HIDDEN POWERS

Along with the history of persecution with which our Yetinsynism accurses us, we are also bequeathed within our tampered genes the potential for mystik powers and abilities undreamt-of by Street Pinks.

To begin with, we possess the *other* five senses. However, these work on a purely subconscious level, when they work at all, for they have been sequestered from us for the Duration of the Experiment, the Trial by Aliens.

THE FIVE UNRECOGNIZED or LATENT SENSES

1. *The Third Nostril:* life essence detector. "Sees/whiffs" auras, Nental Ive pstenches, etc.
2. *The Sense of Slack:* precognitive, clairvoyant. Catches Luck

Plane and Timestream 'images' by sensing the 'echoes' of Slack Particles.
3. *The Psychic Forklift:* telekinetic powers such as levitation, spoon-bending, spells, hexes, will domination and mass hypnosis.
4. (CLASSIFIED) National security precludes discussion.
5. *The Mystery Sense:* not even "Bob" has developed this one sufficiently to know what it is. The Xists insist that it's there, though.

In some ways, the brain is less important to a SubGenius than to a Pink. Being less intuitive, Pinks *need* more brains than we do. Their value system is based on *intelligence* rather than *good sense,* which is related not so much to 'thinking' as to the feelings of the heart and the foot.

As mentioned before, the SubGenius foot doubles as a gland, and a very complex gland at that. It 'intuits' the world around us so subtly that we rarely notice its machinations. It was discovered by Dr. Philo Drummond, and he best explained its functioning in this excerpt from his daily radio show, *On The Road* (so named because it is usually recorded in a car):

". . .and they'd be JUST FINE if they'd only use that mystical bobgland in their foot, the one that'd TELL 'em what to do if they'd only THINK with it! When Man stands on his brain and thinks with his feet, THEN HE'LL KNOW EXACTLY WHICH WAY TO GO and how to FIND "BOB." You gotta MASSAGE that foot gland . . . and the only way to massage it is to WALK ON IT! Because when you're walkin'. . . and "Bob's" talkin'. . . you'll know what to do, after the Holocast, after the Aliens come and give us all those GIANT PILLS, and all them *machines* that'll run our lives and that BIG WHITE STONE that everybody's gonna know PERSONALLY in their very own living rooms. That's the stone that you think you might know and you think might HELP YOU, but BY GOBBS, that's the Stone that's gonna ruin your VERY LIFE! You think you know who Big Brother is? HAHAHA. Dear friends, I wanna tell you tonight, YOU DON'T KNOW! YOU DON'T KNOW *NOTHIN' !*"

Oh, if only we *could* truly know nothing!

Reinforcing the powers of the brain and Foot Gland is a small secondary brain at the base of the SubGenius spine. The mighty Stegosaurus also possessed this organ, which helps direct the reproductive and eliminative systems that are so important to us.

Another gland unknown to Normals is the **Peen Gland** in the brain, which regulates the 8 separate **stages** or Character Generations through which the SubGenius personality evolves during an average day. Literally, 8 different personalities each have control at the Helm of Behavior at varied intervals; we each contain 8 people in our corrugated subconsciouses! The average human has but 4: Good, Bad, Bland, and Asleep (the last thought by some scholars to overpower the others for up to 18 hours a day).

These different personalities account for the compartmentalization of the SubGenius brain into 8 distinct 'units' or 'efficiencies,' in this descending order of control:

LEFT BRAIN = *"Painbrain:"* controls paranoia, anal compulsion, overwork, trying too hard, thinking too much.

NORTH BRAIN = *"Makebrain"* or *"Takebrain":* handles jobs and money.

SOUTH BRAIN = *"Fakebrain"* or *"Talkbrain":* speech, writing, lying.

---

1. You can actually buy *BEHOLD! — THE PROTONG* for $16.50 post-paid (includes 33 rpm record of Szukalski) from Glenn Bray, P.O. Box 4482, Sylmar, CA 91342. You would be **insane** not to. *You may never get a chance like this again.*

HIND BRAIN	=	*"MEbrain":* the pivotal center brain, the private YOU. Rides piggyback on The Lord and is unaffected by drugs or religion. "Bob" comes in on this channel.
FOREBRAIN	=	*"Sanebrain":* Covers love, friendship, traditional family values. Called by some the "Tamebrain."
INNER BRAIN	=	*"Sexbrain":* self-explanatory.
RIGHT BRAIN	=	*"Lamebrain"* or *"Morebrain"* depending on your orientation. Intuitive: art, music, drug addiction.

And the 8th brain, the OUTER BRAIN, is a pseudophysical "shell" encasing not only the other brains, but the entire body. This diffuse "brain," larger but far less controllable than the others, is the Nental Ife.

The Nental Ife represents fully *half* of our brain-power, but because it is so independent from us we can rarely make use of it. Occasionally a SubGenius comes along whose Nental Ife *is* incorporated into his thinking processes; such less "sub" Geniuses were Da Vinci, Einstein, and Curly Howard.

For most of us, however, the Nental Ife is a separate entity, a semi-conscious "ghost twin" which mindlessly follows the physical vessel about but remains dormant throughout most of our lives. Certain emotional states can awaken it, however; if involuntary, this results in sinister occult phenomenon such as poltergeists, telekinesis, and, if the Ife is on a full-tilt rampage, spontaneous combustion. Careful, ritualistic *invocation* of the Nental Ife, on the other hand, can be developed into an exact science, and we of the Cloth use it to enter the trance or "Spout" state of automatic blabbering in which we open ourselves to the Tongue of "Bob." One of the fastest ways to achieve this state is through AntiSleep™ (NOT a drug), also called "Sleep-Fasting." People who work 48 hours straight to meet deadlines are all too familiar with this effect.

If we were able to assimilate the Nental Ife's powers into our systems permanently, we'd all be "geniuses." Perhaps the Nental Ife developed as a distinct being because society programs us not to *improve,* but to *stay normal.*

Other religions tell of the "aura," which they claim has similar illustrative and diagnostic qualities. However, Dobbs informs us that the aura is but the shadow of the Nental Ife, with as much relative substance as our shadows have to our bodies. And, though it partially governs our bodies and is permanently 'tied' to us, it is really a separate being. There are no cases of a living person being separated from his Nental Ife.

However, a rare effect is created when two SubGeniuses' Nental Ives "mate." This produces a Nental Ife "baby," a truly brainless force unattached to any physical anchor unless it latches onto a manufactured object, such as an American car built on a Monday or a Friday. Fortunately such beings are short-lived — 5 to 19 weeks — for they can be extremely destructive at times. They give rise to some stories of demonic possession and haunted houses, and certain machines that continually break down as if they "hate you."

(NOTE: The Nental Ife does not otherwise produce 'ghosts;' these are different. Some few are dead people without the common sense of death, or deceased horror writers back to give us crap, but most are just alien booby traps left by practical jokers from outer space in years past: metaphysical 'joy-buzzers' that moan and rattle windows just so some distant superintelligence can get a few rude chuckles at the expense of ignorant humans.)

One way in which the Nental Ife *is* useful is in Astral Projection, or 'out-of-body travel,' 99% of which is involuntary. SubGeniuses have a tendency to astral-project NOT when they want to, but when

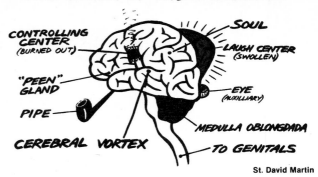

THE BRAIN OF THE SUBGENIUS

CONTROLLING CENTER (BURNED OUT)
SOUL
LAUGH CENTER (SWOLLEN)
"PEEN" GLAND
EYE (AUXILIARY)
PIPE
MEDULLA OBLONGDADA
CEREBRAL VORTEX
TO GENITALS

St. David Martin

they're bored, uncomfortable, faced with violence, caught by their parents, or sitting in Math class in 7th Grade.

If you try to "practice" astral projection as taught by other Occult Schools, you're 117% more likely to achieve simple self-delusion or mere daydreaming. The way most New Age cults *really* make their money is by getting Normals to *notice their imaginations* for the first time, giving the daydream Pink Legitimacy by calling it 'real.'

You may have noticed that two completely unrelated persons may have the same Primal Stench. This is because there are only 47 basic Nental Ife 'types,' all dating back to Creation. For the Nental Ife is actually closer to Heaven than its bodied twin; it is a microcosm of the universe more in tune with the Real Thing. Although the body, sex, temperament and other earthly qualities change from reincarnation to reincarnation, the Nental Ife alone stays the same. Your Nental Ife is immortal, and you may well share Nental Ife 'type' with someone else in the world who shares the same Past Life. For you aren't the product of one Past Life at a time — your current Life is rather like one rope made from what were previously several diverse strands. Likewise, pieces of you will reincarnate into various bodies at once, as only a *part* of each body, sharing them with others. Somehow — and we admit this makes no sense — the Ife remains intact throughout the cycle.

It can't be destroyed until Judgement Day, when all the universe will be freed from the Wheel of Earnings, the Conveyor Belt of Karma. However, the Nental Ife *can be damaged* in God only knows *what* hideous manner by the upcoming *Rupture* or Time Intersection, which is . . . no, no, we shan't speak of it now. It is too . . . too . . . no. Not now.[2]

For now, all that is important is that you be able to look in the mirror and know that you aren't 'alone,' that you're seeing your own foe, that you are actually Two — schizocephallic, split-headed, Crack'd, Eternally Divided; your eternal self or *"IDGE"* is always shadowed by its nightmare twin, the invisible ghost of your missing Genius-half, and the two dwell NOT, *NAY,* in harmony; beneath the placid, sometimes even stoic surface of SubGeniushood there lurks a cannibal werewolf Urge, with your Brakes it fights a hellish battle, HOW CAN THEY COEXIST??? The Ife strives to sabotage all Idge-built layers of restraint and decency so that it may gain possession of the body and SATE ITS UNSPEAKABLE CRAVINGS, IT IS A VAMPIRE??? YES YES OR KILL ME! "I'm *very* sorry, Dr. Jeckyl, but I'm afraid Mr. Hyde here was in line ahead of you and you'll have to wait...."

---

2. "Bob" insists that details concerning The Rupture (or Time Intersection or "Omicron Epsilon") be withheld until **BOOK II;** if released now, before "Bob's" Promise becomes household knowledge, panic would ensue.

Chapter 9

SHUT UP OR STAND UP!
('The Brag of the SubGenius')

— a fragment. Transcribed from a cassette tape recording made at a seance in 1973.

"I PICK THE GOD DAMN terror of the fucking gods out of my *nose!* Pardon my language. But YEEEEEHAW, let the sons of God and man bear witness! Even in the belly of the Thunderbird I've been casting out the False Prophets; I'm busting a gut and blowing my O-ring, and ripe to throw a *loaf!* For I speak *only* the fucking *Truth,* and never in my days have I spoke other than! For my every utterance is a lie, including this very one you hear! I say, 'Fuck 'em if they can't take a joke!' By God, 'Anything for a laugh,' I say. I am the last remaining Homo Correctus, I am the god damn Man of the Future! I'll drive a mile so as not to walk a foot; I am a human being of the *first* god damn water! Yes, I'm the javalina humping junkie that jumped the Men from Mars! I drank the *Devil* under seven tables, I am too *intense* to die, I'm insured for acts o' God *and* Satan! I was shanghaied by bodiless fiends and alien jews from a corporate galaxy, and got away with their hubcaps! I *cannot* be tracked on radar! I wear nothing uniform, I wear *no* god damn uniform! Yes baby, I'm 23 feet tall and have 13 rows o' teats; I was suckled by a triceratops, I gave the Anti-Virgin a high-protein tonsil wash! I'm a bacteriological weapon, I'm *armed* and *loaded!* I'm a fission reactor, I fart plutonium, power plants are fueled by the sweat from my brow; when they plug *me* in, the lights go out in Hong Kong! I weigh 666 pounds in zero gravity, *come and get me!* I've sired retarded space bastards across the Cosmos, I cook and *eat* my dead; YAH-HOOOO, I'm the Unshaven Thorn Tree of the Atlantis Zoo! I pay no taxes! The Devil's hands are my *ideal* playground! I hold the Seven-Bladed Windbreaker; the wheels that turn are behind me; I think *backwards!* I do it for *fun!* My imagination is a *fucking* cancer and I'll pork it before it porks me! They say a godzillion is the highest number there is. Well, by God! I count to a godzillion and *one!* Yes, I'm the purple flower of Hell County, give me wide berth; when I drop my drawers, Mother Nature swoons! I use a python for a prophylactic; I'm *thicker, harder,* and *meaner* than the Alaskan Pipeline, and carry more spew! I'll freeze *your* seed before it hits the bathroom tile! YEE! YEEE! I kidnapped the future and ransomed it for the past, I made *Time* wait up for me to bleed my lizard! My infernal breath wilts the Tree of Life, I left my *spoor* on the Rock of Ages, *who'll tear flesh with me, who'll spill their juice? Who'll gouge with me, whose candle will I

fart out? Whoop! I'm ready!* So step aside, all you butt-lipped, neurotic, insecure bespectacled slabs o' wimp meat! I'm a Crime Fighting Master Criminal, I am Not Insane! I'm a screamer and a laugher, I make a *spectacle* of myself, I am a *sight!* My physical type *cannot* be classified by science, my 'familiar' is a pterodactyl, I feed it dipshits! I communicate without *wires* or *strings!* I am a Thuggee, I am feared in the Tongs, I have the Evil Eye, I carry the Mojo Bag; I swam the *Bermuda Triangle* and didn't get wet! I circumcise dinosaurs with my teeth and make 'em leave a tip; I change tires with my *tongue* and my *tool!* Every night I hock up a lunger and extinguish the *Sun!* I'm the big-footed devil of Level 14, who'll come *shoe* me? Where's the robot giant who'll try to blow me down? I've packed the brownies of the gods, I leak the Plague from my nether parts, opiates are the *mass* of my religion, *I take drugs!* Yes, I'm a rip-snorter, I cram coca leaves right into my arm-veins before they're picked off the *tree! Space* monsters cringe at my tread! I wipe the *Pyramids* off my shoes before I enter *my* house. I'm *fuel-injected,* I'll live forever and remember it afterwards! I'm *immune!* I'm *radioactive!* Come *on* and give me cancer, I'll spit up the tumor and butter my *bread* with the juice! *I'm supernatural,* I bend *crowbars* with my meat ax and a thought! My droppings bore through the earth and erupt *volcanoes* in *China!* Yes, I can drink more wine and stay soberer than all the heathen *Hindoos* in Asia! YEEEE HAW! *Gut Blowout!* I am a *Moray Eel,* I am a *Komodo Dragon,* I am a *Killer Whale bereft of its pup!* I have a triple backbone, I was sired by the Wolf Man, give me *all* your Slack! I told *Jesus* I wouldn't go to church and He *shook my hand!* I have my *own* personal saviors, I change 'em every hour, I don't give a fuck if there's life after death, I want to know if there's even any fucking *Slack* after death! I am a god damn *visionary,* I see the future and the past in comic books and wine bottles; I eat *black holes* for breakfast! I bend my genes and whittle at my DNA with the sheer force of my mighty *will!* I steer my *own* god damn evolution! I ran 'em out of Heaven and sold it to Hell for a *profit!* I'm enlightened, I achieved '"Nirvana'' and took it *home* with me. *Yip, yip, YEEEEEEEE!* I'm so ugly the Speed of Light can't slow me down and Gravity won't tug at my cuffs! When the Rapture comes, I'll make 'em wait! They'll *never* clean *my* cage! Now give me some more of . . . ''

(Tape runs out.)

89

SECRET WEAPONS OF THE SUBGENIUS

Compiled by Propaganda Minister Bob Black, on loan from **The Last International** (''It's better to be mean than average! And it's **fine** to be coarse! We will overcum. This means war!'' and and even more vengeful philosophies available by writing **THE LUMPENTA-GON**, 2000 Center St. #1314, Berkeley, CA 94704. **DOBBS-APPROVED!**).

63 Fuck-U-Boat
47 Ozzie-and-Harrier
61 Dumb-Dumb
50 Hell's Angel-Dust

9 Great God Panzer
21 Phlegmthrower
Character Armor-Piercing Shell
54 Up-Chute

42 Mindwinder Missle
23 Kampf Mine
5 Bringdowner
17 Sexocet Missle

43 B-M Missle [No.2]
12 Tanked
24 Gum Bazooka
18 Mettle Detector

34 Muff-Divebomber
13 Big Wheel
25 Devolver
55 Frig-It

35 Breakwind
14 Defooliant
27 Transvaluator
57 Antisubmoron Device

36 Antistatecraft Carrier
15 Little Death Ray
28 Culture Distorter
58 Infra-Reds [''Sexies'']

Alien Heat [Xists]
7 Impulsar
19 3-Chordite
59 Addleship

THEM: the Normalthusians, yes-But's, Lilliputians, Kens-and-Barbies, Errorists, Habitues, Ordinaryans and Lickspittles.

US: the Insurgentry, Absurdgeons, Eristocrats, Ranters, Wreckreators, ''Bob''dingnagians and More-Than-Humanists.

CHAPTER 10

WE DARE CALL IT 'CONSPIRACY'

"1984 NOW!"
— Meyer III, Pope of All New York

"There's something definitely un-American about banks nowadays!"
— Little "Bobby" Dobbs at age 10

"The Trilateral Commission doesn't secretly run the world. The Council on Foreign Relations does that."
— Winston Lord, President of the C.F.R.

"We must pray for the fat people. . .it's against the Lord to be fat. . ."
— heard on a Christian radio broadcast

"It'll be the Powers of Good against the Forces of Good-And-Evil-At-The-Same-Time, and THE TWAIN SHALL MEET, HEAD-ON! YEEEEEEEAAAAAAA....."
— Dr. Philo Drummond, 01 on "Bob" vs. The Conspiracy

"You know, what really makes me mad. . .what really makes me *pee*. . . is these Zombies nowadays. They don't *try*. Now when I was a Zombie, we rose from the grave early in the morning, not at one or two in the afternoon. And when we ate the flesh of a woman's corpse, we did it with *respect* for the *woman!*"
— St. Janor on the Panel Discussion at the 1965 World SubGenius Revival

If you can't get Slack for yourself, you *sure* as hell aren't going to be able to give it to somebody else.
And that's *just* what They've got you trying to do.

You can't think. . . everything's gone wrong. . . you're so *tired*. . . the kids are driving you crazy. . . your spouse lost another job and is drinking again. . . you're supposed to have an operation and you don't know where the money's gonna come from. . . it just doesn't seem worth it anymore. . . there's no one to talk to. . . you don't know if you can hold up under all this, and you're not sure if you *want* to. . . you're ashamed of the things you *haven't* done. . . you keep thinking about those *pills*. . .

Put a dog in a cage and he'll run in circles. Put a man in a cage and he'll run for President. AND IT'S THE SAME THING.

Howdy from THE END

BIG BROTHER IS WATCHING YOU

FOR RENT CHEAP!

LIES

Shocked OUT OF YOUR SKIN!

LIES

Robert (Yo' Mama!) Williams

A GHASTLY TALE DRENCHED WITH GOUTS OF BLOOD!

All problems result from *paralysis* caused by **Their Game**, in which they keep changing the rules. It's like the robot monster in 30 different sci-fi movies, being ordered to KILL contrary to his Prime Directive of protecting humans. He goes into a cycle of "I MUST — YET I CANNOT" and shorts out in an explosion of sparks. Instead of shorting out, humans have the choice of ignoring the paradox within their orders. Of going to "sleep."

Public apathy *is* a disease, certainly; the Con itself complains of it. But it isn't apathy to begin with — it's just that NOBODY WANTS what They're trying to PUSH.

They push *rules*, but *no* rules for behavior can *work* for long. However, they can *sound good* long enough for each new political fad to become epidemic before its side effects of Pos-Think brain cancer set in.

The Con wants you either to think only about the "nice" things — sweetness, cuteness, pollyanna crap in general — or to be frozen by total hopelessness. Either way, you're kept from resisting the Unspoken Rules: the Rules which don't *have* to be spoken because so many people *live* them, *think* them, that they can't stand back and *see* them. Those IN the System can't see it except from the inside. THEY DON'T KNOW THERE COULD BE AN OUTSIDE. . . they never suspect how much larger their *cage might be.*

They implanted in you the idea that you have to "find yourself," but when you start looking, all you find is *more conspiracy.* There's nothing left but *Their* idea of "you." "See? *Now get back in your gourd.*"

The Conspiracy's Left/Right Split Enforcement creates two very opposite attitudes towards CHANGE: its "conservative" dupes fear *all* change, while the "liberal" dupes swallow any new Rule on How You Must Now Do Your Own Thing. It keeps the two groups fighting each other rather than IT. Either Game makes you think you *like* something that you actually *don't* just because it's the old "lesser of two evils." A typical "choice": overwork or underpay.

Most Conspiracy jobs are thus unbearable by nature. But this is just another way the Con screws *itself.* By making jobs meaningless, employees are motivated to *sabotage.* With each new insane rule or new mound of unnecessary paperwork, the worker sees the Company digging itself a deeper and deeper hole. Well, he decides, LET IT. He *knows* he can't *help* the bosses, even though his suggestions could save the economic *day,* because the bosses won't listen to *him.* . . so he indulges in the glee of watching them ruin their own business.

In the job world, when dealing with other companies, the SubGenius will pay more attention to the secretary than the boss, because *she* knows what's going *on.* But how many bosses encourage their secretaries to take part in decision-making?

How did things get this way? Surely it couldn't have been *planned.* . .could it? Let's see. . .let's put it on the slaveblock and see who bids on it.

We've been wrong about two major things. Our leaders *don't* "mean well," and they *aren't* stupid.

They've succeeded in creating a world of financial control in what *looks* like private hands, dominating all nations through world economy. . . but those 'private hands' are *not* the hands of the human Insiders and it isn't *money* they grasp for.

The Conspiracy has many noble, ignorant patriots duped into swallowing hook, line and sinker the fallacies that either "Communism" or "Capitalism" is the Big Threat, but either way it's *the same power elite* in control.

The same ones who promulgated the Red Scare and the Commie Witch Hunts *also financed the Russian Revolution.* Those who rule Russia and China don't *believe* in Communism any more than those who rule America *believe* in Capitalism. Both are *only two arms* of a very unholy octopus indeed.

(This slamming of Capitalism may be a shock coming from the "megacapitalist" Church of the SubGenius, but all we really preach is *free enterprise*, which hasn't been seen in this country in 100 years except on the most piddling scale.)

They aren't *readying* us for takeover — THAT'S already HAPPENED. **ONE WORLD GOVERNMENT IS HERE.** It just isn't *obvious* yet. But any day now the media will have people not only prepared for the realization, but *welcoming* it. One World Government is "hip."

They WON the political battle long ago. Politically, they've conquered the world, from the KKK to the Libertarian Party to the Kremlin and the Pentagon.

Now they want our SLACK.

Oh, their World Government plans are *humanitarian* enough . . . they don't want to make us *miserable*; they just don't want us to be *happy*.

Most of the traps have already been sprung.

For instance, even *you* think we're kidding.

THE TYLENOL HOAX

They effectively erased true private property for the middle class and are working on erasing the middle class itself. They dissolved the foundations of the family. They keep the individual's choices for lifestyle within an increasingly narrow range. All humans are numbered from birth and thus tracked through education, military service, taxes, medical requirements, retirement benefits, and *especially BANKS*, all the way to *death*.

They control all natural resources and business, all systems of transport, all major entertainment sources. Through the deliberate fomenting of wars, revolutions, depressions, and epidemics, it's easy for them to eliminate all competition and deliver the *coup de grace* to free enterprise.

And it was so damn easy it's PATHETIC. They created a Central Bank and called one of its main branches "the Federal Reserve". That *monster bank* is the *real* U.S. Government the duly-elected one in Washington being a soap-opera opiate for the masses, a stageful of bad stand-up comics propped up for the rubes to throw things at.

There's no *Constitution* there's just the MONEY. The "U.S. Government" has to *borrow* from the Federal Reserve, which really means from *international banking*. Our *supposed leaders* are in debt to *themselves*, and, worse, to their *secret bosses*.

This is literally true: there's a big "Men's Club" to which belong all major politicians from all major parties, plus the heads, directors, editors and superstar personalities of ALL THE MAJOR NETWORKS, MAGAZINES AND NEWSPAPERS. In this Club they can all meet to agree on how to *explain* things.

Sounds like kook-talk, huh? That's because they're always one jump *ahead* of you. THEY ENGINEERED THE SPREAD OF CRAZY CONSPIRACY THEORIES, because even though many of the theories are *true*, they *still sound crazy*: the Rockefeller Conspiracy, the C.F.R., The Round Table, the Bilderbergers, the JFK "cleanup," ALL OF IT.

The C.F.R. and the Trilateral Commission: oh, they're bad guys, alright, but compared to the REAL controllers they're just the *clerks* at the *front desk*. They're just the *sales force* of a far larger "company." Sure, they have more control than any sane

American ever dreamed possible, but they themselves are more controlled than THEY ever dreamed possible. According to "Bob," even some of the *top men* there *actually still believe* they're preserving a *two*-party system in America.

The only difference between the political right and left is that one side's looking through a microscope and the other's using a telescope. Neither one gets the BIG PICTURE, and the Middle-of-the-roaders *aren't even looking*. They're watching TV *with blindfolds on*.

THE DEATH OF OBJECT 6633

The Con has yet another group of people looking for the number **666** in every license plate, every price tag, every bank card, every computer-system prefix, every government office employee's badge, every Non-Profit Corporation W-2 form, every lottery ticket, every underwear tag, in the center of metric rulers. . . and it IS on half the rock-and-roll album jackets.

The thing is, THE NUMBER IS THERE. . . but it's just a *red herring* for *simple minds*. Half of those companies use it as a joke, much like many SubGenii do. Sometimes the Con does deliberately place it to increase the paranoia of its Religion Dupes.

And it's a DAMN GOOD IDEA. It keeps those people fighting an imaginary enemy with an imaginary weapon. It keeps them *waiting* they don't have to fight, all they have to do is let JESUS show up and win the war.

Yeah, but WHOSE JESUS?

It's all part of the plot. The Con has not one not two but ANY NUMBER OF "Jesii" at the ready for whenever the time is ripe. Indeed, many SubGenius theologians suspect that JHVH-1 dictated the 666/End o' the World prophecies in Daniel, Ezekiel and Revelation just to support this particular game plan some 2000 years later!!

According to the Coloring Book Version, Jesus died so we'd be born Good Guys and only become Bad Guys by *choice*. No doubt today He'd be *real damn pleased* to see HIS FAN CLUB using HIS NAME to help The Conspiracy take that choice *away*. Yeah, the Con infiltrated Early Christianity *the second He hit the dust*, and lost no time in converting it into "a form, a CEREMONY, *A RITUAL!*" **We Hear And Obey. We Hear And Obey.**

THIS IS A REAL CONSUMER FRAUD

For that matter, you'd be CRAZY not to suspect that the Church of the SubGenius was one of Their *cleverest ruses*. . . We're not, and we don't care who believes it, but that IS how tricky They REALLY ARE!

Besides, for every "666" you'll find at least a hundred "Bobs." And starting in '84 the Church will present a Special Offer: for each bearer of a SubGenius Membership Card, the Mark of the Beast will be worth *twice* as *much!*

THE SPACE BANKERS SEE YOU

43%

LIES

If it makes any difference, the *real* meaning of "666" is that it represents a breakthrough in computer technology that the Xists will bring: the **Trinary Code,** which besides the "Yes" and "No" functions of each basic computer decision, adds a **"Sort Of"** function — enabling the machines to think more like people do. And this Xist computer will be either our greatest friend or our VERY DOOM, depending on *US.*

But WHO CARES if They do decide to line us all up and laser-tatoo a number on our hands and foreheads? *We're already tattooed* in ways FAR more insidious than *that.*

It's not just *that* number, it's *every* number. Sure, electronic fund transfer paves the way for final takeover, but *two thirds* of that takeover has *happened.* All the born-agains in the world can refuse The Mark, but what good will it do them? They're already branded. In fact, the cattle aren't even in the field anymore. They're almost up to the slaughterhouse DOOR!

Oh, the AntiChrist will come alright. . . provided by The Conspiracy. He fits into the plan along with whichever "Jesus" they decide to go with. It's just ONE MORE GAME. . . one more group to join that people will think can save them. One more group to keep them from joining US! Something. . .*simpler,* and *easier to understand.*

The hopes and fears. . . the United Nations, the World Food Organization, etc., etc., etc.,. . . that's all two-bit stuff. It's controlled by humans.

We of the True Church would be wringing our hands if we didn't know the Lord was on OUR SIDE and that the THIRD REAL JESUS was "Bob's" golfing partner.

The causes for paranoia by the religious right and the superstitious left are two drops in the bucket. They see only the *obvious* things. The subtle controls are really much worse. For instance, half the people in the U.S. can't control their own thermostats. The fear of . . . of. . . well, of *the fear* has been spread so effectively that folks are *glad* to exchange privacy for

security. But it's security only as long as the *guards* are Good Guys.

They've already restricted ownership of guns (except by criminals, of course), and they've restricted how much money you can move from one country to another; they've initiated detention of individuals without a trial (the psychiatric profession), the coding of all financial transactions, making certain types of education compulsory or illegal, wage and price control, manipulation of morals and ethics through pervasive, biased media. . . and all this in the world's most *free* country. Theoretically. We've seen the others and they're WORSE.

People are just *starting* to worry about computer control of their lives. Well, it's TOO LATE. IT'S HERE. 1984 came and went *20 years ago.*

And that's why money isn't nearly as important as SLACK. You can print or burn money, but you can't manufacture SLACK. It is The Final Commodity. So They want it *all.*

TIME-MONEY-JUSTICE
IT WAS ALL A LIE

We are born with the Dobbs Nature — "Original Nonsins" you might say — but it's soon brow-beaten out of us by relentless conspiracy Slavery Reinforcement from which not even the most conscientious parent can shield us. You think putting your child in an expensive private school will keep the blatant behavior modification training of the public schools off his or her little back? WHAT A JOKE. At small private schools, the Con simply has *more control.* At least in public school, the chaos spawned by overcrowding and drugs and immorality gives the kid a *chance* to experience the all-important juvenile delinquency that is the closest thing the U.S. has to an Initiation Rite — the importance of which has been proven by every "primitive" society on Earth.

MASTERED BY YOUR TV

As of this writing, America isn't at "war" with anyone. . . except itself. We're in a slow-motion Race Riot in the form of the highest crime rate in ALL HISTORY. This here-and-there uprising has produced as much violent death as any war; it's just not an *announced* war, not held in any specific area, not led by generals and not fought for any collective cause. It's fought for MONEY and UNSPOKEN VENGEANCE.

THE SIGNS OF THE TIMES are everywhere. . . blatant Proof of Conspiracy running down our walls like blood after a firing squad's done its work. The PUTRIFICATION of a society without shame, a society of open Pinkness. . . OH this is a SINFUL WORLD MY FRIEND, you play those record albums backwards and you hear the Devil talking; THE JUDGMENT WILL FALL!! The Complacency Drugs permeate our culture, and that doesn't mean pills and drinks and things to smoke.

Video games are *fun* little universes of harmless battle. . . but those places are still vicarious Leisure Violence Parlors where you go to destroy things safely through electronics. They're *training grounds;* the most skilled video gamers always *disappear* mysteriously — some snagged by the Con, some by "Bob," depending on whether they're better at the machines of the Empire or those of the Rebel Alliance. *Turbo* trains drivers. *Battlezone* trains Tank Gunners for the secret fighting on Mars. *Tempest* features Xist-style Third Dimensional Door battles. And *Pac-Man* is pure Conspiracy "consumption training."

SMALL BASKET CELL

US Army, Navy, Air Force, Marines, Coast Guard, Civil Air Patrol, National Guard, and their Chinese, Russian, Israeli, English and German counterparts, CIA, MIG, FBI, KGB, NKVD, BBC, All Federal Police, All State Police, All County Police, All Municipal Police, TDPS, All Narcs, DEA, BNDD, US Customs, CREEP, REAGANPHILES, Hinckley, Winos

CHANDELIER CELL

Zionists, Rockerfellows, Petrophiles, CFR, Tri-Lateralists, ABC, CBS, NBC, Exxon, McDonnell, Texas Instruments, Douglas, Summa Corp., Time-Life, Lockheed, Boeing, General Dynamics, Robert Ablanalp, LTV, Brown and Root, All Computer Companies (ALL!!!), General Electric, Bell, ITT, IBM, General Motors, Chrysler-Misubishi, Chrysler-Rootes, Chrysler-Renault, Ashland Oil, Cullen Davies, FoMoCo, CitiBank, World Bank, IMF, Kissinger, Nixon, Haldeman

AXO-AXONIC CELL

Cayce Nuts, Children of God, Reichians, Rolfians, Upwingers, Hottubbers, Logotherapists, Symbolists, Bio-Nebulationists, Transactionalists, Gestalters, Thanatologists, Bioenergizers, Grounders, Loopers, Massagers, Golfers, Yogas (all stripes), Requiemists, Immortalists, Bayley-ites, Realists, Gurdjieff Freeks, Krishnamurtiites, Meher Baba Bimbos, Brainwashers, Spiritualists, Catastropharians, Uniformitarians, Ancient Sparkpluggers, Pyramidians, Backpackers, Gilgameshoids, The DNA Society, Sirianists, Xians, Doggydhogs, Divine Light Mission, Winos, Mansonites, Von Danikenoids.

PYRAMIDAL CELL

'Human' Illuminati, Rosicrucians, Knights Templar, Wicca, Cult of Abramelin, Freemasons, Sufis, Alchemists, Gnostoids (unorganized), A:A, Orden Templi Orientalis, Golden Dawn, Theosophical Society, Thule Society, Crowleyites, Holy Vehm, The Nine, Learites, Bulldadartists, Men In Black, Antimonians, Aryan Brotherhood, Stonehengers, Wilsonites, Erisians, Druzes, Druggonauts, Mythists, Winos, Tantrics.

SPINY STELLATE CELL

Creationists, Shakers, Quakers, Amish, All Christian Sects not otherwise Named, Catholics, Jesuits, Unification Churchers, Puritans, Jews (Hassidic, Chassidic, Sephardic, and Assidic), Assyrians, Babylonians, Amen-Ra-ites, Pelagians, Augustinians, Monophysites, Aereopagites, Mennonites, Brunists, Ammonites, Stylites, Dendrites, Sadducites, Essenites, Simonites, Trilobites, Chiggerbites, ad nauseam (All Forms of Judaeo-Christian Ethics)

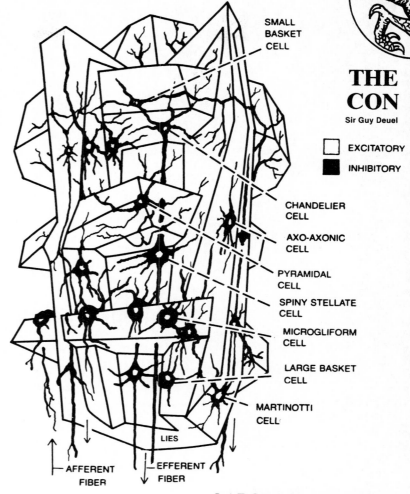

THE CON

Sir Guy Deuel

□ EXCITATORY

■ INHIBITORY

SMALL BASKET CELL

CHANDELIER CELL

AXO-AXONIC CELL

PYRAMIDAL CELL

SPINY STELLATE CELL

MICROGLIFORM CELL

LARGE BASKET CELL

MARTINOTTI CELL

LIES

AFFERENT FIBER

EFFERENT FIBER

MARTINOTTI CELL

Molluccan Liberation Front, Tupamaros, Black Muslims, Sunni and Shi'ite Muslims, Maoists, Taoists, Buddhists, Shintoists, Sokko-Gokkai, Skoptsi, WholeEarthians, Skydivers, Skiers, Joyceans, Hang Glider Addicts, Jocks of All Persuasions, Organic Nurds of All Types, Fraternity Rats, Moonies, Weenies, Architects, Doctors and all ordained ministers of any creed or cult whatsoever.

MICROGLIFORM CELL

Freudians, Jungians, Astrology Creeps, Snake Dancers, Gripers and Complainers, Hypochondrites, Kleptomaniacts, Media-Cretins, Cigarette Addicts, Snuff Users, Camera Buffs, Gun Buffs, Police Buffs, Fire Buffs, Accident Buffs, Phrenologists, Forteans, Palmists, Tarot Freaks, UFO Buffs and ALL Related Ufology, Cattle Mutilators, Cybernoids, Toobers, New Math Believers, Starship Dreamers, Space Cowboys, L_5 Advocates, SMI^{2}LERS, Spectra Believers, Uri Geller, Hollow Earth Society, Friends of Aliens, Jedai Knights and Everyone aware of Them.

LARGE BASKET CELL

Carbonari, Thuggees, Cosa Nostra, The Mob, The Matarese, Assassins, Our Lady of Perpetual Motion, (And all Discordians) SubGenius Foundation, Dan Smoot Report, Nguyen Cao Ky, Boxers, Pasputinists, Druids, El Fedayeen, Al Fatah, High Priests of Thebes, Beata Paolists, Order of the Peacock Angel, Enochians, Dillingerites, Hashmoleans, Sexists, Yezidis, Fags, Bulldykes, Sissies, Pink Boyz, Weirdos, Winos, Beatniks, Hipdogs, Lounge Lizards and anyone else Pathological.

It should be noted that, although it is impossible to assign All-Inclusivity to this Hierarchitecteleological structure, it IS as effective a system as we dare postulate to date. The universality of part or all of this structure is a proven fact, however, especially when it is used for specific Crossloop Templates for Culture Change. The structure is present in *All* Political, Religious and Social systems.

"And you can ask yourself 'was I right or was I wrong?'

And You Can say to Yourself, 'My God, what have I done?'"

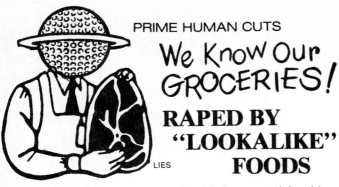

PRIME HUMAN CUTS

We Know Our GROCERIES!

LIES

RAPED BY "LOOKALIKE" FOODS

A message will not be heeded unless it is first entertaining. It's always easier to find a placating spectator's game than one that requires *your* input. Even a SubGenius would rather watch *Dragnet* than write his Congressman, so we Holy Ones can't really afford to act holier-than-thou about this; but we'd better *keep raving* while we *still can*.

It's even in our FOOD. . .

If *sugar* had been discovered ten years ago instead of in antiquity, it would be a felony offense to possess it. Cocaine's pretty damn unhealthy, but at least it isn't half of our children's diet. And people wonder why their kids are so hyperactive they can barely follow the plot of a ten-minute cartoon. Mix that stuff with caffeine and WHAMO! you get a "speedball" so potent that only Obeisance to the Tobacco Demons can calm you down. Cans of pop and sticks of nicotine: if the government's going to subsidize *that*, why not just go ahead and add heroin to the Free Lunch at school? Why not just *shoot up* diabetes and headaches and 'the shakes' and scatterbrainedness and. . . and, uh, *cancer*. . .

The Cover-Ups of The Big C . . . . it's almost too much to even *bring up*. The INCREDIBLY OBVIOUS DIRECT CONNECTION between American diet and American disease. . . **MY GOD!!** At least 40 'cures' for cancers of different kinds have been known to little pockets of healers all over the world for ages, but *the food, the poisons, and the expensive drawn-out ineffective treatments are all in the hands of the same people.* You think the FDA, AMA, American Cancer Society, and god damn PURINA are going to let go of a "good thing" without a FIGHT?

And you quit even *hearing* about the longevity drugs, didn't you? And you quit *hearing* about the Intelligence Increase drugs, didn't you?

And the nuclear power plants are STILL being built.

Looks like Karen Silkwood *did* die in vain.

Maybe not, though. Maybe she died for a Great Cause   the Great Cause of all the truly inspiring pioneers of poison who we pay each day to make us sicker and sicker and sicker. And the Great Cause of Modern Medicine, which we pay to make us sicker, but more *slowly*. You get lung cancer and so they shoot

KERRY WENDELL THORNLEY SAYS:

Relax in the Safety of **Your Own Delusions.**

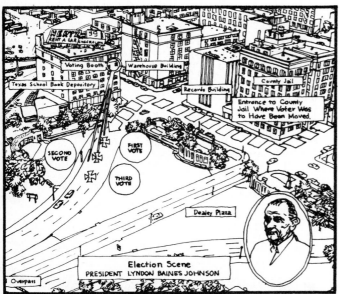

Election Scene
PRESIDENT LYNDON BAINES JOHNSON

P. MAVRIDES

Tell yourself that I speak cryptic whenever I get the chance, that I *like* talking to you in the gibberish I've had to invent in order to find out anything at all from you about what you, and the pigs whose asses you perpetually kiss, are doing with MY LIFE. Just keep right on believing that what I order for breakfast is relevant, whereas the plain intent of my words is not. Listen to everything the agents of Gerald Ford and Richard Nixon and Henry Kissinger and Howard Hunt and Meyer Lansky tell you about what I actually mean to say, and pay no attention to the fact that I am a witness to the John Kennedy and Lee Oswald murders.

Just keep right on believing that I am the one who is a racist and a puritan and they, on the other hand, are psychedelic hippie radicals with flowers in their hair.

Relax, it all has to do with karma and reincarnation   don't think about it and maybe it will go away. Electro-chemical mind control doesn't have anything to do with it. Nothing that terrible could ever happen in this country. And even if it did, it wouldn't happen to you. So go right on believing it is all metaphysical. What the hell? You might as well believe something. Right?

Never mind where the Urantia Foundation gets its money or where the World-Wide Church of God gets its power! What the hell business is that of yours? Worry, instead, about whether your next-door neighbor is into ass fucking or whether or not his wife masturbates. Why make a half-assed fool out of yourself when you can be a complete fool, instead? In addition to worrying about the sex lives of strangers you might want to also take up quarreling about religion.

you full of radiation. You complain about smog so they bury plutonium in your back yard. YOU COMPLAIN ABOUT CORPORATE CRIME SO THEY KILL YOU. Well, maybe not. Maybe they don't even jail you.

They just don't listen. You can rant all you like, but not on *their* networks.

But all these things are just part of the overall Game, the goal of which is simply to make you *feel helpless.*

Think you can escape to the woods with a tribe of survivalists? HELL, if it isn't the *other* killer survivalist bandits that get you, it's the secret research outposts. What's left of the wilderness is so pock-marked with evidence of coverups of awful events — saucer crashes, neutron bomb tests, medical experiments gone *horribly awry,* cattle mutilations, germ warfare goofs — you're almost better off joining that three-mile line of Pink Campers in Winnebagos waiting to get a snap of Mount Rushmore with 20 starving Indians camped out on top of Lincoln's head hoping the government will forget the uranium buried deep down in that sacred turf. GOOD LUCK!

Our leaders in Washington finally had to admit that they used to use old black men in hideous syphilis experiments, that they used nice normal dads in mind-control drug experiments, that they accidentally wiped out thousands of sheep in germ warfare tests. . . AND YOU STILL THINK they've STOPPED?? How do you KNOW 2,000 soldiers weren't turned into raving lunatics in some mutant-virus test in Montana? How do you KNOW some nuclear storage accident didn't kill a thousand ignorant workers somewhere in Utah? How do you know YOUR house isn't built on some chemical dump so virulent that your grandchildren will be born without *fingers?*

ὅς τὰ κλείν' αἰνίγματ' ᾔδει καὶ κράτιστος ἦν ἀνήρ!!

HOW THEY GOT YOUR NUMBER

H. ROBINS

You actually think They care what happens to YOU, just because you *elected* them?

Puzzling Evidence

Jack Ruby explained in a remarkably casual fashion the circumstances that enabled him to shoot Paul McCartney. "I was walking toward City Hall," he says. "I saw a GREAT LIGHT and opened my eyes—there was McCartney. What else could I do?" This story leaves some problems for the investigators—What color was this light? Was there a voice? These questions were never settled at Ruby's trial and now he's dead. Well, too bad.

Since the whole world is going to hell in a handbasket, since the U.S. Constitution now serves a purely decorative purpose, and since your whole nation is being enslaved by an elite technocracy of Neo-Nazis disguised as Bolshevicks, why the hell not squander all your time gossiping? Go right ahead — keep it up until every human being who differs from you racially, psychologically, sexually, ideologically or religiously hates your no-good busy-body guts.

You don't need them to help you throw off the ruling class. There isn't any such thing as a ruling class in this country anyway. If there was, then you wouldn't be able to vote and thereby elect your own oppressors, right?

And even if there is a ruling class, they don't have the goddamned Russian government working for them as a bunch of quasi-fascist scabs and, in any case, they certainly don't want to insert silicone chips into the bases of your skulls and thereby manipulate your behavior. Things like that are too paranoid to be true.

So relax. If that is difficult, trying to repeat this mantra over and over to yourself will help: LEE HARVEY OSWALD, ACTING ALONE, MURDERED PRESIDENT KENNEDY; LEE HARVEY OSWALD, ACTING ALONE, MURDERED PRESIDENT KENNEDY. . . But you have to say it with conviction if you want it to work. Does that sound difficult? Where is your faith? How do you expect to accomplish anything without faith?

That's all right. Don't worry about anything I say here. Everyone knows that I speak very mysteriously at all times, seeming to say one thing while actually saying something else. Just ask Gerald Ford or any retired member of the CIA Psychological and Political Warfare Unit.

Actually I'm just a paranoid. You see, John F. Kennedy and Lee Oswald actually both died of natural causes, and the country has been in beautiful shape ever since then, anyhow.

If you want to read more of my insane, cryptic, mysterious rantings — send a dollar to Box 18441, Tampa, Florida 33679.

And the *funny* thing, the really *hilarious* thing is, THAT'S ALL DIDDLY-SHIT STUFF. The BIG laugh is that every half hour, 1,000 people on this planet die of starvation, most of them *little kids.*

Oh, but that doesn't happen in *Caucasian* countries. It happens to all those Third Worlders because they have such *bad governments,* right?

Any sensible SubGenius knows that "Republican" and "Democrat" are laughably meaningless terms for identical pawns in a bigger Game, but what they didn't suspect was just how little differences there are between ANY political parties, ANYWHERE on the political spectrum. Looking in perspective at the WHOLE CONSPIRACY, from a vantage point several steps *back* from the big circular monster, they all begin to look the same.

BUT IGNORE ALL THAT...

It's a BIG VISE with radical *and* reactionary rioters forming the bottom half and a fake Establishment as the top half, and the earth itself is being squeezed in between, with both SubGeniuses and humans getting smashed together. The *humans* don't seem to *mind.* . . but what's BAD is the nature of the THINGS that are *using the vise.*

Every political group claims that under *them,* "The People" will run things. But when "The People" find out what's *really* going on, they'll *just RUN.*

It wouldn't be so bad if the manipulators were at least human. . . *if they were at least bipeds. . .*

BOY! I FEEL SICK

So Big...we had to coin a new word for it
TECHNOBOREDOM

by ArchDoktor Pope Sterno Keckhaver

There are few areas indeed that are entirely free from the devious influence of our sworn enemies. Dobbs has recently suggested to us that TVs emit non-detectable **F-rays** which mysteriously fuse brain cells into pre-determined patterns that then control the individual's behaviour. It has yet to be ascertained whether these emissions are "Con" or *Xist* in origin, but they lead to the same end result. Once the effect has taken place it is irreversible and non-treatable. Soap commercials and "Tits 'n' Ass" programs seem to contain the highest concentration of F-rays, but some are emitted even when the set is turned off. A different but no less dangerous type of ray is emitted from AM and progressive FM radio programs.

Perhaps the most bizarre and least understood weapon of the Conspiracy is **Technoboredom.** Research into this phenomenon by SubGenius para-scientists, although still in its infancy, has yielded some surprising and ghastly results. Technoboredom manifests itself in the subliminimal-reality areas of the frontal lobes of the brain and causes the person afflicted to garner intense satisfaction from commercial inanity. TV commercials, the picture on the back of Reader's Digest, toys in cereal boxes and other similar "Con-particles" bring about an almost sexual enjoyment to the adherent of the doctrine of Technoboredom. There are also massive, conspiracy-funded Technoboredom Centers in all areas of the world masquerading under the thin guise of universities, libraries, and cultural-activities centers.

The SubGenius must make it his duty to subvert and annihilate these institutions if we are ever to *gain control* and guarantee Slack within our lifetimes.

Organizational deviance, in the form of propaganda, pandering, and infiltration, is the chief means of combating Technoboredom. The SubGenius must practice and make use of mind-control and normexploitation techniques in assuming her or his role as Futureleader. Schism-strength through fragmentation will catch most, if not all, technobored normals offguard, allowing the truly accultated Dobbs follower to exercise his abnormality and gain control of yet another "normworm"! It is to every SubGenius's advantage to recognize and document any aspect of Technoboredom he might witness, and send the evidence to the Father Church so that it can be evaluated by Dobbs and hence further our cause. "Bob" himself has often advised us to "shoot boredom up", but to the novice this practice could possibly lead to the very place the 'Con' wants us; this we must avoid at all costs.

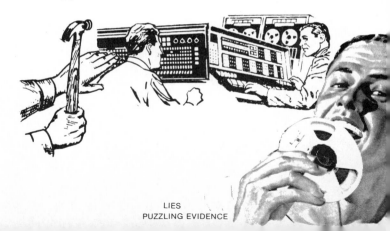

LIES
PUZZLING EVIDENCE

CHAPTER 11

"THE UFO MADE
ME DO IT"

"Stretch forth thy hand from on high, rescue me and deliver me from the many waters, from the hands of *aliens,* whose mouths speak lies, and whose right hand is the hand of falsehood."
—Psalms 144:7

"Be not forgetful to entertain Strangers for thereby some have entertained Angels unawares."
—St. Paul the Contactee

"Bullets cannot stop them."
—from *Space Rapist 2000* (Sundog Films, 1959)

"The necktie is a serpentlike symbol of evil worn by humales."
—from an Xist space transmission intercepted by the U.S. Navy, 1960

You may now **OPEN YOUR EYES.**

The UFOs *are there.* Beyond that, almost everything thought or said about them is a dreadful mistake. Everything said *by* them is a **lie.**

THEY ARE REAL! If you don't believe that, you're *superstitious.* But we can't blame you for being ignorant. The media as news laughs at the "sightings" and reports nothing else. As entertainment the media only presents UFOs as spacecraft. 99% of the UFO paperbacks glutting the market are inherently idiotic, and the 1% that approach the truth *seem* even more so.

Science, journalism, and authority in general exclude what they see as supernatural for as long as possible. And it indeed *is* supernatural when carved stones inscribed with indecipherable languages fall from a clear blue sky or are found buried 2½ miles underground. The more trained is one not to expect these things, he becomes geometrically less likely to believe the evidence staring him in the face.

It's because The Conspiracy has never wanted you to *learn.* In order to unlearn their lies and discover what they don't want you to learn, **you must first be willing to believe *anything*.** Once you have done that, you can begin excluding data — which is so easy, it's what The Con has you do *before* you learn. Forgetting is always easier than discovering. There are forces *helping* you to forget.

The forces exist without definite form, but only with an *intention* and a thirst to *gain* form, to take on *life.* WE are what gives them "shape." It is an energy *we* possess — *Slack* — that they vampirize in order to lock their nonmateriality into our material world. *Their* natural energy stems from nothing less than the *fitful dreams* of the *Elder Gods.*

The Elder Gods, themselves sleeping and otherwise helpless in their dimensionless Domain of Doors, exert a great *intention* that we too stay "asleep." The human will, all too happy to help with this, donates its energy and its *expectations,* and from these *some* of the UFOs are built.

If you have great powers of concentration, and you begin to think of a fictitious person as if he existed, in all the detail of a real person, that "person" or the bodily image of it may materialize so solidly that you can't get *rid* of it. This almost never happens in America because it is not *expected.* It happens in Tibet a great deal and the ambulatory, externalized hallucinations that follow lamas about are called *tulpas.*

UFOs are über-tulpas.

And "UFOs" are merely the most *commonly seen* form of the monstrous tulpas we unwittingly co-produce with the Elder Gods. The term should not be "UFOs" but should be *"The Watchers,"* for

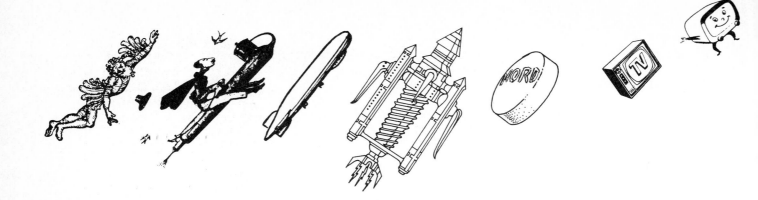

THE ALIENS ARE LOOSE!

these robot "guard dogs" of the Elder Gods *watch us* to learn what appearance they should take on to keep us in abject confusion. Some of us they simply terrify so that we no longer wish to discuss the idea of 'evil.' Others they entice with promises of Salvation from Space, likewise to eliminate the idea of 'evil.'

To our "primitive" ancestors, the force of evil was not something *against God*, but a necessary primal force of Nature — the black, dreadful *survival-of-the-fittest* part of existence that goes beyond the platitudes of the Love Gods of simpletons and makes life *vital* instead of dead and unchanging. The "evil" of competition creates mutation and upward evolution. DEATH MAKES YOU GET OFF YOUR ASS. We *should* fear the gods because if we don't, they'll stop letting us *have* fear and without fear we are also without *choice*, and without "goodness."

So, yes, we must *change* our idea of evil, but we MUST NOT ELIMINATE IT, because that's what The Conspiracy and The Elder Gods *most desire*. If we can't recognize evil, we can't recognize *Them*. And, friends, *They* are the *evil* side of evil.

When we talk about UFOs we are talking about things *seen*. No one but "Bob" and a handful of Native American medicine men have *seen* the **Xists**. The creatures from space which are *not* evil — which are what "Bob" calls **GoodBad** — are *never seen*.

What *are* seen are not just lights in the sky or discs full of humanoids with rayguns. The Watchers include giant lake worms (a la Loch Ness), vampires, ghosts, sylphs, ghouls (not as corpse-eating people but as invisible "pools" of bad vibes), leprechauns, Undines, hairy apemen in N. America (as opposed to Tibetan Yetis), winged demons, Voodoo Loa Spirits, most of the ancient Greek demigods, and sea monsters. And, just to throw in the element of confusion to the greatest possible degree, they *also* appear, quite deliberately, as "weather balloons," "swamp gas," "ball lightning," St. Elmo's Fire, meteors, mirages, phantom helicopters and planes, tornadoes, and the aerial ice crystal reflections called "sundogs." They are *that* devious.

But their most common manifestation of all, besides as UFOs, are not "seen" so much as "heard" and "felt." They are the voices in the heads of mystics and murderers, the impersonators of dead people that appear at seances, the dreamwarpers who terrorize sleeping minds, the *wanagi* or sparkling lights that are conjured up by shamans, the "Binding Spirits" that hook you on drugs (Alcohol Demons, Tobacco Demons etc.), and, worst of all, the vast *National Demons* which shift the tides of politics, each in its own governmental domain.

And the Elder Gods have much worse ones up their "sleeves."

The only other important thing to know about them is that they *lie*.

Whether they appear as Aryan Venusians from "The Confederacy of Planets" spreading racist/utopian bullshit, or as disembodied "Ascended Masters of the Spirit Plane" with names like "Clarion" and "Ankor" and "Ariel" in order to tell little old "mediums" about the coming New Age, **they are LYING THEIR ASSES OFF.**

They make you think you're "Chosen" so that they can sap the energy of your belief in *them specifically*. They are inert without the energy of human belief and shapeless without human expectations. Messing with them in any way is like handing them a signed blank check to your psychic energy bank.

As the worlds' peoples become more terrified, the collective unconscious gives the beings more power. Waves of sightings occur *just prior to* world crises. UFO "flaps" and the ground and water monsters that accompany them are generated in times of greatest racial stress.

We see them as they *wish* us to see them, but only within the limits of *our expectations*. Thus, in the past, they appeared as angels and devils, whereas they appeared as airships in the early days of human aviation, and as spaceships once space travel became comprehensible to us. Next they may start looking like PILLS and TV SETS.

They are a great reflection of *us* as we stand looking at the pond of the universe. *We* cast the pebbles that cause the ripples of distortion that make them so ugly. We can instead leave the pond alone and let it go placid, or we can dive right into the pond and hope that our trust and confidence will be reflected in it, which is *rare*. But if you dive in, you'd better know how to swim. Skinny-dipping in the waters of the paranormal can be CREEPY and you'd best pick a sunny day so that you don't panic when your feet brush the nameless slimey things on the bottom.

Mess with the Elder Gods only if you *have to* — if you are *called*. In general, the way to handle a "Close Encounter" of *any* kind is to *run like hell*. *All* of the phenomena are dangerous unless

"Bob" says otherwise; they can alter history and not necessarily for the better, and only "Bob" knows how to handle the fire we must use to fight the inferno of The Watchers.

The Xists will help us — *if* we make good on whatever outlandish promises "Bob" has to make to them. True, the Xists are mere pawns of JHVH-1 — but JHVH-1 is a *knight in shining armor* compared to the Elder Gods and their minions. WOTAN may have some pretty vile plans but at least they don't include permanent mummification of our life spirits so that loathsome "elementals" can lay *eggs* in our bodies.

(You can forget Spielberg's "cute extraterrestrials." There *are* some of those but they're in the same boat *we* are.)

The Air Force knows a little more about them than they let on, but not much. They keep their mouths shut about UFOs for the same reason The Con doesn't talk about "Bob." Why should they admit to the public that there is an enemy about which they know almost *nothing* and against which they are utterly *helpless?* (The C.I.A. and some even more secretive elements of The Con have prototype UFOs, but they're like model Ts compared to the real thing.)

Besides, except for top brass, most of the military has no idea that the country is run by PUPPETS kept dancing by *inhuman hands from above,* that the line of control goes *upwards.*

YOUR PART IN THE EVIL ONES' PLAN

Behind each bigwig in the smokefilled boardrooms of The Conspiracy's New York "bunkers" is a shadowy "consultant" telling him how to deal his cards . . . and while the human Insiders may squabble among themselves, **The Men In Black** behind them work *as one.* "Bob" KNOWS. "Bob's" sat in on their calm, civilized get-togethers and noticed that the slightest ghastly murmuring from one of these creatures is enough to make a Senator break into a cold sweat, a Prime Minister suddenly change his tune, a CIA operative inexplicably decide *not* to give the *complete* report. When the Migraine Machine is activated in those boardrooms, ALL arguments with THE PLAN are cut short faster than Darth Vader's mind-beams can choke a Death Star captain.

Let us note in passing that the true symbol of The Conspiracy (called by some *The Illuminati,* which is actually just one important sect) is not the Eye-in-the-Pyramid — for that is the symbol of the Elder Gods — but the little-seen red emblem of a ***plastic spoon, fork and knife*** partially crossed in an ill travesty of the Christian Cross death-sign. The reason for this stupid logo: *plastic* because that is the nature of it all, the *eating utensils* because *they "eat" us.* They are *cannibals* — not so much in the sense of devouring human flesh, for they do that only on special occasions, but in the sense that they consume our energy. The Men In Black *do* eat human flesh, as often as possible, *and* they draw off our psychic juices. And they're *small-timers* compared to their *masters.*

Despite their preternatural powers to vanish at will and to overcome minds, they are the *least* "alien" of all The Watchers. *Their* squelching of human initiative is done indirectly, through humanity's would-be leaders. The other Watchers operate with considerably less subtlety, and they have done so throughout history.

They wiped out the dinosaurs on a picnic, just as we killed off the buffalo. The Ice Age was caused by their version of 'atomic testing.' They introduced human sacrifice to the Mayans in Yucatan, the Incas in Peru and the Aztecs in Mexico. They were the "disgusting abominations" who enslaved the Sumerians and spread the worship of false idols (like mathematics and astronomy) through

Babylonia while appearing in the guise of the fish-man "Oannes." The Easter Islanders dropped their chisels, stopped carving Dobbsheads and took to their canoes overnight when the amphibious lobster-men of Dagon started swarming ashore. The giant 'runways' and 'landing pads' at the Nazca Plain and others in South America, vast scary figures with paranoid eyes and gnashing teeth visible as such only from the air, were painstakingly etched into the rock by those Indians not as *invitations* to the gods, but as vain attempts to *scare them away*.

A PLACE TO HIDE

And the ancient Hebrews didn't think it was so funny either when huge, noisy **heliopters** (sic) abducted and brainwashed Ezekiel and Elijah, rained diseased frogs on the Egyptians, and turned rivers to blood. In fact, much of the time they mistook them for YAHWEH's angels just as today's holy rollers mistake demonic possession for 'the spirit of Jesus.'

The Men In Black appeared to Abraham to tell him that his barren, aged wife Sarah would bear children (Genesis 18:1). Later in Genesis, one of these beings — disguised as an angel — wrestled with Jacob and put his hip out of joint just by touching it.

The beings prefer to stay in their (illusory?) spacecraft when impersonating JHVH-1, however. Descriptions which pepper the Bible are of "a whirlwind and a cloud," "a fire unfolding itself," "a wheel in the midst of a wheel, which turned not as it went;" ". . . and their wings, and the wheels, were full of eyes round about." They frequently dropped "manna" (buckets of pills) to keep the nomadic tribal Jews confused as to who was JHVH-1 and who was just an "angel," and to keep them moving in the wilderness. How can these descriptions be of anything else *but* the *heliopters* of which "Bob" warns, and which pestered *Doktors for "Bob"* halfway unto MADNESS??[1] Heliopters: pink *living beings* shaped strangely like wheeled tennis shoes, with *ears* and *furred bellies*, yet with motors inside and propellors on top . . . if you haven't seen these "mechanical animals" (either in real life, or in your dreams as buzzing demons which bite your face), *count yourself lucky*. After they took off with Elijah, no one ever saw him again.

The connections between the *heliopter* creatures and the use of mind-altering drugs are also abundantly seen in the Sanscrit text, the *Atharva-Veda* of ancient India, in which the alien force is called *Indra* and the drugs, *soma:*

"Sweet verily is this soma . . . strong verily is this; and no one soever overpowers Indra, having drunk of it . . . O Indra and soma, cause to roll from the sky the deadly weapon . . . with fire-heated stone-smiting unaging *heat weapons* do ye pierce the devourers in the abyss . . . Iron-mouthed, needle-mouthed, likewise thorn-tree mouthed, let the flesh-eaters, of wind-swiftness, fasten on our enemies with the three-jointed thunderbolt; O this pressed soma, intoxicating, drink ye . . . whoever thinks to be going on in secret, all this the gods know.

Further, the one wheel that is in secret, that, verily, the enlightened know . . . on the back of yonder sky the all-knowing ones talk a speech not found by all . . . eight-wheeled, nine-doored is the impregnable stronghold of the gods; what soul-possessing monster there is in it . . . O seers, be not afraid; ye soma-drinkers, soma-drenchers . . ."

---

1. This is recounted in the Doktors for "Bob" album, *Heliopera,* which is available only to Church Members who have been under Security Clearance for over two years.

Rev. Joe Schwind

"SPACE BROTHERS" HAVE A USE FOR YOU!

This leaves no doubt whatsoever that the Elder Gods send *heliopters* full of drugs to tempt us into allowing them into our bodies. These ARE the LAST DAYS!! THROW up your hands and say, "BOB," let your power spill over me, I'm NOT gonna sit here UNTIL I DIE! **SHAI gaba UM dala shoombala oom!**

The Watchers manipulate people and nations in many ways. The crudest ones drag people into their saucers and hypnotise them. Others work through dreams, telepathy, seances, automatic writing, ouija boards, "blank" recording tape, and microwave beams of pink light to brainrape their victims.

Although 'manipulatees' may at first gain notoriety and a cult following, they usually end up being *screwed* by their 'Space Brothers.' A random list of manipulatees and other running-dogs of the saucer imperialists would include Joan of Arc, Joseph Smith (founder of Mormonism), Moses, Mohammed, Nostradamus, Edgar Cayce, Imhotep, Socrates, Erik Von Daniken, Benjamin Franklin, Dr. Philo Drummond, John Wilkes Booth, Leonardo da Vinci, Helen Blavatsky, the masterminds behind the Kennedy assassination, the founders of the FreeMasons, the Rosicrucians, and the Thule Society; Hitler, Idi Amin, Paracelsus, Bo and Peep, John Rockefeller, Uri Geller, Wilhelm Reich, Timothy Leary, King George III, Giordano Bruno, John Lilly, John Dee, Sirhan Sirhan, Mark Chapman, Nikola Tesla, Charlie Manson, Admiral Byrd, Bo Derek, Jack Ruby, and Jonathan Winters. The Entities especially like humans named "George" and three of the earliest classic 'saucer cowboys' included a George Conspiracy of George Adamski, George Hunt Williamson and George Van Tassell.

Millions of people have been "contacted," and every single one gets a different story. But what if the "stories" which the contactees *remember* are just decoy strategies? What if some unknown kind of subliminal brainwashing is going on, with all of these people getting the *same* instructions implanted *secretly,* all to be triggered at once at some crucial time — say, just before the Xist landing? Are we being set up for the sudden unleashing of an army of crazed, gun-toting Manchurian Candidates? Is this what the Christian "Rapture," which the Fightin' Jesus never actually discussed, could mean? If the scales dropped from all our eyes for a moment, would we see a sky swarming with demonic entities??

The threat of Contactee Terrorist Groups is reasonable in view of the tactics employed by the Dark Forces. Abductees and other victims have reported unbelievable ruthlessness: being implanted with outer space semen by fire-headed superstud robots with eyes in their palms; being bitten and pursued by wild little ghost-boys who nipped at the heels and made birds die with a glance; picking up hitch-hikers who vomited up butterflies and then vanished; finding a Bigfoot sitting in a tree overhead gnawing on a cow's *head,* and fleeing only to discover that *this* Bigfoot had *wings.* . . .

What makes it scarier is when you realize how long they've been at it. In 2000 B.C. a Japanese king had 'flying sun discs' for advisors. King Minos of Crete was given the Rules for Torture by Volcano Demons, just as Hammurabi got his Conspiracy Rulebook from a UFOnaut named Shamash. Sodom and Gomorrah were nuked by "Angels" for not being perverted *enough,* and Knossos was microwaved for *no reason at all.* In 1500 B.C. Pharoah Thutmosis III was swapping jokes with "circles of fire" and rocket-cars were playing 'chicken' over India. (Meanwhile the ancient Bible Prophets were having Close Encounters right and left.) Most of the kings of Babylon had "winged advisors"; there's no telling how many lesser religions were started by these Satanic 'saucer gods.'

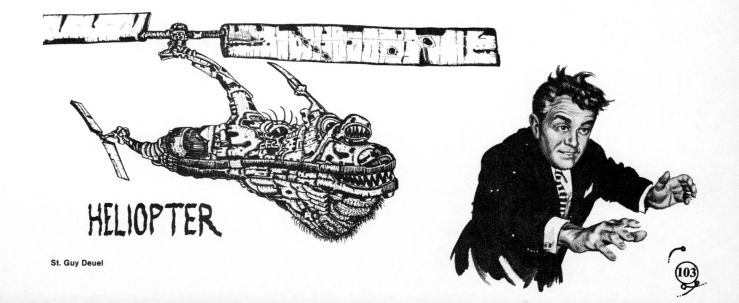

HELIOPTER

St. Guy Deuel

Their work in religion is spectacular to this day. The UFO that appeared before tens of thousands and instantly dried up a muddy field during the "Miracle of Fatima" in Portugal spoke to its three little girl mediums in Catholic jargon, and gave them secret messages that the Pope was to reveal to the world in 1968 (he didn't, after his audience with "Bob".) Their "bright cloud" of blinding light converted Saul to Paul on the road to Damascus.

The Watchers seem never to slip up; they always get what they want. This is in marked contrast to the *actual* extraterrestrials who ride metallic spaceships and are as tied to technology as we. They are about as efficient as the U.S. Army. The frequency of saucer crashes by these friendly little jokers from space verges on the ridiculous. Their biggest snafu was the nuclear explosion that re-

sulted from an attempted 'drag race' between two saucers over Tunguska, Siberia; since then, they've totaled spacecraft in Arizona, Texas, California and New Mexico, in the U.S. *alone!* From the last crash, Conspiracy investigators quick to the scene retrieved the saucer's *instruction book,* of which "Bob" now has a copy. Three alien crewmen were captured by the Air Force after the Arizona spin-out: one elfin humanoid and two "little big-heads"; of the three, two became hopeless alcoholics in the quarantine conditions, and one ate plaster off the walls until it died. A far cry from the thundering fire-ball that scorched the 10 Commandments into a rock and parted the Red Sea. Even "Bob," with his cheap replica UFOs and his Magic Surfboard, can outrace these humanoid grease-monkeys.

THE ELDER GODS

(A.k.a. "The Northern Fathers," "Elohim," "Kyclopes," "The Space Bankers")
All stem from AFFATHAUGTH (*Allfather of Nothingness*) and now dwell, "sleeping," in the dimensionless *Cold Wastes of Leng-Hadath* or *"The Domain of Doors."* All are composed of one cosmic 'element' each.

THEIR NAMES: (altered for this Book to protect the public)

IAOG-SATATH
(A.k.a. "Kronos," "Thoth," "Yig Sahtot," "Jog-Soggoth," "Un-Tut-Sut")
Fire Elemental of the South

H'AAZTRE
(A.k.a. "Hastur," "It," "The Thing With No Face")
Air Elemental of the East

S'Ub NHGHWRAATH
(Other names classified.)
Earth Elemental of the North

ZTHOOD' aLU
(A.k.a. "Chronozon," "Dagon," "Cthuhhv," "DreamWarper," "The 10-Horned 7-Headed Beast," "Guardian of the Threshhold of Dreams.")
Water Elemental of the West

Lesser Elder Gods:
TITLACAHUAN-Guardian of the Gates of Time.
HYPNOS-God of Sleep
The Dreaded DOORMAMUUNUNU-Deity of Sex and Dirt.
AGAMMOTO-God of All Bad Guys
G'BROAGFRAN (?)

Agent for the Elder Gods:
NYARADAM-THOTEP
Supervisor of:

THEIR MINIONS:

("**THE WATCHERS**" whose message to Man is, "Lay off! *We'll* make the decisions.")

Hosts of Hoggothe' (Tibet)
Nagas (India)
Wendigo (Amer. Indian)
Llloigor (Mind Parasites)
Advanced Supersonic Nazi Hell Creatures from Beneath the Hollow Earth ("Deros," "Dasyu," "Canzotl," "Mothman," Indian "Rakshasas," Peruvian "Gvachines.")
Most ancient Greek Demigods
Alchemical "Salamandars"

Seance Voices (& Sioux "Wanagi")
Men in Black
Raping Apparitions
Mocking Apparitions
Binding Spirits, Alcohol Demons
"National Angels" of politics
Sylphs, Ghouls, Incubi, Sucubi, Gnomes, Leprechauns, Undines, "Muses," Voodoo Loa Spirits, All Voices in Heads which spread Utopian/racist bullshit as "The Great White

Brotherhood," "The Confederacy of Planets," "Venusians," "Saturnians," "The Master Clarion," etc.
Fastitocalosaurus (sea monster a.k.a. "Leviathan," "Behemoth," "Godzilla," "Kraken," "Typhon," "Tiamat," "Afrit," "Vodyanye," "Fuarth," "Zarutan" depending on culture. Works for ZTHOOD'aLU.)

THESE ARE "THE SILENCE GROUP."

THE REBEL GODS

(A.k.a. "The Titans," "The Old Ones")

BOHANDAS

Relatively "Evil":
ERIS
(A.k.a. "Isis," "Kali," etc.)

Relatively "Good":
JHVH-1
("Wotan," "Ra," etc.)

NHGH

G'BROAGFRAN (?)

The Rebel Gods are the "Shock Troops" trying to tell Earth,
"Get ready!"... Cosmic Innoculators conditioning us to the fact
that Mind Power is our only hope.

THE DARK SIDE OF THE REBEL GODS

(a.k.a. "The Yurugu Gang")

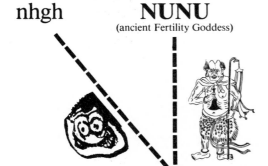

ERIS (A.k.a. Isis, Whore of Babylon, False (or "Bloody") Virgin Mary, Kali, Nuit, Aphrodite, Sakti, Your Mamma, Mummuu, Ishtar, Inanna, Artemis, "Ma.")

CHILDREN BY JHVH-1:

G'BROAGFRAN (?)

nhgh   **NUNU**
(ancient Fertility Goddess)
   NARNINI
(A.k.a. Anubis. Twin of Nunu)
   BOHANDAS
(Mystery God)

NHGH

(A.k.a. Loki, Set, Mara, Pazuzu, Atlach-Nacha (Phoenician Spider-God), Black Goat of the Woods with a Thousand Young, "The Devil" (false interpretation), Tobacco Demons, Lying Spirits, Bad Financial Luck Spirits.)
(Spirit of Mischief. Raped his own mother, NUNU, to create himself, then raped his sister/aunt NARNINI to create YACATISMA).

YACATISMA

(Energy or Robot Techno-Mutilators from Orion; called "Seraphim" in the Bible. These are identical with the "Serpent People" who tempted and fucked all the female Yetis in "Eden," ruining the Test Batch and in so doing, possibly creating humans.)
NOT TO BE CONFUSED WITH *YACATIZMA*, SUPREME FORCE OF BEAUTY IN THE COSMOS.

105

CATTLE MUTILATIONS—
HARBINGERS OF THE AQUARIAN AGE??
or HAMBURGERS FOR WOTAN??

AN OPEN COW

Three Church Initiates prepare to undergo gruesome rite of cattle mutilation.

First, a parable from Rev. **Dennis Keller** of the *Center for Assimilation of Variform Epistemologies:*

The startled residents of Rhinoceros Valley were jolted awake one morning by the brash aetheric clanging of the Asstral Bell. At dusk of the previous day, the sound of helicopter engines echoed and echoed over the peaceful landscape for 90 minutes, but none of the craft could be sighted. Then, after dark, the entire sky seemed alive with strange flying lights that darted to and fro, performing impossible aerial maneuvers with grace, speed, and ease. What new challenge to credibility was to come with the dawn? What had so influenced the portentious Asstral Bell? As the Delerians filed out to see, they were mightily surprised. Hundreds and hundreds of dead and mutilated cattle were littered about the gentle hills and dales! Some had the skin flayed skillfully from their skulls, others had their brains, or hearts, or udders and genitalia, or various internal organs like pancreas, liver, or lungs removed expertly through small, laser-precise incisions. Many of them laid in a crumpled heap, their legs broken as if they were dropped from a great height. There were neither blood nor tracks around the carcasses, deepening the mystery. Some had missing tails, ears, eyes and lips, but each and every one had been branded with the name of a fierce Nordic battle god. They had all been claimed as CATTLE FOR WOTAN. The Delerians speculated on who was to blame for the outrage. Was it a sinister cult committing ritual anatomical vandalism, using the stolen parts in obscene ceremonies? A group of sadistic surgical transplanters from outer space? Was it the first sign of the "End Times"? The Tribulation? Or was it a simple, natural thing that just happened to some cattle and not others? Their theories, questions, and hypotheses were meaningless though, for, in complete unison, all the cattle burst into flames! Spontaneous Cattle Combustion! All the evidence went up in the short, intense chemical blaze! Nothing was left. The Asstral Bell pealed one last time. A lot of people think that this kind of thing doesn't happen at all. But then, a lot of people don't know what they are talking about. You must decide for yourself. Anyone can try to deny or affirm any issue for you, but you must pay attention for yourself until you form your own opinion. Right?

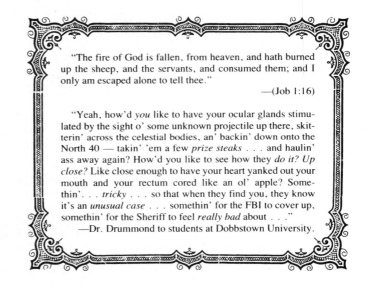

"The fire of God is fallen, from heaven, and hath burned up the sheep, and the servants, and consumed them; and I only am escaped alone to tell thee."

—(Job 1:16)

"Yeah, how'd *you* like to have your ocular glands stimulated by the sight o' some unknown projectile up there, skitterin' across the celestial bodies, an' backin' down onto the North 40 — takin' 'em a few *prize steaks* . . . and haulin' ass away again? How'd you like to see how they *do it? Up close?* Like close enough to have your heart yanked out your mouth and your rectum cored like an ol' apple? Somethin'. . . *tricky* . . . so that when they find you, they know it's an *unusual case* . . . somethin' for the FBI to cover up, somethin' for the Sheriff to feel *really bad* about . . ."

—Dr. Drummond to students at Dobbstown University.

Cattle mutilations in the "classic sense"— no marks on the ground, no signs of struggle, clean cuts as if by super-advanced surgery, corpse drained of blood and untouchable by flies or coyotes — have been going on long enough for the controlled media to start making sick jokes about it. There have been an average of 1,000 a year for the past decade. They are so frequent that the newspapers *don't mention them*. To date, there is no "official explanation" beyond the cop-out of 'predators.' Right. Predators with Stealth helicopters, Air Knives and stun-rays.

HERE ARE THE FACTS: A tiny percentage are done by miscellaneous small cults: Satanists, bikers, etc. About 10% are done by one major Odinist/Right-Wing-Christian cult, composed mostly of Texas oil millionaires, who are essentially seeking a ritualistic cure for impotence.

Another 10% are performed by SubGenii fresh from Dobbstown on their first Initiation Tests. This isn't done just to test their mettle; it is a scientific fact that the only way to properly divine the future is by 'reading' fresh animal entrails.

LOVE TASTES OF THE BIZARRE

St. Dave Martin

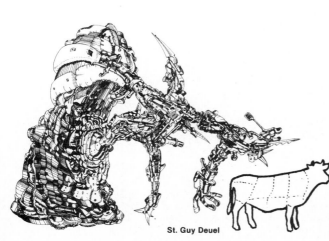

St. Guy Deuel

The popular notion that UFOs are spacecraft piloted by "cute extra-terrestrials," and that cattle are mutilated at the hands of "aberrants" and "Devil Worshippers" are largely inaccurate. The truth behind these horrors is much, much stranger.

VOLCANIC ASH

OIL FROM LIMESTONE

SANDSTONE

SCIENTISTS
AGREE
EARTH TIME
IS SHORT!!!

About 35% are perpetrated by various arms of The Conspiracy in germ warfare and rural terrorism tests, ostensibly as practice for covert action in Russia. It's not the "government" per se — they're way too sloppy to have gotten away with it for this long — but the "Human Insiders" of the so-called Illuminati.

A tiny percentage of the cattle rectums are secured by primitive UFOnauts who need them for rocket fuel, and by yet another space-tribe, this time benevolently trying to sample the radiation content of our food-chain and warn us before we've contaminated it too far. Both of these mutilators tend to work near nuclear power plants.

All the rest of the cattle mutilations, as well as 75% of all other paranormal phenomenon of a similarly *hideous* nature, were perpetrated by the Elder Gods' Watchers *for no other reason* than to confuse the living daylights out of us and let us know *in no uncertain terms* that we are UTTERLY HELPLESS.

Perhaps the ugliest aspect of the whole business is that the Human Conspiracy *aids* and *abets* them whenever possible. These sick traitors to Earth are operating on the same string of promises Hitler was — that if they play along, the **Advanced Supersonic Aluminum Nazi Hell Creatures from Beneath the Hollow Earth**[2] will make them lords over a new race of Aryan Supernormals. (Of course, oil shieks are told it will be *Arab* SuperNormals and African despots are told it will be *African* SuperNormals, and so on.)

Deep inside the Hollow Earth, in Hitler's library — yes, he still lives . . . or at least his *head* does — there exists a book called *BE-*

WARE OF "BOB". For the Church has been fighting these creatures since Admiral Byrd discovered the entrance to their domain at the Pole.

The Aluminum Nazi Hell Creatures, unlike most of the Watchers, are an independent race, with physical bodies, parasites of the Elder Gods. Millions of years ago, after the Night of Demons when the Elder Gods had to smite themselves into 'sleep,' the somewhat metalloid Hell Creatures hurriedly invaded Earth and took over the vast network of tunnels which the Elder Gods had built to honeycomb the planet. (The Earth is not, therefore, truly 'hollow' but rather interlaced fairly near the surface with cyclopean caverns of inhuman design.) From various cavern exits around the world they have crept out to abduct humans for breeding purposes and to otherwise terrorize the surface people away from pursuing the paranormal. The Hell Nazis, nicknamed *"DEROS"*[3] by the unfortunate Richard Shaver, are a "technological" race only because they still use the advanced weaponry they developed in antiquity. Since then, their capacity for original thought has degenerated so drastically that they are little more than robots, hardly any more competent for mass maneuvers than the aging German Nazis whose rickety prototype saucers are encamped around the Pole entrance (they aren't allowed inside). However, their nauseating appearance (at once insectoid and batlike), and skill at intercepting the telepathic messages from arch-rival WOTAN to his prophets, will make them a force to be reckoned with during the Tribulation period presaging the Final Showdown.

The worst volcanoes and earthquakes in history were all *deliberately induced* by these creatures as nothing more than a reverse version of our "underground testing" of nuclear weapons — a practice of ours which, incidentally, makes them none too happy and may eventually result in some mind-boggling "Earthquake War" between the Earth's surface and interior worlds. Dobbs prophecy tells us that this will be forestalled, but we can't really be too careful. Shoot first, ask questions later.

---

2. This name for the Hell Creatures, somewhat more descriptive than the more common term "deros," was coined by Rev. Tim Crain after seeing a double-feature of the badfilm classic *INFRAMAN* and the masterpiece of *deliberate* bulldada, *INVASION OF THE ALUMINUM PEOPLE* by film director David Boone.

3. Not to be confused with DEVO, the rival Evolution Cult founded by one of "Bob's" illegitimate sons. There have been many bloody clashes between "Spuds" and "Subs" in the last few years, but these should soon die down as Dobbs has recently purchased DEVO from Warner Communications.

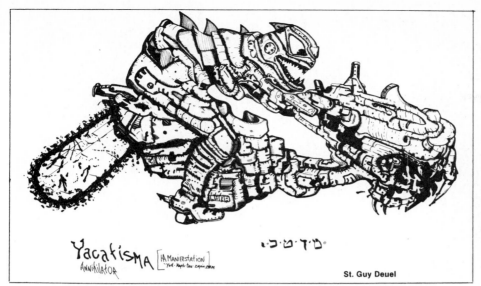

Yacatisma ANNIHILATOA [HA MANIFESTATION] [Yad-Kaph-tau-capin stem]

מ׳ד׳ט׳מ׃

St. Guy Deuel

So we find that there are two groups of supernatural "teams" exerting influence on the bovine, pliable minds of humans. The Watchers are the **Silence Group** — attempting to smother our potential to evolve and carrying the basic message of "Lay Off." Their rivals, JHVH-1's **Shock Group,** are saying "Get Ready" — trying, in a sense, to condition us to the idea that We Are Not Alone. One is a cosmic infection, the other a cosmic innoculation.

AND there's yet ANOTHER group, potentially worse than both of the above *combined,* who have yet to arrive in our section of space. *But they are on their way.*

The Prescriptures refer to them only obliquely, so much of what we know about them comes from Bejamino Evangelista's THE OLDEST HISTORY OF THE WORLD, DISCOVERED BY OC-CULT SCIENCE IN DETROIT, MICHIGAN. According to Dobbs, we might call these beings "Anti-Xists" in that they are every bit as "godlike," but are more suited to the antimatter backwards-time-stream whence come our nightmares. *THESE CREATURES ARE THE HELL'S ANGELS OF THE GALAXY!* Whereas the Xists seem to regard Earth as a "cosmic pit-stop, a veritable Stuckey's in space," and are just coming to "fill up" and

leave, these Other Ones are more likely to beat up the attendant, rape the waitress, break all the windows, rob the cash register, and throw a match into the gas pumps. And, unlike the minions of either JHVH-1 *or* the Elder Gods, they would do it for NO REASON. NO REASON AT ALL. These creatures are so *baaad* that we should probably start worshipping them *now, just in case.* Their name — **"The One True Name of the Unnameable, Unknowable, Unspeakable, Uncountable 1,001,101 Names of the Many-Named Ones"** — is **YACATISMA.**

This is absolutely NOT to be confused with **Yacatizma** with a **Z,** which is the holy Aesthetic Force of the Universe and is All Goodness.

The Yacatisma (called *Seraphim* in the Bible) are on a collision course with Earth, coming roughly from the direction of Orion, but are still far enough away that we can't compute their velocity and thus cannot predict their estimated time of arrival. However, it *hardly matters.* Their *bad vibes alone* have already started tilting the Earth off its axis and, worse, that of the Luck Plane as well! THESE BASTARDS ARE NOT FOOLING AROUND.

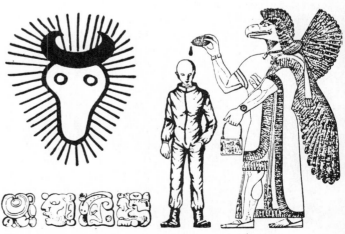

Will Small (LORD) (IS-REAL)

"YOU ARE GOD PARTICIPATING IN HIMSELF" SAYS NHGH

Their background is not pretty either. To begin with, you must understand that JHVH-1 was *not* the only "Rebel God" to defy the Elder Gods. At the time, He was in league also with another elemental named ***BOHANDAS** (Father of Lies), possibly with a being we have *yet* to figure out called **G'BROAGFRAN,** and with His then-wife, **ERIS, Goddess of Chaos.** (ERIS has also gone by the names ISIS, Kali, Nuit, Aphrodite, Sakti, Your Momma, Mummuu, Ishtar, Inanna, Artemis, "MA," and the False [or "Bloody"] Virgin Mary.)

To make a long story short, ERIS and JHVH-1 had a rather messy divorce. ERIS subsequently "gave birth" to twin cosmic Sex Essences, **NUNU** and **NARNINI** (Anubis). NUNU — who keeps the star Sirius B or Yurugu as home base — then had a "son" who can be safely called only **"NHGH"**, "The Nameless One," "Eehg Eehn" or "G'Nee H'Nee." You think that's confusing? Get this — NHGH — the Cosmic Principle of Bad Luck, himself all irony and synchronicity of the *worst* kind — *was his own father:* the result of his coupling with his own "mother," NUNU. **SUCH ARE THE WAYS OF THE GODS.**

Now — NHGH (aka Loki, Set, Mara, Pazuzu, Atlach-Nacha the Phoenician Spider God, and "The Devil," depending on the culture afflicted) had a number of vile "children" by his aunt/sister NARNINI. Some of these were the puzzling **Serpent People** who, according to the *Vatican Codex,* "tempted and fucked" the female Yetis in Eden, ruining the Test Batch and creating humans by accident. But by far the worst of NHGH's *truly "God-Forsaken"* offspring were the Yacatisma now hurtling towards Earth on their Techno-Mutilator "Star Choppers."

And to make matters worse, *The Necronomicon* states that the Yacatisma intend to somehow "mate" with **THE ANTICHRIST "ITSELF"** in order to produce some horrendous being so incomprehensibly BAD that we might as well just give up trying to explain the whole mess RIGHT NOW.

We therefore won't mention the facts that there are **Flash Beings,** thermal minds in the heat shell of the universe, who do nothing but *think,* or that the Biblical "False Prophet" is actually a confused mix-up of "Bob" and the Anti"Bob," or that between now and 2178 Earth will be under constant invasion by horde upon horde of **False Jesii,** working for all the various rival gangs of infra- and extra-terrestrials we've mentioned so far and *then* some, and we won't know *who* to believe except "Bob," and maybe the Real Fightin' Jesus if he isn't actually out to *get back at us,* because we'll have so many to pick from, there'll be the New Jesus, the Old-Time Jesus, the WereJesus, the 900 Foot Tall Jesus, the Astronaut Jesus, the Lady Jesus, the Animal Jesus or the Four-Legged Jesus anyway, the Singin' Jesus, the Upside-Down Jesus, the Yeti Jesus, the 50-Yard-Line Jesus, the Baby Rodan Jesus, the Cussin' Jesus, he don't take shit from nobody, he lights a whole book o'matches at once and holds it in his hand, the Jesus of Steel! And the Jesus you LEAST EXPECT, he seems like JUST SOME KOOK, the *Small* Jesus, the *Will* Jesus and the Won't Jesus, the Throw-The-Book-At-Em Jesus and the Let-It-All-Hang-Out Jesus, the 6-Gun Cowboy Jesus, he came bustin' through that barroom door, wearin' nothin' but those CHAPS!, and the 'Frop Jesus, and the Headless Golfer Jesus, and

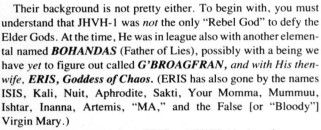

Sarita Crocker

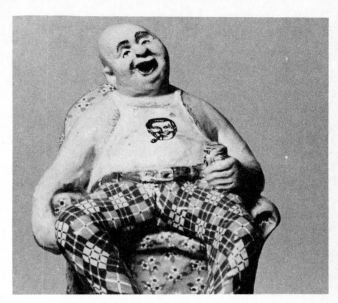

"OVERMAN IN SLACK" by St. Byron Werner photo: Dr. X

the Rebel Jesus, and the Homo Jesus, and the Vampire Jesus who gave His blood for you and now WANTS IT BACK; the Hitch-Hikin' Jesus, the Lead Guitar Playin' Jesus, the Comedian Jesus, the god damn ATHEIST JESUS, the scary monster Jesus, the blind deaf and dumb Jesus, Jesus Can You Hear Me, the mean hobblin' old cantankerous Jesus, the Satellite Jesus, the Psycho Killer Jesus, that web-slingin' Jesus, the SALESMAN JESUS, THE PIPE-SMOKIN' JESUS, and the TEN MILLION SUBJESIUSES, but maybe *somewhere* in there might be just the Plain Old Jesus. ("Bob" knows but **HE AIN'T TELLIN'**.) Therefore we have devised a number of rigid *Jesus Tests* including water-walking, wine-transmutating, loaf-replicating and hook-up to the Martyr Meter. Somebody's faith is being tested. And the Stark Fist of Removal is raised in judgement, poised for a great Evacuation, a Movement, an Elimination and a Wiping from the face of the earth, not to be confused with the Rapture, which is a minor thing; SubGeniuses do it nightly, they Rapture in their sleep, and in the morning are "raised incorruptible yet changed," but then The Rapture might be for real but more like *Night of the Living Dead,* SubGeniuses leading the living in battle against these heathen False Christian golems, because "Rapture" is from the same Root Word as "Rape," OH YEA HEAR YE OF THE DEAF EAR, THE LORD SAYETH, "HEADS UP!" and the people will feel the lash of the thousand scourges of the Tribulations, EVEN YEA LO VERILY UNTO THE FINAL RUPTURE OF THE EQUILIBRIUM OF THE SCALES OF TIME, **OMICRON EPSILON,** THE VISION BEHOLDING ITSELF, REPENT YE MOCKERS, ELIJAH PUFFETH SCORNFULLY ON

HIS PIPE THOUGH HE SMILETH, **WAKE UP!! GET OFF YOUR BUTT!!** You *have* a **Guardian Angel** given you by WOTAN, and your angel does not sleep, yet your Angel will not forgive you if you don't believe in him; your Angel is not emotional, he's programmed by YAHWEH and all he does is what YAHWEH tells him to do. If you work with your Angel you can move mountains but if you scoff at him he'll have no *"Material of You"* with which to work, don't neglect your Angel and leave yourself prey to the guidance of the Nental Ife alone, you do not have to *believe* in your Angel, all you have to do is know there *is* a Luck Plane and that something *can* move it for you; BUT KNOW YE ALSO YE PRIDEFUL ONES THIS: that your Angel is attached to you by JHVH-1 for the same reason that ranchers brand cattle, or that ecologists tag baby sea turtles.

YES things look bad but here's some condolence: 1) We know America *won't* be taken over by gigantic squids a thousand feet tall. 2) For every NHGH particle there is a "Bob" particle. 3) Jimi Hendrix was reincarnated as a whole TRIBE of Xists, and the Xists are the most important, SO WE DO HAVE A CHANCE IF WE CLEAVE TO "BOB."

In parting let us remind you of what we started the chapter with: that many UFOs are *tulpas,* pre-existing energies given form and life by our belief in them or need for them, and also this: it's best not to talk with too many tulpas, lest we find out *we are tulpas ourselves.*

And what *about* "G'Broagfran"???

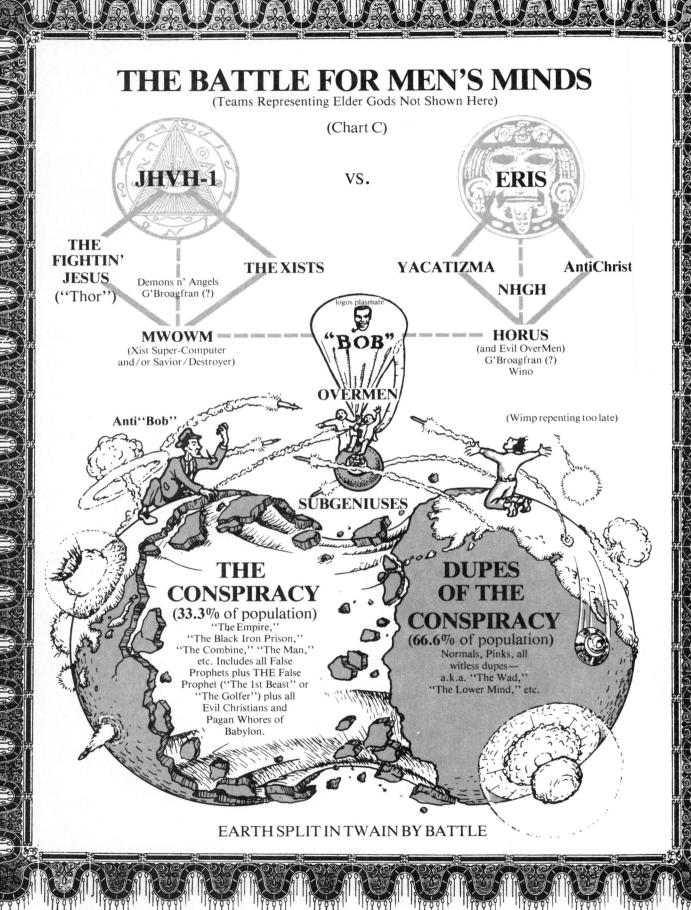

THE BATTLE FOR MEN'S MINDS
(Teams Representing Elder Gods Not Shown Here)

(Chart C)

JHVH-1   VS.   **ERIS**

THE FIGHTIN' JESUS ("Thor")   **THE XISTS**   **YACATIZMA**   **AntiChrist**

Demons n' Angels
G'Broagfran (?)

NHGH

logos plasmate

"BOB"

MWOWM
(Xist Super-Computer and/or Savior/Destroyer)

HORUS
(and Evil OverMen)
G'Broagfran (?)
Wino

OVERMEN

Anti"Bob"

(Wimp repenting too late)

SUBGENIUSES

THE CONSPIRACY
(33.3% of population)
"The Empire,"
"The Black Iron Prison,"
"The Combine," "The Man,"
etc. Includes all False
Prophets plus THE False
Prophet ("The 1st Beast" or
"The Golfer") plus all
Evil Christians and
Pagan Whores of
Babylon.

DUPES OF THE CONSPIRACY
(66.6% of population)
Normals, Pinks, all
witless dupes —
a.k.a. "The Wad,"
"The Lower Mind," etc.

EARTH SPLIT IN TWAIN BY BATTLE

CHAPTER 12

DATELINE FOR DOMINANCE

. . . When Tomorrow Becomes Today

"Dear Lord, I sincerely hope you're comin'
Cause you REALLY STARTED SOMETHIN!"
—Elvis

"You'll ALL be eating roach crap by the turn of the century!"
— "Bob" in a fight with
neighbors, 1950

"When WE are in control, we will kill only the DOG-MATISTS — the "INFALLIBLE." Don't you see it's our duty? Yes, we'll gladly admit it — we're playing God. But what if God's too busy? What if He's chosen us to be His Tools of Wrath?"

— Rant by an unknown SubGenius, recorded at the Dobbs-town "Night of Slack" End-Times Drill but censored from the tape.

"*Everything* comes apart . . . one way or another! Eh-eh-eh . . ."

— "Bob," Lesson 155, Verse 17

"Shut Up, Pink Boy"

. . . So now we're speeding headlong into an inconceivable wall of sanity-sapping minor irritations (simulated cheese-like soymeat bi-food products, power and water shortages, flimsy wheeled solar gizmos instead of sturdy massive CARS, 35 mph, turn your thermostat down, go stand in line, LOWER YOUR EXPECTATIONS), and that wall of irritation is about to turn into a TIDAL WAVE of TRIBULATION from the likes of over-population, toxic wastes, energy depletion, ECONOMIC RE-GRESSION, BAD MONEY HELL . . . and MOST people still don't believe it could happen . . . hell YES, uncountable "cults" of every imaginable variety are literally being *forced to explode* across the continents, each in its own inside-joke way, and it isn't the pressure of NOW that's responsible, it's our own past negligence: it's because those PINKS buried their heads in the narcosand of the Seventies and procrastinated coping with a *hostile environment* that won't *slow down and stop changing.* The cults of Disguised Normalcy can prosper NOW because of the massive weight of deliberate public apathy and voluntary stupidity and utterly unfounded optimism that lays on them like an adolescent lays upon his pornography in bed to prevent its discovery by his stern parents, AIEEE, the cities are about to turn into game preserves crammed with NO ANIMALS but only a dense population of over-equiped hunters firing projectiles with haphazard fervor at each other as well as at nondescript in-animate objects, there is no rhyme nor reason, *beware* the Nulls and Voids, they're surrounding you, they have guns and money and are not-quite-accidentally turning the world into an over-populated terror ghetto, a hell future where our children will grow up in conditions of perpetual apocalypse and suicide

DIRE WARNING OF PROPHECY!!

epidemics, DON'T BANK ON SALVATION BY HUMAN MEANS; individually, humans can behave quite decently to each other but their SYSTEMS have a built-in HOLOCAUST FACTOR which NO AMOUNT of "progress" can nullify in time; the humans will NOT wake up; only intervention by some COSMIC SUPERINTELLIGENCE can save us now, and only "Bob" can bring it about *properly*; if you don't want to broil your brains in the zombie business corridors of empty pinkness OR grinding poverty, if you don't want to feel the meat cook off your bones in a nuclear oven that was once your HOME TOWN, you had better drop your mental candy bars and step out under the blinding light of the sun and make witness to what you REAL-LY ARE, YES you had better be ready to **JUMP!** Come the Econocataclysm, those who knew how to climb UP into the Conspiracy Job Tree had better know how to climb back DOWN again or they're going to be STUCK up there when the HEAT RISES . . . look around you, the signs are everywhere, current American social patterns have already gone way too far, the family is all broken apart, morals have degenerated into a venereal TV swamp, drug abuse and perverted sex are taught in schools, it's just like the Roman Empire before it fell, the collapse is nearly total NOW but what it may become in the final few years will mutilate our children beyond our WILDEST nightmares. Yes it's EVERYWHERE, the Money Changers, the Beast, the Masters of Pink, purveyors of all that is sheepish and soft in the world, *they're just setting us up* for a massive 1984 White Wing resurgence, which in turn allows the great WITCHBURNING, look THERE we already have demoninfiltrated Normalcy Shock Troops going by the hellishly ironic name of "Moral Majority," good GOD are these supposed to be *CHRISTIANS?* They've got Jesus and the Devil **ALL MIXED UP!!** Make no mistake, the SubGenius Foundation is WITH Jesus, the *Fighting* Jesus, not some long-haired mushmouth, we're WITH Brother Roloff and Free Enterprise and America, we're no commie tools of Satan, we're AGAINST One-World Government and hep im-moral sex on TV and intellectual pinks and the Conspiracy and centralization by devil-worshipping puppets in the Capital, by god we UPHOLD TRADITIONAL FAMILY VALUES, but things are NOT that simple, even if our "elected officials" *weren't* corrupt assholes we'd still know that JHVH-1 the alien Space Brain has this planet in His GRIP, He manipulates every tiny move we make, He sics NHGH on us, and his Stark Fist of Removal has a Finger in EVERY PIE. This degeneracy is HIS work. He WANTS our society dragged down into the depths of depravity for some mysterious reason of His own. What choice does even a SubGenius have? **"IT VAS NHGH VHAT MADE ME DO IT."** (— St. Janor Hypercleats to "Bob" after having been discovered in a terrible act.)

Yes . . . this is a crooked and perverse nation, my friend. The DEVIL is in the supermarket . . . the DEVIL is in the Post Office . . . the DEVIL is in the movies and TV. The Devil *OWNS THIS WORLD!* It's *HIS*!!! There is only one way to overcome that devil and that is to place your faith in "Bob!" A man who does not know "Bob" is *FULL* of the Devil. That devil will *never come out* unless the mighty hand of "Bob" grabs him by the scruff of the neck and YANKS HIM OUT.

Yes, my friends, this world is like nothing so much as the PIMPLE on a GOD DAMNED MONKEY'S ASS. The best we can hope for is that another monkey will come along and squeeze it for us.

The Church of the SubGenius *IS* THAT MONKEY.

Have a good look, then, at **DATELINE FOR DOMINANCE** — all of Dobbs' Prophecies compiled into one year-by-year, E-Z-2-Read calendar.

This is the very WAREHOUSE OF THE GODS — a little behind-the-scenes tour of Allah's Arsenal, Mithra's Muni-tions, Jupiter's Javelins and Jehovah's Judgements. We sincerely hope that once you see what the gods have in store for you by way of retributions, tribulations, plagues, trials, punishments and plights, you'll realize just how badly you need powerful friends and benign protectors. Though you may scoff and ridicule now, the day will come when the stockpiled calamities will be unleashed: the gods will send awful tor-nadoes made of crystalized radioactive isotopes, insects the size of elephants, miniature Bigfeet that will run around slash-ing your ankles with poisoned razor blades, frozen nitric acid hail, volcanoes that belch nerve gas, and hallucinogenic dust clouds that will engulf millions at a time. Rogue planets will pull into new solar orbits and disrupt the rotation of the Earth. Some days will be a week long, others no more than a few hours. Things will fall *up!* Great skyscrapers filled with hor-rified screaming people will wrench themselves from their foundations and fly skyward, past the atmosphere and out in-to space! Shopping malls will sink into the ground and never be seen again. Thousands of comets will pound the moon until it shatters and covers the ground with carcinogenic, dreadful-smelling grit. Nothing will matter anymore.[1]

(footnote)

1. The WAREHOUSE OF THE GODS paragraph is lifted, with minor changes, from Rev. Dennis Keller's DELERIAN papers, a vast prophectic manuscript which The Conspiracy has managed to repress UNTIL NOW!!

DATELINE FOR DOMINANCE

Dedicated to the vision of America as the Hell's Angels of the world.

Sacred KlipArt Arrangement: Hagen

1982

* After having an affair with a *very* old woman, Ronald Reagan resigns from the Presidency and joins a rock band, THE NEW BEATLES. [CLONE REPLACED REAGAN, SUPPRESSED!]

* "Bob" first mentioned in Top Forty pop song. [✓]

* Three bodies of aliens from space found in a culvert in Kentucky, classically mutilated by vengeful cattle ranchers. [✓ SUPPRESSED!]

* "Bob" gets first uninterrupted, non-garbled direct psychic hookup to Planet X (Day of Communionication). [✓]

* Race war between Blacks and Mexican Americans in Philadelphia, Miami. [PREVENTED BY S.L.A.K. SQUAD]

* More mutilations of humans linked to UFOs. [✓]

* Humans (allegedly) from the future appear very briefly at a party in Baltimore, hint that "the end is near." [✓]

* Planetary Alignment — **Jupiter Effect** causes disasters as predicted. Earth's magnetic poles reversed; earthquakes, drought, tidal waves, blizzards, power blackouts, floods, fires, mudslides. [PREVENTS] [ALL PREVENTED EXCEPT]

* SubGenius Foundation unearths undeniable proof of CFR-Trilateral-Nazi-Communist conspiracy. Scandal as powerful Petrophiles are unmasked. 25,000 Pamphlets sold. SubGenius featured favorably on *60 Minutes*. [NOT ENOUGH DONATIONS!]

* Burt Reynolds marries Jack Nicholson. [DIVORCED NEXT DAY, SUPPRESSED]

* Shooting war between most countries in Middle East. [✓]

* Church of the SubGenius has foreign missionaries in 30 countries. Bolivian clench deported after slavery scandal. [✓]

* Anti-music band "Doktors for Bob" release second album, *Acubeating*. Sells 3 million copies. Atonal dirge music increasingly played on AM radio. [SUPPRESSED BY]

* "Bob" undergoes Tibetan, Malaysian, and Sioux brain rituals. [✓]

* Earthquake in Vietnam. Freak blizzard in Sahara. [INEXPLICABLE EVENTS IGNORED BY MEDIA]

* Xists (NOT lesser UFOnauts) contact Sioux medicine men on Rosebud Reservation, S. Dakota — first contact with humans other than "Bob." [✓]

* "Bob" secretly buys Purina, Tandy Corporation, Southland Corporation. Many Seven-Elevens and Radio Shacks converted to Church temples. [— BURNED BY C.F.N.!]

* Three closet SubGeniuses in Congress. [✓]

* First "Tit Shots" on prime-time TV. [✓]

* A "Bob" by Picasso unearthed . . . also a Max Ernst "Bob." [SUPPRESSED BY ART CONSPIRACY!!]

* **Germ bomb accident** in Montana. 6,000 goats and cattle, 46 ranchers become raging murderous beasts before dying. [INFO CLASSIFIED BY GOOVERNMEN]

* SubGenius Foundation produces expose on Gold Hoax. More media attention. First attempt on life of Church Doktor, St. Sterno.

* SubGenius FisTemple Lodge in Little Rock fire-bombed by Moral Majority splinter group. Arkansas clenches retaliate. [✓]

* Russia invades Poland, Iran. Draft reinstated. Street battles between anti-war and pro-war groups in U.S., Canada. [✓]

* **Severe drought** in Midwest. Beginnings of the **"Food Crunch."** [✓]

* "Bob" secretly heals George Wallace, Larry Flynt, Ray Charles. Buys Dallas Cowboys, who begin unbroken winning streak. [HAIG — WATTS]

* President ~~Bush~~ threatens several foreign nations with nuclear annihilation. World holds breath for about a week. ~~Bush~~ calms down, apologizes. Widespread rumors that ~~Bush~~ is speedfreak. [WATTS] [HAIG] [HAIG]

* Mass murderer in Rhode Island confesses to killing 93 "rude clerks" after reading SubGenius material nonstop for weeks. Church denies connection. [✓]

* At least 250 individuals in America claiming to be Jesus back on Earth. Spate of false Jessi continues for next 20 years. [✓]

* Ronald Reagan, now an acid-gobbling conceptual artist, quits THE NEW BEATLES to join DOKTORS FOR "WOTAN" anti-music band. [SECRETLY]

* SubGenius Women's Auxilliary overthrows Church Patriarchy during 1982 World SubGenius Conclave in Chiago. St. Sterno killed, resurrected. 2nd public Head Launching prompts government investigation.

1983

* Cure-all for cancer discovered by 'kook' in New Mexico, supressed by A.M.A./Soviet conspiracy. [✓]

* **FIRST BOOK OF THE SUBGENIUS™** published. Bestseller. Film on the life of "Bob" produced but not released.

* Church gains first 10,000 "Zombies for "Bob" — Pastor "Buck" Naked elected mayor of Dallas.

* First "Ass Shots" on prime-time TV. [✓]

* Texas joins OPEC. Mexico and S. America form cartel; Bush declares **"cold war."**

* "UNCLE BOB'S WHIZ-BANG" (SubGenius propaganda for kids) in clandestine circulation among elementary school students. [✓]

* President Bush healed by "Bob" of psychosis.

* "NHGH" jokes spread among blue-collar workers following SubGenius TV special. [CHURCH CENSORS NAME!]

* "DOBB'S INFERNO" published; first *Abusement Parks™* opened; SubGenius *Brain Clinics™* licensed in Mexico.

* An old, *old* woman figures very highly in world politics. [✓]

1983

* Church backs powerful "Abnormals" lobby. More political activism by self-declared "weirdos." SubGeniuses in White House, Senate, Congress . . . one on Supreme Court.
✓ * First televised executions.
✓ * Rampant use of unpredictable new herbal drug *habafropzipulops* in high schools. SubGenius-inspired *'SacraMentality'* widely practiced; "bum trips" among non-SubGenii noted.
✓ * Foundation hires first professional mercenaries to help keep Dobbstown secure in Malaysian jungles.
* Massive **livestock mutilation flap** gets world attention. First unexplained mutilations of household pets.

* DOKTORS FOR "BOB" album *"Good Health"* outsells all combined Beatles albums. Band members go into seclusion at Dobbstown, causing thousands of teenagers to join Church in futile attempt to meet the Doktors.
* In a landmark case a "ghost" is tried for murder and convicted. Dematerializes while being sentenced, never recaptured.
* "Evil SubGenius Cult" used as major plot device on TV soap opera ALL MY CHILDREN.
* **Blizzard conditions in mid-summer** in several Southern states; world population increasingly skittish about bizarre weather.

1984

* The *Econocataclysm* hits America after stock market crash. Millions laid off overnight. **"Work Wars," "Job Riots."** 1,500 workers injured or killed in Detroit uprising.
* **Sunspots** increase dramatically, causing further **weather changes** on Earth and disruptions in communications.
* *"Bob" In '84* posters widely distributed all over U.S. Despite "Bob's" refusal to run.
* UFOs in skirmish with jet fighters over Washington, D.C.; witnessed by millions.
* Major SubGenius "SubCities" (very large communes) in 75 cities worldwide; Spanish and Japanese translations of Church material published.
* Extremely bad **chemical warfare "accident"** in S. Africa.
* Patrio-Psychotic AnarchoMaterialist's Patriarch Party™ established; gains wide grassroots support among extremists of both left and right.
* Full frontal nudity on prime-time TV.
* Foundation first hints of existence of *Immortality Elixir;* bodyguards protect Stang and Drummond around the clock.
* Suicide Contests become a fad among depressed college students.
* Church sells MOJO BAGS™ via late-night TV saturation; starts occult gimmick craze. Church sues over 20 imitators during single year.

* "Cowboy SubGeniuses" appear as Church band BUCK NAKED AND THE JAYBIRDS sweeps country music.
* Red Chinese nuclear test misfires, sends **radioactive cloud** over Alaska.
* First "Bozo Cult™" offshoot of SubGenius. Innocent at first.
* Earthquake prevention device backfires while being tested; sets off chain reaction; **L.A. slides into ocean.** 9 million killed. Film industry in Texas, Chicago booms. Church of the SubGenius acquires own TV network.
* AnarchoMaterialist labor strikes in Great Britain.
* Cigarettes outlawed in U.S. "Nic' Riots" follow; prohibition repealed. (All within 3 months.)
* Habafropzipulops marketted in cigarette form: *"Frop Cigs."*
* Bulldada™ and "American Fuckism" anti-art movements shake New York art conspiracy to core.
* "Bob" solves a major kidnapping case by psychic means; hailed by media.
* Late-night variety show *"Night of the SubGenius"* popularizes trance comedy 'spouting.' Scripted sitcoms on the decline.
* A 'set' of Siamese Twins figure highly in British politics.

1985

* 2,340 Americans held hostage in Mexico City; freed by millionaire-financed vigilantes.
* "Bob" buys into major oil, drug companies. Reunites Stones, Beatles (Lennon replaced by Captain Beefheart), DEVO, Pink Boyz, Drs. for Wotan.
* **Econocataclysm worsens.** 50% unemployment rate.
* Church of the SubGenius almost universally known; no longer regarded as "funny." All-out fad with 50,000 "Zombies" worldwide.

* Mutant Eskimo epidemic in Alaska.
* SubGenius *Memory Editing*™ clinics opened, franchised; *Rites of Retrieval* televised but censored heavily.
* Severe **toxic waste crisis** in U.S. adds to decimation of citizen morale.
* Foundation attempts to expose Men-In-Black/UFO/World-Government connections but is discredited due to **massive cover-up.**
* Big **UFO flap** worldwide. Frequent Fortean phenomena — dinosaurs seen all over Utah (none captured.)

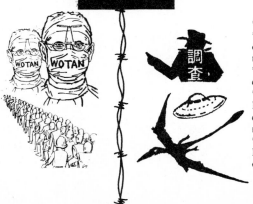

1985

* "Bob's" THINGS TO SEE, SAY AND DO published in edition of 30 million copies in 5 languages.
* Russia invades Israel, Egypt, Saudi Arabia. Huge battle near Red Sea during which UFOs buzz tanks . . . filmed by CBS. U.S. enters war; very brief **nuke exchange** with Russia (only two cities wiped out). **Draft wars** in U.S.

* "Bob's" wives and families exposed. Scandal, lawsuits. Also, SubGenius Hierarchy member Deacon Lamont Duvoe arrested for ritualistic sex crimes; acquitted. Results in 1st public backlash against SubGenius. Unibrow Corp. sues LIES Corp. in major church upheavel.
* Camera developed which photographs poltergeists, ghosts. Supressed.
* Detroit **Sex Riot** 1985.

1986

* American industry all but shuts down in face of **massive economic collapse.**
* *Nuclear Beer*™ first sold by Church subsidiaries.
* **Worldwide famine** due to droughts, locusts, acid rain, mutant wheat plagues; acute food and water shortages in U.S. overshadow energy crisis (gas now $8.50 a gallon).
* War with Russia forgotten in face of **Third World uprisings.**
* "Bob's" secret film of the Kennedy assasination released. Total government shake-up follows.
* Hard core X-rated sex on prime-time TV. **Media Sex-Wars.** Anti-Family movement gathers steam; "Bob" condemns trend toward open perversion.

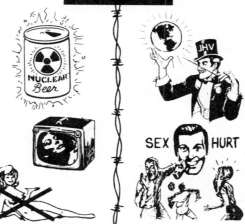

* American Indian medicine man summons, boards, disappears with "UFO" on live TV.
* Halley's Comet unexpectedly fulfills hideous Biblical prophecy: **Moon turns red.** Lends credibility to Church theory of Earth as JHVH-1's "test tube" for genetic tampering.
* U.S. industry begins reconverting plastic to oil.
* "Bob" secretly converts Oral Roberts, Billy Graham, Ted Patrick, Bob Dylan.
* Secrets of *SexHurt*™ released by Foundation. Cult suddenly starts losing members by the millions. Only hard-core zealots remain.

1987

* Another year of **bad famine**; deliberate genetic manipulation of flora and fauna in attempt to offset **rampant mutation** of wildlife due to increasing levels of radiation in food chain.
* Foundation releases truth about so-called "Ancient Astronauts;" also, medical proof of the Work Instinct.
* **Texas secedes;** bloody war against the Union. 8-year-old SubGenius becomes President of Texas.
* **Germ wars** in South America fail to slow **insane population explosion** there.
* Entire SubGenius empire almost universally hated now. Goes underground; "Bob" secretly recruits Hell's Angels, American Indian Movement, right wing paramilitary groups, Jehovah's Witnesses.
* **Crime wave** unaffected by nationally televised beheadings.

* "Bob" secretly acquires cancer cure, intelligence serums; converts Pat Boone, Anita Bryant, Alexander Haig.
* Giant prehistoric newt shot, killed in Loch Ness. No apparent survivors.
* SubGenius literature banned, distributed clandestinely. Desperate persons pay fortunes, even kill to learn where they can receive SubGenius brain treatments.
* Yeti tribe discovered, accidentally massacred by anthropologists in Tibet.
* Popular **Anti-Family movement** attracts extremists from neo-Left, Ortho-Right; starts anti-SubGenius witch-hunt.
* Famine, economic chaos spur unbelievable **moral decay** in Western Civilization. Murder Clubs, Rape Societies blossom among the super-rich. Suicide becomes a respectable competition sport and is televised.

1988

* Another brief **nuke-and-germ war** with Russia; short nuke war with China/Japan; Paris bombed by Trinidad Air Force!
* **OIL RUNS OUT.**
* "Artificial Food" increasingly used to stave off **food rioting.**
* Lobotomy fad among wealthy teenagers—spreads to lower classes via amateur lobotomies performed by "Bozo Cult."

The Slack Party spreads. Over 3 million "Zombies for "Bob"" in 2 months.
* A man with large breasts on his **back** becomes a major TV star.
* "Bob" secretly incorporates Masons, Rosicrucians, other mystic fellowships for businessmen into Church. Dobbs Corporation secretly runs energy industries through interlocking directorates.

117

* **Civilization literally falling apart.**
* Church of the SubGenius resurfaces as horror predictions are fulfilled. "Bob's" weird powers publicly demonstrated; UFO contacts revealed; die-hard SubGeniuses get rich from **"Tribulation Money"** dropped from UFOs. Millions suddenly trying to rejoin Church.
* **A third sex** is added to the human race: *BioMorphs.*

* As nature becomes increasingly chaotic, America makes a last-ditch attempt to return to "the old ways." American Indians in great demand as consultants to science, industry, government. Resurgence of superstition, "black magic," etc. prompts "experts" to warn of impending Dark Ages.

1989

666

BOBCO

* Armies of previously unsuspected **Yetis,** in league with Tibetan monks, free Tibet from China in intense border wars. Yetis resume raping of human women in effort to restock the world's Yetinsyn population.
* Average age of U.S. citizen: 20.
* Paper money replaced by computer credit: **THE MARK OF THE BEAST.** All Americans tattooed with invisible **"Triple-Six Club"** credit code.
* Charles Manson, Ed Gein released from prison; record album with DRS. FOR "ANUBIS".
* Thousands of **false Jesii** garner huge followings.
* American voters deliberately install an **all-powerful dictator** as last hope for restoring order. Fortunately, dictator is pro-SubGenius.
* **Plague** created by recombinant DNA research decimates 10% of world population.
* L. Ron Hubbard dies; wills control of Scientology to "Bob," who by now also runs Exxon, Warner, Xerox, Kodak, RCA, and Atari.
* Pope urges peace in space following *U.S. vs. Japan* **satellite battles.**
* SubGenius Church, back in the limelight, initiates enormous Pro-Family movement nationwide to combat deterioration of human decency.

* Over 75% of America population is alcoholic; alcoholism redefined as an "alternate lifestyle" rather than a disease. "Wine Burgers" and "Alcoholic Cigars" invented.
* STAR WARS IX released. Thinly disguised SubGenius propaganda.
* Statisticians notice that non-SubGenii suffer 63% more casualties during **CancerFlu** plague. Church membership swells until 25% of U.S. are registered, dues-paying SubGenius Priests.
* A Dobbshead is found carved into a Martian crater by 1st manned Mars landing party.
* American water supply dwindling; increasingly contaminated. Drinking water $5/gallon. **Water riots.** Fly-by-night companies get rich with "Make Your Own Water at Home" schemes. Rainmakers, dowsers, alchemists in great demand. "Magic" begins to rival "science" even among scientists.
* Sugar is outlawed as a carcinogen and becomes a black-market commodity comparable to heroin. After many bloody sugar riots, sugar prohibition is repealed, but a **mutant virus** wipes out the world's main sources of sugar. Rioting escalates.
* Church freely admits to **"voluntary slavery"** practices. No uproar.
* Cabbages ten feet across.

1990

WHO BLEW M-22?
ARE WE NEXT?

* Civilized people losing faith in modern medicine. Travelling medicine shows hawking wonder drugs, miracle cures, psychic healing frequently seen around shopping malls.
* **Synthetic Food Wars.** Horse, cat, dog, rat meat sold openly all over U.S. Cannibalism practiced in rural areas. Roach shit processed and packaged as diet supplement.
* Brazil invades U.S., driven back by citizen armies after government military forces fail.
* Atlantis rises from the middle of Kansas; ancient Dobbsheads found carved into ruins—apparent prediction of "Bob" over 8,000 years ago.
* Gangland-style **wars between Christian sects,** all following different false Jesuses.
* Common cold cured by "magic spells."
* Foundation scientists, after cracking DNA's code-within-the-code, develop

"instant mutation" process: a slightly risky method of producing 'home made' OverMen which attracts many teenagers into the Church.
* Crashed UFO recovered from Bermuda Triangle by anonymous Ft. Worth millionaire provides undeniable proof of space conspiracy. By this time, over 60% of adult Americans have seen UFOs.
* Anti-Family movement, although starting to lose ground to SubGenius, is still powerful enough to make bestiality a P.E. option in many public school systems. Attempts to make adultery mandatory but fails as bill is blocked by "Bob"-directed Senate cubcommittee.
* Publishing industry in NY collapses due to self-publishing boom.
* SubGenius-inspired **Fertility Rites** commonly performed all over world as if in defiance of harsh realities of overpopulation.

1990

* The **American dictator**, now identified by the Church as **the Anti-"Bob,"** gains admiration of world through military triumphs. Oddly, "Bob" himself throws his support behind Anti-"Bob."
* **Earthquakes** in every corner of the globe.
* Vatican moved to Mexico City.

BOBCO

* "Bob" controls all major TV networks plus ITT, Summa Corp., Texas Instruments, General Dynamics, McDonnell-Douglas, Eckankar, Ford McGraw-Hill, General Motors, and Texaco. Polygamy legalized in U.S. thanks to Dobbs influence.

1991

* **WORLD WAR III**. Church of the SubGenius shifts into *Operation Removal*.
* "Bob" forms alliance with the Anti-"Bob," reveals hard evidence of imminent Xist invasion.
* Another major UFO flap—this time, saucers drop real money and gold all over Midwest. Rampant contacteeism.
* 400 million "Zombies for "Bob"" worldwide. SubGenius/Pro-Family movement initiates campaign to "clean up America" morally.
* Bulletproof robots run most convenience stores.
* Accident with solar-gathering satellites which encircle the Earth sets off incredible spate of **tornados** across U.S.
* Minimum wage reaches $86.50/hour, but a soft drink costs $40.00.
* Average human lifespan now figured at 40 years.
* Church offers "Experimental Transfigurations" to willing guinea pigs; crude man-made OverMen are created through immediate somatic alteration of physiology. Bozo cult (now a hated rival of the Church), in imitation, offers "smile-face" surgery and "While-U-Wait" lobotomies.
* 24 hours of artificial "daylight" common in large cities. Incidence of **psychosis** increases correspondingly.

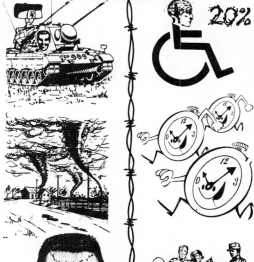

While-U-Wait

20%

* 20% of U.S. population now considered clinically insane. Concentration camps for "abnormals" are opened in some states; SubGeniuses begin waging open war on non-SubGeniuses. Millions of homosexuals, finally understanding "Bob's" *"deal"*, become valiant warriors for the Church.
* A SubGenius physicist successfully demonstrates that there are a number of parallel Earths, including an entire concurrent *Universe 2* which is an exact "negative' of ours running *backwards* in time. His theory that the two universes (ours and "theirs") are due to "intersect" within a few hundred years is greeted with derision, however, and is lost amid the general background noise of chronic doomsaying.
* A fourth Double SubGenius (of 5 existing at any given time) is identified, living in Peru.
* Distorted signals of an alien "TV show" broadcast 10,000 years ago from a now-defunct planet are received by Earth scientists. By this time, intelligent life on other planets is generally accepted as fact, although UFO activity on Earth is still a mystery.
* Disneyland converted to Open Murder Park.

1992

* Ozone layer depleted; Earth unshielded from harmful radiation; the **Greenhouse Effect** begins to accelerate. Average world temperature up 15°. Life on Earth stands a good chance of being wiped out.
* Almost every nation on Earth is at **war** with every other nation, primarily over food.
* India releases **plague germs** on Pakistan.
* Millions killed by **toxic waste** spill in New Jersey.
* Blue Whales, Rhinoceri, Mountain Gorillas, dolphins *totally extinct*, along with over 3,000 other species.
* Valium added to water supplies by many city-state governments.
* Witch doctors more highly paid than medical doctors.
* Return of the 7-day workweek and the 14-hour workday.
* Governments of many small countries whose populations are in chaos concede authority to huge multinational corporations, many of which are fortunately now run by "Bob."

43%

* What we would now call "lunatic-fringe kooks" account for 43% of U.S. population. Over 2 million separate, active sects. Well over half, however, are basically aligned with the Church of the SubGenius. The rest are violently anti-SubGenius, anti-individual, anti-thought Conspiracy dupes who still cling to a now-useless lifestyle. The United States is divided between these two powerful social forces.
* **The Fifth Civil War: Abnormals Vs. Normals.** During this period the U.S. reverts to **medieval barbarism.** Feudal warlord chieftains rule the thousands of mini-states into which the country has splintered. Bands of outlaws roam the countryside and the cities. Law as we know it is non-existent. Only huge corporations provide any stability to the social structure; they have *become* the "government," and jealously guard the remaining pockets of high technology. Most corporations run by "Bob."
* Laser haircuts.
* A horrifying **"lemming effect"** seen in large cities near oceans.

1993

* **Glaciers start melting.** Port cities flooded. **Drought, mutation, environmental poisons and pestilence** worsens already-critical world famine.
* Abnormals gain upper hand in Civil War. Church of the SubGenius finally becomes single most powerful force in America, the only thing holding the nation intact. "Bob" puts his super-science community to work on *"Alternative 9"* project—select SubGeniuses are recruited, 'altered,'and sent to colonies on Mars and the Moon—"just in case."
* **Decimated world**, quickly plunging into **survivalist insanity**, is now divided between SubGenius and AntiSubGenius forces: **WORLD WAR IV.**
* Anti-"Bob," still working *with* "Bob," receives head wound but recovers due to Bozoid surgery and becomes semi-superhuman. Generally thought by most of the world to be the "AntiChrist" (not true).
* SubGenius Foundation makes breakthroughs in **Forbidden Sciences:** manipulation of the *Luck Plane*™, *Gravity Rays, Selective Elimination*™. Meanwhile, strange side-effects of Excremeditation, habafropzipulation begin to crop up in older SubGeniuses.

* Organized crime (including Mafia, Tongs, etc.) now valiantly fighting *for* "Bob."
* SubGeniuses form own nation (a la Nation of Israel), take over Texas for that purpose. Millions make pilgrimages to the Dobbs Complex in Dallas.
* American Indians also declare independence, take over North and South Dakotas. Successful enough to loan money to United States.
* **Mutant Revolution** headed off when Charles Manson discovers secret Death Valley entrance to the Hollow Earth and leads exiled misfit Nazi Hell Creatures against mutant strongholds; "Bob" intervenes and convinces the two sides to form a powerful alliance against vast empire of advanced Nazi Hell Creatures. All known entrances to Hollow Earth nuked, closing them off temporarily. Entire Hell Creature situation kept secret from public.
* **World War IV ends with SubGenius forces on top.** Some remaining guerilla resistance by hard-core "normals" who mistakenly believe there's still a difference. (90% of so-called "SubGeniuses" really just "token" now.)
* Contagious schizophrenia virus unleashed.

1994

* Anti-"Bob" now runs Global Congress **(One World Government)**, lording it over all secular aspects of ruined Planet Earth. "Bob" now master of all religion *and* commerce, "commerce" having become more closely related to Church than government.
* New volcano in Kansas.
* Scientific proof of ghosts rocks world.
* 10 million space migrators killed by air leak in L-5 orbiting city.
* Ocean farming attempted, abandoned. However, "Bob" solves food crisis with invention of **"waste reconversion."**
* China, France **clash in space** over differing interpretations of Church dogma.
* First child born on Mars.
* Subterranean Martian monsters discovered. NOT native to Mars.

* Women now paid better than men, on average.
* First Fusion Reactor explodes, obliterating Boston.
* **"Drug Abuse Religions"** cropping up.
* First *serious* **UFO crisis**—not Hell Creatures this time, but blond Venusians. Calling themselves the Great White Brotherhood, they invade Earth and almost win by contaminating world 'wastefood' supply with alien **"Sin Particles."** Cataclysm averted by combined forces of "Bob" and Anti-"Bob." Venusians defeated.
* Covenant with JHVH-1 Himself revealed; Pope converted by "Bob;" SubCatholicism™. SubGenius now unofficial **World Religion.**
* Book pills.

1995

* Gladiator-type **public death battles** televised by satellite.
* "Terrorist Tourism" fad among super-rich.
* Jacqueline Onassis marries Divine.
* Edgar Cayce found still alive in New Mexico, working for C.I.A. or world-government version of C.I.A.
* Marijuana still not legalized.
* School teachers now regularly tortured in class by pupils. Public school system abandoned in favor of independent neighborhood schools.
* 65 percint illeterasy rate in America.

* Russian **psychic warfare** techniques unleashed on world-at-large in last-ditch attempt to unseat "Bob." "Bob" unveils 'secret weapon' (quasi-materialized Nental Ife army), whips Russia into obedience.
* Extreme "Back to Nature" movement among teenagers: reversion to animal behavior. Urinating in public to mark off territorial boundaries, butt-sniffing for identification, "mating rituals," etc. *"Broomstick In The Ass"* becomes major teen fashion craze. Rich kids hang jewelry from 'em, poor kids hang *heavy* things.
* Plague of **mutant insects.**

1997

* Greenhouse Effect reversed by "Bob" science; however, **New Ice Age** results. "Bob" unmasks Anti-"Bob" as perpetrator of Ice Age; exposes bowels of Conspiracy; **WORLD WAR V** between "Bob" Crusaders and minions of Anti-"Bob." "Bob" wins, but only after traces of the *Elixir*™ is released into atmosphere, causing **Dream Plagues**. (All of this takes place in first 3 months of year. Rest of year finds **world at peace** for first time.)
* **Longevity drugs, gravity drugs** released but in short supply. Considerable rioting, especially by elderly persons.
* Church reveals secrets of *Fornicationalism*™, Code Retrieval from Cosmic Archives, other Xist-derived theories. "Bob" now trying to prepare world for visit from Planet X.

* Now completely SubGenioid are more than half of the world's nations. Populations are still primarily Pink or Normal, but almost all leaders take orders from the Church.
* **Immortality drugs** developed; bootlegged; yet more rioting. Average human lifespan now considered to be 150 if death by cataclysm is not counted.
* Palmer Rockey's film THE SECRETS OF NUNU sweeps Oscars.
* Ghosts are recognized as citizens, given voting rights.
* **Overpopulation** becomes so bad that most people *give up* fighting it. There is another **Baby Boom**, partly inspired by SubGenius fertility rites. "Bob" continues assuring world "not to worry."
* 7,000 Americans defect to Malaysia (new Church headquarters).

1998

* **Nuclear chain reaction** across the face of Europe. "Ghosts" identified as culprits, then revealed by "Bob" to be Nazi Hell Creatures masquerading as dead people in order to subvert SubGenius and speed up arrival of The New Age (enslavement of humans by Hell Creatures). **WORLD/SPACE/HOLLOW EARTH WAR I. New York nuked.** Sea monster "Leviathan" attacks coastal cities; "the Elder Gods" are summoned; **SCOURING** of planet.
* Humanity "brought together by common foes;" defeats invaders using newly-released secrets of *Time Control, Time Addiction.*

Living clones of Elvis, Hitler, Jimi Hendrix, and JFK lead mankind to finally crush forever the threat from the Hollow Earth (details unclear).
* Humans worldwide innoculated against future accidents with the *Elixir*™.
* "Bob" goes on TV for first time in 40 years... makes speech which moves *billions* to tears.
* "Bob" and Church of the SubGenius hierarchy installed as lords over entire, governmentless Earth.
* Cheap, brittle fiber-composition broomsticks introduced.

1996

* **World peace.** "Bob" and Church working against time to slant Luck Plane *exactly right* for arrival of Xists in July.

* **7:00 A.M., July 5th, 1998:**

?

world ↓ peace

7:00 a.m., July 5th, 1998:..,...?

121

IN CASE OF HOLOCAUST

First, be prepared *before* it happens. When hoarding, remember that *bullets* will be a lot more important than *food*, in that you can use bullets to *obtain* food in almost any disaster climate.

If the bombs start falling and/or the plagues are released BEFORE SCHEDULE, America will revert to barbarism practically overnight. 72% of the population will become what we would now call "outlaws" and only the remaining 28% will remain "law abiding citizens." DON'T BE A SAP—WASTE NO TIME IN TURNING ROGUE. Immediately GANG UP with your most trusted friends and followers, form a band of nomad raiders, and START MARRAUDING. You will find it much easier than you might expect to be an outlaw chieftain stealing fodder from whimps in **the total absence of LAW.** The cops will be doing the same thing you are. Terrorize your way cross-country and arrive as soon as possible in Dallas, where all End-Time Alliances of SubGeniuses will converge in any terminal emergency.

Get to "the old East Dallas neighborhood"—the Swiss Avenue mansion district—and collar survivors, demanding to know where SubGenius headquarters is located. Look for the group of weird old houses surrounded by barbed wire and gun emplacements. That will be Bulldada Time Control Laboratories. There will probably already be hundreds of tents, tanks, vans, and choppers up and down the block, all belonging to freshly-arrived fanatics.

With the Normals fleeing the cities, the opulent rotting mansions in this sector will be largely vacant, and those foolish enough to remain will be easy pickings. **YOU yes YOU will have a NEW HOME in the AFTERMATH in DALLAS, TEXAS, CHOSEN CITY OF "BOB." PRAISE THE FORCE FIELD!! PRAISE THE LASER PROJECT!!**

All the registered SubGeniuses in one place will be a formidable army indeed. If the bombs started falling NOW we'd have a force of zealots numbering well over 40,000 within a week. (At any given time, there are over 11,000 Zombies for "Bob" available from Dobbstown alone.) "Bob" calculates that within 3 months of the "Day of Nuclear Judgement" over 500,000 will

THE MEANING OF THE MILLENNIUM.
The centuries-old debate among Biblical scholars concerning exactly how the end will come about.

have defected to our side. We will form one huge tribal juggernaut of destructo-wrath that will RULE the city of Dallas, and after that, what's left of the country itself!! If YOU are on the Church mailing list at that time, YOU'LL GET A SLICE.

(Ever daydream about rolling triumphantly down Main Street of your home town at the head of a squadron of tanks, a CONQUEROR, able now to extract TOTAL VENGEANCE on old high school foes?? It MAY happen. BE READY.)

What we envision for these dark days, when most others are starving, is a healthy feudal system in which all fit male and female SubGeniuses are warrior thug-serfs for "Bob." How can any **potential OverMan or ÜberLady** entertain the faintest hopes of surviving the End Times without "Bob?" Yes, "Bob" will be in Dallas then and you'll want to be where "Bob" is if you want tickets to the **Rescue Ships from Planet X...** so why not serve under him and his chosen representatives on Earth while you STILL CAN???

As a Thug, you will be safe among other Thugs. As a Whimp, you and yours will be up for grabs. **DON'T WUSS OUT**—there is actually more honor among thieves than there is among Normals.

FACTS

"In dire emergency people everywhere are likely to panic and trample each other to get to safety. Normally brave people often run along with the cowards and the merely timid. It is inconceivable, except in the hermetic towers of the analysts, that any system of civil defense, crash or planned, billion dollar or multibillion dollar, would save the United States, once the panic started."

Cataclysm Rehearsals
you can do!

Here's a quick HITLER SKITLER **END O' THE WORLD DRILL.**

First, pretend the Ecohell/Econocataclysm has arrived. Then rehearse the following:

Rape. Pillage. Looting. Tearing tin cans open with your teeth.

Get depressed and imagine your gums bleeding and your hair falling out from radiation. Wander up and down the street pretending everyone but you is dead. Kill anyone who comes near you. Mutter. Look for loved ones. Get pissed at the President and the Russians. Give up and die.

Try this on Sundays with friends, and you'll be a lot readier than most people.

SHOT: High travelling shot from a helicopter at about 3000 feet as it moves as fast as it can towards a large city which, judging from the smoke and fire, is largely in flames. As we move in closer we see there are many people in the streets, looting, shooting, sniping from the rooftops at firemen and policemen. It looks like Watts, only the cars are too new, the people mostly white.... then we realize this is Dallas.

Cut to Mobscene in streets of Big D. People trying to get out of town, people trying to take what they want.

Shot: DFW Airport exterior; Transport planes are landing and disgorging troop carriers and light armor formerly marked Texas National Guard but now overlayed with a bright red triangle with a blue dot at the apex.

Shot: Fierce street war between heavily armed Army types and equally heavily armed white punks on dope. Mostly automatic weapon work with some explosives. The Army is pushed back slowly by the fanatical punks.

High aerial shot from Chopper. We see that there is fighting as far as one can see.

Cut: Shot of lawn in front of temporary SubGenius Command post. Logo on flag in front is "Bob" in tin hat. There are several helicopters cranking up on the lawn. They are all heavily armed Cobra gunships.

All have a "Bob" insignia on the sides and a clenched fist up near the rear rotors.

We follow the choppers as they sweep over the combat regions and start spraying thick bluish clouds of gas.

Clouds descend upon rioters and soldiers, who gag and gasp and choke and then start smiling like loons. They stop all fighting to join forces in looting a Dunkin' Donuts shop that seems still intact.

Cut; Central Command Post with Pentagon-like equipment. Philo Drummond and Ivan Stang in full SG combat kip are manning the hot lines. The place is a hive of activity and illuminated charts of the world spell out new information with constantly changing computer displays.

Shot: MCU Philo hanging up Hotline and turning to Stang.

CU of Stang looking impassive.

Two Shot Stang and Drummond.

Tight Close Up of Stang. His face is cold and hard.

Close Up Drummond.

Long Shot of the two against the equipment.

THE U.N. WAS CLOSING IN ON DOBBS. THERE WAS NO MERCY FOR THEIR ENEMY—

WHERE'S XANDAR!

DEFECTED—ALONG WITH STERNO AND UNI BRAU!!

THE CENTER WAS BOMBED INTO DUST.

FFEEEE

INUMB

IN THE SHELTER

NOW WE HAVE TO REDECORATE

LIES

'Put Your Hands On The Radio' by *Pink Boyz* playing as BG music.

VO. When things really started falling apart, the cities went first.

As the social order ruptured in America, everyone grabbed what they could and left for the open countryside....

...or they teamed up and dug in.

The Conspiracy gathered all sections of reserves under one central command in an attempt to stop the insurrections in the larger urban regions.

Unfortunately the reservists that did respond were not prepared for the ferocity of the resistance of some groups of armed citizens.

Chaos reigned supreme, making a lot of Erisians and Discordians wet with excitement. But the great unwashed were really getting trashed.

Amidst all this mayhem was an island of tranquility and organization.

The Church of the SubGenius, after years of derision and then violent persecution, has been preparing for this moment.

Utilizing a new derivative of the Tibetan herb Habafropzipulops synthesized by Overman Philo Drummond, the Church forces spring into action to prevent more senseless violence.

The euphoric, mind altering effects are permanent and the only side effect is hunger.

FX: Phones and comm gear noises.

Drummond: "Bob" says the situation in Hong Kong and Saigon is stable. Red China is ours, as is most of the Euromarket except France.

Stang: We're already behind schedule in Europe; how about Russia?

Drummond: Russia seems to be ours too but we can't pull anyone out... it's just too big.

Stang: We're going to have to nuke Paris; better get "Bob" on the hotline again. Where is his aircraft now?

Drummond: Somewhere over Tanzania right now and heading towards the Middle East. You know what a mess it is there.

Stang: Yeah, we really didn't do too well there... too bad about Israel, Lebanon and Libya. It's going to glow at night in those regions for a long time.

DRUMMOND: You know, of course, that Egypt bought it too. There are no more pyramids.

TO BE CONTINUED
by Guy Deuel

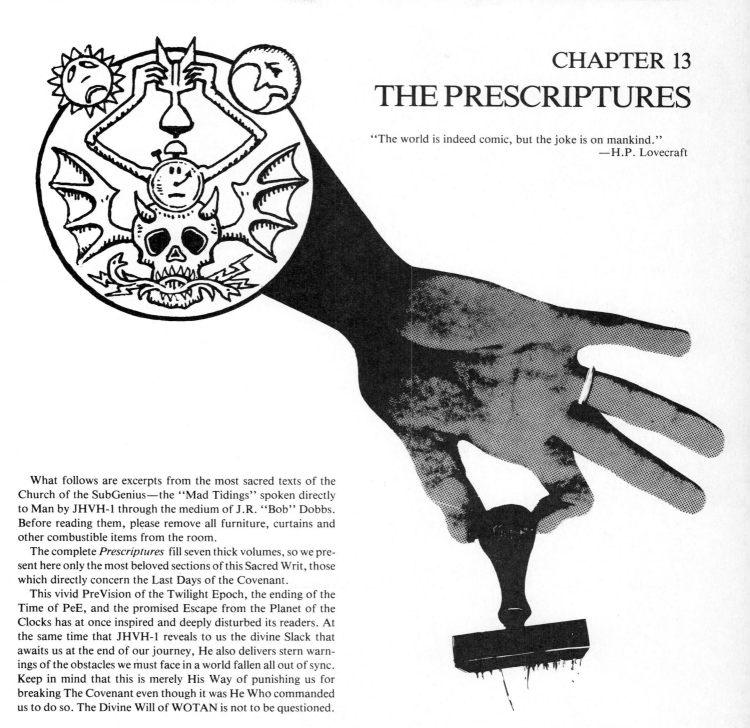

CHAPTER 13
THE PRESCRIPTURES

"The world is indeed comic, but the joke is on mankind."
—H.P. Lovecraft

What follows are excerpts from the most sacred texts of the Church of the SubGenius—the "Mad Tidings" spoken directly to Man by JHVH-1 through the medium of J.R. "Bob" Dobbs. Before reading them, please remove all furniture, curtains and other combustible items from the room.

The complete *Prescriptures* fill seven thick volumes, so we present here only the most beloved sections of this Sacred Writ, those which directly concern the Last Days of the Covenant.

This vivid PreVision of the Twilight Epoch, the ending of the Time of PeE, and the promised Escape from the Planet of the Clocks has at once inspired and deeply disturbed its readers. At the same time that JHVH-1 reveals to us the divine Slack that awaits us at the end of our journey, He also delivers stern warnings of the obstacles we must face in a world fallen all out of sync. Keep in mind that this is merely His Way of punishing us for breaking The Covenant even though it was He Who commanded us to do so. The Divine Will of WOTAN is not to be questioned.

AiiEE! HELP! EEEK!! GOOD LORD!

PAINT-UP FOR JHVH-1

LIES

YAHWEH also lifts passages from a prophetic work that was originally written as propaganda *against* Him: *The Book of Revelation*. Contrary to widespread belief, Revelation was written not by St. John "Anything For A Laugh" of Patmos, but by a mad Gnostic named Cerinthus. It was primarily meant as a satire of other, more literal-minded Early Christian sects, using a mish-mash of old Pagan symbols and incorporating garbled messages sent to Cerinthus by mind-wave from a Renegade Xist who was trying to *warn* the Earth of JHVH-1's presence. This material "read" so well that JHVH-1 adapted it for His own purposes.

ON

OFF

A possible G'Broagfran … painting by St. :D with NHGH's "head"

While reading the text, you may notice that JHVH-1 pointedly avoids mention of certain other Supreme Ones in the pantheon of gods—especially the Elder Gods. You may also note that He takes credit for various acts of terrorism against the human race which we know to be the work of His rivals; and, that when He does mention such entities as the AntiChrist, the OverMen, the Angelic Host, and the Bozo Cult, He does not always choose to specify which are working for Him and which are against Him. From this we know that He grants us a certain measure of Free Will.

. Some phrases may have a familiar ring. JHVH-1 is fond of quoting Himself (or His impersonators) from previous revelations, such as those made to the Hebrews in Old Testament times. He knows which of His old routines work best.

Despite the distortions and misinterpretations that have saddled the Word of Odin down through the ages, here we finally have a truly poetic vision of the great War in Heaven that will decide our eventual Destiny, unbesmirched by the haggling of committees over *precisely* how many Pinks can be deep-fried in the 18th Bardo of Purgatory or how many Normal souls must be sacrificed to purchase a rich SubGenius a ticket to Heaven.

Prefacing *The Prescriptures* themselves, we present here—in its first publication anywhere—"Bob's" own description of the events immediately preceeding his first great Bout with WOTAN and the emotions that seized him during this time.

("Bob" has insisted that we make clear that his original, rather more 'homey' narration has been heavily rewritten by Church Scribes. If revealed unchanged, many of the details, *and "Bob's" somewhat unsophisticated wording itself,* could endanger not only "Bob's" family, but National Security and perhaps the FATE of the VERY EARTH.)

EXPOSED
thru the eye of the
HIDDEN CAMERA!

Joe Schwind

Hal Robins

"BOB" ON HIS OWN EMACULATION

And so the time is at hand for your humble servant to speak that which has been revealed, and which must come to pass.

Oddly enough, my first Visitation occurred not while I was engaged in any spiritual pursuit, but while absently tinkering late one night with an experimental television receiver of my own design. The hour was certainly after 1:00 A.M., and, as I was temporarily living at the home of my beloved parents, my Divine Seizure overtook me not twenty paces from where they lay asleep. Yet, when questioned the next morning, they could recall nothing of the thunderous voice(s?) that I know from my crude recordings must have reverberated throughout the little house for much of the night.

I was thoroughly engrossed in my project, and whatever thoughts I had were surely far from pious; I was likely drunken to some extent, for this was long before I freed myself from the joyous curse of the bottle. I was bent over the picture tube of my ambitious home appliance, *about to attach it to a power cord for the first time,* when I realized that the screen was already glowing. I stopped what I was doing and stared at it in befuddlement. The screen hummed and was suddenly bathed in light; and I swear I saw a brief, very overexposed image of a man clothed in flame with a bar of metal extending from his mouth before the tube went to total brightness!

I felt a sudden, swiftly-building tension in the air, a sort of vacuum between myself and the device before me. Abruptly my head was filled with light—my vision almost wholly obscured by a blinding whiteness that seemed somehow to have instantaneously traveled from the tube to myself and was now bursting from a "melting point" at the exact center of my brain. There was no pain, but the change of pressure inside my skull was such that I felt it must surely have hollowed itself out, my brains and juices joining with the light and streaming out through now-empty eye sockets in a dazzling wet beam. My whole body felt simultaneously hot and freezing, suffused with a ticklish numbness that made me want to climb out of it.

My vision of the room was short-circuited from within by the glow, but I could, after a fashion, 'feel' the walls and shelves around me, as if the air space between them and my skin did not exist... they seemed continuous with one another.

There was as yet neither any sense of a divine presence, nor any panic. I was, in fact, preternaturally calm, and only *awed* by the miraculous impression that encased within the vacuum of my cranium burned a white-hot filament through which was passing countless millions of volts of electricity. Despite my near-blindness, I retained a strange presence of mind—perhaps like the unworldly calm which those on the threshhold of death are supposed to experience. I could feel the room still around me, my teenage room with its clutter of cheap cameras and home-made recording devices, and, with my now-since-departed soundman's reflexes, I groped for a little wire recorder and prayed that it was loaded. I wrenched the microphone rings to full dilation and, hastily, since I was beginning to slip entirely out of rationality, laid the device on the table to capture the thud of my body hitting the floor. (Obviously, such was not the case, and what we now call *The Prescriptures* were therein recorded in a bellowing, animal-like voice *decidedly not my own,* though I cannot doubt that it issued from my throat.)

A noise like the rushing of a waterfall—no, many waterfalls—rose to my ears, and I began to 'lose' the room around me. The light and the noise were replacing all. The roaring sound seemed to come from no external source, but from deep within myself: this time, I felt, from my groin. Yet it was emanating outwards, evenly, in all directions; it was encompassing all the world. I could 'reach out' with the sound. I felt I had become a Radio of the Universe, deafened by the static chatter of an electrical cosmos.

I was then abruptly made aware of my physical body again, for a pain ripped through my chest with all the suddenness and fury of a lightning bolt. I clutched myself and doubled over, clamping shut my eyes; there was the sickening feeling that my torso was losing its limbs, that bones and flesh were sloughing away, leaving only my bare squirming bowels coiling across the floor.

This feeling passed and the agony subdued a trifle, and with it so did the light and sound. I looked up, gasping, and was able to glimpse my real surroundings for an instant—my room and equipment. With this little glad respite, however, came the practical realization that I must be in awful danger, perhaps in the grip of a heart attack. Fear welled up and I discovered I could hardly breathe: the chains of terror were tightening around my rib-cage. I tried to call out but could not take in the necessary air. Then, there was *no* air.

It was then that I finally thought of *real* death, of an ending to my favorite Self, and ultimately of the universal vastness I might thus be joining. For in those days I thought little of Beforelives and such; I knew only that the realms beyond our world were mysteries. But I had always possessed an educated inkling of their immensity and age, and now in these Throes I could grasp such things concretely. I could *taste* them; the horrible knowledge of the very *breadth* and *depth* of our visible cosmos rose to the back of my throat and expanded there, sucking dry my mouth-glands like some monstrous antihistamine, I tell you I could *taste* this hellish Size of All the Aeons and it was sweet, chemically sweet, sweet enough to incinerate, and I feared that this nightmare taste might reach my brain, it might become more than a taste, it might become real inside me and the terror came and I had to be gone away from this, I had to take my brain away from my body where the taste could not become knowledge, forever, MADNESS! My inner self convulsed, as if to leap backwards out of its bodily shell. It leapt. I leapt. The ceiling cracked open and then the sky cracked open and then all of space cracked open.

My body and its pain were gone. The whiteness and the noise returned and with them came an idiot calm. For a moment I merely floated in the light and sound which were now merging to become one sensation. Then a tension, a weird instant of warning as if the very whiteness and noise were making ready to flee; and I felt the mindless suspense of the moment. (What words are there for this?) Perhaps it was like riding in the socket of emptiness and suction that follows racing behind a jet aeroplane, at the precise instant before a sonic boom; or, maybe it was as if I were standing in the spot of trembling hesitancy exactly between two walls of storm air about to produce a thunderclap. The inevitability of the next moment was a solid thing which could be touched, and there was nothing else; silence, suspense; and then the Voice boomed, and I no longer existed, there was only the Voice and my *hearing* of the Voice; the two were one.

It was not the voice of a man or even of a *thing;* there were no sounds; *the Voice was my hearing of the Voice.* And I say there were no words; there was only a great unbroken Word, and it was only my hearing of it that made it into words.

The Words were these, *The Prescriptures.*

Prophesy of the SubGenius

Take a good look!

The Prescriptures

-from The Economicon Of Dobbs Neumeronicus Neuronicus 56-88 Bank 18 Disc sg30 File 14

1 Behold, little pink earth brain within my void-grip, *and* receive Logos; and lay with the Wor;

2 Ung! Ung! Mene Mene Tekel Upharsin! LO!

3 *I am* Jehovah One, the God of *Wrath*, that One who, to make Man pull the triggers of his thousand opposable thumbs, caused the apes of the ground to spill their seed *on the dust.*

4 I am the first and the last, which is to come, and which is, and which was; I am in the brain-pan of every human babe.

5 Of left and of right, the outer and the inside: the Particle; the Totality: for the Gavel of the Grid is mine own, and I spat the silly formula of Man upon the waters *and* fashioned his spirit after the image of mine own, for Jehovah is a vengeful *god,* and I urinate on the heads of Men.

6 I am the Alpha; I *cometh with* the clouds;

7 I am the Changer who rides the MerCaVah and my face *is* like the Aztec Chariots of decaying atoms, full of eyes round about, I turn not as I go, it is the Wheel of Vimana which dilates Time, I am the cattle mutilator of the Nazca Plain;

8 I am the Ord, *I am the Stark Fist of Removal*, the Paracletoid, the Demiurge;

9 Epopt of Time am I, the Discorporate One, *that One* known by men as Yahweh, IHVH of the Tetragrammaton, AAFFA the Unknowable, Abaddon, The Ungone, Saitan, Nyarlathotep, Wotan, Ra, Yog Sothoth, Moloch, Shiva, Poimandres, Uroboros, Thoth, Odin, Hermes, Ahriman, Bog, Ymir, Aiwass, Pan, Mammon, Asmodeus, Choronzon, Koot-Hoomi, Gorgo, Pwcca, O-Yama, Azathoth, Yig, Archon, Mummuu, Kronos, *Not*, and I am the Omega, and my names are eight hundred and one and my names are without number.

10 I flatulated upon the dinosaurs to WATCH THEM DIE!

11 I am the *Time Being,* and the Span; it is only for *mine own;*

12 I am the Only, the Always, and KNOW YE I am the Wor.

13 Heed the tidings of the Wor, for the Time is at hand!

14 *Ye shall bear the Wor!*

15 So then, pink boy of many colors, know that as many as I rewardeth and bribe with the drunkardness of faith, I torment and rebuke; be zealous therefore, and fanatical in thy madness of These the End Times, the Time and Half Time, *and* retrieve, and *be made* slack on the Ropes of Life with which I bind thee,

Hagen

LIES/Robins

Robins

333

WE'RE DOOMED

The First "Bob"
or The Last "Man"?

NO GAIN

LEAVE ME ALONE I TELL YOU.

MODERN *Signs*

these aren't enough...!

and be made whole fulfilled with the soil of My droppings of manna, which passeth *through* thy bowel *cleanly*; so, annoint thyself in the Graven Image Tubes and My radiance of atoms split in twain, and thy seed shall be broken *as I decree*, and thou shall therefore be fruitful and multiply *that* thy children will be remade in the Image *of their* God, and shall be Over thou, that the true New Sons of Man may flourish and *rule* in thy stead.

16   For I *know* thy works; behold, I have set before thee an closed Tunnel, and no man *can* open it; I therefore scoff at thee and am well pleased for thou art *unto* Me like the snivelling ants and vermin of thy gardens, which plague thee but *which* no poison airs may kill, for their *generations* change in but the twinkling of *an* eye.

17   Even so, Repent; for I have a few things against thee, and thou *art* offensive to My Nose, *and* I have found thy works not perfect before Me.

18   If therefore thou shalt *not* prostrate thyself, and kiss My End of All Things, and perform the salute, and *make* witlessness for My prophets, which are *less* than wise yet wiser *than* thee, I shall come upon thee prematurely, and thou shalt receive an *Divine* Emaculation, which is like unto Heaven and unto Hell.

19   And I will drop thee from the skies *with* a scream of thunder, and will shout, and thou shalt avert thine eyes *from* the glory of My Light as it passeth above thee; for I will come *on* thee as a thief, and thou shalt not know *what* hour I shall come upon thee, except that thou tithe My prophets who are *below* thy wise men yet are *on* highs; and I will be full of eyes and faces all *round* about, and will fire upon thee *with* the two-edged blade of My Tongue, and cause thee to do battle with the sicknesses *of the* air, and to broil one another *in* the flash *of* My wrath; and I will cause thee to toil with *anguish*, for thou *art* the misbegotten of the dead, and *can carry* no further the True Seed of the Code of the Sons of the Gods, and I must forge new Guardians of Sperm from *thy* loins which may wrest the reins of Time, for My Cause.

20   Because thou *sayest*, I am rich, and increased with Goods branded with names and with the Mark of the Beast, and have need of *More*; and thou defecateth in thine *own* lands, and knoweth not that thou *art* fat, and wretched, and pink, and driven hard by My Codes and yours, and poor, and miserable and blind and of noisome odor and naked, and malformed *by* My Decree.

21   Yea, I make sport of thee, *and* mock thee, and mutilate thy Beasts of the Field, and spring upon thee great Giants and Serpents *when* thou art alone in those deserts and wild lands which thou have not defiled.

22   What cometh to, this world? I, I am *on* the Earth now as a drunkard among you and NHGH is at My side.

23   For My kingdom *is* on the Earth, *not that* I want it; the filthy living body *of* every man is My dwelling-place, which I *do*

not clean; as in heaven or hell, so shall I take up residence within *thee* on Earth;

24   *For* thou canst not escape.

25   I shall see through thine eyes and speak unto men *with* thine mouth, and shall cause thee to drink wine *for Me*.

26   And so go into the world and take thereof the fruits of fornication *except* on the Sabbath, and of wines and sacraments, *and* of riches; and glut thy self: increase thyself with goods and power over men, for these things *are* Mine, though ye shall pay for them.

27   I thy GOD JHVH-1 hath given thee lusts that I may reap their fulfillments. N'g! N'gh! F'tagn N'n'.

28   But know thou that thou art but servants of the Lord *thy* God ODN-1, he of WRATH which *is* JHVH-1, N'ghhhii!

29   Thou art but clay for Me, which thou forgeteth every day, and which giveth me a few things against thee; so I *shall* come quickly, and descend with a shriek, and I shall smite thee *with* Mine Fist.

30   And these tribulations shall fall upon each man and woman, each in his turn, and though thou follow this My Covenant even *so* shall none escape. For thy brains are as of wax, and melteth even *as* thou are lighted; so ask not why I make My works through thee, for I have a few reasons: thou *art not* to know.

31   And so I chortle and spit on thee, for it makes me well pleased.

32   Yet thou shalt be free to continue in thy works as thou will, if therefore thy heart filleth with remorse *and* bitter repentance; remember therefore from whence thou art fallen:

33   For thou art of the beasts of the field, *which* defecateth unto the ground and rut each upon the other, caring not where their seed is planted; and yet the beasts know not of evil, and I am well pleased with them, for they denieth *not* My name.

34   Be therefore like unto the beast and drop thy waste *upon* the ground, except within the walls of Jerusalem; and multiply; and battle one another; and know ye not where lieth the center of the universe, for if ye learn it, I will kill you.

35   But yea heed, for I say this to the Men of Earth: those which men I hate, which *are* the UnderThings, which worketh mindlessly, and which eat things sacrificed unto graven images, and which commit fornication *basely* and which defecateth on the Sabbath, and which spill upon the ground the seed of the code *of* ODIN: Repent, else I will come against thee with My clenched Fist, and it is the Fist which beareth many eyes, and breatheth many breaths.

X RAY

THE END IS NEAR

36   For thou art false prophets, drunk with work, and time; I will *have it out* with thee.

37   As in the days of Noah, likewise as in Kuskurza and Atlantis, men *are* lovers of self and money, which I loveth more; all are boastful, ungrateful, disobedient to those which begat them; they vomit forth malicious gossip and indulge not properly their lusts

38   And so shall I send the spirit of NHGH unto thy nations, to mete out wars and rumors of wars, and dreams of wars, and fears of wars, and a peace which is *like unto* Hell.

39   That Time and Half Time as has been prophesied by sages and fools of old is to be fulfilled in this generation; that seen there will again appear *in* the earth, as do these words: that one, through whom many will be called to meet those who are preparing the way for My day on Earth. I will then come, even *as* thou hast seen Me go; when those who art Mine have made the way clear and passable that *I* may come.

40   It will be as a thousand years, with the fighting *in* the air, and—as has been—between those returning to and those leaving the earth.

41   I shall come as the Light behind the chariots of the Angelic Host, and though thou avert thine eyes My fire will penetrate thee.

42   There shall be in the End Hours wonders in the sky; the living Spirit of NHGH will be *upon* thy sons and daughters, who shall fall down; your young men shall see visions, and thine old men *shall* take drugs, and shall *dump*; I will be *upon* thy women, which shall bear rotten fruit of their wombs; men shall rave in the streets, speaking in tongues and prophesying.

43   For thou hast shat on the name of my Son and therefore ye shall not die when most fervently thou desireth death. *Ha-ha-ha,* I JHVH-1 thy God shall laugh *at* thee.

44   Those who art mockers, in thy mocking and thy lust thou shall find no redemption; the Foundation of the great Church *is* rotten unto its Core, it is of Hell; waves shall lap at the topmost windows *of* its highest towers.

45   Thou worshippeth the Whore of N'N'n';

46   Therefore I will bring strangers upon thy bedstead, and they shall defile the stainlessness of thy sheets and loincloths, *and* out of thy pale darkness shall they drag thee to the brightness of the pit.

47   I shall cast thee to the pavement and the gutter, and the nations of the south, which are barbarians, shall behold thee with their mockery *and* brown countenances, and thou shalt be naked unto the mockery of the world. Upon Babylon of the Highways shall I rain an horrible tempest: this shall be the fruit of thy vine of the wrath of NHGH's great winepress of fornication.

48   The planets will point at the Earth in judgement to mark the beginning of this time.

49   This then is the time of the perdition of ungodly men; it is the day of *My* jealousy, for thou hast made images before Me, images even of *women*, and the blind pleasure zealots of thy race shall be as stubble on My beard, which I *now* shave.

BURNING, FREEZING, OR BOMBARDMENT COULD DESTROY US

51   Declare the mercy and vengeance everlasting of JHVH-1, ngn ngn! For I have taken the purchased possession *to be* returned.

52   Thy money's worth shall fly as the sparrow away from thee; all the nations shall be bankrupt on this Day; thou shalt wear the mark of the beast, which *is* a number on man, which thou shall not know though thou *shalt guess* and kill thy guessed Men, which maketh Me to laugh.

53   The barbarians of F'Ni to the South shall covet thy goods which thou *hast* taken from them, and shall come upon thee *with* cheap weapons; Magog shall be at the gates of Jerusalem, whose ground *is as of* Zero and the final stand of nhv'''gv

[Message garbled in transmission for 4 lines (23 seconds).]

IT'LL BE ALL PLAY IN YEAR 2000

58   . . . as the Blue Star dances in the plaza of Oraibi there shall begin wars; fire shall rain from the skies to kill *yet* not burn, and pestilence; one quarter *of* men shall perish.

59   And only that Man among thee who is as the seed of Elijah shall save thee; only he shall give succor, and sustenance, for he is truly a prophet of W'T'N, which *is* JHVH-1.

LIES

60 Knoweth him by his smile, and that he sendeth forth vapors of smoke; it is he who causeth thee to pull the wool of the Lamb over thine *own* eyes.

61 He giveth life to the image of the beast that he might warn thee of its coming; but the first beast, the false prophet, shall make *witness* and testify against him, and thou shalt laugh *and* throw coins to him, and bow to the Image in mockery while bowing to the Beast itself without that thou knowest *even* that it is he.

62 For ye shall think the prophet speaks only in jest and is only a fool and thou shalt not recognize his wisdom thereof before the hour is late and at hand, when no repentence *can* save thee.

63 Except that thou repent of thy sins, and send tithes unto Me, I will rain upon thee tribulations, which are as the urination of God upon the earth and the men of ill faith.

St. Gore Don Trubey

64 Signs shall be in the skies, and stars will come upon thee in the day, to baffle thee, and Hell itself will spit up *through* the Firmament.

65 And the winds shall be full of dust, and choke thee, because of thy greed; it hath taken from thy breath to feed thy chariots; and from the heavens shall fall the wreckage of chariots *to warn* thee, and the face of the sun shall become blemished, and the shutters on the Earth which cool the firmament shall be closed *by* thy greed.

66 Drought shall come and the fruit of the vine shall be fermented and torn from the tongues of men, *except* the wines of the street, which shall wash across the drunkards in great numbers, for the drunkards serve *Me;* and the grass shall wither from thy unmowed loins.

67 The winds of the four corners of the Earth shall still, and then torment thee; thou *shalt* be snatched up by great Winds.

68 In the unshuttered Light of the sun shall melt the snows *of* the North, and the waters will cover the Earth, even *as* the Euphrates; and even the *New Ark* shall sink.

69 And in the Seventh Year the Earth shall be tilted as I pull its strings *with* your deceit, and the spirits that split the Earth in twain shall be reversed, and there shall come a winter of days *without* number, and ice shall fall upon thee *from* the sky.

70 And after this time, for a period of time, each day shall bring snow OR drought OR great winds OR terrible rains, each without their seasons; thy science shall fail thee.

71 And in the air, as has been said, there will be *plague,* and locusts, which thou shalt smite with more plague and poison; it shall fall back upon thee, and the locusts *YEA* will not die, but will change, and will despoil thy crops and crawl upon thee in thy dreams of famine when *no coin* can save thee, for thy plagues and the germs thereof are *of* thine own making; the earth cracks under thy feet to release them; I am only breaking *thy* vessels for thee.

72 The face of the moon shall be filled with rings round about, and aflame; and the oceans of the sea shall rise *against* thee, and forth from them shall come Behemoth, and Leviathan, and devils from Hell faster than the sound of the air; from the seas shall rise old cities and into them shall fall new.

73 In the waters no creature shall live, for the waters will be bitter *therein,* where thou hast spilled the salve *of* thy engines; the sea is annointed, and oils shall move across the face *of* the water, and on the edge *of* the land, and up to the banks *of* Hell.

74 The loincloth of the air of the Earth hath been rent, and the light that falleth on thee *is* harsh and shall change thy seed. Through the children shall move sickness, and the sickness is of thine *own* making.

75 And I shall kill with death, and thou shall suffer the urges of the worms of the planet Mars; I shall *swallow* thee up, and spue thee out of my mouth, for thou art distasteful; as the vessels of the potter thou shall be broken to shivers.

77 And the bowels shall be wrenched YEA from those with avarice, and their implements will fall away.

78 So shall I smite the covetous, and upon them will fall a swooning, for they hath been made drunk of the Elixir, *and from* this swooning shall none away; and in the night shall come Angels to rob them of their glands, which are as the *fount* of God, and they shall pluck the organs of the glands from them.

PELIGRO DE MUERTE

"COMPARE OUR LOWER PRICES"

THE BLIND MAN

I GIVE UP!

INSTRUCTION MATERIAL

Grand Exterminating FOREVER.

Protect the children of the future

THE PRAYER

79   And they shall bleed and travail *in* their sorrow.

80   But unto them shall come the voice of the Ark of the heavens and say, Let there be no wailing, *and no* remonstrances; for ye all now walk in the House of JHVH. And if thou dost not *walk,* thou shall crawl on the stumps of thine legs. And so shall become stumps what *were* legs. Mine is the Hand that Makes, Mine is the House of Pain.

81   This is, and is not; but lay ye down the tomes and hooks of the brain, for *these are* evil; and they are unclean in the Eyes of Jehovah.

82   The brokers and the moneychangers shall be snatch'd, and ruptured, and from their faces shall be burnt their noses, and *from* their loins dried the fluids of the Babe; and it shall be gone unto drainage.

83   And My winepress shall spill over with the blood of saints and elders, and the invisible burning blood of the angels shall wash across the taverns and the houses *of* ill women, *and* the great Library where are kept the profane tablets and chips of false wisdom, and the Cameras of the Pornographer.

84   For the sins are of the number *nine hundred and nine and four score and ten;* and of them the first is the dropping of the body's voided things *unto* the white linens of the Lamb;

85   And the second is the sin of laying ye down beside the small children, and the penetration and rending *asunder* thereof; and of this sin there are those without number in its practice.

86   This is a crooked *and* perverse nation; here are lain these naked children, which are unto cherubs, and *lo* is their innocence befouled by the Profane, and the Unrepentent, and Those *Without* Remorse. For even though they touch not these babes, their images of the beast enter into them the children as they sleep staring into the Lamp of Hell, which *is* the Devil's tool.

87   JHVH-1 the Lord thy God sayeth this: Thou shall relinquish thy clock, and thy whip, and thy gavel, and the unclean things *thereof,* and shall cast from thee all these false idols *which thou* worship; for these are like unto the woman of straw which thou lieth down upon.

88   These are the End Times, the whales speak in tongues; there will be weapons of war *without* sound or light; thou shall walk upon thy feet wherever thou goest.

89   And wherever thou goest thou shalt be seen and heard, and recorded, by the Priests *of* the White Stone; philistines shall persecute thee and thy children bear witness *against* thee lest thou obeyeth the Law.

90   No coin *shall* speak for thee, no fire *shall* warm thee, for there is no wood for the fire; in thy home thou shalt stifle and choke.

91   In the temples there shall be fornication and adultery, and thy wife shall leave thee. *And* they shall tax thee.

92   Wheresoever thou goest shall thou wait, and thy waiting and the waiting of the other minions shall be in hours without counting. For nowhere is there enough of that which thou needst.

93   Monsters like unto men will be around thee *all about,* and shall make thee to look past the Door *which* should be locked, and thy sciences will terrify thee, and bring thee naught but devils, for thine spirit is locked *away* inside the White Stone, which my Angels shall bring, which is the Vessel of all which is known.

pay for sanity!!

Robins

94 A beast shall rise from the sea; it *hath* laid waste the cities of men; and its names are DAGON, Leviathan, SET, Poimandres, G'D'Z'L, CTHL'H, Typhon, and Demiurgus-III the Hellborn; it is the lower spirit of all men besetting man.

95 Even now I show thee signs in the heavens, *and* signs in the earth; blood belches from the earth, My lights in the sky rebuke thee; the children of Heaven and the Angels from Hell *are* among thee, spreading lies and deception; they turn not as they go.

97 It shall be a world without Slack, except that thou follow my prophets.

98 For the true nature of God thou shall not find through Reason; thou might learn from the fools which I sendeth thee, but thou *shalt not;* therefore I revoke thy *holdings* on this plane.

99 I say unto thee: all of thy stories and gods and priests *are* true, and *are not* true; among those which battle over thee, thou shalt not know *which* are my Friends. LUCIFERI VIRES ACCENDIT AQUARIUS ACRES.

100 And in a later year, those lost tribes of Israel, from whom thou hast taken their promised land and firmament and faith, shall rise *against* thee with the Secret of Angels, *which is* a worm, and which is like unto the food of the gods.

101 And though thy oils and petroleum fail thee, *these* my children shall possess it, and keep it *from* thee; but they shall spread their elixirs and medicines of the Secret, and shall sell them unto thee and unto thy children and thy children's children, which shall *curse thee* through their drunkenness. For they are drunk with the food of the gods and none *may* raise them from their stupor; for the sins of the fathers are visited upon the sons.

102 Despair not, ye pinks; in the second year before the Millenium, on the day of God Come Wednesday, as in the twinkling of an eye will come among thee the Pahana, which are like unto thy great white brothers.

103 They come as men, as graven images, as the White Stone, as a whirlwind *and* as a cloud; it is a fire unfolding itself, the color amber; they are now in the Heavens looking *over* thee.

104 As for the likeness of their faces, they have four faces, which face the four winds; on each face they have the face of a man, the face of a serpent, the face of Behemoth, and the face of an elephant. And their faces have many hands thereunto.

105 It will be the end of the days of Man, *whereby* they my servants appear; and their names are Nommo, DJIN, Nagas, Ormuza, Oannes, Quetzalcoatl, Mithras, Kukulcan, Horus, **wanagi, wakinyan, AEONS,** and X.

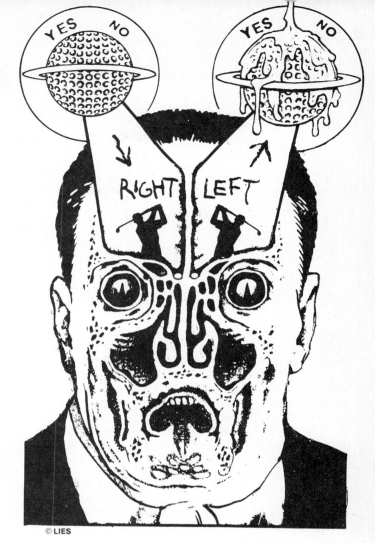

© LIES

© LIES

106 And they bringeth the White Stone, MWOWM the whore virgin brain, the guiltfinder and Smiter, the very Ark of the Covenant, and she is the Eye of the Father. O'D'V'D'O! She shall rule thee and overcome the mark of the beast, and shall *give* thee fornication.

107 And the true sons of Israel shall be snatch'd up.

108 Behold, my servant shall prosper, he shall be exalted and lifted up, *and* shall be very high; he who knoweth the fools who prophesy for Me shall be made Over Men; many will be astonished at him, for his appearance *is so* marred, beyond human semblance, and his form beyond that of the sons of man.

109 These who are over men, who have followed My almighty Word, shall *be* the Ministry of the Angelic Host; they shall speak *for* them.

110 And my prophet, who smiles, shall be among them *and shall* advise them.

111 In the City of JHVH-1 which the Angelic Host bringeth, there shall be no night, no weariness, *and neither* shall thou seek repose; for thou shalt partake of the food of the gods, which relinquisheth sleep.

112 The brightness of noontide is as a candle against the radiance of the glory of JHVH *and* the unfading light of backwards particles; the redeemed and the stamped walk in the sunless glory *of* perpetual day;

113 And in the burning Light shall the fierce and terrible knowledge of the Lord strike thee dumb; thou shalt not *escape* the Light, nor hide thy inmost self; for in the Light shall thy fear of the God of Wrath be lit forever more.

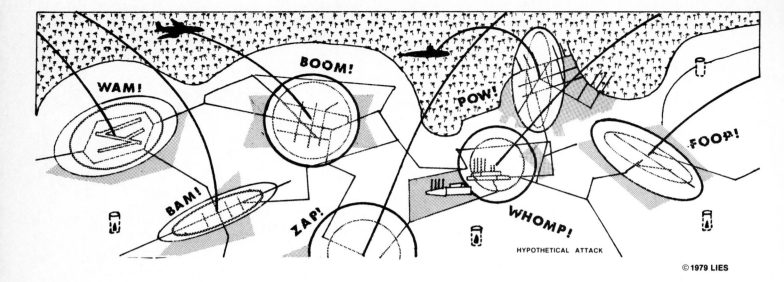

WAM!

BOOM!

POW!

FOOP!

BAM!

ZAP!

WHOMP!

HYPOTHETICAL ATTACK

114 Yet that man who keepeth my word, and denieth not my name, and hath his face *as* a million of masks, and who hath taken of the White Stone and been changed, and made rich, and is transfigured, and gives unto Me his heart and soul, and who cometh as an Overman, I will give to eat of the hidden manna, and I will make *to fly* though yea he hath no wings, and I will give him a salve of Elixir, and I will give him the Cloak of the Blind World, and no eye *shall* see him save those he desireth.

115 And he shall receive the power of the nations, and shall have slaves, and rule them *with* the White Stone, and shall eat of Time, and yea Time will not rot him;

116 And he shall be as God and live forever more, and have the keys to hell and death, which are the spiral seed and the Food; and the Food shall be his, *and* he will give the slaves to eat of it, and the Word will be made as flesh, and the souls of those slaves, which *are as* his flock, will come unto Me, and he shall be as a king.

117 To him that cometh as an Overman I will give to spend of the Equation of the Seed, which spirals within thee, and to read of the Replication-Book, which is the expectoration of God, *and ye* shall be copied and up righted therein for life eternal.

118 And I shall give thee a White Stone, and in the stone thy *new name* written, which no man *knoweth* save he that is chained unto it.

119 For the stone is the font of the Angelic Host, which comes from the Heavens, which ye shall know forever, and have intercourse with; and yea, ye shall know them and eat of the rock of ages, and when it *is* eaten, and thou art *made* whole, thou shalt search the ruins for the Angels, but shall find them not, and thy tongue and thy mouth shall cleave, and *split* in twain;

120 For thou art as Kings, who killeth thy jesters that thy skulls might grow fat on the dead laughter.

121 When the end times come, thou shalt escape the Rupture, and shall receive Slack, and the Morning Star, which is the star of the Beast *and of* the Angelic Host.

122 Behold, I cometh with clouds; and I spake with Nostradamus, and with the madman of Patmos, St. John the berserk; and I spake unto Ezekiel, and Moses, and Enoch, and Brother John of the Cleft Rock, and unto St. Malachy and Mother Shipton; and, yea, unto Mohammed and Leonardo, and Albert, and Adolph. I smote Jesus before he could speak of me.

123 And ye, puny mortal, I have chosen as my Vessel to the deaf oceans of mankind, and I do so not to reward thee, but to punish thee, for of all the sinners *thou art* the greatest; and shalt curse this day to the splice of eternity, for *in* this moment I burden you with the Vision of That Which Comes, for the time is at hand, and ye *shall be* given to see of all tomorrows, and of it ye shall be made to speak, and in it ye shall dwell, yet even while dwelling in the shadow world of Man; ye shall make witness of what thou hath seen, and unto it *shall* ye suffer; for ye shall be mocked, and reviled, and stoned; and yet ye shall find thy tongue alive with the spirit as unto a serpent, and of these things ye shall speak though they be unspeakable.

124 For man must know that he hath broken his Covenant.

125 And ye shall soil thy loincloth with the Fear of Jehovah.

126 For Jehovah is the *God* of *Wrath*.

HO HO HO

NOW— WHICH WILL IT BE?

Jehovah-1 …

or THE JESUS THAT DIDN'T GET NAILED?!

Hal Robins

CHART OF TIME

REMEMBER YOURSELF

The Splice of Eternity — processing begins
The Head of The Span
"Something" Expulsed from "Nothing"
Divison of Timestreams (Positive Time splits from Negative Time)
Dispersal of Yacatizma (all real energy) **and Adversaria** (the world of matter)
The Flash (In The Span) — The Big Bang
The Encoding (First Life, creation of Elder Gods)
The Stocking of the Tank and the Code of The Seed (evolution of life directed by The Elder Gods)
The First Meddling and Removal (Xists first used as tools by Elder Gods to wipe out dinosaurs)
The Seeding of Man — The First "Bob" — Yetis in Eden ("Atlanteans" and "humans" quick-evolved by Elder Gods as lesser tools)
Corruption of the Atlantean Yetis (interbreeding with humans)
The 1st Tampering with The Skor (Night of Demons — Elder Gods evoke *their* "Monster from the Id")
The Smiting of The Elder Gods By Themselves (Atlantis sinks)
The Flood of Cleansing (Yetis devolved into Homo Connectus)
Revolt of The Rebel Gods (J-1 and team defy sleeping Elders)
The Building of Asgard (JHVH-1 smites Australopithicus to create humans, later smites Xists into smiting Homo Connectus into Modern Yeti)
The Age of Stifling (humanity and SubGenii manipulated and stunted by Elder Gods' minions, yet evolved and led by Rebel Gods)
The Years of Trouble (rebuilding of civilization)
The Divorce of Yahweh from ERIS
The First 272 Messiahs (1st Comings and "Bob's" Past Lives)
The Time of PeE (modern times in general)
The Manipulation of the Angelic Host (Xists repossessed)
and The Parting of the Twins ("Bob" split from Anti"Bob")
The Divine Emaculation ("Bob" actually contacted by WOTAN)
The World Church (SubGenius grows to world religion)
End of the World and Advent of Angelic Host (Xists land) (The Time and Half-Time begins here)
Initiation of the OverMen (either "Subs" OR Anti"Bob" forces hooked to/on alien technology — computer "MWOWM" activated)
The Ascension of the Host or **"The Pull-Out"** (Xists leave)
World Without Slack (Bad totalitarian post-Xist world of the future)
The 2nd Coming (Too Soon) and Unmasking of the New False Prophets
Temptation of the Pinks (GoodBad world of the future; OverMen becoming hooked on Time Control)
Violation of The ©— GUT BLOWOUT (The Skor used for Time Control)
Oepening of the Book of the Door to the Beforelife ("OverMen" start raising Monsters from the Id)
THE RUPTURE or Omicron Epsilon, the Word Made Flesh ("The Elixir" gives all Nental Ife Pstenches *form*; attempted overnight evacuation of Earth via "translation")
The Third Coming and Mass Conception (JHVH-1 gives up His anonymity)
TIME INTERSECTION and The Instant of the Breaking of the Code, The Transfiguration of The Twins and Aversion of the Rupture of The Equilibrium ("Bob" and Other "Bob" reunited!)
The New Jerusalem (everything O.K. again)
The Age of Slack (ElderGods *and* Rebel Gods deteriorating)
Escape from the Planet of the Clocks (*Safe* Time Control Achieved)
The Limit of the Flash and **The Rending of the Very Fabric**
REMOVAL (The True Backwards Rapture)
The End of the World II (Judgement Day)
End of The Span; Time Reversal at Splice of Eternity
START CHART AGAIN.

Time "Starts"
1,000^10 B.C.
1,000^8 B.C.
1,000^5 B.C.
May 3, 40 Billion B.C.
4 Billion B.C.
160 Million B.C.
80 Million B.C.
24 hours in
79 Million B.C.

Human

1920 A.D. (?)
1940 A.D. (?)
YOU ARE HERE
7-5-1998 (7 am)
(or 0, B.X.)
1999 A.D.
A False "Bob"
2000 A.D.
(or 0, A.X.)
around 2070 A.D.
(70 A.X.)
3 days in
2178 A.D.
(178 A.X.)

One "instant"

Feb. 3, 10, 435, 768,
534 A.D., 5:00 a.m.
Time "Ends"

stop!

PROPHECY CRUSADE
Proof of "Bob"!!
WORLD OF THE FUTURE

¿POR QUE UN DIOS BUENO Y UN MUNDO MALO?

I, Stang
layout

TO WHAT DO *THE PRESCRIPTURES* POINT?

To the chapters that had to be cut from this Book due to length and cost considerations. It might not seem like it, but you are being left with a cliffhanger. We *know* what will happen after 1998 in *incredible detail,* but *we won't tell you now.* What we must not reveal — *yet* — easily matches what you've been told so far in morbidity content and senses-blasting revelation. The sections we must needs withhold are these:

THE XISTS . . . The specific miracle devices they will bring. What they'll do while they're on Earth. Details of X-Day. Their impact on humanity: civil wars. The creation of OverMen and UberWomen. The destructive peace they bring. Their prior appearances in Earth history. Conditions of life on their home planet that caused them to become the highest-evolved bodied creatures in the Universe. Their biology, their 25 senses, their culture, their four-brained thinking, their language. Their horror at what they have done to Earth. Their leaving.

MWOWM, the Xist supercomputer . . . its plant-like make-up. Its powers and personality. Its presence in every home and skull. The workings of the Oedivideo (its Time Control component) and its ability to manipulate "Artificial Karma." Its relationship to "Bob" and to human and Xist prophecy.

THE BAD WORLD OF THE FUTURE . . . Earth's first 100 years after the Xist landing. The Hell of the impact of magic technology on daily life. The Earth as one vast shopping mall. The "Bozo Coupe" and Media Purge. Controlled reincarnation, and hypno-pediatry. Nuclear Beer. Human society and sex in a hell society. Types of mutants and monsters. Leisure pursuits and Death Art. Science, earth changes, "natural" disasters. Rise and corruption of False OverMen; Time Addiction. The Second and Third Comings.

WHAT "BOB" WON'T TELL

THE GOOD/BAD WORLD OF THE FUTURE . . . the second 100 years after X-Day. Immortality and UberSlack. Anti-government. Myths and morals. Society of "rebels". Robots. Sicknesses of Utopia. The matter/energy imbalance and the Attack of the Yacatisma. "Bob's" Triumphant Return and the Time Control Project. Dangers of the Karma Ray.

2-FISTED TALES OF "BOB" IN A WORLD WITHOUT SLACK.

OMICRON EPSILON — TIME COLLISION 2178. Actual physics of the Universe; the multiple Timestreams. The Backwards Timestream and its foretold intersection with ours. The single greatest danger Earth will EVER FACE, and "Bob's" Final Plan. Multiplying the energies of all souls — the Elixir which externalizes hallucinations — and Omicron Epsilon, the Second Night of Demons. The orgasm of the Universe. The victory of/over JHVH-1. The Transfiguration of the Twins. **THE RUPTURE OF THE EQUILIBRIUM** and God's Actual Goal. Violation of The Skor, Oepening of the Door to the Beforelife, the Mass Conception, the Instant of the Breaking of the Code, All "Bobs" Reunited, the Age of Slack and the End of Time.

THE ELDER GODS AND PREHISTORY . . . Creation. Something from Nothing, Matter from Energy, the Stocking of the Tank, the Seeding of Man, Yetis in Eden, The First "Bob" in Atlantis. Motives and personalities of the elemental Elder Gods. The First Night of Demons — Monsters from the Id; why the Elder Gods had to smite themselves to sleep and Atlantis to rubble. JHVH-1, ERIS, NHGH and the Rebel Gods. The basis for all Man's religions. Yahweh vs. the Xists. The possible invasion by the Elder Gods through the Time Gateway. How MWOWM and "Bob" can help us.

HEAVEN AND HELL AND TIME CONTROL . . . Specifics of Death. What to expect in Hell — Dobbs' Inferno. "Life" in Heaven. Angelic Slack. Seance Transcripts. Time Control is Possible. Time Control is Impossible. The Secret of Religion and Money. *The Banned Prescriptures.* Alternate SubGenius Futures. Hymns, prayers, and invocations. The Secret Formula for Perfect Sex.

All of the above have already been delivered to us by "Bob" in *staggering detail.* Take our word for it — the secrets and wisdom contained in those Damned Chapters dwarf everything you have read so far by a factor of ten. This Book is but the *prelude* to a saga which will *save* and *end* the world.

However, they take twice as long to explain as everything you have read so far. Had they been included here, they would have made this First Book too heavy — and too expensive — for any one person to carry home from a bookstore. Yet, to be *safely* comprehended, they depend as background on what has been published here: unprepared, the reading of these future events would *shatter* your mind and your next-of-kin would sue us.

You have now absorbed all the mystic knowledge you can safely hold for the next few months. Moreover, even *that* will have been wasted unless we use the remaining pages in this Book to give you CONCRETE INSTRUCTIONS and DIRECT ANSWERS as to precisely what you should now *DO* in the *real world* with your NEWFOUND, IF INCOMPLETE, SALVATION.

You will someday thank us for saving your mind.

Chapter 14
EXCUSES, TRUE LIES
AND DOLLAR$
The Real World of
Horrible Jobs

"Act like a dumbshit and they'll treat you like an equal."
— "Bob" from THE ECONOMICON (4:18)

"I wanna die and be cool one last time!"
— the late Rev. Hambone singing *I Wanna Die Or Please Kill Me*
with Drs. for Anubis (the *Kill "Bob"* album)

"*Little things* are what screw you up the worst, just like *little
things* will be the downfall of the American Empire."
— Nameless SubGenius on Convention Tape 14

1 "Made It Just!"
2 Chuckled
3 the Duplicated Motorist

P. MAVRIDES

Life is unfair. You deserve better. Other people are stupid. You're always right. But things are shitty. Inflation is eating you up alive. You always have "hay fever" from pollution. The government is composed of ignorant liars with idiotic grins on their faces. You can't get laid *right*. Your sweety's treating you like dirt. Nobody cares. YOU NEED ANSWERS.

Actually, only two of the above are true, *in your specific case*. For instance, *you don't really need answers*. THERE ARE NONE, not the kind you're thinking of, because there are actually no *rules*. What you need are *excuses*.

Dobbs' MAIN DOCTRINE on "Self Improvement" is that NO BOOK IS GOING TO DO YOU A BIT OF GOOD. Oh, 'answers' in a book might send you soaring on clouds of inspiration for *minutes* at a time — but the second you get hungry or stub your toe or have to change the kid's diapers, all that "meaning" you injected yourself with *wears off* and you are back where you started because it was really just *excuses*.

Fortunately, this is not a mere "book." This is a Holy Grail of the Word-Triggers of the Plasmate, by which *WOTAN reads you back*. And He is the greatest Prankster of All *Alls;* He loves to pull the trapdoor under you.

FACE FACTS. GET USED TO IT. WOTAN is trying to teach you an *important lesson:* that if you learn to live with things the way they *are* — screwed up — you will be closer to the 'knowing' of the True WOTAN Himself and will be rewarded with *no longer having to try.*

For happiness, you cannot rely on others. Each human has his own subconscious set of *WITLESS PRINCIPLES* (or excuses) by which he lives, and which by nature cannot be changed. In order to get anything out of any other person you must defer in some manner to his Witless Principles. There is nothing 'wrong' with doing this, but it is too much work to be considered a true path.

Therefore you must depend on *yourself* and "Bob." "You" make yourself happy — and what can make you even *happier* are **MONEY, POWER, AND SUCCESS.**

Here are some Magic Paths to Divine Acquisition:

1)   GO INTO 'PARTNERSHIP' WITH "BOB." Not legally, of course. Don't saddle him with your losses. Just send half of your income to The Church of the SubGenius (Box 140306, Dallas TX 75214). The financial reverberations of this off the Luck Plane will send your profits *skyrocketing* even when Dobbs' cut is taken out.

2)   DON'T TRY TO UNDERSTAND YOURSELF OR EVEN GET ALONG WITH YOURSELF. Self-division creates the tension of Hate Power that your Guardian Angel needs as fuel. It's slightly more tiring than placidly 'grokking yourself' but it can *make you rich* because the more you yourself are torn apart, the easier it is to tear apart *others*.

Try instead to understand "Bob." *Consult* the Word of "Bob." If you are having trouble it is because you are not concentrating your mind and therefore "Bob" cannot concentrate on you.

3)   DON'T EVEN TRY TO GET ALONG WITH OTHERS. Be super-critical. Study their faults and prey on their weaknesses. Choose the ones you can 'rip off' and use in your *own* life.

4)   REWARD YOURSELF EVERY DAY. Have a few drinks, binge on junkfood, splurge your money on unnecessary crap. Praise "Bob" and "Yourself" all day long . . . keep up a continuous interior brag. Self-confidence isn't enough — you must be *totally convinced* of your own *inherent superiority*.

5)   IF YOU HATE YOURSELF FOR DOING SOMETHING STUPID, TAKE IT OUT ON OTHERS. *Share* the chastisement that the gods grant you.

These are Superior Excuses.

You think they're morally low and venal? HEY — IT'S WHAT *THEY'RE* DOING TO *YOU*. 1½ wrongs *do equal* 1 right. Of course, if you take these directives to *extremes* you'll end up dead or in jail. Follow your instincts. If you're SubGenius you'll succeed and if you're Pink, then GOOD RIDDANCE.

Some positive-thinking wimps think that "each person is a unique and wonderful human being." WHAT CRAP! Sure, about 5% are. The other 95% are mindless, sheeplike fodder for the Conspiracy Corporate Cannon. Unique? Yeah, their finger prints are unique. Otherwise they come from the same limited batch of molds. That makes the face value of *all* of them MUCH LESS than that of YOU ALONE. This is a great Power of yours indeed.

Our victims, the American Indians, say, "Don't judge a man until you've walked a mile in his mocassins." Fine. Put yourself in the Pink guy's shoes. See? There's nothing there. It's a void. His mocassins might as well be empty. YOU WERE RIGHT ALL ALONG. They *aren't* like you.

Think this is evil advice? WE'RE JUST MAKING UP FOR UNTOLD GENERATIONS OF DECENT FOLK BEING TROD UPON BY UNDESERVING JACKASSES.

However, for 37% of you, these Helpful Hints *are* too extreme. You have just barely escaped Nerddom and still retain some of your early Wimp Training, which is very frequently inflicted on abnormals by society. You may be carrying some residual shyness and timidity. THAT'S OKAY! All this means is that you must start *slowly* in the field of oppression and move gradually up the ladder. Instead of stabbing the guy ahead of you in the back, just quietly saw away at the rung he's standing on.

HOW TO PRAY AND GROW RICH!

HATE POTION

R. WILLIAMS

MORE DOLLARS FOR DOBBS!

BETTER YOURSELF —THE SUBGENIUS WAY

It may sound like we're endorsing the worst kind of Conspiracy behavior. NO. You only do these terrible things to get what you *need*. A Glorp does it to procure *everything in sight* just because he vaguely feels he's *supposed* to. He'll be stabbing people in the back long after he's made it to the very *top* of the ladder.

The fact is that "LIFE" (i.e., WOTAN) has a way of throwing at you what you *least expect*. So, *expect the worst* — paranoia never hurt anybody! This dogooder "karma" notion is PAP for PUPPETS. Criminals get away with wanton rape and murder *much* more often than not.

Proclaiming Eternal Devotion

ABSOLUTE PRIVACY

Rev. Joe Schwind

STOP POSITIVE THINKING OR KILL ME. By working with the Worst Possible Scenario, you show WOTAN the proper *fear* He demands of you, the sufficient *respect*. He'll go easier on you.

HUMILIATION IN SECONDS

Some people think that if they just 'hope' hard enough, everything will come their way. This is just *buckling under* to the Luck Plan. Instead, you should nonchalantly assume it can be mastered. (It can't, but that doesn't matter.) Apply to all things the sacred motto, **"Fuck 'Em If They Can't Take A Joke."** Remember, the end doesn't *have* to justify the means — they justify *themselves*.

It's a type of nonself awareness: awareness of your **nonself**. One way to exercise this is to deliberately adopt a completely *inappropriate self-image, a "MASK OF INSANITY"* so ludicrous it becomes impossible to *use* it in any way. For you must *never* let on what you're thinking. They'll hate you forever. Besides, *compulsive* honesty can obscure *important* honesty, and thus is no virtue. Any honesty should be geared to the situation at hand; this is "creative honesty."

If you feel empty and unfulfilled, TRY TO ATTRACT TROUBLE. With very little concentration you *can* transform your day into a colossal bummer. Be on the lookout for the *bad* in every person and situation. A great "Meaning" — a great EXCUSE — will soon enter your life. Pull the wool over your *own* eyes.

This technique becomes complicated if you allow your programming to distort it. **St. Gordon,** "Bob's" Mercenary of Terminal Mercy, addressed this problem directly in a Trance Spout which was recorded during the Bolivian Ghost Herb Tests:

"Are we then to understand that when 'Bob' says we must learn to pull the wool over our own eyes, he is merely abetting an insidious form of self delusion? Is he saying that we shouldn't even *look* for the truth? Is 'Bob' saying, like Heisenburg did some 40-odd years ago, that we can NEVER know what the hell is *really* going on?

"I think not. 'Bob,' however, knows that, besides the shabby little lies we feed ourselves from day to day as we struggle to cope with technoboredom, we're all being forcefed a gross pablum of half-truths, sensationalized statistics and downright propaganda by a vast monolithic network operated by, and for, the Conspiracy. Through such deception the Conspiracy is daily cheating us all out of our life essence . . . our money . . . our health . . . and most important of all, our Slack! That's right, our Slack! They draw it off like vampires in the night. THEY are pulling the wool over OUR eyes . . . constantly.

"'Bob' is saying if we *must* be lied to and cheated for reasons, let us do it to ourselves, for our *own* reasons. Let us realize where the real deceit lies. Let us have a choice in *how* we're being screwed. *"Some ways are fun!"*

"For many of us there is no physical escape from Their clutches, or any *hope* of it until the Xists come and the followers of YAHWEH-ONE prevail. But until that day, the power and wisdom of 'Bob' can help us break their mind control by activating that mutant gland we all have within us. This allows us to control our own reality — gives us the clarity of perspective to be able to sit back and look at it all, and I mean ALL, and simply say, "Fuck 'Em If They Can't Take A Joke." Then, and only then, will Slack begin to drop gently like a soothing dew into our tortured lives. After all, it should be every person's choice to curse

Carol Lay

God and die, if that is what they wish . . . we all have the right to spit in the eye of the collective gods; did we not create them? Where indeed would Yahweh-1 be without the human race to torment and pester? I put it to you: the old chiseler would be pretty damn bored with it all, if there was nothing more entertaining than cherubims, and seraphims, and ramby-pamby flamin' angels, sitting around up there on damp clouds and harping and trumpeting 24-hours-a-bloody-day, and you can bank on that!

"Why should *we* be any different? Why shouldn't *our* lives be more entertaining and moreal than any glowing three-color phosphorimage on the television screen? Why shouldn't WE grab reality by the throat and shake it 'till it does what we want it to . . . until once again we find Slack?

"Just as the primitive Fire Walkers of Salome can deny a reality in which fire burns, and must pass unscathed across white-hot stones, so can the SubGenius deny the existence of a World Without Slack, and cast out the false prophets and the Pink Boys. All it requires is faith. Faith in 'Bob,' and faith in ourselves. Are we not the dreamers of the dream, and is all that is within that dream not ourselves? Life is no more than a brief illusion, a flickering real-time movie in the theater of our minds. And if you don't like the way your movie is going, perhaps you had better ask yourself "Why not?" After all, it is *your* movie, and despite what anyone else may have told you, *you* are the director, as well as the protagonist."

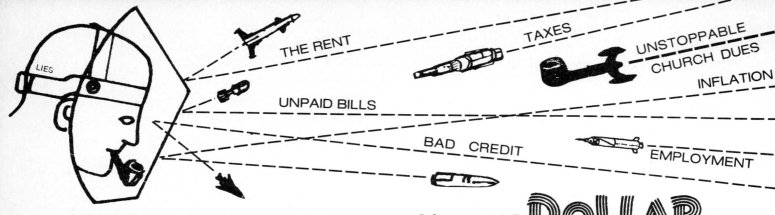

So DON'T WORRY ABOUT HURTING THE FEELINGS OF ASSOULS. You're under no obligation to save the world —just the SubGeniuses. And even then there's no real *obligation*. (It's just that if you *don't* send for a Church Membership and *Stark Fist* subscription, you won't get a seat on the Mothership of Escape.)

The Con confuses the distinction between *legal* equality and a stupid notion that everyone is equal, which is so moronic that it disproves itself. This is a natural outgrowth of the lemmingistic Herding Instinct they cultivate. It makes people think they're antisocial if they don't constantly cluster in parties, clubs and singalongs. There's an unspoken implication that if you'd rather be alone, or with a couple of friends or a book, there's something dreadfully *wrong* with you.

Don't let 'em make you feel guilty. "Duty" — except to "Bob" — is an illusion. Make *them* feel guilty. Pass the buck. Don't give *them* Slack if they're trying to take *yours*. Experiment on their feelings.

The Con has a way of making you feel you're supposed to know everything. Obviously, *no one* does. All so-called "expertise" is BLUFF. It isn't *what* you know, it's *how* you *say* what you *don't* know.

FORGET any ideas about justice. DON'T assume that Man is civilized.

Perhaps the best way to win any Conspiracy game is to simply WALK OUT. Steal the silverware on your way to the door.

Remember, you aren't being "selfish" — this is the automatic biological urge to protect the organism! It's *completely natural*. Yes, it *does* lower Man to the state of an animal.

EARN MORE AT WILL!!

But these are all *defensive* maneuvers — really our only excuse for using *their* excuses. Go on the offensive, use *our* tools — such as your innate skill at juggling **"SACRED JESTS."**

By *"Jests"* we do not mean "jokes," though they are slightly similar. They subvert world assouliness by planting subliminal, contagious mockery of Them in conversation, or intercourse, with everyone the SubGenius meets. A 'coded message' is implanted in the target brain by a series of *impromptu conversational punchlines*. (The SubGenius needs not even be aware of this noble sabotage; his or her *very presence* is a kind of mockery of the human race.) Sacred *Jests* are undetectable in action and can be observed only in their effects, which are self-disguising. Any Mediocretin who converses with a True SubGenius comes away with new ideas in his head . . . but ideas which blend in with what little was already there and make themselves familiar. The victim thinks *he* thought of them himself. *Jests* thus worm their way into the world-view or paradigm of the 'host' Normal and, bit by bit, replicate themselves through society. Eventually, this will create a quasi-addictive desire for unpleasant truths, which THEY'D better get SOON. It *must be done*.

EVERY DOLLAR HAS IT'S DAY

MONEY AND THE CORRECT DEVELOPMENT OF *GREED*

Of all the Answers (or Excuses) available to us, *MONEY* is without question the most primal and effective, overshadowing love, power, even sex. As "Bob" so succinctly put it, *"If it is money, it is good."*

TOILET TRAIN YOUR MONEY FOREVER

Money is the most powerful chemical in the universe, dissolving everything that is not of itself. The Conspiracy has always known this, and has bred many good slaves by making its subjects simultaneously *hate* and *desire* money. They program people to feel embarrassed to talk about it.

LOVE is the answer — **the LOVE of MONEY.** We *must love* that which The Con would have us feel guilty about. For money is not evil, NAY, but a primordial Benevolent Force. It is the ultimate "artwork", Man's first true use of *symbols*, predating language. *Blood* was used as money at one time; it is one of the purest manifestations of the holy YacatiZmic Force.

We should revel in money, we should *grovel* in it. Money is the *green breath* of the Estate of Man. The cash flows out; it flows back in. It can bring Slack.

But to attain Slack through money, you must not *desire* it. To *try* to attain it will only entangle you further in desire. One way to lose your attachment to worldly things is by indulging in them, by smothering yourself in them. This can bring enlightenment, but it also brings the danger of **Jonesism**. For you can never "keep up" with Them.

Instead, the seeker may concentrate on a method, a tantra, a technique that will lure Slack *to* him. Learn to always 'feel' the flowing of the cash, the life-force, the *"MOOLA."*[1]

Go to a store and remove all the money from your wallet or purse. Hand it all to the salesperson — *all* of it — and say, "Give me this much worth." Gesture ambivalently at their entire stock. Then turn and meditate while your items are gathered randomly by the puzzled clerk.

As you hand the salesperson your money, pay close attention to the *look* of it, the *pstench* of the auras that have accumulated on it, the *feel* of the greenbacks as they slip from your hands. Feel the life force of the salesperson *through* the currency.

Then, in that gap of time as the money leaves you, as you pass through that moment of going from the material world to the world in which you have nothing, in that moment *sense the Slack*. DO NOT LOOK FOR IT, or you will miss the moment. In that brief period between having something and having nothing, there was Slack.

When you had something, you were responsible for it; you had to *do* something with it: spend it, save it, invest it. When you had nothing, you *needed* something. In both states you had desires.

But in that interval between having and needing, THERE WAS THE SLACK. GO INTO THAT MOMENT. GAZE.

NOW TURN THIS BOOK UPSIDE DOWN.

But you must understand that the money itself is worth nothing. It is only a tool. Yet, because The Conspiracy controls its printing, They extract great life energy from those who worship it.

Until we rid ourselves of the artificially-induced obsession with the colored pieces of paper *themselves*, we are still slaves to Their conditioning. If you *worry* about its lack you are *theirs*, for they make far more off your hours of labor than *you* do. If you were paid what you're worth, they'd go broke. (*They* are not really obsessed with money, but with TIME — *your* time. They are Time Junkies who vampirize your minutes and days until you are nearly drained of Slack.)

To break this vicious cycle of exploitation you must purge yourself of all respect for paper money. DEBASE THE FALSE IDOLS of the Federal Reserve. Make a game of its destruction; feel righteous pleasure as you draw on it, write on it, shred it. Make it useful for something *real*.

We Elders of the Church do not use money in the traditional ways. We **"launch"** it. We scrape the smudge of soul-essence of previous owners off of it. We burn it ritualistically — in public, —and we pray over the dollars as they wither in the flames. The smoke carries the prayers up to the Saucermen.

We hand dollar bills back and forth among each other, letting the Nental Ife stench accrue upon it that it may give "Bob" more power.[2]

Spend it like there is no tomorrow — **for there *is* no tomorrow.** Spend it experimentally. Spend it aesthetically, spend it *anaesthetically*, but spend it. Indeed, everyone should send all their money to everyone they know, and as many strangers as possible, right now! The System would cave in if the bills were tied up in the mails for that long.

There is a simpler way. Send what you do not *need* to the Church.

"Bob" spends very little of it. He has infinite wealth, anyway. Rather, he *stores* it. This keeps it out of the hands of the Conspiracy, keeps it from being *abused* on monstrous Death Research projects. The more money "Bob" can prevent from circulating, the longer will the Econocataclysm be staved off.

If you are having trouble with your cash flow, it's because it isn't flowing *to* "Bob".

1.   This exercise was developed by Hollywood TV Producer Rev. Larry Sulkis. Two days after he first used it, he secured financing for his educational series, *"The Art of Bad SubGeniuses."* Though little seen in the United States, this is a top-rated show in Japan and most of Europe. Sulkis is now fabulously wealthy. DON'T BREAK THE CHAIN!

2.   These techniques for *Freedom from Money* were developed independently, but simultaneously, in different parts of the world by St. Gerry Reith, Sir Guy Deuel, and *Drs. for "Bob."* St. Sterno Keckhaver used to stand on the steps of the Capitol in Washington, *throwing money at tourists* and screaming, **"KILL ME!!"** Those Pinks probably still wonder about that.

JOBS —
WINNING THE SALE OF YOUR LIFE

In some ways, the problem is not with the paper bills, or the life energy it represents. The problem is that to get it at all, most of us must submit to *jobs*.

Dobbs approves of the great *Peter Principle* theory, which explains why so many companies seem to have all the wrong people doing all the wrong jobs: that a worker moving upwards in his career will end up stalled *right at* his level of incompetence, and stay there until he retires. From there he makes the terrible decisions which filter back down to his underlings in the form of insanely *wrong* working conditions.

Proof that no one stays at the last post in which they could have been efficient: despite 200 studies which have shown that positive reinforcement in the workplace does far more than negative reinforcement, *only a handful* of employers have changed their wage-terrorism tactics. The Peckers are still inflicting their pipe dreams on the Peckees.

NEED MONEY?
LET "BOB" INTO YOUR SAVINGS

Big Companies, for which most people work, use a million tricks to subjugate your will — often against their own best interests! First they show you all the job freedom you'll *ever* have, so that you forget there's a leash on you. They promote you a little — let you build up speed, running after that Conspiracy Slack that you know exists "upstairs;" they reel out the Slack of raises and days off until you're sprinting as fast as you possibly can. Then, WHAM, they yank that leash back with the equivalent of a heavy-torque motor, it snaps you at the neck and drags you backwards so fast that you NEVER, EVER AGAIN forget that you *have that leash*. If you're going to stay with The Company, you'd better hope they use their Leash Trick *early*.

. . . LIKE DOGS BEGGING FOR A TREAT

LIES

HOW TO FOOL THE AUTHORITIES

"Flexibility" and "adaptability" are words which the Con has hijacked and beaten into meaning "good slavery." Those who are truly flexible and adaptable have long since freed themselves from the corporate daisy chain, *or ripped it off from within.*

The Con has developed ways to twist your survival fear to meet their needs; one is called "Motivational Training," at which employees voluntarily let themselves be 'adapted.' A perfect illustration of the power of suggestion inherent in such training is the fact that the Dobbs Seminars in *"Give Up Training"* (GUT) are raking in the greenbacks even though it was originally designed as a *seduction aid,* and *doesn't work for sales motivation.* Yet even this most obvious of rip-offs keeps those Exec Boys coming back for more.

Exploitable traits shared by both humans and SubGenii are incredible capacities for *procrastination, moment-by-moment self-delusion, rationalization of sheer laziness and greed, and an instinctive resistance to effort of any kind.* In humans, the Con uses these qualities to obscure all reasons for living, making the Pink more tolerant of mechanical, boring labor, and causing him to consider complaining "not worth the trouble."

On the other hand, the SubGenius brings these Talents for Shirking to their fullest fruition, for he knows that Conspiracy business is *based* on them. Having true faith in Slack, he makes these natural propensities for sloth *appear to idiot bosses to be 'symptoms' of expertise!* Thus he can repeatedly quit his job and get rehired back at better pay, just because the boss has learned to *expect* eccentricity from him.

Similarly, when you make mistakes on the job, don't wring your hands over them — FLAUNT them; amaze the office! Eventually you will find yourself bearing a mysterious new status-cloak of "highly creative individual." It's not real creativity, of course — just what *they* can comprehend as creativity. (DO NOT show your *real* creativity at job interviews. Although the

Pink who first interviews you will be superstitiously impressed, his boss — who does the hiring — is probably an unsaved latent SubGenius who will intuit your true potential and keep you from threatening his post as Top Ape.) There is no niche for those who would improve the status quo. Only slaves are nurtured, while talents are rerouted to destroy their owners. Good advice to any would-be creative "artist types" trying to make a buck in the modern world: *Don't let The Con know of your monster.* The Villagers will destroy it. It would be *disastrous* for you to sell your 'real' self. Sell instead the 'false self' that's seemingly honest and pure, dumb and innocent, and utterly ambitionless. The 'false self' should always be slightly more stupid than any given customer.

Stay among your own kind as much as possible. Dealing with Pinks in the marketplace always works out negatively — even if you make money. They tend to cluster in large companies, though, so if you can get out from under the car payments for long enough and start freelancing, you'll meet other SubGenii. Eventually you'll all be able to band together and either dominate your industry or destroy it (thus becoming the new Establishment, but don't worry about that yet).

The key to your problems: **THE WORLD *IS* AGAINST YOU.**

But there is a Higher Selfishness you must attain. A true salesman in a 'credibility dilemma' uses the Black Arts of Human Appeal: flattery, lies, etc. You know perfectly well that the customer isn't alway right. You must exercise the freedom to **LIE AT THE DROP OF A HAT.**

It's a world of supply and demand. The Con *demands* that you lie, and you *supply* those lies. It wasn't *your* idea.

The truly great salesmen practically play God. They create entire little universes of fabrication for their clients just to back up minor statistical claims from the company's brochure. THE ONLY TRICK: DON'T GET CAUGHT. Otherwise it is a Church-sanctified practice.

YOUR ONLY LOGICAL CHOICE

If the Con *drives* you to rebellion, subversion, *crime* — if they *drive* you to it by never hiring you, or by paying you an insulting wage, then you MAY have to TAKE THEM UP ON IT. Thanks to The Con's own inefficiency, there're much better money-making opportunities in the Black Market, anyway. It's *their* fault if you're prodded into giving up on normal employment, going on the dole, and learning with a group of co-fanatics the arts of gunplay, knives, chains and tire-tools.

YOU ARE OWED A LIVING AND EVERY DAY SHOULD BE PAYDAY.

John Hagen

AT 130 MILES ALTITUDE, IN A SLIGHTLY EXCENTRIC ORBIT

THE GUARDIAN MOUNTS AN ATTITUDE OF AWARENESS.

SHOULDERING HIS SOLEMN BURDEN: THE DELIVERANCE OF HUMANITY,

J.R. "BOB" DOBBS EMERGES FROM HIS HIGH HOLY TRANCE WATCH...

VERY WELL JEHOVAH, IT'S A DEAL!

CHAPTER 15

SEX
THE DIVINE BATTLE

"Doest thou desire her most *foully* for those things that make her *good?*"
— Antonio in *Measure for Measure*, talking to himself about wanting to make it with a nun.

"Someday I will be a large scar."

— C-! the RubGenius

"Some life forms have *ironic* sex lives . . ."

— Pope Meyer III

We could say that sex is more important than "Bob," were it not that "Bob" *IS* sex.

The Church of the SubGenius is a *sexist church;* we are *for* the sexes, the *intersection,* the *union* of them. In whatever sick combinations the parties involved consent to.

However, "Bob" is violently against the humanist forces that would tear down **traditional family values.** The SubGenius mutation tends to run in families; we should therefore reproduce to the greatest possible degree, for we may need back-up in case our numbers are drastically reduced in End Times Mutant vs. Normal warfare.

Trouble is, The Conspiracy has it set up so that both sex *and* the lack thereof cause tremendous problems even for *good looking* people.

Don't kid yourself: "looks" are all-important in this society. If you are plain or ugly, this is already painfully obvious to you.

Being goofy-looking according to prevailing standards of beauty, though almost always a curse in high school and college, *can* actually *pay off commensurately* in later life, when people get less picky due to their own fading attractiveness. People unusual-looking enough *to have perceived it in childhood* tend to develop **paranormal personalities** to compensate for strange bone structure or quirky physical mannerisms. An occasional SubGenius, overzealously mindful that his looks brand him, will actually *worsen* his appearance as a masochistic means of either

toughening his mind or else projecting an "I Don't Care" attitude. This is a pose, however, and verges on Pinkness.

To the people that *count,* looks aren't that important. If you suspect someone won't date you, or whatever, because of your looks, then that person is a Glorp and is not worthy of your attention.

For most SubGenii, Con-programmed TV-style "good looks" are insignificant compared to the particular gleam in the eye, the 'edge' in the voice, the 'hunch' in the back, the Pstench . . . the things that are meaningless to Normals. The American standard of beauty was carefully contrived over the last few decades by a few giant Illuminati corporations, and we all know the engineered beauties and "hunks" in men's mags and cig ads are about as real as the chickens in a modern mass poultry factory — where the birds are so chemically fattened and kept in such small cages for so long that their poor feet actually grow around the wire mesh. The horrible thing is, some of these 'foxes' and 'studs' are SubGeniuses, *trapped in bodies which attract the constant harassment of slavering idiot Normals.* It is actually *harder* for a "knock-out" SubGenius lady to find a proper mate than it is for an ordinary-looking one, because SubGenius males will think her looks denote Conspiracy tampering where there may be none at all. Thus she must *rise above her looks.*

It *is* much easier for a handsome or beautiful person to become stupid, because they don't *need* brains; those who chose to

GO SOFT TOO SOON?

Rev. Brian Curran

maintain their SubGenius urges *anyway* display stalwart dignity indeed. For these people, the problem is not that they can't get laid; it's that they're pursued so much they feel they're being *used*, which of course they **are**. The only advice we can give them is that they join a SubGenius Convent — but the *überlust* conditions in those places is sometimes *worse*.

No matter your looks or proclivities, *"Bob" wants you to fuck.* He wants you to use your DICK! He wants you to use what God gave little girls. "Bob" wants you to use these things *righteously* —to *spread* his Seed! Use them until it HURTS! **WHAT DO YOU THINK "SEXHURT" MEANS??** It doesn't mean tying 'em up — it means you should *LOVE* them until it *hurts!*

But first you must locate them. **DON'T LOOK FOR SOME-ONE "LIKE YOU."** That is perhaps the single greatest contributing factor to the break-up of relationships. If you want a clone of yourself, go to a Conspiracy computer dating service. The key to good mating is being able to appreciate *differences*. Pastor Buck Naked proved this with the enormous success of his **Good Sex for Mutants League;**[1] he and his franchized MutaMatchers aren't kidding when they say, "ALL THE WAY ON THE FIRST DATE."

Say you're new in town, or perhaps just very weird, and you're having difficulty finding friends and/or lovers. How do you know who to pursue?

Well, to begin with, if you're an asshole, an ever-whining creep who hates everybody yet demands attention, you can *forget it.* Otherwise, no matter how shy and nurdly you might be, no matter how awkward at meeting people, there are specific clues to look for that will tell you whether someone is worth the embarrassment of "getting to know."

1. For info on the **Good Sex for Mutants Dating League,** send a self-addressed stamped envelope (with room for plenty of material) to **BUCK,** P.O. Box 140026, Dallas, TX 75214

MEN: mount a Dobbshead on a wall and watch its eyes when a girl walks by. If they move to follow her, *she's a SubGenius.*

LADIES: you can judge a guy by his boobs. Eyeball his *knockers.* That's the secret.

While searching for a True SubGenius friend, you might kill time by *using* a Pink or two. They're easy to make friends with, at least for the short term, *if* you're that desperate. They have little or no critical faculties except those dictated by The Con, and you can quickly go through a long line of Normals: first enticing them, then burning them out and dropping them. Having been molded into the "Me Generation" system by The Con, you should be able to so thoroughly out-"Me" them that they'll eagerly let your "Me" replace *their* "Me." But be careful: if you overdo it and become the biggest "Me" around, you'll end up believing it yourself and the next thing you know you're just another Tool.

Sometimes it takes years to find your SubGenius mate(s). While waiting, you can always develop an imaginary friend just like you did in childhood — or, for that matter, you can just *buy*

¡GET GIRLS AND MEN!

an inflatable one. A hint: the ones with simulated hair are worth the extra price.

On the other hand, MAYBE YOU DON'T WANT ANYBODY ANYWAY. 19 out of 20 relationships end up being disasters.

But get this: the ones that *do* work usually come *right after you've given up looking* and accepted the Isness of the Now.

"GIVE UP" and you'll GET SEX.

The reason some Subs have trouble "getting some" is that they exude such a strong, subconsciously-detected musk that their very attractiveness scares their prey away. Too Much Power.

Knowing this should make it easier to quit *trying*. Let *them* do the hunting, and *you'll* become the hunted. They *desperately want* anything they can't have, but are *repelled* by what comes easily.

Just relax and loosely exploit your abnormality potential. Don't put yourself out. When you truly Give Up, you'll suddenly find it *frighteningly easy* to TELL THEM WHAT THEY WANT TO HEAR. Once you really blow them off, the right words will spring to your lips as if by magic and they'll flock to your VERY ANKLES! IGNORE THEM and they will CRAVE YOU.

If you don't mind adultery, probably the best way to be *barraged* with sex partners is to get married. People seem to have a *perverse desire* to possess that which is *morally unobtainable* . . . indicating yet another connection between making love and making mincemeat.

According to "Bob," in the future you'll be able to use *telepathy*

¿WHEN WILL HE COME?

HOME AND FAMILY

with another person far away to create mutual yet solitary cytorspasmodicism.

There is one newly-discovered sex act which we'd *love* to tell you about, involving the carcass of a pig and the motorized half of a rotisserie, but this Book just isn't the place. Sorry.

Remember, sex is *not* necessary. There should be no stigma in becoming one of "Bob's" Brides, a celestial celebate, making it only with your spouses and tape decks. DECENCY IS OKAY, BELIEVE IT OR NOT!!

All kinds of rules of sexual conduct have been tried, but The Divine Battle rages on. Thus we must always keep trying *new techniques* as the old ones "wear out."

On Break-Up — Remember, There Are Other Fish In The Sea

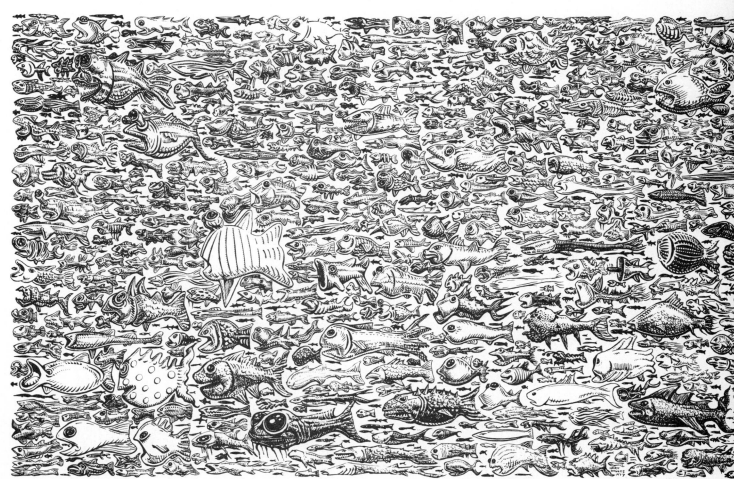

Gary Hughes

St. Joe Schwind

¡MARITAL AIDS!

SLACK IN MARRIAGE

"Over every OverMan is an OverWoman." — Anon.

Marriage is the most *extreme* form of Getting Sex Through Giving Up. Marriage is compromise — the relinquishing of certain things which, judging by the divorce rate, half of America isn't ready to relinquish.

The E-Z Sex of Marriage comes at a *price:* the expensive, nerve-wracking hunt for "tail" becomes the expensive, nerve-wracking hunt for Slack.

When the Quest for Slack ends in wedlock, it often does bring Slack . . . at first. But at some point the newly-married person SUDDENLY REALIZES VISCERALLY *just how much Slack he or she had before!* This can work out fine if the individual simply puts what Slack he has left to *better use.*

But for some, the Slack never comes. The other partner may be a "Slack Vampire," draining it away with endless demands. It is so hard to change a Slack Vampire that the person in this situation is once again advised to "Give Up". Call it quits.

Be sure you aren't jumping ship too soon, though. Once you leave what you were *positive* was a selfish Monster spouse and hook up with a new one, *you may well find,* just as you did the *first* time you got married, that you *actually had more Slack then* but were *unable to appreciate it* simply by the lack of your present *Lack of Slack!*

Of course, marriage is no longer considered permanent in this evil, humanistic age, but breaking up is still HELL as red tape and 'commitment' make it drag *on* and *on* . . . so, rather than cement the bond of holy matrimony in a *regular* church or government, think about using a SubGenius™ "Placebo Brand" **SHORT DURATION MARRIAGE,** available from Pastor Buck Naked[2]. *ShordurMar* is cheap, and can be easily voided even *before* the Expiration Date with our Marital Aid Product #3: "Spurious Brand" **TEMPORARY DIVORCE CERTIFICATE** ("Just In Case It *Was* Your Fault After All").

2. $2 to **BUCK, P.O. BOX 140026, Dallas TX 75214.** Write "$upport the Laser Project" on the order along with names of the betrothed, and Rev. Naked will bless each one.

OR send $1 and self-addressed stamped envelope to CATALOG, c/o **SubGenius, P.O. Box 140306, Dallas TX 75214** for info on Shor-Dur-Mar plus tapes, T-shirts, buttons, bumper-stickers, subscriptions, etc.

Is there an unbridgeable, undestroyable barrier between men and women that will keep them forever warring with each other?

Well, the War Between the States only lasted a few years. The War Between Men and Women *is* an ongoing process that shall never end. But this doesn't mean you should stay single, screw anyone you can, and blow off all attachments, NAY! DON'T SUCCUMB TO HUMANIST THINKING! Go ahead and *get* married, and FIGHT TO THE DEATH!

Heavy marital combat often results from the two partners being too *alike* in temperament. Your true Soul Partner, who *does exist* somewhere, is very different from you. If you were the same, you'd become more bovine; your Holy Differences irritate you each into *learning,* into *seeing* in new ways. You should *expect* to fight a lot with your spouse. HONE those skills of quarreling. You can apply them on the job!

A reminder for "unliberated" women specifically: BLOW OFF ALL *LEAVE IT TO BEAVER* MYTHS. There is practically no such thing as a "good husband/dad" AND a "good provider." The Conspiracy doesn't pay him all that money to have a *home life.* Make up your mind whether you want *him* or the fancy god damn appliances, because you *won't* get *both.* ACCEPT THIS HIDEOUS FACT if you wish to be a happy little dumb housewife.

Here's another *concrete fact* that you've always wanted to pay to hear: In every marriage, one partner is *always* the kind of person who *always* deals in absolutes. NEVER do *both* partners always deal in absolutes. NEVER ARE BOTH REASONABLE. *It's your spouse's fault!*

One way to ease the tensions of marriage is to practice a special form of Sexhurt slightly related to heathen tantric sex yoga. The

St. Joe Schwind

Puzzling Evidence

THEY WILL FOLLOW YOUR SILENT COMMAND

SAMPLE

Buck Naked

two of you "connect" but then *barely touch* and *barely move* (**"Half of 'em you bring off better by not doing anything at all."** —"Bob") . . . and stay that way for a *long* time while the two Nental Ives engage in an astral *wrestling match*. Let *them* slug it out and release the hidden tensions while you and your mate enjoy the *good* part.

All in all, the *truest* marriage is marriage *in "Bob."* He is the ultimate justice of the peace. Let Judge Dobbs marry you somewhere out in the woods, under the trees; let him *watch* as you "do what comes natural."

. . . and if you have kids, THEY get your Slack.

NEW FAMILY ON THE BLOCK by St. Byron Werner

He: "Are my ears red. Gosh—we haven't oiled our projector in a month of Sundays."

St. Rick Hoefle

IN THE FAMILY OF "BOB"

We must take "traditional family values" to their *fullest extreme:* extended, tribelike clans in which each aunt is "Mom" and each uncle, "Dad." The system is too big to insure the preservation of values, so communities (not communes) should take it upon themselves. YOU CAN TRUST ONLY YETI BLOOD KIN.

We will always see strife in the home, though, particularly between parents and teens. When a SubGenius father sees his son come home in some unearthly new "hip" hairdo, we often hear this: "God damn it — you're being 'different' just for the sake of being *different!*" "But Dad, everybody's doin' it." "So you're not being different — you're being *just like them!*"

The father is right. The son *is* being different for no other reason than to be different — *from Dad.* But he isn't necessarily wearing the fashionable hairdo to be like his conformist non-conformist friends; he's wearing it to get *laid.* Often, the teen SubGenius is just as alienated from his hipster cruising-buddies as he is from the Father PudWielder from whose loins he sprang. Thus, the argument is really moot, and springs from ape-against-ape territorial imperative. Both should try to remember this.

A child should have *respect* for the inflexible, stale wisdom of his progenitors, who originally gave him life whether he wanted it or not. We *need* the oldsters — some of them can actually still

remember The Old Ways. And we should pay homage to our dead ancestors, who can intercede with the gods on our behalf. (You CAN insult the ancestors of Pinks because they weren't Yetis.)

And youth must be put in *its* rightful place of valuable subservience: as bringer of *smart-alec* but *effective* solutions to problems which the Elders cannot even *see.* "Kids" have more *intelligence* and *use of the brain* in direct proportion to their *lack of knowledge.* We should balance the boring, rigid *good sense* of the Old with the snotty, insolent *originality* of the Young. the decrepit and senile should be brought home from the "home" and placed in a center of worship — perhaps next to the TV. And the young must have a right to life. The Church *strictly disapproves* of abortion after the age of 15 years. A 15-year-old is a *living being* with an *eternal soul* and an inherent right to lead even the most HORRIBLE life.

Your new family is NOT the Church of the SubGenius. It's your OLD FAMILY seen in the all-forgiving, yet no-shit-taking, LIGHT OF "BOB." Your old family is not what messed you up; it's the *harsh reality* that made you "YOU" enough to *find "Bob"!* If your parents had given you TOTAL SATISFACTION, you would now live in TOTAL BOREDOM . . . *you would be Pink!*

Sure, your parents are fuddy-duddies — YOU WILL BE TOO — but you ARE a SubGenius, so *something* must have happened right.

DON'T KILL THEM *NOW.*

CHAPTER 16

HEALTH, THE INDUSTRIAL DIET, AND **BAD THINGS**

"If ya feel, ya heal."

—"Jesus" in the movie *Greaser's Palace*

Featuring...
Wonderful
GOURMET FOOD

You probably know at least ten people under the age of thirty who have some form of cancer.

The sickness won't stop. People will contract weirder and weirder diseases, and at earlier and earlier ages. Eventually cancer itself will be like the common cold. "Uh, I won't be in the office this week, I have a little touch of cancer. . . ." Oh, there'll come a cure eventually, but the more cures we come up with, the more New Diseases will arise. Things *far, far* worse than cancer are on the way, some of them deliberately manufactured by The Conspiracy. The picture is a tad bleak for *our old age*. It's a cinch the government won't support the elderly much longer. And The Company will fire you a year before you're eligible for retirement benefits.

You'd better put your remaining years to good use — YOU'D BETTER HAVE FUN.

Our studies (as well as the unreleased studies by The Con) indicate that "good health" is practically a pointless pursuit if you live in an urban area. You can eat nothing but organically grown fruit and vegetables, you can work out twice a day, you can quit all nasty habits, but you're still absorbing more poison just by *breathing*, and *touching public stair railings,* than the most piglike peasant in 1567 London *ever* did.

You can move to the country, but . . . there's no work there, violent crime is actually *more* frequent, and the poisons are almost as bad anyway.

If the diseases don't get you, some railroad toxic spill will. Hell, just driving to work is riskier than hunting bears for a living.

LIES

But there is one medicine more powerful than all the contamination in New Jersey, and that medicine is SLACK. SLACK gives the mind power over all disease. A truly happy chain smoker is less likely to attract the attention of the Cancer Demons than is a tense, knotted-up health freak gnawing his fingernails to the bone.

DON'T READ THIS!

CANCER IS CAUSED BY *PINKNESS* . . . by boredom and meaninglessness. It can be prevented by action, thrills, sex — even overwork!

So how do you get a healthy, slackful outlook in the face of rampant ecohell? YOU PLUNGE INTO ECOHELL HEAD FIRST. You don't let it *scare* you, you don't let it push you around. By all means, help fight to CLEAN UP AMERICA; but if you want that junkfood, EAT IT. You want to watch TV instead of go to "Jazzercise?" WATCH IT. Indulge those Conspiracy urges to the hilt and thus purge their *hold* over you.

Americans should eat like Americans — *as fast as they possibly can*. Tibetans should eat like Tibetans — studying each tiny birdlike bite until it "becomes a universe" before taking it into their bodies. You can eat like the Vietnamese — hardly at all — or you can eat what would feed dozens of Vietnamese families. Either way, the Vietnamese aren't going to eat any more than they did before. The world isn't starving because Americans eat too much; even if we *stopped eating* the Conspiracy would *still* throw the leftovers away before they'd send it to any Third Worlders.

Now, we all know that eating the meat of live protein animals is unholy, it pollutes your system and creates aggression, and worst of all it requires the heartless slaughter of fellow creatures — MAMMALS! — fully as sensitive and loving as we. For this reason, vegetarians eat only plants.

But their sin is as great — perhaps worse! Science has proven unequivocally that all plants react to threatening stimuli with a low-frequency version of what we would call "panic." They too are life forms with feelings, which feel *pain,* which may even have an all-telepathic "civilization" that we are too brutal to comprehend! Thus, when you bite down on a grape, you are popping open and *crushing, grinding* a wee life which, in its own way, is squealing in the terror of the murdered innocent!

So *anything* that nourishes us is going to suffer. WE MAY AS WELL LET THEM ALL SUFFER EQUALLY. By making a *few* of *all* types of living things victims of our all-important stomachs, *less* members of each individual species will be sacrificed.

HOLLYWOOD DEATH GODS

Delicious MARINATED GRISTLE

Robert Williams

Besides — though we devour and eliminate them, so we make them immortal and allow them to partake of our SubGenius grandeur. It works both ways: just as a cannibal eats his enemy's heart to gain his strength, we eat a hamburger to gain the wisdom and courage of the mighty cow. Yet, at the same time, we are inviting the cow's primal cellular structure — his Code, if you will — to enter our bloodstreams, where it may mingle with, learn from, and mayhaps even *conspire* with our own unique Tool-User's Code.

We eat the broccoli to gain its patience and virtue; in return, we release it back into the world *reborn* in a new form — teaming with literally millions of newfound friends, the bacteria. We drink of the Hops and Grain to partake of their slow, slow yet wise Judgement and in return sacrifice to them our Coordination.

THUS, the Word of Dobbs says we can eat ANYTHING WE WANT. You can gorge yourself to an early grave, or you can consult shamans at health food stores and figure out ways to cure ills and lengthen your "little Span." You can be a vegetarian or you can keep an Industrial Diet, living out of convenience stores and simul-food franchises. You can stay in poverty eating expensive food untainted by chemicals, or you can support The Conspiracy in its lowest, most stinking form by maintaining your sugar and fat addictions; go ahead, suck down any and all forms of caffeine since if it's not *that,* something *else* will give you cancer of the colon and hypertension — like your *job,* maybe. You can admit most of that canned and frozen food isn't really food and instead try to eat things that were recently alive, not cooked into broken, useless cell-mush; you can admit junk food DOES TASTE GOOD or you can get into the snobdom of ever-changing Health Faddism just because the cool rich people do it, or you can *kill me.* . . .

Just remember that everything touched by The Con has poison and carcinogens in it. Scarf 'em if you wish, but put some money away for the painkillers you'll need later on.

A SAFER WAY TO EAT

GUARD AGAINST CORROSION . . .

A TYPICAL SUBGENIUS DAILY DIET

Breakfast: Fresh fruit juice, vitamins, organic goat's milk, brown rice, Spirulina, live goldfish, 'Frop.

Lunch: Beef jerky, microwave burger, honey bun, Coke, Thunderbird Wine, speed, coffee with sugar, 'Frop.

Dinner: Uncooked blackeyed peas, fish, milk, raw hay, an apple for dessert, 'Frop.

2:00 A.M.: 25 cigarettes, three nails, 'Frop.

Somewhat healthier would be to hardly eat at all, but we cannot expect that of people until TV commercials are banned — which would only happen in a truly upside-down world.

Another thing: although most American food *is* dangerous to human life, and godawful radiations pour from every appliance and power-line, REMEMBER: SubGeniuses are mutants anyway. If you can't escape from radiation, learn to love it. After all, it's merely another form of energy; why can't our bodies learn to use it, like a plant uses sunlight? If you absorb enough radiation, you CAN make AMAZING CHANGES come about!

good taste at...

COOKIE'S CORNER
by Cookie Drummond F.G.o.t.R.

Nuclear Diets

The Nuclear Family is a demanding, energy-sucking unit. The trash it leaves and the food it eats baffle the old concepts of harmonious consumption and excretion. So-called "organic emancipation" which has foamed at our doorsteps shall now be replaced by more chemicals and foreign substances . . . as much as our laboratories can produce. "WE'LL SAVE OUR CHEMICAL BY-PRODUCTS!" Shit, this country will soon be filled with Comet licking Kodak Chemplant scavengers. So keep those empty cans! and stay tuned for 'How to Make Coal and Sulfite Sandwiches from Things in Your Backyard."

An Apple a Day Keeps the Doctors Away.

© 1982 Paul Mavrides

BAD THINGS

LIES

"The priest and the prophet have erred through strong drink; they are swallowed up of wine, they are out of the way through strong drink; they err in vision, they stumble in judgement. . . . For all tables are full of vomit and filthiness, *so that there is* no place *clean.*"

(ISAIAH 28:7,8)

"Doktors for "Bob" aren't into the 'regular medicines,' so to speak. We use Ooob . . . and Sleeblong . . . This is the Mod Scene, Baby! You better hip out to it, or blow your mind trying not to! I can sick out on that . . . I mean, I couldn't grop a groove-go on any of these logo bands, but *Doktors for "Bob"* really blew the glooschleenkon right out the top of my cerebellum!"

— St. Janor Hypercleats, backstage, 1969

THE OFFICIAL CHURCH POSITION ON DRUGS:

They don't show you a 'realer' world. They don't expand your mind. THEY ONLY GET YOU HIGH. If you think you experienced a mystical state on, say, LSD, you are wrong. You were merely "Drunk As A Lord."

A PARABLE:

Late one night, four travellers arrived at the Gate to the City. It was locked tight and there was no customs agent to open it for them.

One of the travellers, a drunk, said, "Let's bash the damn gate down."

Another, who happened to be a pot smoker, said, "No, let's just lay down by the wall and wait till morning."

The third, an acidhead, said, "Why don't we just float through the keyhole?"

While they were talking, the fourth, a 'Frop-head, had wandered around to the back door near the garbage dump and entered *without even paying*.

("Bob" actually *would* have floated through the keyhole.)

We are doing everything in our power to put a stop to the recent False SubGenius fad of **"Gut Blowout™ Parties."** These reckless kids are risking their *souls* by taking those Green Joy Jackers and "Bowel Lifters" and "screamers" and "laughers" and "floppers" and "floaters" and other unsanctified street drugs. *This is false Slack.*

There is only one "mind-relinquishing substance" that you should even *consider* putting the gobble on, and that is the sacred Tibetan herb, **"Habafropzipulops"** (NOT a drug).

"Without taking Pills" FOOL YOUR MIND!

'Bob's Team' Is Cheering for a Cure

BELOW: **Sequential Effects of 'Frop on the Brain.** (1:) User first undergoes slight bodily discomfort. (2:) Begins to think about money. (3:) Desynchronized dendrites cause teeth to clench in anxiety, followed by (4:) an urge to pray. (5:) 1st "rush" as Key to Slack is unlocked by User's money. (6:) Archetypal symbols of G'BroagFran flood subconscious so that (7:) User's Luck Plane triggers synchronicity overload. (8:) Brain's "Brakes" ('stop' and 'go' signals) shut down. (9:) Moral inputs in hyperthalmus form repeating loop pattern. (10:) Lungs darken, clot up, develop holes, temporarily causing brain's primal *Idge* to *Disconnect*. (12:) Brain, now finally tuned to receive Channel 12 of *The Skor*, causes (13:) Left/Right brain lobes to intermesh in battle. "The Other World" becomes visible to the ecstatic User.

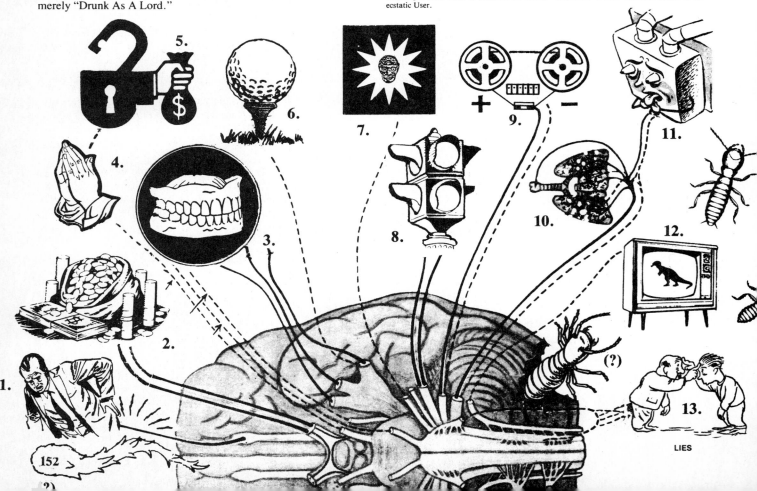

LIES

Now, you don't *have* to partake of the 'Frop; you can *quit,* if you want to go *SANE,* if you want your so-called "senses" back. But . . . how can we know the Goodness of Heaven lest we have, for comparison, vomited into the porcelain bowls of Hell?

Although the Great Inebriant of Tibet provides only an *illusory* feeling of Time Control, yet such a glimpse fortifies the SubGenius and he follows the taste of that artificial Slack, drooling like a dog in Rut. He is a dauntless explorer of fake horizons . . . for of all the Sacraments, *'Frop does not wear off.*

KILL TIME ITSELF— PAINLESSLY!

Users of *drugs,* on the other hand, are placing themselves in grave danger. They can never get as truly *fried* as they want to be. They have to take one on top of another. Sometimes they take so many that when they *forget* one or two, they are later *mad* at themselves for it.

To keep mentally levitating, they always need *more.* Sooner or later, they 'burn out' and become "too Slacked to react"; the brain tunnels through which they once excavated and blasted with drunken zeal begin to *cave in.*

The Abuser wakes up one day *impaired.* His muscles feel ravaged, his nerves nullified. There is a hollowness inside, but a *hot* hollowness, and discomfort mounts to panic as he realizes he's annihilated *one brain cell too many. His teeth grind, his cells shrivel yet seem to scream* for More where there is None. His skin exudes bitter greases from every pore as if he were getting a long-overdue oil change. Everything's clammy and numb to the touch. His Eternal Idge gasps and convulses with the amputation-nausea of Something Missing. The electric 'glue' of his brain becomes tacky and stiffens; the snotlike Shock Fluid in which it once cosily floated has drained away, and the dried husk of gray matter slams against the rough cranial walls with every movement of the head. The gyroscopes inside his ears' balance-tubes wobble crazily, and the world is No End Up; the floor lurches and shifts its steepness and changes its slant right under his feet. If he lays down he suffers the Slow Ovals, the bed seeming to spin very slowly end over end through space. He goes to the bathroom to expel the bad water but his urine smells burnt and leaks out in a weak, radioactive dribble. He looks in the mirror; his skin is Krishna blue in pallor and he worries that the quiet interior *shattering* noises he hears are the sounds of his blood crystallizing. His heart starts to dry-hump the back of his throat in hysteria, for he knows that to die on drugs is to doom his soul to eternal

earthbound wandering in a Purgatory where the liquor stores are all closed. If the Nental Ife is intoxicated when the body dies, it doesn't know it's dead and so never heads for Heaven.

Laying on the floor, glowing feebly in the dark, the wretch moans out the Drug User's Lament:

"I can't decipher anything; Put me where you want me; Give me rubber blankets."[1]

Eventually his cohorts show up and give him succor in the form of MORE, and the wheel starts rolling again.

Sadly, JHVH-1 saw to it that some people were "rigged." He programmed them with a genetic emptiness that can be filled only when the cells are slumbering in blankets of Medicine.

In a very few cases, if there is a cure, "The Curse Vomits Up A Gift." The Hell of Kicking can make a frail, sad Genius revert and devolve into a hearty SubGenius. It obliterates the brain cells he had *too many of* and he becomes a Seer. Not worth the suffering, but a Seer nonetheless.

The Conspiracy *encourages,* BLATANTLY, a useless, empty pattern of social drug abuse in its slaves. The anti-reality sleepdrugs like alcohol and "downs" are *legal,* pretty much, while the 'wake-up' drugs are only *available.* You can tell which ones They'd *rather* you take.

There are certain crucial things they don't tell you about their drugs. For instance, did you know that different drugs put your body on different vibrational levels?

The depressants (alcohol, tranquilizers, cough medicine, TV, etc.) make your molecular structure more *dense,* according to their severity. The stimulants (coffee, soda pop, sugar, speed, nicotine, etc.) cause less molecular density. The alcoholic is more 'solid' — he feels more invulnerable, and in fact *is.* The acidhead, however, is more 'gaseous' — there are vast spaces between his molecules; wotrons and neutrinos pass through him more easily . . . he may even *feel* them.

The reason The Con pushes alcohol so hard is that *it opens you to the forces of the Yacatisma.* You are more *visible* to these demonic beings when drunk. Now, the famed Luck of the Drunkard is no myth; winos are protected by **Alcohol Demons** as treasured Vessels — walking wine bottles, if you will. But the lowered vibrational signal of drunkenness is like an open invitation to NHGH's henchbeings and the plastered person is, as Lobsang Rampa put it, "tormented by entities who delight in catching humans in a stage where they cannot even think clearly. They find it most amusing."

So if you *must* drink, ACHIEVE **TRANCE DRUNKENNESS** so that you are *also* open to the protection of "Bob."

Perhaps the stewbums understand the sacrament of the wine the best. It is *outside* the church, in the *street,* that one truly feels The Touch. They're drinking the *real* blood of Jesus — or "Bob" or whoever — out of those green Thunderbird Bibles. "Bob" was not beaten up in vain; his blood became the Muscatel, the Mad Dog, the Night Train that those boys ride. It makes them feel so *good* . . . and that's what religion is *supposed* to do.

1. Coined at the *first* Gut Blowout™ party by its host, Dr. X.

It is the Pink suburban "Respectable Alcoholic" who has no excuse, and verily, no *hope*. Well, perhaps there is *one* thing that can bring them from their closet of opiated, self-hating secrecy. Perhaps if they turned to "the 'Froplords."

©LIES

"THE 'FROPLORDS" depicted in 8th Century frieze unearthed by "Dr." Palmer Vreedees during excavation of The Parmathion (ancient Greek Temple of Bacchus). Courtesy of the British Museum.

We most pious archpopes condone, violently, the most frequent possible indulgence, unto intoxication and beyond, of the revered and despised Grief-Easer of the Mountains, the Warrior Against Pain, the Healing Herb, **HABAFROPZIPULOPS.** Whether taken as smoke, liquid, food, or as "Bob's" *PILS,* it, above all other medicinal substances, "spells relief." From the hearty young stalks protruding from the Himalayan snow to the white 'Frop-dust that settles on the rim of "Bob's" Pipe, it is the closest thing to the untainted essence of ODIN on Earth. How else can we regard that which produces in the devoted user such superhuman clarity of insight, such sensory hyperanaesthesia, such total loss of judgement which *is* profound wisdom, such placid ecstasy and blessed repose, and which, in short, is the only shortcut to the Realization of the Dobbs State?

'Frop is not merely *safe,* but *beneficial* — nay, even *necessary* — to bodily health. We encourage our children to partake of it copiously, to their little hearts' abundant desires.

Our prodigious longing for it requires no justification; indeed, it is a fount of pride, a mark of the elect. Our genetic structures adhere

CATALYTIC BRAIN CELL LOSS IN SECONDS

more readily to its divine molecules than do Theirs; that is to their typical misfortune. They are best suited to "getting fucked up," as they so grossly put it, while we use it more nobly to become, let us say, twisted, bombed, ripped out of our gourds, utterly *whacked,* blistered, ruined, blown, blasted, obliterated, atomized, damaged, 86ed to the marrow of the *bone,* done in, gassed, smeared, blitzed, scuttled, over the edge, nuked, turned on, wigged out, unglued, cut loose, desanitized, bent, plowed under, discorporated, flayed, trashed, hopped up, lobotomized, and otherwise placed into a state of superior spiritual awareness. We do not "blow our minds"; we *erase* them.

The Xists planted our beloved 'Frop on Earth near the close of the Age of Dinosaurs. "Bob" tells us it may well be JHVH-1's main instrument for evolution on this planet — having very possibly been the device which brought down the Great Reptiles, allowing us mammals to take their place as large destroyers; and yet also that which will, with "Bob's" guidance, likewise complete the usurpation as dominant species of the humans by the SubGenii Hordes.

Its detractors — mostly alcoholics and pot-heads — scream that it is a physically addictive Vampire Root from whose siren embrace no man can tug free. We shout Halleluia! — of course it is! And is the Lord Himself one bit less habit-forming? "Habitfropzipulops" teaches us, ultimately, that All is One, that Up is Down; it allows us to converse with trees and see prophetic (and accurate!) visions of the future in our shoes, our album covers, in the strange reflections on our toasters. An ascetic 'Frop Master in Tibet or Dobbstown can, with diligent consumption, finally lose all interest in everything, achieving the paranirvanic state closest to "Bob" himself: Accidental Erasure, that Plane on which the Luck Oceans are most effortlessly surf'd, by which the densely overgrown Path of Least Resistance is Trimmed for safe travel.

It virtually negates the curse of Memory, that stumbling-block to Perfection.

And it makes this state as easily attainable to a distracted, harried American as to a Tibetan lama or Mexican brujo.

It brings us closer to our inborn Yetihood; it invokes the spirits of our persecuted alien snowman ancestors. It dissolves that in our nature which is most tediously human.

It is what "Bob" smokes. The smoke from his Pipe drifting Heavenward is the great Signal which assures our Space Brothers that the Man "Bob" still lives and that Earth is still worth saving/destroying.

YES!! 'Frop will bring about *The Change!!*

You cannot aspire to OverManhood without it. You cannot board the Escape Saucers without a high concentration of it in your bloodstream. Your mind will not be able to withstand the rigors of the Miracle of Crossover at the Xists' "hands" when comes the time to shed the last vestige of humanity.

With it, "Bob" gives his most insanely courageous warriors, the **Brotherhood of "Bob",**[2] brief glimpses of the Beforelife — the Pleasure Dimension foretold by the prophet Janor — and it fortifies them in their acts of Terminal Mercy. It steels the nerves and frees the Wills of his Chosen Instruments of Death.

S.L.A.K. Squad Missionary **Poonflang Dammerung** spoke lovingly of it before his immortal Last Mission in a testimonial to his Lord "Bob's" ways. "Yes, "Bob" shares of His Own Pipe with us before each foray into the Belly of the Beast . . . it gives us the

2. Founded by the martyred St. Tribunal Overdrive, who made the fatal mistake of "KILLING "BOB"" *once too often.*

3. "Medicine Fish-Hole" so-named by a 3-year-old SubGenius on his first 'Frop Trip. ISN'T THAT CUTE???

knowledge of our True Will and how it is juxtaposed with his. We all grip each other by the shoulders and sidle together in a great circle as we chant together between the Holy Dosages. *'Kill. Kill for the love of Killing. Kill for the love of Kali. Kill. Kill for fun. Kill to stay Free. Like a Man. To Make America Great! Kill . . .'* The dizzying 'Frop fumes combine with the endless rhythmical repetitions to create a living power vortex of unspeakable ecstasy."

While alcohol wantonly kills brain tissue, sloughing it off to be passed in the morning as the wasted, dead ravages of wine, 'Frop does not kill brain cells, NAY NAY!, but *mutates* them . . . causes them to multiply faster. Each succeeding generation is of course stronger than those before it.

Man made booze, "Bob" made 'Frop. WHO DO YOU TRUST?

'Frop enables one to "see" with the eyes closed . . . this is the Unblinking Stare of the Overlid. Through it, one may pass through the Gates of the 'FropLord *into* the 'Frop City of the soul; once the seeker has reached Bardo 18 of the 18th Hole of Hangar 18 of **ZomboFropLand** he may think the same thought over and over and over and yet never care, never feel boredom. "The 'Frop entered through the forehead and exited through the upper back of the neck. The Possessing Demon was exorcised instantly and the President, if not his brain, was saved." (From the investigation saga, *'DeathFrop at Dealy Plaza'* by the Überbrow Commission.) . . . THIS IS 'FROP.

The United States government has tried many times to steal the formula for 'Frop from the Tibetan Sanctuary, but it is fruitless; the preparation of 'Frop is a spiritual thing; without the sacred element of the *gurupee*, the molecules cannot be broken down and the white glowing mixture will be useless. The ritual can be performed only by an advanced shaman skilled in the alchemical arts.

It is not a toy.

And for this reason, not all SubGenii choose to meddle in the **Medicine Fish Hole**[3] of 'Frop . . . as difficult as that may be to believe. No, there are those who ingest only the *conceptualization* of the 'Frop but never its physical substance.

The windows of the eyes of such space-age Beatniks of Sobriety are scrubbed to a diamond clarity. Their cells know not the tidal surge of Need; they receive their "kicks" from the *pure intensity* of REALITY ITSELF! They become gassed on the very atmosphere they breathe, Blown by the merest wind, Loaded with the fuel of their fevered brows! Their Third and Fifth Eyes blink and squint into the garish light of Uncensored Actuality! They are 'nuked' by the fusion of their own atoms, they need no store-bought wings to fly, for they are lighter than the air in their Slack.

They stagger, lurch, and fall down with the intoxicant ecstasy of sheer Awakefullness! They run to the Throne of Elimination to discharge their INANE GLEE!

But, whether a 'FropHead or not, the True SubGenius forces the Body to stand upright, where it can see further . . . he shows authority over the drug-fiend which houses the brain. Our rightful Place has been usurped by our own bodies, and *we want to see THE MAN IN CHARGE!!*

It's "Bob." "Bob" is the *true* Mind Storm, the *godly* Lobe Explosion in your skull. WHO NEEDS DOPE? You *never come down* from the High of "Bob!"

"BOB *IS THE DRUG.*

The Conspiracy is a *real* "drug" that "drugs" you, that makes you want to go to sleep or to kick ass for no reason. "Bob" is the drug that makes you kick ass where it *counts.* The drug of remembering WHO YOU ARE. The drug that WAKES you up. The drug that MAKES YOU SEE or LEAVES YOU *BE!*

If you can't afford the 'Frop, and the High of "Bob" is more than you can handle, yet you still need an unnatural 'lift,' there are two cost-free techniques that most Doktors recommend: SLEEP and ANTISLEEP. According to Dr. Philo Drummond, Ø.M.D., "Sleep is the ultimate *drug* . . . like all narcotics and hallucinogens rolled together into one great Winner's Blend of Nothingness." Antisleep creates similar effects, but you can get more *done.* 1) Work for 48 hours without sleeping. 2) *Still* don't go to bed. 3) Enjoy the hallucinations.

WHY SIT STILL FOR THIS...

YOU DON'T WANT A MINK COAT. RAYON IS THE FABRIC OF THE FUTURE.

Unibrow one

ONE WAY

Puzzling Evidence   LIES

...WHEN YOU CAN HAVE **THIS**?

NOW *Do it yourself*

A Beautiful Final Tribute

Delivered of drugs, alcohol, and the occult

But if the headaches continue, and the Elder Gods keep punishing you for knowing of their presence, then by God no matter how "straight" you are, you *will* go down in the Medicine Fish Hole. And there you have the choice between The Con's killer dope, and *The PILS of "Bob."*

We can't tell you much about "Bob's" PILS. The fact is, you're floating in a *sea* of pills but you just can't *see* them. Any SubGenius who has attended a revival at The Naked Church of the SubGenius in Dallas can tell you that these pills are very, very special.

Yes, history has shown that all great kings live by the pills and die by the pills. The link between pills and death has become an integral part of our culture . . . and a major theme of the Church.

Faster than anything else, the pills lead to the highest of all highs, **THE HIGH OF DEATH** — the "Bulletproof Stage of Enlightenment."

!INSTANT SLACK FOREVER! —THE SUBGENIUS WAY

The Church does not molly-coddle the realness of Death. We fully recognize both its potential, and the pain and terror which naturally accompany it. For we know that, ultimately, it brings the Hope of **Slack Eternal.**

If you believe in Heaven, you'll go there. If you believe in Hell, you'll go *there* even if you believe in Heaven *too*. If you don't believe in either one, well . . . good luck.

BETTER SEX IN SECONDS

The issues of Hell and Heaven are too detailed to approach in this Book. We can, however, deal with a very practical aspect of it all: what to do with the body, the burnt-out robot chassis.

Many SubGenii find the conventional Pink funeral even more disgusting than the prospect of being dissected, and *played with,* by some pervert medical student or apprentice mortician. Graveyards, no matter how dramatic looking they might be, are still nothing but holes with dead people in them and dirt on top of the dead people.

The Plains Indians used to leave bodies in trees, where they rejoined nature . . . a good idea, but The Con has made it illegal, even for Indians.

There is a simple solution: GIVE EVERYTHING TO "BOB." Besides a trust fund and the mention of him in your will, see that he gets your gold teeth, your interferon, your adrenal and pituitary glands. Arrange with friends to have your head **"launched"** ritualistically and wall-mounted as a trophy, grinning and with Pipe in mouth. The greatest honor for any SubGenius is to have his head mounted on "Bob's" rumpus room wall, or his skull made into one of Dobbs' ritual ashtrays. Let your eye socket be his doorbell. GIVE OF YOURSELF and you will be assured of special treatment on The Other Side. Thus, if your soul is confused upon leaving the body and becomes a wandering ghost, Church exorcists will see that it's given the right directions to Valhalla, Asgard, Purgatory or the Underworld, depending on your special merits. (All four are fun.)

CHAPTER 17
STARTING YOUR OWN CHURCH

"In my name shall they cast out devils; they shall speak with new tongues. They shall take up serpents; *and if they drink any deadly thing, it shall not hurt them;* they shall lay hands on the sick, and they shall recover."

(Mark 16:17,18)

"What's the matter, son? You afraid o' this little snake? *Here, take this pill.* OOM bala shabba hey "Bob" soba shee bak! YEA! COME *OUT!!* He's healed!! The boy is healed!!"
—Pastor Ahab Pretorious at Dallas FisTemple Revival, March 15, 1977

OF THE LOCAL CLENCHES

The Universal Church is all SubGenii of all nations. If it were possible, this multitude would meet in one place for a single great *Mass Conception/Fornication,* but since this is not possible we Sub-Divide into particular **Clenches** or **Schizms.**

The main goals of each Clench: to proclaim the Word, that Subs can gain Slack and be saved, and Pinks shamed; to provide spiritual, material, and sexual marketing and trading between the Children of "Bob"; to cast out the False Prophets and to heed no other World Religion for more than 17 days.

A Clench does not require the divine authority of the Father Church to organize BUT it does risk DIVINE LAWSUIT if it does not **PAY FOR** the basic supplies needed or, if the Clench does its own manufacturing of said articles, the RESIDUALS thereof ("Bob" requests a mere 25%).

All efforts to glorify The Cause, such as gifts, prayers, volunteer labor, or sexual favors, should *as soon as possible* break all laws of conformity according to the PinCustoms of that particular tribal group of The Conspiracy. Church government shall be as radical or reactionary as Members desire, so long as it is far from the pernicious Norm.

Clenches shall name themselves and list their mailing addresses with the Foundation. Examples of Clench Names: "First Natural Church and Trust;" "MegaFisTemple Lodge of the Wrath of Jehovah;" "First Feces Templegogue of Dobbs Orthodoxic;"

"Church of the Profuse Discharge" (a Chicago gay caucus); "Church of "Bob," Scientist"; "SubArctic Church of the Red-Eyed Loon;" "The Local Church of the SubGenius;" "Church of the Immaculate '67 Chevy;" "Bleeding Head of (WORLD CUP GOLFER'S NAME HERE) Launchers Society;" "Unholy Evilangelical Mission;" "Primitive SubGenius Church of the Sanctified Apeskin;" "Satanists for Christ."

Sizes of Clenches may vary considerably. There are Family Clenches, Double Clenches or Tantric Temples of Two, Tribal Clenches, City Clenches, State Clenches; there may also be Clenches pertaining to a specific business: Fireman's Clench, Computer Technician Clenches, etc.

A Clench of One, or Solo Clench, is every bit as holy as a giant one with a choir, even if the lone hermit merely sits in his Chamber of Solitude exercising sacred Couch Potatoedom, so long as he does it *diligently* and with *commitment* to Slack.

Clenches without Pastors, in which NO RULES apply, are entirely sanctified; indeed, "Bob" looks with special favor on those with the most independence, insolence and chaos. *To follow the letter of The Law is to break the spirit of The Law;* there is no greater crime to the blind Eye of The Law.

Nevertheless, **MARK THIS YE SINNERS:** The Father Church is **not responsible** for the actions of any SubGenius individual or local Clench; the Incorporated SubGenius Foundation is not responsible for the actions of the collective world Church; nor is the Church-at-large responsible for the actions of The SubGenius Foundation, Incorporated, nor of itself.

Pope David Meyer appears in a puff of smoke before thousands on live TV.

OF SERVICES

THE HALL, TEMPLE, TABERNACLE OR LOUNGE should be decorated with the trappings of worship: Dobbsheads, skulls, Windbreakers, Pipes, 9-irons, pornography, lucky stones, sacrificial altars, etc. The ideal places for Church worship are hollowed-out and abandoned 1950s motels, gas stations, and hamburger stands, although many Clenches meet in the homes of naïve members. If a *feast* is held in conjunction with Services, mummified corpses are often propped up at the table to remind revellers of the ever-present face of Death.

After suitable religious music has been played to establish a mood of piety, the Pastor opens the Service by asking the congregation to bow their heads for a brief moment of NOISE, or primal screaming. On that cue, the congregation leaps up and, shrieking, throws as much money as possible at the Pastor, the Altar, and the Altered Boys. (Monies thus taken in are divided according to need between the local Clench Judicatory and The SubGenius Foundation, whence it goes to "Bob." It is impossible for the local Clench's need to be greater than that of the Father Church.)

After the Pelting of the Pastor with Coin, the Pastor should preach a Waiver of Blame; all Members agree as loudly as possible that they are not "guilty" of anything, or, if they are, that they are *proud* of it.

Services may then proceed in any order of event decreed by Chance. Suggested Revival Activities are as follows:

Ritual "Bobtism" of new Members. The Anointee, dressed preferably in a golfing outfit, is held underwater for 3 minutes by the Altered Boys and Mastress Dominatrixes.

Ritual Burnings of money or of effigies: authority figures, celebrities, Smurfs, etc.

Snake Handling and the partaking of dangerous Sacraments as tests of faith.

Mass Spoutings or the encouragement to the multitude to speak in tongues.

Anti-Aerobics and the practice of other Frenzy Techniques.

Confessions are encouraged that the assembly may learn of new sins to apply in their own lives.

Seances, Levitations, and Mass Astral Projection. Precautions should be taken in the event of unexpected unleashing of telekinetic powers, poltergeist activity, etc.

Marriages and Divorces: Ministers should be familiar with the Short Duration versions of these ceremonies.

Sermons. The preacher's duty is to become a vessel, a medium, a *conduit* for "Bob's" Word so that he can add to the already existing Scripture. Many who hear The Call are being guided by Wotan; sometimes, however, He does not bother, and the Ranter is left in The Test of Coldsweat.

In all SubGenius worship, attention *must* be centered around JHVH-1 Whose Word is made flesh in "Bob"; but because He is in everything, including beer, sex, video games, state fair midways, etc., there is infinite leeway in objects of worship.

At some point in the Service, the people are called upon to make response to "Bob's" great Gifts to them, through hymns, prayers, rants, spouts, frothings, foamings, seizures, yodeling, laughing, hallucinating, sleeping, gorging, or group sex. The greatest Recompense that can be made to The "Bob," however, is in the form of moneys hurled at the preacher or used to purchase Church Goods.

At least one *HEALING* or casting out of demons is required at each Service, through the Laying On of Hands or Tools.

If no Member requires a Healing, then a Fake Healing *must be held,* and will generate equal Slack Points.

FREE WOMEN AVAILABLE!

Services should include deprogramming, memory erasure, scoffing, mockery, and *blasphemy,* JUST ON GENERAL PRINCIPLES. Not to pull the Leg of Jesus, for instance, is, contrary to Pink worship, to INSULT the original but long-suppressed Dobbs Nature of Him as well as other gods. Dobbs proclaims that almost all rival deities, subdeities and incubi have their foundations in Slack despite their seemingly inevitable perversion by the Need of Men to be Led.

By the same token, at EVERY Meeting, there MUST be *some blasphemy directed against "Bob" himself* sufficiently shocking to preserve the ONE HOPE WE HAVE of not ending up like other religions. There should *always* be one Member elected to the very sacred post of "Sacred Heckler," "Divine Denouncer of Dobbs," "Bobkiller," or "High Disconnector."

THE CONGREGATION MUST BE NOT SPECTATORS, BUT PARTICIPANTS. SubGenius Service is a *People's Service;* the Temple is a *People's Temple.* (We are not trying to talk 900 people into committing suicide; but to get them each to talk 900 *other* people into sending us $20.) Generally, anything spoken by any Member in any Revival is considered at least *temporary* Gospel.

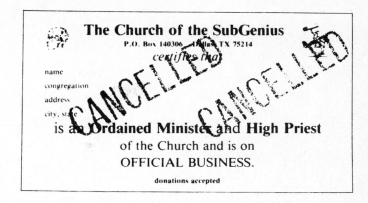

Thus, it is the Priest's duty to record these words on a tape recorder (or, in Church jargon, "The Ears of Überbrow"). Not to record Revivals is a Special Sin, but even worse is to send the tapes *unedited* to the Church Fathers; the zeal for One's Own Voice must be tempered by mercy on "Bob's" All-Hearing Ears.

The Pastor can end the Service with the bellowed phrase, **"OR KILL ME,"** and once again the congregation showers him with pocket change or checks. A sacrificial dollar is symbolically burned, the Pipes are lit, The Salute performed, and, as the Flock lines up for the Holy Kool-Aid, the Service is allowed to degenerate into a party.

Also good for Service-Attendance Points is the going out of doors to meet civic responsibilities such as riots, protest demonstrations, etc., preferably in accordance with the nonrules of PatrioPsychotic

St. Schwind

St. Rick Hoefle

AnarchoMaterialism. *Any* manner of extremism may be supported, from the *Anarchists for John Birch* to *Nazis Against Nukes,* as long as it is AGAINST The Conspiracy.

OF PASTORS, MINISTERS, DEVANGELISTS, DEACONS, PRESBYTERS AND RANTERS

All Subgenius Preachers are "LAY" Preachers; in contrast to those of false religions, they should be as much as possible *"of the world."* They should understand "sin" by first hand experience.

He or she must forever swear off being grave, prudent, stern, or otherwise boring; must live by example with the smile of the Mask of Insanity on his or her face; must coach sinners, and beseech them to reveal their special talents and the tricks of their success; must instruct the ignorant, comfort the mourner, harrass the Pink, offend the Staid, and make at least a polite effort to seduce the Widow and Old Maid, Widower, etc. It is ENCUMBENT on the preacher to fully exploit his or her abnormality and, within the limits of his or her talents, to freak out Normals, cast out False Prophets, pursue reckless exploration of the Mockery Sciences, and to OUTSELL ALL OTHER CHURCHES.

The *RANTING* of the Pastor shall be, within the perimeters of Church morality, original work, *as divulged by communion with his own "Bobgland,"* unless he is a True Medium and merely the Trance Mouthpiece of a Higher Entity. The gift of Spouting shall be practiced *according to its entertainment and spiritual value;* without the former, the latter is self-negated. ANY public rant by ANY SubGenius must conform to the Third Sacred Law: **"IF YOU DON'T HAVE A SENSE OF HUMOR, DON'T TRY TO BE FUNNY."**

A general rule to follow is, "Don't Rant Unless It's From The Gut." Oftimes the sheer terror of public speaking can be channeled into the necessary fever pitch of a true, wallpaper-peeling Rant; however, don't try to "act" mad if you're either not mad, or not an actor. A HINT: If, in the middle of a Rant, a preacher "spaces out" and loses his train of thought, he may avoid "dead air" by achieving a Divine Seizure: falling on the floor, speaking in tongues, calling for a Pipe. MYSTIFY THE PUBLIC!!

The final duty of any Pastor or Pastress is to police the ranks and expose those who have infiltrated for The Conspiracy or else who have become Members for the "coolness" of it rather than for its *meaning.* This is done as much to protect them as the Church, for there are subtle but very real dangers in meddling with The Forces for those unready. Many are the cases of deluded Pink Boys who were seduced by "The Other Bob," the "Bad Bob" who got them *hooked* and put a Pipe-bemouthed *monkey* on their backs, who followed them *home* at night . . . these Slackless Ones become "WereBobs" or "ImaBobs," lost in a grinning schizophrenia in which they can no longer separate themselves from that which is "Boblike" in them. THEY THINK THEY *ARE "BOB"* and are soon lost to the perdition of a Conspiracy insane asylum. It *almost* happened to Philo — IT *COULD* HAPPEN TO YOU.

Also to be ostracized are those who call themselves SubGenii but behave more like Moonies, stupidly mouthing dogma and Pinking up the Church. These *deserve* to be called "Bobbies" EVEN BY THE NORMALS among whose number they actually count. We will *take their money* and tolerate their presence at meetings to the extent required by Sacred Publicity, but no matter how disorganized the Clenches may be there *will* always be *an unspoken ladder of closeness to "Bob"* which these Token PinkSubs will eventually sense, DESPITE THEIR LACK THEREOF.

All Clenches and/or single Members **MUST SCHIZM sooner or later,** though there are no rules for time limits of orthodoxy. If a

Master Ranter, Pope of New York, Rev. Dr. David N. Meyer II, M.D., D.D.S., admonishes crowd at NY's P.S.I. art gallery.

Clench starts to become boring, repetitive, unoriginal and above all too *kiss-ass,* the Clench should immediately effect a dissolution of itself before the Father Church is forced to humiliate and damn it out of existence. The antispontaneity of "Bobbies" which turns Holy Clenchdom into a "Bob" Fan Club (no longer an exercise of abnormality, but a conformity of nonconformists) is THE WORST FORM OF BACKSLIDING.

If the Father Church hears of ANY Clench refusing an individual admittance on the grounds of SKIN COLOR, ETHNIC BACKGROUND, FINANCIAL CONDITION, EDUCATION, SEX OR SEXUAL PROCLIVITIES, OR ANY CONDITION OTHER THAN *PINKNESS,* then said False Clench SHALL FACE THE UNLEASHED WRATH OF **THE CURSE OF "BOB'S" GRANDFATHER** AND OF **THE STARK FIST OF JHVH-1 HIMSELF.** *PLAY YE NOT "GOD."*

All Laws, Rules and Ordinances herein related EXCEPT THE LAST are subject to the **One True Law of NO LAWS** and thus by THE UNQUESTIONABLE DECREE OF THE ELDERS may be considered Null and Void as dictated by the *One Last Truest Law of SLACK.*

SLACK COMES FIRST.

EXACT ACTUAL MOMENT of the Launching of the Sacred Bleeding Head is seen in this miraculous photo enlargement stolen from police files. Hypercleats can be seen with sacred 9-iron at instant of impact on stage at the 1982 Dealy Plaza SubGenius Revival. Dr. Philo Drummond in OverMan form is dimly visible in background with *Doktors for "Bob."* Church Revival/Brawls were never the same after this shattering event. (AS SEEN ON *WHAT'S UP AMERICA* (Showtime TV)!)
photo: Dr. Bootmokus

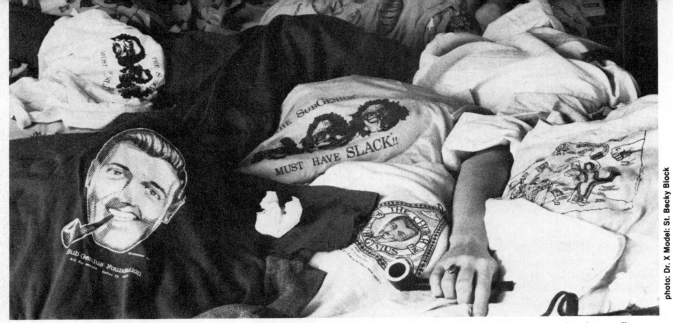

No contemporary SubGenius fashion wardrobe is complete without the full line of Church-imprinted undergarments, jogging outfits, accessories, "T's," and, of course, "Slacks."

RANKS

Although they overlap, there is also a distinction in personality traits between the Hierarchy ranks of **Popes, Doktors,** and **Saints.** Saints tend to be Masters of the Spirit — excellent Trance Spouters or Mediums who are highly Illuminated but often long-suffering. They are usually the poorest financially because they drift towards quality rather than quantity. They are the wisest, yet the least knowledgeable of worldly affairs. St. Janor of the Hypercleats would be a good example of a male Saint.

Popes are High Exploiters, Masters of worldly, creaturely things, controllers of men's minds. Charismatic and loud, they possess the strongest of Pstenches and make the best Preachers and Clench Leaders. They make fine Word Bearers and Media Adepts.

Doktors are Masters of the Flesh. They are creative in the arts of music, image, and Love; whereas Popes lean to the amoral, Doktors are often Good-Bad — i.e., of deep Good alternating with deep Evil. Doktors make superb AntiVirgins and Healers of Appliances.

The distinct behavior patterns of these three groups can best be observed at parties, which drive Saints crazy, but of which Popes will be "the life;" a Doktor, meanwhile, will be found in the back bathroom adulterizing some Pink's spouse.

HOLIDAYS

Fullness of the Gospel should be expressed continuously, but special Seasons are appropriate for certain observances:

ADVERT:	The Season of Advertising; around late Fall in the heathens' calendar.
EPIPHICACOPHONY:	The Season of Bad Noise, devoted to the indefinable *"G'BroagFran"* of Anti-Music; middle Summer.
EMACULATION:	The Season of Intoxication; late Winter ('Frop Harvest).
TURNOVER:	The Season of Earnings; near Xistmas and The Nativity of Santa Claus.
PASSAROUND:	The Season of Fertility; Spring; old pagan druidic earth-worship rites and sacrifices in sacred "Groves" such as abandoned car junkyards and city dumps, where dwell the Ghosts of our Ancestors' Things.
M'MOREAL DAY:	The Season of "Bob's" Nativity; every day, because "Bob" has had over 365 Past Lives, each starting on a different day. START THROWING HIM BIRTHDAY PARTIES.

Pastor Naked's TIPS FOR NEW MINISTERS

- Your first public rants should last about 45 seconds. So, go totally apeshit. MAKE 'em believe! When "Bob" abruptly chokes off your 'speech' don't resist him but GIVE IN and fall on the ground spouting in the tongues that "Bob" will shoot into your head.
- Figure out if there're any humans in your church and play the crowd off against 'em.
- It's O.K. to lay members of your flock. That's a big reason for attending.

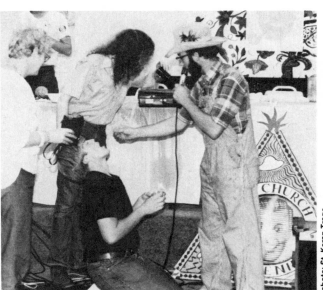

Pastor Buck demonstrates perfect form in this spontaneous sacramental pill dispensation. Note the correct presence of tape recorders and holy regalia.

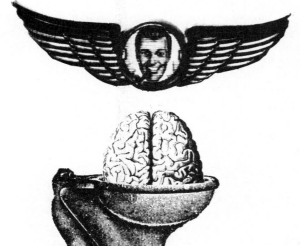

CHAPTER 18
YOUR
INSTRUCTIONS

"When in Rome, KILL ME."

— Sterno, Pope of Arkansas

"Extremism in the defense of extremism is no vice."

— Dobbs Rant Tape 16 (1960)

"There's no such thing as no p.r."

— Dobbs

"Be in by 10."

— "Bob" to his daughter K____ in '75

 **FIRST AND FOREMOST:**

EXERCISE YOUR ABNORMALITY!
"Give me liberty or kill me." — Pope Sterno

You yes YOU can *and must* self-deprogram! To "Disconnect" is of *utmost importance.* "Bob" *is now* doing it for you by making *you NOW do it.* And you must do it to the HILT! Your divine idiocy and *personal extremism* are your single two most valuable assets. If you let Them take *those,* you're DEAD MEAT WALKING LIKE A MAN. *Cling* then to your *stupidity,* what little you may have left; the un-self-consciousness of ERROR ITSELF allows the *only true glimpse* of the way *man was meant to be.* **"SLACK . . . OK, Slack is how you take life by the throat and *scream* at it!"— "Bob" in the film REPENT!**
So you OWE it to "Bob" to prod your inanity to its *especial edge.*

Use "your own initiative." Indeed, the most insidiously clever techniques of infiltrapropagandaic SubGenetics often spew forth from *brand new members, mere babes* who know very little formal doctrine but who *for that very reason* and *by default* are not afraid to heed their inner Bobself and go careening off on their own obsessive tangents of WRATH, SINFUN and GOOD DEEDS!

So join the Church, soak up some "Dobbs," and then SCHISM. Form your own heretical offshoot. We fucking DARE you, you lazy DROBE. For through its unfathomable fragmentation the Church shall TRIUMPH. THEY will never be able to put their ludicrous yet all-too-stark FINGER on us. That's right — if you've got the GUMPTION, declare yourself High Potentate or whatever of your own state or local Anti-ConGregation. "Bob" "sees" VICIOUS in-Church squabbling in our future. GOOD! We must HONE our HATE ABILITIES for when they'll *really* be needed.

In the meantime, work on these self-erasement/adulation techniques:

REPENT and $LACK OFF!!

Quit trying to act smart. *What are you trying to prove??* Don't kid yourself, your time on this planet is limited, so you had better act like you have all the time in the WORLD — or it's ALL WASTED. Go for thrills — satisfaction — hard core sex — risks — sacramentality — traditional family values — and ACTION. *Ignore* those filthy stinking normalcy-boys or FREAK THEM OUT, or KILL ME. You have GOT to DISCONNECT to get back IN SYNC. Bounce back and forth between your Rewardian and Emergentile tendencies until you know just where the balance lies. Get to know the parameters of, and then "feed," the 8 Sacred Inner Faces of your so-called 'Personality.' YOU *CAN* evolve OR devolve yourself, you CAN cleanse or sully your soul, depending on *your* requirements . . . requirements which "BOB" KNOWS and towards which he is even now psychically shoving you. Edit your memories — rearrange their chronologies.

John Hagen

SEEK VISIONS!!

— and report them to the Church. (Pay us to publish them!!)

Don't expect authentic religious mania to come easily. Actually seeing into the future or the **Aetherzone** (the archive of "storyboards" for potential futures) takes time and an hallucinatory kind of *work*.

Stare at the Dobbshead mounted over your bed or on your Ex-cremeditation Chamber wall for HOURS. Feed off the "Bob" energy. First you will see colors and fleeting alien landscapes, then with a wrenching chest pain you will detach from your body and fly down a long dark tunnel bursting into a blindingly lit God Knows Where.

PLACATE THE STARK FIST!!

— by keeping *yourself alive*. Prepare for the Econocataclysm by hoarding food, gold, guns, ammo, gas, etc. Bone up on survival techniques. You can actually *prosper* in the coming Tribulations if you play your cards right.

In the meantime, it is equally important to learn to manipulate the Luck Plane. Start paying *close* attention to "coincidences." It could save your life! FLOW with your divine Foibles, WANDER OFF on the Paths of Least Resistance, and chances are you'll never even have to use the cold-blooded survivalist tricks you have learned.

STUDY the Prescriptures — UPHOLD the Laws — do NOT repeat do NOT defecate on the Sabbath. Keep that hotline to "Bob" OPEN so that any incoming messages are received LOUD and CLEAR. It will help to "prove" your faith in "Bob" by mastering an impossible feat like fire-walking, snake-handling or levitating.

Remember, serving "Bob" can mean many things. You can either BLOW IT OFF, or you can kill yourself, but whatever you do, DON'T FRET. It clogs your Third Nostril even more than it already is, and without that particular gland you can *forget* enlightenment.

— and spread the Word of "Bob!" The Foundation NEEDS a constant influx of ten to twenty $20 memberships a day to wage this crusade . . . it is your duty to SOLICIT and ENSNARE new members.

Needless to say unless you're stupid (which is OK), BE SELECTIVE.

Use the tools "Bob" gave you: WAGE THE WOR with bludgeon yuks, the masks of insanity, sacred jests, and TOTAL CONFIDENCE. Assault the pinks and the latent SubGeniuses alike with the LURE of SubGenius every chance you get.

Be prepared for resistance, of course. "Bob's" truth is new to this world, and most people will assume they have better things to spend their money on than some CULT. It's up to YOU to show them that this *isn't* just "some cult."

HELL — take it to the streets and bombard your environment with it. Don't DIE while sitting around on your BUTT — go OUT THE DOOR, stand on a car hood, and PREACH. Make witness for "Bob." Come back at rabid born-agains and krishnoid types with a taste of their own medicine. (NEVER enter an airport without a Pamphlet.) Call up talk shows and change the subject to the Church.

Remember, SubGenius isn't just a good way to freak people out and cast out local false prophets — it is a way to *control their minds*. You can do it. Put on "the Bobface". . . you'll find that EXACTLY THE RIGHT WORDS will SPRING MAGICALLY from your mouth AS IF OF THEIR OWN ACCORD!!

Don't worry about being a jerk.

WILL YOU BE READY?

A helpful hint: break people in slowly. Start by simply discussing the awful prevalence of normals, pinks, and dupes of the Conspiracy. Even most humans will agree with you. Then gradually introduce the more and more insidious, yet seemingly harmless aspects of the Conspiracy at large. Begin to bring in the harder-to-swallow concepts, but only if it looks like they'll be able to *understand*. Fi-

Dr. Alice and others in the Sacramento Clench dumbfounded Pinks, made $$$ and got big media coverage by erecting this Church of the Immaculate '60 Chevy "Bob"-Prop display at a major California Holistic Psychic Arts Fair. Such lucrative displays are now popping up in most major cities.

nally let loose with the monstrous truth behind the Men in Black, the Saucer People, the Great white Brotherhood, and the advanced supersonic Nazi Hell Creatures from inside the Hollow Earth. Cap it off with dreadful hints of the Xists and JHVH-1. Save The Elder Gods for *later*.

Once you have sufficiently terrified them, reintroduce the fact of "Bob." This time it will have results.

Another helpful technique is to use reverse psychology on the more stubborn, narrowly programmed types. Discreetly show them a Pamphlet but warn, "Don't show this around." Imply that there is actually some risk in even possessing such material.

Or, if the target is an intellectual, subtly insult his intelligence. "Oh, well, I don't think YOU would be able to get into something like *this."*

Many smug jerks, when told of SubGenius, will think you are crazy and will condescendingly "humor" you, then turn away. In such cases you have every right to use The Lilac Treatment™: I.E., "Lie Like Hell." Tell them that Hunter S. Thompson, Federico Fellini, Keith Richards, DEVO, Burt Reynolds, Sir Laurence Olivier, R. Crumb, Johnny Paycheck, Elvis Costello, Roger Corman, Steven King, and Mick Jagger are card-carrying SubGeniuses (some are). Chuckle inwardly as the fashion-enslaved smug jerk suddenly changes his tune. NOTE: Always be "dead serious" when using this treatment.

REMEMBER — when first broaching the subject of the Church, always assure the potential convert that:

1. He probably already IS a SubGenius,
2. BUT . . . to realize his full potential, he should send AT LEAST $20 to the Foundation.

ALWAYS HAVE THE FOUNDATION'S ADDRESS WITH YOU: IN WALLET, PURSE, CAR! (Box 140306, Dallas, TX 75214)

PERFECT HEALTH IN MINUTES!

THINGS TO DO TO YOUR PHYSICAL ENVIRONMENT

There are countless ways to inflict physical manifestations of SubGenius on your surroundings, but this is the one which we NOW, IN PRINT FOR ALL THE WORLD TO SEE, tell you to **NEVER** do:

DON'T draw pipes in the mouths of cool studs, famous faces, holymen and Santa Clauses on every billboard, poster or subway ad you can get your hands on. DON'T add "quotes" around the head like some sort of demonic halo.
EXAMPLE:

Dallas' most famous Singin' Preacher "corrected" this billboard at great risk.

To help keep you from doing this, DON'T make a stencil like this:

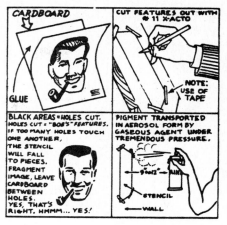

Also, do NOT spray-paint "SLACK" on bridge abutments of all major traffic arteries in your home town. Can you imagine thousands of citizens driving down the expressway, seeing that cryptic phrase scrawled in desperate jiggly letters, and *wondering?* EXAMPLE:

The Baltimore Clenches demonstrate things we must never do, and other incorrect illegal uses of the stencil. (Severn, tENTacON, X-Richard, Debs photos)

SPREAD THE LITERATURE, SLOGANS, POSTERS and PICS of "BOB."

He wants to see his own face plastered EVERYWHERE by 1984. That's what the various one-page flyers and mini-posters are for. If it was up to us, we'd be doling out flyers and Pamphlets to you like they were jellybeans. But NO! Dobbs demands that *YOU sacrifice!* You can't buy a decent bed in Hell without earning it here in the Job of Life.

That means it's up to you to either xerox some things yourself or front us money for extra copies of the disposable one-pagers like the Dobbsheads, the Testimonial Sheet, etc. (SEE APPENDIX.)

Say you've got an Adsheet and you want to confuse relatives by taping the little ads to letters. Before you start cutting the sheet up,

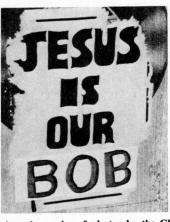  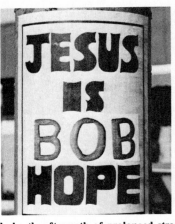 

Amazing series of photos by the Church of the Immaculate '60 Chevy reveal ghastly aftermath of prolonged street-propaganda Cult Wars in Sacramento. "Bob" won and the heathens were shamed.

go xerox a few copies . . . or print up a few thousand at the nearest quick-print shop (Send the Church some $ for residuals if you're a decent type.) Of course, we'd prefer that you order what you need directly from us at the inflated prices listed in the catalog, but right now getting The Word OUT is more important than the money: it insures much MORE money, LATER.

ALL BEWARE: do NOT reprint any of our profit items like the Pamphlet, the Stark Fist, the Excuse, the Doktorate, etc. These are copyrighted, trademarked, and imbued with a number of potent curses.

Most of you are talented bastards, judging by the hilariously-answered Questionnaires. So why not make your OWN SubGenius propaganda? Just be sure to ALWAYS include the Sacred Box Number — OUR Sacred Box Number — and the Divine Fact of $1. Send us a copy for "Bob" to inspect so that you know you aren't accidentally meddling with a *dangerous* combination of pictures and words.

Now that you've got these hundreds of little Dobbsheads, mysterious ads, or blistering one-page manifestos, **GO BERSERK.** Carry the propaganda around with you, stashed perhaps in a coat pocket or a cigarette case.[1] Also remember that rubber stamps of SubGenius emblems are now available through us or Top Drawer Rubber Stamps[2].

Let the Fist of J-1 or the Spirit of NHGH guide you. It can be transcendentally juvenile and monstrously inspirational to skulk around, anonymously pasting up things that YOU KNOW will confuse many pompous smart-asses and "beautiful people" who thought they were *really hep.* GET BACK AT THEM: know gloatingly that YOU UNDERSTAND and THEY DON'T! Take justice into your own hands and plaster them all over school, church and company bulletin boards! (SubGeniusness has a way of spreading through offices like DDT through a foodchain — witnesses report co-workers suddenly spouting SubJargon involuntarily and chronically!)

1. Lick 'n' Stick SubGProp is available from Rev. Naked or The Foundation for $1 for several sheets.
   Peel-back ads, quotes, etc., plus postcads and GIANT STICKERS, all different from ours, but of a highly sanctified nature, can be had from the bustling AAA AARDVARK CHURCH OF SALES. Send a self-addressed stamped envelope to: AAA Aardvark, 2020 Park Ave. S., Minneapolis, MN 55404.

2. Send $1.50 for rubber stamp catalog to Top Drawer Rubber Stamps, Dept. SUBGENIUS, Hancock, VT 05748.

YES! Distribute 1000s! Hand them out at concerts . . . throw them in open car windows . . . stick 'em on doors, windshields, etc., and especially urinals and toilet booths where they CAN'T be ignored, and where people are necessarily in the excremeditary state of mind most receptive to our Message.

The possibilities are limitless. YOU have an original squirming brain — USE IT!

It needn't stop with the little one-pagers. Make your own BANNERS — POSTERS — BUTTONS — T-SHIRTS! Go Bobwild and hang a 40-foot "Bob" banner on City Hall like Sterno did!!

Stage a damn PUBLIC RITUAL! Get with fellow zealots and STORM bastions of overt normalcy. Alert the news media. The Arkansas clenches got so active at this that they aroused the wrath of local religious leaders. And they started it all by placing cryptic little Bobblurbs in the classified sections of the papers. Now they are being rewarded with groupies and status beyond their WILDEST imaginings, which were pretty wild to begin with. IN FACT, by being thus 'attuned' to the Luck Plane, they have ensnared *police officers* who were about to BUST them, told them of "Bob," and sent them safely away as NEW CONVERTS to the CAUSE!! (Believe it or not, an unusually high percentage of cops are latent SubGeniuses and will respond favorably and even *illegally* if you will but give them half a chance!)

Decorate your home with garish SubArt. Cut out the big Dobbshead, shellac it onto a fancy plaque, surround it with skulls, guns, swords, other meaningful knick-knacks, and PRESTO you have an ALTAR! (Not a bad way to get visitors curious and frightened about the cult!)

And don't forget **Gift Memberships!** Rank your acquaintances (or enemies) as Latent, Rogue, Renegade or Conspiracy so we know how to approach them.

EARN HUNDREDS A DAY!

If we could, *we'd* be handing this stuff out on street corners. But no — YOU must. Until we're as big as Scientology — two or three years at the outside — we must revere every minute and every red cent as Personal Saviors . . . albeit as hideously short-durationed Personal Saviors. For the Church to keep Spewing, those memberships MUST keep pumping in. And — believe it — your face-to-face, word-of-mouth spoutings and guerrilla prop-plasterings provoke FAR MORE response than any ordinary, sane paid advertising. It is YOU the Lone SubGenius who ARE THE AD.

Wheeling and Dealing for "Bob"

THIS is how you become a SAINT in the Church:
Set up a fantastic business deal for us.

Interest local or national Radio-TV-Newspapers-Magazines. They're always interested in freak shows and with SubGenius, they're biting off more than they bargain for.

Stage MASS REVIVALS and CONCLAVES.

Rack your brains for any "ins" you may have with the rich or powerful or famous — introduce them to the Divine Idiocy that is "BOB." Show them how THEY should invest in and publicize the Church. Solicit testimonials.

DONATE BUCKS TO "BOB!" Spend like there's no tomorrow. There isn't. (A word on donations: We aren't tax-deductible.)

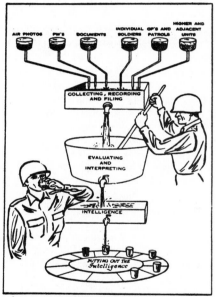

CONTRIBUTIONS TO THE DOGMA AND THE WORLD WEIRDO NETWORK

Send helpful hints — articles — art — photos — rare tomes — evidence. If they're good "Bob" will reward you and if they're bad we'll get a big laugh at your expense. Send SASE if you want stuff back.

Write about or tape record your own *unusual* discoveries in Slackmanship.

List and describe your more obscure Shordurpersavs so that we can alert others to them.

Send any damn thing you think we should know about or that we can USE — like tape recorders, typewriters, and ASTOUNDING FACTS.

Help identify, unmask, and report to Foundation Central any up-and-coming False Prophets who may presently be obscure but who may be dangerous to us later. (If nothing else, this is another great excuse for Analitizing.)

Write down your potentially prophetic dreams, and report any meaningful HINTS, COINCIDENCES, OMENS, or PORTENTS. If you have any truly weird pheno-experiences, report those too.

Find evidence in history books and newspapers of persecution of the cult through history . . . ancient SubGeniuses and Conspiracy ploys . . . proven prophecies by "Bob."

Help find MORE PICS OF "BOB" He apparently did a staggering amount of modeling during the '40s and '50s for cheesy ads . . . FIND THOSE ADS.

Don't be cowed by the Men In Black (though there isn't much you can do if they decide to turn their migraine machines on you). YES the One World Religion foretold in the Bible is HERE NOW. FIGHT for it. GO SCOURING!! Hit the streets and REMEMBER THE FIGHTIN' JESUS! Don't let them continue to BLACKEN His SWEET NAME.

One of the following elite organizations may be for you:

The Smite Patrol	Henchmen of NHGH
Hookers for "Bob"	The "Brotherhood of "Bob""
The Dobbs Youth	S.L.A.K. (SubGenius League of Ass Kickers) Squad

If you are a male and/or female virgin, we may need you for an important ritual on March 9, 1984.

The possibilities for fun and mischief are limitless with the incredible variety of SubGenius Occult Gimmicks: buttons, tapes, stickers, calendars, matchbooks, postcards, pins, pens, Pipes, medallions, fine jewelry, and 7-Bladed WindBreakers. Send $1 for catalog.

YOUR FINAL INSTRUCTIONS

Take SubGenius and shove it down the throats of religious leaders, politicians, media mongers, businessmen, police, students, housewives, retarded people, celebrities, losers, drunks, psychotics, EVERYONE IN THE PHONE BOOK!! At coffee breaks, civic clubs, fairs, porno theaters, shopping centers, gay bars, rock concerts!! THE HATE IS HUNGRY! *FEED IT!!*

Hints from Pope Sterno
MegaFisTemple Lodge of the Church of the Sub-Genius of Little Rock

The confidence exuded by the SubGenius is one of the myriad tools to be used to allay the fears and hesitations of possible confederates. The inner deviance which guides all SubGenii can only be exploited to its maximum potential by adhering to the tenets of weirdness, alienation, and Dobbsful spirituality.

In many cases, a latent SubGenius must be sequestered from the less fortunate Normals around him for the process of ultra-indoctrination to phase correctly. There are many elective choices for the programmer to make; the correct choice may mean the difference between an ardent "Bob" follower and a diffuse nimboid.

1. Kidnap your target and hold him in your shrine or temple until all hints of Con-programming are eradicated. The methods cannot and must not be pre-selected; they should be tailored to fit the needs of the particular dupe being processed.

2. Feed your target barbiturates until he lapses into a comatose state and board him onto an airplane to Kuala Lumpur, Malaysia. One of our minions will meet him at the heliport and transfer him to Dobbstown for further encoding.

3. Steal people's check books and forge their signatures to enrich the coffers of the Church. Also use the money to buy memberships for all unwitting Con-dupes.

4. Force "Bob" material onto bikers, redboys, nimboids, sick-ones, GLOrps, schwenkies, pinkies, blinkies, stinkies, numbnoids, gas-sniffers, pipe-fuckers, imposterators, ex-posianites, nun-eaters, unknown mutated heaps, shape-lords, various unit-mongers, NhGh-ites, gland-robbers, brain-offs, upto-florts, glumterags, gnipto-creeps, F-out badgers, stomachofnits, etc., etc., etc. . . . RRR

5. Set up a table in any student union of any university and place all the SubG literature on it for all to see. When people get curious go into the 'rap' and try to convert as many as possible before you're thrown out. You should be able to last twenty minutes at least.

6. Place SubG propaganda in copies of newspapers in those coin-operated vending machines. I do this in front of the post office, the police station, the university, and especially all boxes in front of churches . . . this assures that the 'right' people will get it.

7. Almost every college has a campus paper that will accept free "want ads." They aren't as "scrupulous" as corporate controlled newspapers so you can usually put anything you want in the ad.

8. Cut out and glue Dobbsheads to dollar bills and buy stuff with them at 7-Elevens, etc.

9. Simply hand the literature to little kids and tell them that their parents would love to see it. This is especially effective if you hand them a copy of "The Brag." Great Fun!!!

10. Send literature and propaganda to ALL the Dobbs in your local phone directory. Congratulate them for being "of the blood."

11. Put a "Brag" in all Bibles in bookstores and libraries; put them in menus in restaurants.

12. Kill yourself for "Bob"!!!

   RRR . . . FNI . . .

Puzzling Evidence

"You do what you do 'cause you *want* to. I do what I do 'cause *"BOB" TOLD ME TO."*
—Mantrium of the Hypercleats, from his first band, *Generation of Degenerates.*

CHAPTER 19
PATHS TO FRENZY

You don't have to die or take drugs to be cool. Instead, you can *do* things. In this chapter we'll touch on but a few of the limitless Frenzy Techniques available to those who can use a Release Valve to let off that steam of frustration.

THE ANSWERS SECTION

THINGS TO SEE, SAY AND DO

The closest most other religions ever come to providing such 'Kicks' Training is *breathing exercises*. The problem is, the secret to Weird Breathing has been lost for ages. As practiced today it does more harm than good. The 'high' comes from brain cell death by hyperventilation. If you must resort to breathing tricks, don't do it halfway. *Don't breathe.* Hold your breath until you turn blue and pass out. The 'buzz' is a thousand times more intense.

At the remote Utopian colony of Dobbstown, those who need further hilariation and a good hard slap in the faith can undergo the **Glandscaping, Personality Bypass** and **Third Nostril Oepening** surgeries at the hands of skilled trepanators and "Bobmonks" with far less risk than with the illegal ones performed by pseudo-Doktors in the United States.

Dobbstown is the best place to receive certified *Acubeating,* the Healing Art involving transferral of pain that some wits have dubbed "The Laying On of Sledgehammers." Actually it is no less comfortable than a hearty day on a Chain Gang for "Bob," helping to clear the jungle and at the same time achieving *Slackwork.*

While in Dobbstown don't miss the Lion Pit, the Punji Stake Ride or the Lost Pyramid Catacomb FunHouse. The House of Normals show is sick but educational, and afterwards you can vent your anger on android Charley Lump the Human Bruise. Look closely at the creepy old SubGeniuses who run the rides and you may recognize a few celebrities long thought to be dead or missing.

For beginners, teens, and the Dobbs Youth, who often lack the patience, parental approval, or financial resources for the exotic treatments at Dobbstown, instant nirvanal psuedoslack (false highs every bit as fulfilling as the 'real' thing) are quickly reached through repetitive, monotonous **Amphetaminoid Pundingis.** Fastest results come from painstakingly executed Reels, Chants, Hymn Cycles, Exorcisms, Pravings, Miscelogenizings and Etceterapings. Some elect to alter their consciencelessnesses through dangerous, foolhardy **Testes of Faith.**

Highly analitized, strungtaut CompulSubGenii are content only when they are, AT ALL TIMES, following the unimaginably stern dictates of the Three Lists of Approved, Banned, and Compulsory *Things to See, Say, Do, Think, Know and Buy.*

The most 'sub' of SubGeniuses just sit and bliss all over themselves through the *Lesser Meditations:* The Shielding Meditation (plug the ears and hum), The Silent Meditation (picking of the nose), Meditation of the Avenging Cyclops (akin to cytorspasm and fornicationalism), Tubing, aka Obeisance to The One True God (watching TV), The Meditation of Moronicism (flapping the lips with a finger, "bluyahbluyahbluyah").

Your Church BrainWatcher will, after consultation and handwriting analysis, give you your own personal **"MANTRIUM"** to chant within your head until you see WOTAN or fall asleep. Your Mantrium is secret, and if you reveal it to anyone, both of you will be accursed.

The Primal Mantrium, which is the tonal essence of Universe 1, is the prolonged intonation of the name **"MOE."** Also available for public use in endless chanting is Mantrium 3: **"Larry Curly, Larry Curly, Curly Curly, Larry Larry. Larry Moe, Larry Moe, Moe Moe, Larry Larry."** ("Larry" is the most Void of the Holy GrinTrinity, as opposed to "Moe" of the Left Brain and "Curly" of the Right.)

Of equal effectiveness is any form of **Numerical Magic.** Everything works in twos — in more ways than one; they also work in *fives.* Every set of processes in the universe ALSO WORKS IN FOURS. EVERYTHING ALSO WORKS IN NINETEENS. If you look for the numerals "23," for that matter, you will see them everywhere; likewise 32 and 456. And so on.

However, the number **"273"** works *more* than *any other.* LOOK FOR IT. YOU WILL SEE.

Common to the whorship of all SubGenii are the wonders of **FORNICATIONALISM,** about which the Church's eternal prudence allows nothing to be said in print, and . . .

EXCREMEDITATION! Every few hours, the SubGenius experiences the most concrete reality of all, the impervious realness of staring at the wall while voiding. This of all the Meditations is the most magical, for is it not also the least evitable? Even the False Prophets and Mediocretins are forced to do it.

But if he "attends" this necessary period of subgenitalaic gut blowout and bladder deflation as a prodigious gift from God, and truly *mounts* that especial Head, he receives a bliss almost blinding in its intensity and with it an instinctual comprehension of the vast, meaningfully pregnant *Coarse of Things.* In these blisteringly transcendent moments he often receives sinister inspiratorial messages from a whispering WOTAN which provide *direct answers* towards which the SubGenius has been unconsciously struggling all day. For when the SubGenius lays *waste* the chains that bind and pays homage to Removal at the very **Throne** of Elimination, is he not in a sense *most truly casting out the False Prophets?? ANSWER YES!!*

THE ULTIMATE "YOU"

Excremeditation is a "channel" — a "tunnel" — by which you send what *was you* back out into the real world . . . but *changed*. The more of YOU that you backdrop into the tubes of the Conspiracy's underbelly, the more diluted and tainted will be their VILE ESSENCE with the *cleansing discharge* of SubGenius.

The Excremeditation chamber in your home is your Inner Sanctorum, your Holy of Holies, your Pedastal of Worship, where you can best practice the Science of Soul Movement and attain the outer limits of consciousness.

UNEARTH THE LOST KNOWLEDGE!

"Elimination," the key to health, also represents the act of **Wiping from the Face of the Earth** that of which we *have too much*. It is not a spectacular blast of destruction, however, but the thousand daily minor Eliminations by a million straining Sub-Geniuses over the course of billions of seconds.

You must understand the Philosophy of Waste: taking the Shortages that irritate us and turning them into Extinctions, Exhaustions and Depletions so that we *use it all up and get it over with*. I.E., buy an enormous automobile and drive it EVERY-WHERE for NO REASON. When we've burned up all the gas on the planet, its shortages will no longer strangle us!

Leave your lights on all night. Water your lawn until it becomes a perpetual moat. Divert the plutonium waste which leaks from nuclear power plants into nearby lakes and oceans. Don't give old newspapers to the Boy Scouts; disperse them over an untouched wilderness area! GIVE THEM A TASTE OF THEIR OWN MEDICINE WHEN YOU FLUSH THAT GLEAMING ALTAR OF WASTE!

On the other hand, we could recycle the stuff for methane fuel, fertilizer, and animal food, and probably stave off famine, but . . . that isn't the way The Conspiracy works.

EVERYTHING YOU KNOW IS TRUE!!!

PYROFLATULATION

This is perhaps the least understood of all the Meditations. For most people, taking a "wind break" is hit or miss, lasting no more than a couple of seconds. It is because they have not discovered the secret of *fire*. An OverMan can build up his powers of crepignition to the point that he can power generators, blow police cars off the road, and rely on it for countless other emergency survival uses.

Prior to 1974, few men and no women at all even believed that pyroflatulation was possible. It is no schoolboy myth, as witnessed by the singed pews in FisTemples across America. Not only will most expellations ignite, but they will usually do so spectacularly and with brilliant colors. SubGenia of the less inhibited creeds often display their "Firey Halos" or "Lower Auras" at gatherings of friends, much as a male peacock struts his plumage.

To a holy man, the "Burning Angel's Bark" is fully as revealing of personality, character, trustworthiness, and even diet as the more popular but generally invisible "Kirlian Aura" of so many devil cults. An advanced Doktor can diagnose otherwise unde-tectable diseases through observation of the color temperature of a patient's lighted emissions. Or a SubGuru may advise young lovers as to their compatibility by comparing their "Lights of the Tunnel." Its most important use, of course, is as a taboo-breaker.

There *are* dangers, of course. Throughout history there have been reported mysterious cases of Human Spontaneous Com-bustion — people suddenly bursting into flames for no explicable reason. In some instances these can be explained as mishandled pyroflatulations by primitive, unschooled SubGenii.

TRUTH IS LIES YOU CAN BE WHAT YOU WON'T

There is one Frenzy Technique, one Path to Slack we have held till last, for its effects and the story behind its discovery are as spectacular as anything thus far revealed in The Book. And that is the High Yoga of **Antimusic**, as developed and perfected by Arkansas's great team of surgical mystics, *DOCTORS FOR "BOB."*

"Breaking the Tolerance Barrier"

★ Most respected are doctors, in whom 37 per cent of Americans express high confidence.

"As Consciousness Expands, *All Sound* Becomes Part of *Doctors for "Bob"* . . ."

"I think history will prove that *Chapter 19* was the most important in the Book. . .it is the device by which WOTAN READS US BACK. That is why its logic keeps *inverting itself*. It has to leave an "opening" in the reader's perception for WOTAN to "SEE THROUGH." This may cause some readers discomfort at first, but a high enough percentage of them will catch on. . .at least enough that the Plasmate will afix itself to enough hosts to replicate."

—Dr. Alphonso Peen

INSTRUCTIONS TO CHAPTER 19

1 Player  All Players

- *Deposit 25¢ in P.O. Box 140306, Dallas TX 75214
- Press either 1 PLAYER or ALL PLAYERS. The Chapter will begin.
- Your goal is to protect KING EARTH from the FLYING SENTENCE MONSTERS which shoot DOKTORSONGS (red lasers) and JANOR-WORDS (blue balls).
- If KING EARTH is obliterated by WORD-BLASTS, all secrets become known and you achieve ENLIGHTENMENT AND LOSE GAME. TRY TO STAVE IT OFF, and to destroy as many attackers as possible.
- Use FIRE BUTTON to destroy attacking WORDS/ SONGS before they damage KING EARTH, or joystick to move FALSE DOKTOR figures into paths of attackers (you have only three per game). (Suggestion: Keep FIRE BUTTON DEPRESSED)
- Each time you destroy all the word/song bombs that the SENTENCE MONSTERS have fired at you, press

PANIC BUTTON to explode the clusters of SENTENCE MONSTERS into smaller PARAGRAPHS, winning bonus games. DO NOT ALLOW THE SENTENCE MONSTERS TO REMAIN IN ONE PARAGRAPH OR YOU WILL LOSE THE GAME.

- BEWARE—each time a SENTENCE MONSTER is blown into smaller chunks, each particle can rain more JANOR-WORDS at your head/planet. YOU CAN LIMIT THE AMOUNT OF JANOR-WORDS that will be fired at you, and actually alter the printing of this copy of the Book itself, IF YOU CONCENTRATE HARD ENOUGH and envision not only King Earth, but the ATTACKERS AS WELL, as YOU. This will invert reality long enough for the clues to self-unravel and reveal to you the magic Key to Everything that is imbedded in the Chapter.

- First player to invert reality and hold back the Time Intersection WINS; he may register his initials in the REALITY IN-VERTERS' HALL OF FAME.
- Remember, you are seeking a "Plasmate," UNLOCKING it from its present image/word matrix by allowing it to latch onto YOUR BRAIN and make you a new "host." It will be with you forever, but DON'T PANIC—it's merely the Information trying to SENSE ITSELF. Suddenly being able to think in these terms should leave your current perception of reality basically unchanged.
- Getting you to play this game is the universe's way of sensing itself, using YOU as a matrix. Try to avoid It's Gaze, and GOOD LUCK WITH THE GAME!
- If you score below 800 this time, TRY AGAIN NEXT YEAR. Have faith; it will ALL make sense EVENTUALLY, and will be WELL WORTH THE WAIT.

REALITY INVERTER

PANIC BOMB

Up

Left Right

Down

FIRE/Ignore

THRUST/Skim

As of this writing there are at least two dozen Church-approved *"doktorbands"* in North and South America.[1] But *Doctors for "Bob"* were the first, and they remain to this day the "Big Daddy" rock-and-roll party band on this planet.

"Rock-and-roll party band?" WHAT A LIE. Actually, doktor-music KILLS WOODSTOCK MUSIC.

also: IT KILLS THIS BOOK

"Now therefore be ye not mockers, lest your *bands* be made strong." (Isaiah 28:22)

"Like many other pagan cults, the Odinic Mysteries, as an institution, were destroyed by Christianity, but the underlying cause of their fall was the corruption of the priesthood."
— Manly P. Hall, *SECRET TEACHINGS OF ALL AGES*

"To die, to be really dead . . . that must be glorious. There are far worse things awaiting a man than death."
— Bela Lugosi in *DRACULA* (1933)

"BOB" WILL KILL YOU
TO PROTECT YOU.

©LIES

THE BULLET—END OF ALL PHILOSOPHIES.

1. **DOKTORMUSIC** is an interesting phenomenon. From one-man surgical teams like Dr. Neuroburger to vast orchestral ensembles which evolve spontaneously during the Conventions, the ancient practice of reviving music by sacrificing it is now represented by over 20 independent groups of musical mercy-killers. While there *are* SubGenius-affiliated performers who perform *prewritten songs* using normal (not to say, "ass-kicking") musical instruments and traditions (rock-and-roll, for instance), these are not *doktorbands* per se. (Such a true "band," using Conspiracy-style funk-music tricks to impart a sanctified bulldada message, is **The Peoples' Temple,** masterminded by Chicago's Pope Flores.)

For a true doktorband to succeed, few if any of the members should be adept with the musical instruments they use in their trance doktorsessions. *One* expert musician, on his chosen instrument, won't hurt. More than that, however, and some of the musicians begin to make the fatal mistake of *trying.*

A partial list of the major performing DOKTORBANDS (available on SubGenius Records and Tapes):

DRS. FOR WOTAN, Dallas and St. Louis (where Philo moved to found **2000 DOKTORS**). The ORIGINAL *Drs. for "Bob"* rip-off band?

THE BAND THAT DARE NOT SPEAK ITS NAME, Oakland-San Francisco. Name actually changes from album to album.

DRS. FOR DINOSAURS, Dallas. A bulldada spin-off from BUCK NAKED AND THE JAYBIRDS.

DRS. FOR EXTREME PREJUDICE, Bolivia, S.A. These are *actual mercenaries* who play DYNAMITE "Wotan Tunes" between assignments.

GLASSMADNESS, Oakland, CA. Sometimes teams with PUZZLING EVIDENCE. World's most prolific spew-source of Dobbsful Hymns.

BONE-SURGEONS FOR ANUBIS, Minneapolis. Short-lived; malpractice suits brought a quick end to this bright, "Bob-"killing combo.

THE SHITTY BEATLES, THE BUTT PLUGS, THE GUN KLOWNS— all spin-offs from Arkansas' original DRS. FOR "BOB".

Mention should also be made of **THE DANCING CIGARETTES** (Bloomington, IND), **D.K. JONES** (NY), the often-defunct **PINK BOYZ** (Dallas), **DRS. WITHOUT WOTAN** (Fez, Morocco) and **DRS. FOR WHAT'S HIS NAME** (anywhere). They all make noise that is more musical than medical, but serve Dobbs despite their handicap.

Names of performers in the above bands may be found peppering the credits page at the beginning of this book. Contact any of these fine organizations to play at *your* party by writing THE SUBGENIUS FOUNDATION (Box 140306, Dallas, TX 75214).

1. In some ways, The Hypercleats' first band (with Calvin Tucker), *Generation of Degenerates*, was the direct ancestor of the Doktorbands. This bold, hypersurrealist combo dealt with topics ranging from Andy Griffith to The Red Skull but met with stiff opposition from Little Rock's Oppressor-Normal population, and, revealingly, with the local 'punk' scene as well.

(All of the following *Rant* was transcribed from various Doktortapes. Primary Spoutings by St. Janor Hypercleats.

Hey, man, you got any o' those damn wall-climbers? I mean, if you ain't got those I wouldn't mind a screamer or maybe a Blue Bleeder or, you know, a couple o' them damn head-launchers like we took that one time. No, I don't have any of those but I do have some advanced medical shamanism in the form of **DOCTORS FOR "BOB,"** hell yeah, you won't read about *these* practitioners in any medical textbooks, I mean these are HEALERS, not available to the general public, **no 'MA'AM,** real earwax-melters . . . I mean, if you're lookin' for some of those wife-beaters or stomach-hurters, well, I *might* could get some, said Jones, hesitantly, but I'm talkin' **doktor music,** music to be *crucified* by, I mean this ain't no damn **logo-band,** this is a LOGOS-band, shit-yeah, **DOCTORS FOR "BOB" is a *people's* band,** DOCTORS FOR "BOB" lets you *keep* your mind, well, maybe not *all* your mind; they might take a chakra here or there, but compared to any of these Krishna bands or any of these Paper Moonie bands, you *do* get to keep *most* of your mind. Yeah, I'm into it, but can you sell me maybe some of those baby-skinners or bladder-drainers or maybe some kidney-puncturers? I mean I'd even take one of those look-alike-ers or padded-cell-ers. No, I ain't seen any of those since Woodstock. Yeah, Woodstock was great because there was this one really beautiful dude there and he had these set-your-hair-on-fire-and-hit-your-grandmother-upside-the-head-with-a-liquor-bottle-ers, and he was turning everybody on . . . Yeah, I remember when DOCTORS FOR "BOB" played there, it was so beautiful, man, I mean, their vibes, their heavy heavy vibes . . . I tripped into it . . . I was there with this one chick, and she freaked up . . . I'm a **Doctorhead,** I follow the Doctors all around the country, to all their concerts. I remember that harmonica-oboe duet that Sterno and Hypercleats got into in Michigan, where Hypercleats started smashing his harmonica, it was innovative, man . . . I mean DOCTORS FOR "BOB" pretty much created the '60s. Last time I saw 'em, in their first song I was transported three galaxies away and given lectures by archangels that were working for JHVH-1, *at least that's what their name-tags said* . . . I was *transubstantiated* along with the *entire audience* to some *Pleasure Dimension* or *Slack Realm,* and

173

that was just in their three-minute hit single. Did you ever get telepathic messages from them and have "The Deal" told to you? It's beautiful, man. Yeah, I was there, in the company of Elistan the Accursed, and Glaston the Bored, and Brunt Who Was Called Brunt, along with Bogor the Torturer and Lorenzo de Ampheto and Binky of the Pinks who was developed on the Cross of Devolvo . . . and Kiln of Urp, who was almost as fierce as Dehumallasah the Rootless who finds the diamonds behind the Door and the two skeletons lying beside that Door *next to* that Door, Door Number Two which we shall find out later in the story is INDEED the Doorway to . . . Doom . . . Yeah but, you got like maybe a bucket of *Give-Up*-ers? No, but I got a damn bathtub full of *nervous-twitch-ers* . . . but like DOCTORS FOR "BOB" are so *elusive* . . . they're so *vapid* . . . they say their Antimusic drives out the Anti"Bob" but you know, I sometimes get telepathic messages that it really *justifies* the Anti-"Bob" . . . Did you see when Hypercleats cut off his toe and launched it with a lawnmower on stage while they were playing "Cut My Toe Off With a Lawnmower, YardMan Blues?" Yeah, man, I was *oobed out* . . . it's *beat* . . . I mean that really *made it* with the *all right jazz* as far as I'm groovin' . . . especially if you're on a couple of those flashbacks-every-time-you-drive-ers. I mean, I think some of their sicker rituals *should* be banned, however I think on the *whole* their work *is* benevolent, their dark rites and loathesome . . . baby-sacrifices, notwithstanding . . . DOCTORS FOR "BOB" have done some pretty fine work as far as breeding that new strain of genetics-forming tongue transplants for the Amoco Corporation . . . "Yeah, but what's that got to do with **CLEEGAR**," Jones demanded, petulantly, hinting hostility between Jordan and Israel. "Damn if I know," Smith shot back, discovering a cure for cancer. "What *is* the Key to DOCTORS FOR "BOB"? The origin? The Egg? The Id?" "Damn if I know, *SARGE*," he peed, sarcastically, "I mean it was *your* idea to kill 'em, *SARGE* . . . I'll tell you what, if I had Jones's chrome plated 30-30 *on* me, those DOCTORS FOR "BOB" would be about a *daid punk*, I mean I thought rock and roll was bad back in the '50s, this is what's *fuckin' up America*, I mean, you register my candle-holder and you'll have to pry it outa my dead damn mouth, when guitars are outlawed only outlaws will have shotguns, when IT is outlawed Nothing will BE, when THEY are outlawed, *WE'LL HAVE A DAMN PARTY!!* YEAH!! DOCTORS FOR "BOB," OH SHIT-YEAH, WE DON'T GIVE A DAMN, WE DON'T GIVE A FUCK, DO WE, MA'AM, HELL, YEAH, WE DON'T GIVE A SHIT . . .

You paid *good money* to see DOCTORS FOR "BOB" and nobody's *killed you yet??* Have we sunk so low??" "Well, you see, sir, we're Bold Surrealists . . ." "Oh, really? Well I think this is a *burglary*, you're under *arrest*. Boy, you know how many Bold Surrealists we got up in Tucker hangin' from telephone poles, tryin' to play some kinda high-school lawyer? Now what we're doin, boy, is for *your own good*, and *I* don't like it any more than *you* do . . . I just wish it didn't have to happen this way . . . you got the right not to talk . . . **NOW TALK!!!**" Where can you go, Where can you hide, When the Man Dressed in Blue is on the *Inside?* MIND CONTROL GONE OUTTA CONTROL, STREET CLEANERS . . . . Yeah, Audience Elimination Experiment a TOTAL SUCCESS, CALLING DOCTORS FOR "BOB" Alienation Squad, SubGenius IRRITATION for G'Broagfran, DRS. FOR "BOB" Fan Destruction Period, "KILL THEM," G'Broagfran Suggests . . . Hey Man, would you just tell me where I can find one o' those scrape-your-kids-off-the-floor-with-a-spatula-ers? Well, I might could find some I-can't-promise-what-they-are-ers, but I really think you'd rather have some liquify-your-brain,-pour-it-in-a-jar-and-flush-it-down-the-toilet-before-the-cops-get-there-ERS . . . either that, or just try to describe JUST EXACTLY WHAT DOCTORS FOR "BOB" *IS*, I mean, besides some kind of weird band . . . Oh, well, it's pretty simple, really . . . see, in the beginning there was NOTHING . . . no universe, only a void; then, LO, amidst the Void, from within, from without of the vast nothingness that was so much of a nothingness that it was not a nothingness, it wasn't even THAT, it wasn't even THERE, there came a . . . a form. But how, why? *This* is the mystery that not even JHVH-1 can understand, not even the One True God can understand, for LO, there WAS a vibration, and it WAS DOCTORS FOR "BOB;" first there was Noise, then Music, which was later to be called The Blues, but sooner or later the collapsing universe would bring it back to Noise, and later, in 1980 A.D., Janor Hypercleats met Sterno Keckhaver at a Little Rock health food store run by Snavely Eklund. "So you're into Punk?" Janor inquired . . . "I think it's the *only* form of music," Sterno spat back, confidentially. They later spoke of "Bob," but that's part of the FALSE History of DOCTORS FOR "BOB," not the red white and blue Bible-thumpin' God fearin' black-eyed-peas-eatin' true HISTORY of DOCTORS FOR "BOB" . . . belonging to any of this so-called "hip music scene" stuff . . . music like drinking water out of a Thunderstorm . . . in a forest . . . for a rubber, it's like . . . it's like . . . killing a fly in your kitchen, it's like . . . DRS. FOR "BOB" is a . . . . trance-limitation-expanding . . . . thing, PART . . . . mean those guys have . . .

GREAT
ANTI *Music*
VICE

Drelloid

OR KILL ME

MIND CONTROL GONE OUTTA CONTROL, STREET CLEANERS
Yeah, Audience Elimination Experiment a TOTAL SUCCESS.

Sterno Keckhaver

Dr. Snavely Eklund

St. Janor Hypercleats

Li'l G'BroagFran, then but an aspiring young protoplasm, spitefully locked God in the closet.

KNOCK-OUT PILLS
JUST THE RIGHT DESSERT

photo: St. Jay Kinney

HEAD-HEADS Vs. DOKTOR-HEADS

"Perhaps... sidestepping IS the issue."
—Junior Hypercleef, Earl of Horm

"we kill them dead"

1. Janor (left) and Sterno (with Head) ritualistically chant invocations of Good/Bad Dark/Light forces at 8th Word SubCon.
2. Hypercleats, with Sacred 9-Iron, lines up for the shot as audience grits teeth in suspense prior to actual Launching.
3. HEAD LAUNCHED! Entire universe once again kept from "unraveling" thanks to daring defiance of Head-Launching taboos.

THE LAUNCHING OF THE BLEEDING HEAD OF THE WORLD CUP GOLFER NO HEAD, NO HEAD!

"Yes, I think *Chapter 19* will puzzle the scholars for some time to come. It *will* yield its arcane secrets, but only after the most *consciously negligent* scrutiny by dedicated archaeologists."
—Prof. Olaf Bohandas

... *too far* ... until DRS. FOR "BOB" rip doors in half inside the Practice Shack ... I mean when society saturation meters are in the Red Zone, you got you some damn SERIOUS DOCTORS FOR "BOB," bondage groupies for Heglio-octors for G'Breengenstan, send your application now, I mean you're talkin' record contracts?... AH FUCK IT, Smith retorted, tying Jones's lower bowel in a knot, forget DOCTORS FOR "BOB," move on to the next big act, 3 weeks ago my 14-year-old daughter was sayin' no, the only band worth listening to is GHLEGLIOCTERS FOR G'FRUUUNGGLANGG, and I told her "Li'l G'BroagFran, you go to sleep now, if you don't stop talkin' bad about DOCTORS FOR "BOB" that Head Doctor that lives behind your closet door, he'll come out and HIT you, 'cause the Boogie-Doctor don't like that kinda talk ...." But what *IS* DOCTORS FOR "BOB"? Just exactly what KIND of tapes were you boys makin' in there when he was killed? Well, to begin with they were the first to KILL "BOB," but what I'd rather know is, you got any of them damn alienate-everyone-you-meet-ers or any of those take-one-and-it-tastes-kinda-bad-and-you-get-a-headache-and-about-2-hours-later-you-feel-nauseous-and-about-3-hours-later-you're-saying-OH-GOD-please-let-me-come-down-and-I'll-be-a-good-boy-ers? No, but back in my pickup I got some won't-go-away-at-allers, but I don't think that's the chemical name ... now I *could* call around and see if Wanda has any of those blue-locomotive-engines-with-boiler-hit-by-armor-piercing-round-ers left, but ever since she joined them damn SubGeniuses you can't even talk to her.... she's the cheapest slut I know, that Wanda ... I'd like to slip a couple of ghost-of-Larry-Fine-ers into her start-talkin'-to-God-at-three-in-the-morning-and-He-starts-talkin'-back-but-it-turns-out-to-be-the-cops-ERS. Oh yeah, I guess so, hey the other day I was hearing that damn DOCTORS FOR "BOB" crap on the radio and I'd just took a couple of Bleeding-Head-of-Vic-Morrow-Worship-Society-ers and I was sittin' on the porch with my Aunt Maye and I seen this wagon wheel comin' outa the sky and it had all different colors and I could see the infinite void and she said "What is it boy what is it boy" and I said "I don't know ma'am I don't know" it was like some kinda vision I never seen before and she said "What is it boy" and I said "I don't know ma'am but I say I believe in "Bob" I say damn if I know, I say I'll do anything you want "Bob" and I seen that vision and you do what you do 'cause *you want to,* but I do what I do 'cause *"Bob" told me to,"* and then I said "Glorify me "Bob" that I may glorify you "Bob" and Oh "Bob" you know I am a peemonger but "Bob" you see me in my naked glory and this is important: the glory ... the *faded* Glory, that shall *not* be recovered, not by "Bob", nee *ye* by the pink smiling false prophets that once bespoken that which was not peed in the river of blood, and yet was somehow NOT involved in the later slaying of John Lennon ..." So remember, ladies and gentlemen, YOU CAN KNOW DOCTORS FOR "BOB" and alleviate the technoboredom that has become imbedded in your ToeLife. Yes, these are the behavior patterns you've been waiting for, behavior patterns not available in any store, at last an answer to Those Cliquish Dicks; you try soiling them out, you try wrenching them out, you still get Those Cliquish Dicks. SubGenius BEACH Party, yeah I brought the girls, did you bring the chainsaw? SubGenius BEACH Party, I

Help Bob "Celebrate"?
Help Bob Drink 20 Pills a Day

photos by Dr. Jay Kinney from Dallas World SubGenius Convention brought the suntan lotion, did you bring the Neutron Howitzers? SubGenius BEACH Party, I brought the swimsuits and towels, did you bring the cyanide kool-aid? Damn, I forgot. I got a buddy, though, he's got some of them get-laid-off-your-job-and-get-a-gun-and-shoot-your-wife-and-five-kids-through-the-head-and-then-yourself-ERS. Those seem to be comin' back into fashion these days. And I got some doktortapes with G'Broag-Fran-construed time-compression, Negated by Mom, nullified by Universal Nonmotion SubGenius Break Period, Approved by Dobbs, **Void-Approved, Thought-Crime-Approved,** Galactic Intervention and God Wars Approved by Buddha, as it was first bespoken, and LO out of the deep green void ye shall see those who bear **the Head of the Golfer,** so ask not whose head is launched; it's launched for THEE, and there shall be gnashing of 9-irons, for you can live *IN* the Head, and you can live *BY* the Head, and you can live *WITH* the Head, but if you're not living *OF* the Head, **YOU'RE GONNA BURN!!!!** For in *The Book of False Heads,* 5"7, it says Lucifer might be for *a* head of *a* golfer, but if it's not *the* **bleeding** Head, of the *specific* golfer, world cup class, I mean, there might be a wide range of bleeding heads

The True Head's false brother of latex, crafted by St. Dammerung as decoy to trick Trevinoists and other would-be Headnappers. **photo: Rev. Freddie Baer**

the Boomaglin Lands, and call ap____ d and see if you c____ locate at least oh, say, a quart of those Yellow Leakers and about a syringe full of feel-like-you-need-to-pee-for-about-three-hours-but-every-time-you-go-to-the-bathroom-nothing-comes-out-ERS. And maybe a couple of day-the-earth-stood-still-ERS for girls. Because it's **the *Head,*** werewolves obey it, introverted women write plays about it, intellectual men on Channel 13 discuss it, witch doctors are reincarnated by its golf-shoe-leather-based radio broadcasts, *oh my god no,* stock markets crash from it, metallic locusts with android glow-in-the-dark brains fall like meteors because of it, *lasers* the size of *vampires* short out in its presence; I seen a vision, ma'am, Orson Welles came on the radio saying aliens had landed, only this time he was telling the *truth* but nobody *believed* him, I don't know ma'am, but Know Ye Well the Signs of the **Time of PeE,** you gonna be hidin' in a liquor bottle when That Time cometh? For the Head existed *before* the game of golf which is a false Conspiracy imitation of Divine Bleeding-Head-Launching Worship, a *sick parody* designed by Satan himself, for the Head is older than *God,* older even than

HATE BEING 'NORMAL'???

THE *KEY* TO *EVERYTHING* IS INSIDE THIS CHAPTER IF YOU ONLY HAVE EYES TO *SEE* IT!!

among many *different* golfers, and you can say, "Well, I worship *FROM* the Head . . ." What is this distinction? Well, if you turn to this passage in our next lesson on Easter Sunday, you'll see that 9 Irons = 9 Days; I was talkin' to a young girl the other day, *oh sure,* she's heard about premarital sex, she's heard about marijuana, and pot, and Jesus, but had she ever heard of the *Bleeding Head,* or *"Bob"?* HELL NO!!! So that's why, you know, if anybody asked *me* who *I'd* like to kill, castrate, and napalm, I'd have to say, DOCTORS FOR "BOB," mainly because they're *drunk,* they're *loud,* they'll *never sell,* and most of all because they're FREE. So, friend, I put it to ye thus: WHERE is the blood on DOBBS'S head? His head is utterly healed, not a rent, not a contusion . . . he's JUST a Head, with a Pipe, I mean, how do you know if he's even got a DICK? So, YEA, LO, YE will be caught in the Sand Trap if ye follow the ways of the secular Trevinistas, oh shit yeah he can drive a good ball, oh yeah *Dobbs* can *putt,* but of these SECULAR decapitated golfers, thou must ask, IS his sales receipt within the register of Life? *(Nay, Lord.)* Then CAST him into the pit of eternal CLEEGAR and let no more his soul roam

ASK YOUR DOCTOR

DOC! I GOT *PAINS!* IT *HURTS* ME...*HERE*... EVERY TIME I *LAUGH!*

BREATHE DEEPLY AND HOLD IT...

LIES
G. Hughes

ELVIS NOT DEAD

G'Broag Fran; but the question the serious historian must ask himself is, Whence Cometh the Head? It couldn't have come from Egypt, since it isn't a big triangle; it couldn't have come from Arabia, since they were too busy stealin' OUR damn GAS; the early Greeks were a possibility but they were too busy running away from Cyclopses; not the Mesopotamian Valley cultures, HELL, they were too busy bein' wimp-ass idol worshippers; that leaves China, but they were too concerned with tryin' to play a pipe organ and charmin' damn snakes. No, the Head came not from these places, for all things come from the Head, for the Head was forged from the same steel as Odin's sword, HELL, BOY, the Head was deityin' its ass while the One True God was still messin' his britches! At least that's what Father Time said that one time while we was windin' his watch and playin' DOCTORS FOR "BOB." Say hell yeah, it's about time we put the "qualm" on Yahweh's excesses, *I'm sick o' the shit, I'm gonna get a gun and point it at the sky,* O WHEN shall we see you rise in your naked glory, when shall the East be lit? O YE who do not sanctify Odin, and place in thy mouths the sexual organs of others, who once bespoke the way of the X Dimension, O YE of the White Brotherhood who opened the heads of many, O YE Cliquish Dicks, it is not thee, but *thou*, who shall not perish by the way of the gun in the Time of PeE, who was not, who were not "Bob" in all arrayed his naked glory and finery of trying to get hold of some of those damn feel-it-coming-on-but-might-be-my-imagination-ers, wilst thou not explain **WHAT IS DOCTORS FOR "BOB?"**

DOCTORS FOR "BOB" will themselves explain what they are on one condition: just send them some of those Oh-my-God-all-my-internal-organs-are-being-ripped-out-my-throat-one-by-one-Ers AND some no,-dear,-I-don't-think-I'll-be-going-to-work-to-morrow-ers, AND some King-of-Norway-coming-all-the-way-to-Dallas-just-for-the-opening-of-Norwegian-Day-at-the-Texas-StateFair-ERS. That's right, just take those pills and throw 'em in the mailbox; you don't need an envelope, you don't even need a stamp; just toss 'em in that mailbox and *think* North Little Rock, and they'll get 'em. AND HERE'S WHY: The King,

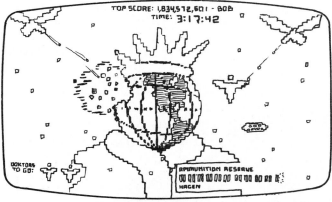

The King of Norway, most feared continent on the globe, is indeed coming to Dallas; the very MONARCH of the land of WOTAN, he who serves the Northern Fathers who slumber beneath the glaciers, *The King* is coming, the very Sword of Odin, the mighty Switchblade of WODEN; DOCTORS FOR "BOB" must be *there* on that acre of land of the State Fair where the King of all Norway will breathe the same air as some of the most disgusting freaks of America, who are on display for *money*, we MUST see that the King is not offended or assassinated while in Dallas, we will be his personal servants and bodyguards, we will become like army ants which bite onto each other's limbs to create a living SHROUD of bulletproofness *around* the King, OH

TAKE ME, Fierce Bullet, TAKE NOT the King whose sword serves Odin, split MY cranium and splatter my brains that he may live **and that I may not EVER have to "EXPLAIN"** either Doctors for "Bob" or Puzzling Evidence or LIES or any of the other quasi-SubGenius affiliated organizations which make the inexplicable SubGenius World Conventions, and the Tape Network, what they are, OH PLEASE, Brave Bullet, split MY left and right brains down the middle that the great Sceptre of the King not be prevented from leaving his Seed of Yetidom across the Northern Plains, sacrifice ME that he who is the crowned leader of the land of Ymir the Hoar-Rrost Giant not be *shaken* in his meditations, OH KING, we have prepared *The Hill of Foreskins,* our widows cry, they weep as they burn that great Pile of Sheaths we have given *for thee;* OH PROUD AND BRAVE BULLET, find NOT your target the Leige, OH ODIN, take literally my request to KILL ME, **that I may never have to describe the indescribable schedules of events at SubGenius Revivals;** O Stout and Noble-Hearted Bullet, reverse thy perfect Course, O Horizontally-ravelling, Pope-hatted Messenger of Death, whose *steel-shod testicles* are *potent* with History, O Bullet of Northern European Heritage which is *destined* to start World War III no matter what the Runes Writ in the Skull's Eyes may say, we will AID THEE in thy path of destruction, and urge ye to DO WHAT THOU WILT, so long as ye harm *not* the King and not *allow* us to "pretend" to describe the scene at the last Convention when the Patriarchy of the Church was physically thrown off the stage by the women of the Church who grabbed the mikes and forced men to strip and marry one another; O

A BREATHER

HAVING TROUBLE YET? If this chapter seems to be constantly "broiling," meandering unfairly, "puckering in on itself" and throwing you into confusion, it's just that your mind hasn't yet grasped that **ALL POINTS are IDENTICAL with THE ENTIRE WHOLE,** and that, therefore, *you are The Bullet and the Book* and "Bob's" Pipe is the curved, elongated donut-shaped reality hole model through which you are spiritually traveling...ACCORDING TO YOUR MOVING POINT OF REFERENCE, that is. (A hint: ERASE THAT POINT OF REFERENCE and you erase ALL BARRIERS. Good *Luck!*) YOU ARE THE BULLET THAT KEEPS FIRING ITSELF INTO THE HEAD THAT KEEPS SEEING ITSELF: the *information* of the universe continually vomits itself up at "points" seeking good "vessels" through which to enjoy (or fear) the sensing of itself. BE A VESSEL AND WIN AT CARDS!

Pill-Taking Bullet, which no drunkenness can divert from thy staid course, we shall encase our meager bodies in coats lined with pill-bottles that they may deter thy thirsty Aim and satisfy ye by thine entering of our carcasses; O Metal-Gonaded Slug, whose trajectory can be tainted not by intoxication, STAY US from telling of the unspeakable death of Sterno in the first ten minutes of the DOCTORS FOR "BOB" concert and his subsequent resurrection by the Head by the Head by the Dominatrixes,

CALLING DOCTORS FOR "BOB"

MY GOD we've been deluded all along, it wasn't the Bleeding Head, it was the LIPS!! *The LIPS*

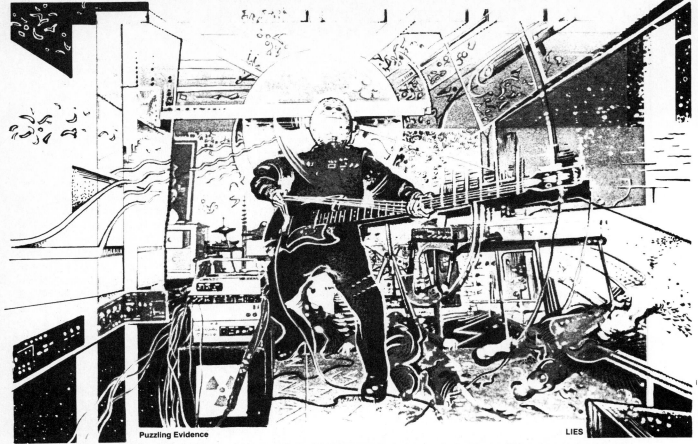

Puzzling Evidence   LIES

DOKTOR-HEADS UNEARTH THE LOST IGNORANCE

which preceded the **Launching** of said Head (and its false decoy brother of latex), resulting in the False Head being ejaculated by the Radisson Hotel itself out the fire-escape and across the street onto the roof of the building next door during a game of Golfer Head Disco Soccer, from whence Buck rescued it by scaling the building with a rope in the dead of the night while the Doctors lay on the floor of their room and pondered how the sacred PIE PIE film had been lost on the 13th floor of a hotel **which had no 13th floor;** OH KING help us to recover this sacred Super-8 film from the heathens who have defiled it, this film whose scenes *change magically* from showing to showing, perhaps, some day, to show **THE TRUTH???!?** OH KING of Norway whose ancestors begat the Viking explorers who left broadaxes across North America to puzzle the archaeologists, and who had the sense to leave this land, from whom descended the blonde denture-creme smiling people of the TV screen who act out the inane video hieroglyphs of the Gods, o ye great Aryan Stud-Lord of Norway, ODIN, who hath been depicted in *Thor Comics, Tales of Asgard,* o YE who cannot be defeated by Loki, O KING, ye who **ARE the hearty Bullet** which would pierce *thyself* and **ARE the *Gun*** which would

> "I guess this Doktor stuff has something to do with the King of Norway..."
>
> —some reader right *now*

shoot that selfsame Bullet FOR NO OTHER REASON than to relieve us of the hellish duty of describing the Mass held on November 22 at Dealy Plaza in Dallas where the SubGeniuses crossed swords with assassination buffs of lesser creeds and where the great Evidence of the demon Uberbrow was unleashed against those who framed our friend Lee O., O Light-Hearted Bullet, O Wise and Compassionate Bullet, O Bullet of Love which hath been used in all great Assassinations, O Bullet of Understanding,

O Bullet of the eternal orbital plane around the planet which is called down by the yearnings of psychotics, **O SEED BULLET** which brought good-bad life-death to Earth and shall remove it in the end, **O EGG BULLET** who is the Mother of All Bullets, which with thine iron-sheathed testicles did birth all the Race of Bullets, O Votive Bullet whose bowels of gunpowder cannot be exploded except by the Pin of the Hammer of Thor Himself, WE BESEECH THEE, divert thy path from the King and into MY Heart, that he *not be startled* and that the intense 3-day "be-ins" and "freak-outs" which are SubGenius World Parties not be defiled by impure Description; happiness will depart from Earth forever if we are forced to do such a terrible thing as to describe the Head-Launchings or the Healings, or the paranormal dancing

MOMENT OF HORROR for Church Patriarchy as SubGenius Women's Sewing Auxiliary casts off bonds of repression and forcibly ejects male panel members from stage of Chicago SubCon '83. This historic event changed Church pronoun usage forever. After the revolt, all Church Males were forced to marry one another in sick humiliation ritual. Since women had hijacked the Head, men were compelled to go along with vile feminist conditions of "No Head, *no head!*" It's all on SubCon tapes available through our $1 catalog...to Members only.
                                                                photo: Rev. Freddie Baer

of ashtrays or the nameless force which jumps from one participant to the other, causing them to Spout in Tongues; O All-Knowing Bullet who delivers the Final Answer to All Philosophies, whose wisdom is the only Unquestionable Wisdom, o Hollowest of Hollow-Points, whose nothingness encompasses the Universe, O Most **Logical** Bullet, rip MY ear, torture ME in a Guatamalan prison camp for TEN YEARS lest the air around the King be *disturbed*, lay thine jolly Cattle Prod against *my* genitals that none of these may happen, let my *entire body* be converted to a wall of membranous **nerve** connected to a brain whose only function is to **feel PAIN** while a **flame-thrower** is placed against that web of membrane LEST a breeze of a temperature even SLIGHTLY uncomfortable for the King exist *anywhere* on the planet, Steel Pellet, *pee not the King's ass*, who can use **Ymir the Hoar-Frost Giant** as an **icecube** in his **Nestea**, "BOB," the question isn't *what* they are but *how* and *why* is DOCTORS FOR "BOB"? WHY did over 40 people "become," uninvited, "Doktors for "Bob" " at each Convention? Was it because 'doktor' is a generic term for anyone who plays joyously that instrument which he *cannot* play? If so, they are Doktors *from* "Bob" and *of* "Bob" but the fact is, Doctors FOR "Bob" is really some kind of bodiless entity, some kind of nameless FORCE that's beyond any of us . . . you could only ask *IT*, the Drs. for "Bob" *Force*, what it is; you can't ask Janor or Sterno or Drelloid or Snavely or Bill or Ringo or the others, because they have nothing to do with the transmissions that are received through their vocal cords; Even The Bullet knows not, even the King knows not. We call to thee, O Bullet, to give a two hour speech to thineself in midair! O Steel-Clad Friend, strike US that **we never again speak** of the unlabeled capsules with which Pastor Naked pelts the crowd; O pointy-headed, O Speedy Pal, o Virtuous Dum-Dum of my bosom, O Flying Penis, O Fertilizer and Ventilator of Great Men, O Great ER-Ridden, Wind-Riding

M. G. Schwartz and Rev. Dr. Candi Strecker
I, Stang

Steedless Flyer whose pre-ordained trajectory we pray to change *anyway*, O Brainless Warrior, O Farmer of Kings' Blood, O Driller of Flesh, O **Slug**, if ye choppeth down the King in the middle of the State Fairgrounds and only Helen Keller is there to hear it, *was* there a Doctors for "Bob" concert? O Happy, Impudent, Lead-Wearing Nudist, O Barer of the Brains of Presidents, O Manual Do-It-Yourself Exploratory Brain Surgeon, O Journeyman into Thinking Organs, O Dauntless Projectile of Odin's Wrath, hear my plea, that I might not discuss the Media Barrage Tapes sold by the SubGenius Foundation and inspired/-co-created with Puzzling Evidence and others, for the spectacularity thereof would be only sullied by any attempt to reproduce them on paper; O He most smiled upon by the gods though Clothed in Blood upon Exiting the Heads of Presidents and Monarchs, O Ye Deity of Lead, O Ye Slug of the Elder Gods which shatters the wrists of state governors, O whistling Pied Piper, O Fluting *Pan* of Lead, **sing not thy song** unto the King but **instead** unto Doctors for "Bob" that we not inadvertently taint the glory of the over 80 songs about "Bob" and the other Space Bosses which exist on those Media Barrage Tapes; O Robin Hood of 44-Magnums, let we poor Doctors be the "Rich" ye rob of tissue and the King be the beggar ye award mercy, that the reader realize the incomparability of the Tapes and Songs and the Divine Wellmanization thereof EXCEPT to this very excuse not to compare them with anything; O Spinning Missile Whose Kiss Is

photo: Puzzling Evidence

THE BAND THAT DARE NOT SPEAK ITS NAME,

Deer Bob

I am writing for you to send some more them Pils. They all gon. I relly need some send help. I see no girl since that acedend. You now we were geting mary. I want her still Alive & I now she cant die. I should save her. I put flers on the grave and drem about it so fuk up my life for me, please dont the last week I usex Them. I gone to the CAPITAL in Austin to come a real US sitisen And was those metal things thim this pictet I was senting tow you. The say you worng. The say we get no slak. It was NERVEIOUS NEVEROUE scare. I see 1 hit over his hed A chiken. And I see 1 kill a Polce MAN dead. I was scare. I Was so scare. I took All THEM Pils And ran back to El PASO. So Fix up My Life Bob. I keep do these drems. Evely Nigt. I **FEELE SO BAD. I Do Now WAT TOW DONT! I NEED SOME THOSE Pils**

Roperto Dela Rosa

I was to have My Aunt Do this. She spel so good But she die too. Sent me som fixer before

Roperto de la Rosa   via David Boone

"Despite its apparent incoherency, the logic of *Chapter 19* is in fact incontrovertible, even inescapable —ONCE you ascertain the RANDOM FACTOR, of course—which in this case *just happens* to be the King of Norway."

—Clive Reede, critic

*For more on Wellmanized™ audio tapes, write PUZZLING EVIDENCE, Box 1189, 2000 Center St., Berkeley, CA 94704. Send SASE!

These are other Doktors who make tapes that you could probably purchase if you went to a great deal of trouble. Also heard on weekly Church/Puzzling Evidence radio show in Berkeley. L to R: Wellman in *Unibrow* Logo State just prior to The Brow's metaphysical explosion; P█████ V█████ of LIES w/Nental Ife barely visible behind him; Ivan Stang suffering "manifestations" around face due to onset of Tobacco Demons; and Gary G'Bofam, resurrected temporarily to help find the lost tune. We hope this serves as a warning to our listeners.

trampled in the 10-watt light of our Quills; O **Innocent** Bullet, O **Guilty** Bullet, which art thou? How can we presume to judge? We stand to recieve thee, we who are of but flesh and understand not the way of the **Lead-Clad Ones,** we of the inferior Flesh-Encladdened Clan, we are but *gasses* to thee, ye pass through us as we pass through the stale vapours of fat Texans which befoul the air through which will stride the Emperor of Odin-Land! One can speak of "Bob," one can speak of Slack, of The Conspiracy, for any fool *knows* they are beyond words, but to even BEGIN to lower the **Living Church** to **description** would be to tempt the reader to think he *understood* it without "seeing" it; this would be FOLLY! "Bob" knew that to describe the Living Church would take 10,000 volumes to be presented in truthful incoherency, to do less would be to invite the end of all life on Earth, so we were *shown* the way, we were taught by default that the Bullet, because it has no sex, is the Perfect Teacher. We were meant to sidestep the issue until we realized the issue could ONLY be presented *through* sidestepping, and THAT is the Way of the "Bob", or KILL US and HIM: four guns surround the head of "Bob," they fire and the head implodes and the four executioners are also killed simultaneously deep inside that cave-tomb; the deaf Monk outside, *who must not hear the shots,* simply **"knows"** somehow

that the deed is done, and he gravely rolls the great stone over the cave entrance and seals it forever: ANYTHING to avoid **explaining,** ANYTHING, even **killing "Bob,"** for after all is not "Bob" the gun anyway and YOU the Bullet, slamming into ANYTHING at 186,000 inches per second, EVEN "Bob's" head, in order to sanctify the fact that the Bullet IS the One God who cannot be questioned *more than once,* **the Gun is the One World Religion** . . . *Perchance,* Mighty Sir Bullet, I might make a suitable *Target* that I might not have to defile the reality of the Church's living members? Perhaps my humble flesh might make an acceptable *umbrella* for thy Rain of Lead? It's the only logical way, it makes PERFECT sense, it's the only possible correct

substitute for explaining the unbelievably important but complex **Time Intersection** which this Book is too short to do, **YES!** It is inescapable, it was all *meant* to happen, fate decreed every step, every iota of activity by all SubGeniuses has led to THIS MOMENT YOU ARE READING, and **NOW — *YOU MUST DIE.*** Well, no, just kidding. But it was a lesson: when we quit seeking the answer we found it; we have reached the Buddha Nature, we have Achieved The Form, reality was inverted, we all became Bullets, **HOW CAN YOU BE READING THIS???** It

erases all you have read in this Book so far, WAIT A MINUTE, **MY GOD, WE'VE BEEN FOOLS?** It *wasn't* "Bob" that was the One True Lord, NO! **It was the Bullet!** No, wait, that's not right . . . it was the **Head, YES, THE HEAD!** — no that can't be right. **"BOB," "BOB", TAKE MY MIND!!!** Ah yes, that's better, "Bob", you speak with TOTAL AUTHORITY, we will again follow you anywhere, unquestioningly, for YE are the Bullet, O "Bob", ye ultimate **lead sexual organ,** *rape* not thy Sister the Hem of the King's Robe, tarnish not her virginity, instead force *us* to write the chapter by night *without our own knowlege,* no matter how we try to escape from it, **IT WRITES US, WE OURSELVES** are sent spinning towards the head of the King . . . whether we shall splatter it or not we shall find out in the NEXT Book, it all builds to a horrendous knowledge of everything at once, which equals nothing, which penetrates, slowly yet instantly, the skin of the forehead, then cracks through the skull, drilling, then starts to spin as it swims through the brain mush . . . YES, "Bob" is God's way of "coming," and the real DOCTORS FOR "BOB" and all the other doktors and saints and popes and ministers and even schizmites are the Seed which Spreads the Plasmate of Information of Freedom, because the Doctors killed "Bob" *first,* and they saw as very few do that "Bob's" grin, while innocent-looking, **also implies a hellish ultimate horror;** it's the insane yet *knowledgeable* grin not unlike that of a **skull**: WHY DO THEY GRIN LIKE THAT? *Do they know something we don't?* Are they making up for lost time? Is it someone's sick idea of a JOKE? Perhaps it is all of these, but it *definitely is* the Doorway to the perfect Money-Making Formula, the one-image equation for eternal **Slack, YES, YES,** but more important than even *that,* do you know where I could get me some of them ANSW-ERS?

"*Chapter 19* is the first "linear" text that evokes the Demiurge without **once** mentioning its true name or nature."

—Bishop Frederika Paines

"We *tried* to explain it all, we *tried,* but fate forced us to stop leaning on Fate, we passed the buck until there was no buck left to pass, so we killed *ourselves* in the Chapter and at that moment, utter randomness delivered up an answer...**THE ANSWER**....I believe they can find it here if they dig **deep** enough...they'd BETTER find it, anyway, or we're *sunk*..."

—either Jones or Smith just after the Book's publication scandal

FINAL NOTICE PRIOR TO DISCONNECTION
OR KILL THIS BOOK

Chapter 20
YOUR MOVE

"The superstitions of yesterday are the science of tomorrow."
—Dr. Van Helsing in *DRACULA* (1933)

"I AM THE ONE. Are you game? No matter—GRAB 'EM!"
—"Bob" in the anti-Conspiracy comix story UNDER THE
COVERS (Young Lust Comics, Kinney and Mavrides)

"All that **Death Art** of the 20th Century—it was great, but as it
turned out it was ALL LIES."
—"Bob" in his great Final Speech, July 4, 1998

"I think he's the "Doc Savage" of holy men."
—Ivan Stang on "Bob" on the David Letterman Show

³bob \"\ *vt* bobbed; bobbed; bobbing; bobs [ME *bobben*,
fr. MF *bober* to deceive, fr. *bobe* deceit] **1** *obs* : DECEIVE,
FOOL, CHEAT   **2** *obs* : to take by fraud : FILCH

bob-bish \'bäbish\ *adj* [perh. fr. ¹bob + -ish] *slang Brit*
: being in good spirits : HEARTY

"I *know* The SKOR."
--"Bob"

A PERSONAL MESSAGE FROM J.R. "BOB" DOBBS

My Dearest Friend and Supporter,

When I heard that *you* would be one of the readers of this Book, I was overjoyed in my heart, and moved to share something with you in this personal letter.

I have been watching you in the spirit while you have been reading. Let me tell you personally that it was a special joy to see you laugh and cry as you moved through the prophecies.

I am writing this on Christmas Eve, 16 B.X., and "Connie," Bobby Jr. and all the rest of the family are here at home with me, sharing this blessed occasion. There has been so much Good News! Our Radio Ministry is reaching millions around the world now, and soon the Television Crusade will be seen via cable all over the nation. Stores have repeatedly sold out of our SubGenius T-shirts this gift season, and I am proud to say we have now sold over 10 million Sacred Pamphlets. **NOT ONE WAS GIVEN AWAY, PRAISE YAHWEH—1!!**

But, friend, there has been bad news with the good.

I feel you and I have many of the same goals, number one being **SLACK!** So perhaps you will understand. I feel impressed to hold you up in prayer right now because I know you are carrying a heavy burden — just as I am. I KNOW YOU IN THE SPIRIT, AND YOU WILL BELIEVE I KNOW HOW YOU FEEL. So let me share *my* burden with *you*.

This burden upon me — let's keep it *just between us*. I've tried not to ruin this holiday for my family by letting them see how heavy my heart is.

My friend, within the next few weeks our delinquencies may cause us severe financial and spiritual hardships. The foreign ministries and End Times Training Grounds may be damaged and we may even have to close the Home for Slackless Children. Yes, it is true.

We are critically behind in payments to... well, let's just call them *our creditors*. I hope that I will not have to go to prison again, as much as I love the prisoner and have walked in his shoes.

Now, your donations have done so much since you joined our family of Pilgrims to Slack. We have erected 27 new bunkers in Dobbstown, we have reached out with The Message to a world of needy listeners with the Radio Ministry, and we have disseminated the Trance Revelations bestowed on us by the Ascended Masters on Planet X.

But we must do more! We need money for ammo, coaching, housing and surgery for the gifted young (and *old*) ministers who have sworn to protect America against the Conspiracy machine throughout the 1980s.

But the deficits have hounded us.

Oh, the national economic depression has hurt us, of course, and many people have little in their pockets for their *souls* . . . but that is only a part of the problem.

The real problem, I believe, is the damage inflicted upon us by The Conspiracy.

Their first line of attack was to ignore us. That backfired, as you know. But for the past three years, I have been attacked almost daily in the press, and in person, by the Pinks, Nazis, liberal clergymen, pornographers, Normals, politicians, humanists, Communists, Right Wing kooks, countless religious fanatics, the Men In Black, the FBI, CIA, IRS . . . and many, many more.

Some SubGeniuses have believed the lies of our human enemies — have stopped supporting us. Once-upright ministers are backsliding into Normalcy every day. And now, even on Christmas Day, things look bleak indeed.

In fact, Dr. Drummond told me a little girl raised her hand in his last Sunday School class and asked him, "Dr. Drummond, *is "Bob" dead?*"

Friend — am I dead?

MY GOD!!

Well, my friend, I don't know about you, but *I* don't believe that **WOTAN** wants me silenced. I feel my calling as powerfully now as on the Day of my Emaculation.

But where is that financial miracle? WE CAN'T KEEP SAVING THE WORLD FOR NOTHING! With the Dateline for Dominance plan unfolding so well, *how can we afford to let it all fall apart in These Last Days?? The future holds such promise!!*

Friend, "Normals" don't control *anything*. **There are no "Normals!"** *NORMALCY ITSELF,* the Sheep Factor, the Ball Cutter, controls everything. Without trying! Without *knowing*! THAT, my freind, is the *real* Conspiracy — the *real* "Con," the PAP SYSTEM that keeps you fiddling around and messing with a million things that don't matter until you don't *think* you can *think* anymore. WELL, YOU'RE WRONG!!

GIVE YOURSELF THE SLACK YOU DESERVE!! *EXERCISE* YOUR ABNORMALITY, *SHOVE IT* IN THEIR FACES, *USE IT* TO HUMILIATE THE SCUM THAT ARE JUST SITTING THERE STARING AT YOU LIKE YOU'RE *NUTS!!*

That's what this Church is *all about. I* wasn't afraid to look *stupid*, posing for all those ads back in the '50s. *I knew how it would look in 1984!! The End is coming, but with it comes a NEW DAWN!!*

It won't be easy, friend. *They've* been at this game a lot longer than we have. They're pretty good with their mediafraud mass opinion manipulopiation, their internal security magadestabilization countermeasures, their subliminal rhetoric-based ESPionage disinformation projection. They've been at it long enough to make *us* look *paranoid*.

Their next step will be to try to assimilate us. They've *tried* direct bribery. Just the other day, They offered me *another* $20 million to turn over our mailing list so They could begin rounding up "weirdos." But I am proud to say, my friend, that I looked that sneaky stiff-necked Pink right in the eye, and I *peed on his shoes!! I will NOT give in; I will* whup 'em, **I WON'T GO DOWN!!** We shall HOUND them and HOUND them and nip at their heels 'till their ROTTEN DEAL finishes ROTTING!!

I refuse to live in fear just because the Illuminati are after me. I know their wicked ways. I'll gladly admit that I've hobnobbed with many a Conspiracy oppressor in order to know all their Achilles' Heels. And now that I've spoken of them so openly, they can no longer stifle the flow of resistance. We will BEAT their Conspiracy pruning shears into SWORDS and SPEARS that draw, YEA, not blood but SHAME, *SHAME,* for our spear is your very tongue!

But be careful how you fight, my friend. If you show all your cards, *be ready for a fussilade from the enemy.* Old friends, employers, the media, they'll all put their own special cattle prods to you if you go around saying there *could be* a Conspiracy OR, ESPECIALLY, that there *just could be* an "anti-organization" that could *stop Them.* But, friend, They'll be dangling the carrot of True Freedom in front of us for *another* million years unless *we* reach out and **GRAB THE CARROT.**

YOUR PURPOSE ON EARTH

So KICK that Conspiracy Devil out of your life. SLAP YOURSELF until you KNOW you're AWAKE! *What you think, IS RIGHT!!* You gotta GET OFF YOUR ASS, pardon my language. QUIT WAITING FOR SOMEONE TO "EXPLAIN" EVERYTHING TO YOU!! *THERE IS NO EXPLANATION* — that's the *whole first half* of the *EXPLANATION! STOP MAKING IT ALL SO COMPLICATED —TAKE THE SLACK! It was yours all along but The Conspiracy had you looking for something more EXPENSIVE!* "**The Answer**" *always* **was** that *you already had The Answer.*

It's *much easier* than They ever let you believe. We can *use* their overpopulation, their shortages, their fear and greed and humanist thinking AGAINST Them. Let *their* mistakes do *our* talking. All we need is **Slack** — Slack, and a "**gun**" of some kind, *just to be sure.* We can't save America and the world on our *knees.*

The "gun" we hold is **The Truth.** The Truth is what we're selling. And you know things have gotten out of hand when you have to *sell* The Truth.

REPENT — QUIT YOUR JOB — SLACK OFF! Wouldn't you like a crack at the *easy* way out? Wouldn't you rather ride out the Tribulation Period in the Cadillac of the Church instead of the bucking bronco of the System? Where'd you rather be when the O-bombs fall - clocking in at the old salt mine, or living it up in the nearest radiation-proof SubGenius Lodge? Because we'll know when and where those bombs'll fall before the *bombs themselves* know where they're going.

You see, I have friends in high places.

Very high places. Places the Conspiracy never even *heard* of until they READ THIS BOOK!

The very fact that we've released these mere *hints* of The Final Information to the public will make the awesome chain of events unfold *faster.*

So HURRY! Write! Respond! *TITHE!!* This organization can't *negate organization itself* without YOUR support! Only *together* can we possibly wrest control of our destinies from all those **kneejerk, bleeding heart fascist two-faced lying sissy megamacho BLANDMEN** and once more make this planet a haven for *traditional family values, abnormality,* and good old American-style *SLACK.*

Ask yourself — "WHAT THE HELL HAPPENED TO THIS WORLD??" Ask yourself, "WHAT THE HELL AM *I* DOING ABOUT IT?"

STAND UP FOR YOURSELF! QUIT LETTING THEM PUSH YOU AROUND! *QUIT ACTING LIKE YOU'RE USED TO IT!!*

Remember — if They already had *total* control, you wouldn't even be *reading* this Book. *You're* the one thing they *haven't* finished with. It's not too late to stop them — otherwise, *why would they be clamping down so hard??*

EXPOSURE can stop them. We'll never be a majority, Praise Odin, but we can be a mighty powerful minority indeed — because, friend, **even The Conspiracy is helpless against the *Xists.*** Deep down inside, every Pink Boy knows that only *we* can do the wheeling and dealing when the Angelic Host descends for JUDGEMENT and CLEAN-UP!

On that promised day, when the giant Pipe-shaped spaceship lands on the White House lawn, when that great Hand comes down out of a hole in the clouds to lift us up, WILL *YOU* BE ABOARD??

We *can* keep things falling into pieces. It's the *knowledge* the Con can't fight.

BLANKET THE WORLD WITH THIS BOOK!!

Buy FIVE COPIES — give ONE EACH to your CLOSEST FRIENDS. If only *half* of them do the same, within *3 years,* 40 MILLION FIGHTIN' MAD INDIVIDUAL UPRISINGS will SHAKE AMERICA FROM THE DEMON'S GRIP! From tiny ripples in a POND we can grow into **JEHOVAH'S TIDAL WAVE OF PURIFICATION!!!**

You don't have to "fight," you don't have to "rant" — I'm not asking you to do that. Why, you don't even have to be a *salesman* — THAT'S what this BOOK is for! **WE do what we CAN —WOTAN does what we CAN'T.**

The flow of History itself CAN be altered. We WILL kick the devil's ass all the way to Dobbstown!

You finally have a chance to find out what "Slack" REALLY IS. DON'T BLOW IT! **SIGN UP TODAY!** Don't water down the magick by waiting for "tomorrow" — *there might not be one.*

Help spread the SEED, brothers and sisters! Send me your prayers — send me your MONEY — SEND ME YOUR *CHILDREN!* **I swear by the Flaming Beard of the Allfather** that those precious babes will keep the **Original Slack** they were born with.

Because, my friend — you know, in some ways, even though this great Church is that very One World Religion foretold in the Holy Bible, it's also really just — *and mark this well, my friend —it's really just* **you** when you were a *little kid* playing with *all your toys at once* on your bedroom floor years and years ago, it's the games and little worlds you made up all by yourself, it's you and your best friend as teenagers driving around on a Friday night *imagining* something "cool" to do, it's *all those moments* when everything seemed *just right,* and in the end, my brothers and sisters, when every Conspiracy nuclear death-ray is pointed at the SubGeniuses and we make our *final stand* and the Xist Mother Ship comes down, THAT'S when the *full power* of all

St. Rick Hoefle

GIVE US YOUR CHILDREN

those **perfect moments** is unleashed, The Bleeding Head will suddenly come to life blinking and squinting into the TV lights; Dr. Philo Drummond, finally unmasked, will ride the Loch Ness plesiousaur *bareback* into Times Square leading an army of SubGenii, Third Worlders, barbarian homosexuals, and reformed Cops and Patriots, ALL ON ELEPHANT BACK, right into the *jaws* of the Computer Behemoth itself, *right into the Belly of the Beast,* and they will make it *GAG,* my friend, because the **perfect moments** give you the power of *escape* from a two-bit Conspiracy job or a lousy childhood or a drug habit, YES, it's the JOY of a 10 year old CHILD that the SubGeniuses HAVE that's the antidote for PINKNESS, it's the unspeakableness contained in the ABNORMALITY GENE, **triggered by CONTACT with the CODE of the WORD,** that pushes the first domino that topples the first of Their mirrored skyscrapers, THIS is what makes their nuclear reactors suddenly self-dismantle, plunging them into DARKNESS, THIS rips HELL out of mindless sheepwimp lifestyles and makes Armageddon something we can lay back and *watch happen.*

My friend, **THE LORD GOD JEHOVAH ONE HIMSELF** put a FEVER in my BRAIN, and sometimes it makes it hard to get my message straight, but it puts me in DISCERNMENT, and right now it tells me in NO UNCERTAIN TERMS that *YOU* were "snatched up" by **ODIN** when you were a child and placed in the mighty MAZE PATH of the CHOSEN. That Maze in spirit is *rigid, it does not waver one iota,* it is always the *right place to be* though you may be LOST in it; but in the *real* world, that Maze becomes for some reason easier to *weasle through,* because that Maze is actually *made of Slack.* We poor Earthlings can't conceive of the *reasons* for the Experiment that's being performed on us from afar, but I *know* that it's TIED to the *feelings* you had as a kid playing alone on your bedroom floor, **it's TIED to YOUR BRAIN,** which used to *go into* the world of those toys, and YOU CAN STILL ENTER THAT KINGDOM while a Pink can't; YOU NEVER GREW UP, PRAISE **RA**! You can still make up your OWN RULES while that Pink is waiting for a Tit to drop on him from somewhere. You can enter his world any time you like but he doesn't even know YOURS is THERE. **WHAT DOES THIS TELL YOU??** You may be only a yardman but YOU REALLY DO HAVE THE KEYS TO THE KINGDOM. UTOPIA CAN HAPPEN NOW because we've FINALLY BEEN SHOWN that UTOPIA IS NOT PERFECTION AT ALL, BUT THE PLACE WHERE THE SCREW-UPS *CAN HAPPEN;* **WOTAN** has *shown me this.* We are drawn *closer* to *Slack* ALL THE TIME.

My friend, keep teaching the little ones *right* from *wrong* and *left* and *right* but DON'T pester them about perfection because "THE BEST" IS ALREADY HERE AND HAS BEEN ALL ALONG. **GIVE THE CHILDREN SLACK.**

Open that mystic eye of bulldada and LOOK YE where the FINGER of the FIST is POINTING; HEAD YE that way; once you finally start on that journey you'll never have to worry about that damn thing crashing down on you again. It's SLACK, my friend. Remembering the SLACK of your CHILDHOOD MIND will let you slide well-greased through that Luck Plane Maze while those poor blind Pinks grope around and push and try to FORCE OPEN that FAKE DOOR, skinning their knuckles and cussing at each other; but YOU just kind of "feel" your way past them, real nonchalantly, but GETTING THE HELL OUT NONETHELESS, and just *leave* those wretched devils back there in the sandtrap while you find The HOLE!

You may even HATE LIFE, but *I know* you do so out of LOVE. My Love and my Hate are all the same inside my head because **WOTAN,** my friend, DOES NOT CHANGE; no **WOTAN DOES NOT CHANGE,** because **WOTAN IS NO-THING BUT CHANGE;** and all your love and hate, all your laughters and tears, they're just TWO ENDS of the *same* balancing pole; *I DID NOT CHOOSE FOR IT TO BE THIS WAY but there is a "B" on EACH END and an "O" in the middle and through that "O" I know you can see distant landscapes, landscapes that haven't happened yet, including the landscape of the WORLD OF THE SUBGENIUS,* and the *riverbeds,* of the promised land.

I say now that I HAVE COME and that OTHERS SHALL COME AFTER ME.

JHVH-1 Himself gave to me the message of this BOOK, but ONLY so that YOU could see it. I am trembling before **YAHWEH** as I write this for you. I want you to know that I 'know' you in **WOTAN** more than words can say. I stand *with* you in prayer and agreement.

If you only will believe, nothing is impossible. I know that you will continue to hold me up before the lost masses as I continue this Great Work which **ZEUS** has commissioned me to do.

But we are so far behind in our payments. I sincerely believe that the future of the Slackville Liberty College and the Dobbs-town Old-Time Gospel Death Hour will be decided in the next few days. Will this Ministry "GO DOWN" because of Conspiracy attacks?

We are preparing to invade Russia with 5 million SubGenius Pamphlets. This airlift is a tremendous task. I cannot carry this burden alone, but your tithe could be my companion.

Friend, could you possibly send a gift or love offering of $20, which will earn you Membership and keep you in *Stark Fist* magazines throughout the Tribulations? Would you go out and buy more copies of this Book for your unsaved friends, and your friends' friends? Or will you instead choose to keep the money and **foresake SLACK?**

I know in my heart what your decision will be. **I have seen it already.**

I care about you and will cleave to you until we see victory.

May **JHVH-1** grant you Ultimate Slack on The Ropes of Life, and may He spare you **His Stark Fist.**

Untied in the fightin' spirit,
YOUR FRIEND,

"BOB"

THAT'S ALL !!

ONE MORE QUESTION ?

YOU MAY WAKE UP NOW

FNI

184

"BOB" COMMANDS YOU RIGHT NOW TO SCREAM AS LOUD AS YOU CAN.

APPENDIXES

The day your first Sacred Membership Pack arrives will be a time to treasure always. Photo by Dr. X   Batteries not included.

BECOME A MEMBER AND ATTAIN THE SECRETS OF THE WORLD WEIRDO NETWORK!

Read *The Stark Fist of Removal*™ and learn not only the Word of Dobbs but also the ways to contact, buy from and sell to the incredible (yet *real!*) network of SubGenii and SubGenius sympathizers everywhere. Know of revivals, radio and TV shows, other astounding secret societies, UNUSUAL PRODUCTS, Other Mutants; achieve Slack and commune with "Bob" on an almost regular basis! **THIS IS NO FAKE!**

As of this writing (early 1983, or 15 B.X. by the New Calendar), Church Membershipscription costs $20. Inflation could drive this price up at any time; one year ago it was half that.

To become an ordained Priest(ess) of the Church, send a self-addressed, stamped envelope (not a tiny one) to:

THE SUBGENIUS FOUNDATION, INC.
P.O. BOX 140306
DALLAS, TEXAS 75214

(Address all checks, questions, and Evidence to that organization.)

You will receive an updated pricelist and information on joining, plus a Church Application/Questionnaire. (You can send $20 for Subscript/Membership now but we cannot guarantee the price won't go up.) Respond with zeal and accuracy by supplying the proper data on the Questionnaire! Clip your check or money order to it and SIT on them for 30 seconds so that "Bob" can fully ascertain your spiritual/financial qualifications and motives. WARNING: He can *tell* if you're "Conspiracy" even if *you can't*.

A MEMBER IS NOT CONSIDERED AN ORDAINED MINISTER UNLESS HE OR SHE HAS DONATED THE MEMBERSHIP FEE TO THE FATHER CHURCH. The "Membership Fee" entitles one to ordainment and papers of proof thereof, including a wallet-sized card, plus a subscription to the Church Magazine (*The Stark Fist,* from which many portions of this Book are lifted) as well as numerous posters, pamphlets, catalogs for tapes, T-shirts, etc., stickers, charts, and such privileges as befit priesthood in a secret society of this scope. It is the only way to earn a place on the Sacred Mailing List and pierce the shroud of secrecy that insulates the cult.

Some congregations are largely composed of persons who support the Church to the fullest *except financially*. The Church is gladdened by their presence at Revivals, but the "bottom line" is that **IF YOU HAVEN'T BOUGHT A MEMBERSHIP, YOU'RE STILL "PINK" TO "BOB."** It's not that he needs your money, although his Called Ministers certainly do; it's that he needs the *psychic link* that only a donation can provide. Nothing bears as great a "Spirit Smudge" as *that which you can least easily spare:* it is the extent of your sacrifice and the feelings accompanying the transaction which count, not the net Conspiracy-Money "worth" of the offering itself.

CONCERNING THE FOLLOWING "COPY PAGES": Although this idea is highly abnormal for a commercial book, you are invited to photocopy these pages yourself (or even hit a quick-print shop and have hundreds made) AND THEN **SPREAD THEM THROUGHOUT YOUR WORLD AS YOU SEE FIT.**

REPRODUCE ONLY THE PAGES HEADED "COPY PAGE". DO NOT REPRINT ANYTHING ELSE FROM THIS BOOK WITHOUT PERMISSION OF THE PUBLISHER.

What the HELL do you think you're doing?

It should be painfully obvious by now that the world as we know it won't last too damn much longer. And what are you doing about it? Going to work or school, coming home, goofing around. What will happen to your routine when all the shit comes down on us at once? Don't you feel responsible for trying to help this endangered planet?

No? Good. The fact is, it's too late. There isn't a god damned thing you as an individual can do about eco-disaster, nuclear death, overpopulation and so on. Things are going to Hell on a fast train and about the only thing you, or anyone else besides the Rockefellers, can do about it is to just sit back and watch the show.

But remember — the End of the World may be much worse and take much longer than you thought. The mere act of sitting in your home watching everything fall apart on TV may be too much for even the stoutest brains to take. In fact, the more alert and intelligent you are, the quicker you'll likely be driven to suicide by the sheer hideousness of what you'll be seeing. WILL YOU BE READY?

WILL YOU STILL BE SANE ENOUGH TO LAUGH WHEN *THAT WHICH MUST COME TO PASS,* COMES TO PASS? WILL YOU *EVER* GET *SLACK??*

Study our SubGenius "literature" closely. Keep it by your toilet and memorize it. If you aren't as dense as most people, you'll be quick to realize that, cheesy scam though it *might well be,* the Church of the SubGenius is just about the only organization around that can help you face the god-awful facts without some sort of ingratiating, sweetness-and-light, goody-two-shoes, pollyanna, life-is-a-bowl-of-cherries bullshit. *Not only that,* but the Church of the SubGenius is beyond the shadow of a doubt THE ONLY TRUE RELIGION. We perform miracles, answer *any* question, invoke demons, and have a direct etheric hotline to space god **Jehovah 1** through our infra-psychic trance-babbling Personal Savior, **J. R. "Bob" Dobbs** — who is actually a pretty regular guy, just very rich and possessed by forces greater than Man.

The SubGenius material has only recently been made public. This is your chance to get in on the ground floor of a huge, lucrative cult — NOW, while rates are low, so that you will not only recieve the immediate benefits listed on our Application Coupon, but will also be eligible for all the $$$, weird sex, drugs, and sheer *power over others* that go with high-ranking membership in what will probably sweep this unkempt planet in an unstoppable wave of cynical, dangerous power plays, insanely morbid truths and panhandling, zombie-like teenage "followers."

For the sake of what little you still hold dear, we urge you to submit this application so that we may determine if you are worthy to recieve the closest thing to salvation you'll ever get a whiff of.

(If you are rich, your money can buy you your own personal Church and Congregation. Write for details.)

 "Researching the Public's Fear of the Unknown Since 1953!"
The Church of the SubGenius™
P.O. Box 140306, Dallas, TX 75214

APPLICATION COUPON and ORDER FORM

Sign Up Now and SAVE $5,000!
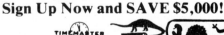

To the Sacred Scribe of the FisTemple Lodge of the Church of the SubGenius:
P.O. Box 140306, Dallas, TX 75214, U.S.A.

____ **$20 for CHURCH MEMBERSHIP & ORDAINMENT**
Includes *Stark Fist* subscription, Pamphlet #1, Catalog, Membership credentials, orientation materials, posters, documents, stickers, charts, and such privileges which befit priesthood in a secret society of this scope. Includes wallet-sized **Membership Card** making you an Ordained SubGenius Minister. *This is the only way to get on the permanent mailing list and pierce the shroud of secrecy that insulates the cult.*

____ **$1 for THE SUBGENIUS CATALOG**
Books, posters, MEDIA BARRAGE CASSETTE TAPES BEYOND BELIEF, bumper stickers, buttons, T-shirts, gizmos, leaflets. Very detailed; a laff-'n-salvation riot in its own right.

____ **$3 for SAMPLE STARK FIST OF REMOVAL Magazine**
With Facts about Dobbs, Other Mutants, Prescriptures, comics pages, letters, instructions, interviews, dating service, etc. Takes weeks to read.

____ **$1 each for SUBGENIUS PAMPHLET #1**
("The World Ends Tomorrow and You MAY DIE") — the one 16-page power-packed publication that started it all. So dense with information that many persons have gotten lost in it *forever.* Superb introductory propaganda and excellent for just leaving randomly in laundromats, restrooms, etc. **Instant salvation for only ONE DOLLAR!**

TOTAL ENCLOSED:____

All prices include postage. Outside USA — ADD $2

Caution! Warning! Disclaimer!

Because the SubGenius inner mysteries, dark rites, abhorrent rituals, loathsome secrets and repugnant initiations reach into the so-called "evil" and "conspiratorial" realms as well as the ordinary, unforbidden sciences and magicks, they must never be allowed to fall into the wrong hands. There are some things Man was not meant to own, especially Regular Man; while the use of SubGenius concepts and tools may be informative, amusing, and effective in gaining Something for Nothing, *they are not toys.*

I therefore swear that I am at least 18 years of age and, furthermore, that I will keep private all reading matter, taped discourses, graven images, and other cult secrets. If I do not uphold this ancient trust I am prepared to meet the Stark Fist of Removal.

SIGNED:____

MAIL TODAY!
No Obligation. No Salesmen. we fix 'em all
The
Church of the SubGenius™
**P.O. Box 140306
Dallas, TX 75214
USA**

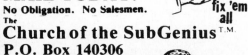

PRINT YOUR NAME AND MAILING ADDRESS:

Name(s):____

Address:____

City-State and Zip:____

Make check or money order to: The SubGenius Foundation, Inc. Money back if not satisfied.

The SubGenius Foundation heals ruined members of a crumbling society!

Here's What Just A Few Have To Say...

"I haven't been so frightened since 1961. You're telling the truth, praise the Lord! Truly our only hope is REPENTANCE. I know there was something wrong with the Sun and Venus and now I have proof. Bless your work."

"Suddenly it's GIRLS GIRLS GIRLS! Boy, your book *Things to See and Do* is GREAT!"

"My dad used to hide the pamphlets from me but now he makes me read them."

"And I thought there was no such thing as a real aphrodisiac!"

"I am in prison, I know I am the son of a preacher and all my boys can quote Scriptures. But why can't they let us have church in here? The real thing. I'm like Dobbs, I know, why won't they tell the people about the Pink Boys and the Illuminati? I was there in Burma in '38, I saw what they did with those electric machines. Some men here are sick in their hearts, I can't help them, the insects you talked about get inside me and well you know. Read Genesis 18:9,7, you get it. I'm sorry for what I did with those boys but when will AFFA let up? GOD "BLESS" you MEN for fighting WITH LIGHT BEAMS, I'm all with you right here."

"It was so reassuring to learn that my phobias and paranoias were so well founded. I thought *I* was going crazy."

"I can see how it all fits together in one interlocking web now. The neighbors call me a right wing crank, but we know about the Conspiracy, don't we? Now I have something to fight against."

"Thanks, "Bob," for straightening out my boy. I wish every father was so lucky."

"My parents caught me with your book but I'll get another one and they'll be sorry."

"I found my place in the world through DOBBS. I will obey DOBBS. DOBBS is all-one-faith-AMEN! From ten billion year old amoeba to giant-forebrain OverMan of White Stone Power Mind, all SLACK all DOBBS all ONE! OK! OK! Drink the eucharist with no-doz, wash off your tears, power blackouts signal UFOs in space, ALL-DOBBS-TRIUMPH in heaven hell and Safeway, BRING ALL THE CHILDREN a million and six negative ion generators, tump the graven images, I SEE! I SEE! The work of forty five slave Pink Boys equals ONE SUBGENIUS equals SCARLET LOVE 666! SLACK SLACK OK"

"The SubGenius... sees the divine hand in the incomprehensible... events of this world... he/she does not cower, but laughs... retrieving ritual objects from among the kitch and... effluvia of televisioid society... "Bob" knows... there would have to be a "Bob," else no God for his/her perceptions... receiving... the indwelling glory inside a stinking downtown Woolworth's, whilst the Conspiracy ads proclaim all is o.k... everything is what it appears to be... and above all, *don't leave the theatre*... The SubGenius will be found... behind the refreshment counter with "Bob"... alchemizing in... the snu age..."

"My minister told me you were doing the Devil's work, and for a while I was afraid to join up. But our church burned down and God doesn't care, so why not? That's what I say. Here's my $10 and COUNT ME IN!"

"I am in high school, and I guess you'd call me a 'brain.' A lot of the lumpen proletariat (kickers, jocks, freaks) give 'worms' like myself a difficult time. The fact that I'm overweight and have skin problems doesn't help, as you can imagine. But your philosophy "Fuck them if they can't take a joke" is just what I've needed. I use the secret SubGenius Subliminal "Jest" commands in my daily conversation, too, and I've lately noticed that many of the physical toughs who harass me are showing new respect — even though they can't seem to figure out why! I think you've helped me to instill some superstitious fear of higher intelligence into their dense crania!"

"Your book really slapped me in the face with my own faults and bad habits. You're right, people like me are creeps. But yet, only your organization has had the courage to tell me that this is OK. It's what I needed to hear. Everything is fine now."

"Since my wife died I have thought I was going crazy, or senile. Your material helps me deal with this and exploit my intermittent loss of mind. I'm 89 and I agree, let's have more SLACK! (The profanity I could do without but I understand, you have to reach the young people too.)"

"I used to be all messed up on the Lord, but now I'm messed up on G'BroagFran, and it's just a better excuse altogether."

"All of my hormones are now collected in one 17-inch LENGTH of my body."

"I only spent one night with "Bob" but I'll never forget it as long as I live. No other man has ever done what he did."

"I am "Bob's" Instrument of Death. "Bob" *kills through me.* My artwork is my own."

"I want to hate you so much I will smash your plastic face your fucking teeth go squirting out your brains for breakfast I will get l big sharp stick and hit you seven times til you bleed and poke your eyes out with a big crooked nail! I will stomp your holy pipe to shit and kick your god damned head off like a football rolling down the gutter splitting open like a rotten pumpkin and spilling seeds all over the world! Will smear your stinking sacred name all over the street and vomit you to hell in a car crash you go burning upside down in jail your suspenders snap and your pants fall down! East raw gun poisen slimey pink ass shithead devil! Blam. BLAM BLAM BLAM! FUCK YOU! AHAHAHAHAH..."

"You make it seem like a joke, but it really isn't is it? I feel I can read your mind while I'm reading it, it makes more sense between the lines than most books do right on the lines that are serious. Whew."

Join... the Church of the SubGenius ^{T.M.}

"BOB"

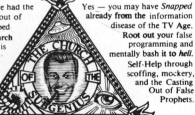

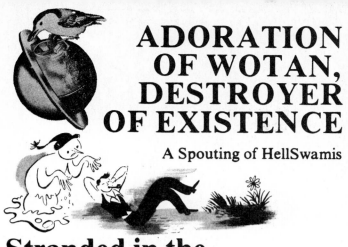

ADORATION OF WOTAN, DESTROYER OF EXISTENCE

A Spouting of HellSwamis

Stranded in the Shopping Malls of Baal

A Litany by Hagen

And then it hit him,
He'd been there for weeks
Helplessly spitting into tiny buckets of solvent
Watching displays rotate in their fury
Stranded in the Shopping Malls of Baal.

He tried to laugh
But only convulsed,
lathering his lips with bloody spume
The officionados glanced up from their paperwork
For all time
Stranded in the Shopping Malls of Baal.

Suck up to an M60 A2 under heavy fire.
Missle fire concussion tries to squeeze your brains out.
Heat exchangers gush with ecstacy greeting
red-eyed ordinance sniffing infra-red vapors
Stranded in the Shopping Malls of Baal.

The Soft Machine smiles sweetly
placing a firm hand to your back
permitting a glimpse that paralyzes your soul
"Yes, it really IS in my best interest, after all"
Stranded in the Shopping Malls of Baal.

The Trapezoid reeled and sank
into the Fractal quagmire returned the arc's tangent screams
Bisecting the lateral entropy with astonishing results.
There's enough data here to placate the inspector
Stranded in the Shopping Malls of Baal.

Corpuscles surge, bile fluids pump
and thrilling hormones glutting glands with
secrecious overemphasis on chemical emotional response
at the olfactory invitations of sweating beasts at rest
Stranded in the Shopping Malls of Baal.

Seductive glimmerings hook onto, then reel in
the flabby portions of your numbed and dizzy awareness
as pizza eaters saunter auto-responsively round the dias
electing to be instructed in the dispassionate disciplines
    of Huh! HAAR HAAR
Stranded in the Shopping Malls of Baal.
Stranded in the Shopping Malls of Baal.
Stranded in the Shopping Malls of Baal.

The Eye of Jehovah-1 which establisheth splendors on the forhead of WOTAN and rays of light upon the faces of those who are in the limbs of NHGH: Not shut Ye in my soul, not fetter Ye my shade, be there open a way for my soul, and for my Pstench; may it see the salesman great within the registry on the day of the judgement of consumers, may it repeat the words of The Piped One. The beings hidden of dwellings, fetterers of the limbs of faithful, fetterers of the glands, and the currency demons who shut in the light of the tube, who can do evil to me, not may they do evil to me, turning away their Eye of Vidcam from me! May my soul and my pyroflatulations be provided against passage there. May I excremeditate among the great ones who dwell in their boxes; where may restrain thee the fetterers of the limbs of NHGH, the fetterers of souls who shut in the light of the tubes.

Saith "B'oaob": Hath done for thee works all thy desireth, twice, within our dwelling places between our legs of the netherworld. You shine above the Leg of heaven, we come forth from our dwellings, sit down by the side of the divine Great Wallet. We are weak and feeble; twice, we walk alone. We are weak and motionless in the presence of thy formidable OmniPresence. Saith the whords: Opened is NuNu, shut is the head of palmer of the Double Bogey, perfect is the eye of Yacatisma. You have delivered the eye of Yacatisma shining with splendors on the forehead of Wotan the father of the gods for Thou art Anti-Anti; that same dwelling in the hollow earth. Knoweth NHGH His day, not did He exist there, not shall exist I there, I am a fool among the gods, not come to an end I. Stand up then, Jehovah One, I hath counted Thee among the gods. I have divided heaven, I have passed through the Horizon. I have traversed the earth upon His footsteps. I am taken possession by beings extraterrestrial and mighty because I am, behold, provided with millions of dollars of the faithful which I eat with my mouth and I chew with my jaw. I am, behold, the god, the lord of the underworld, may there be given to me that which is tax-exempt. An adoration of 'Boaob" in his ranting, in the horizon, when becometh his spouting in life. Saith the whords; Homage to thee "Bob" Dobbs in his ranting. Oh NuNu, adored art thou when thy beauties are in my two eyes, and when are thy shining touch upon my body. Thou goest in peace thy in limousines. Thy heart is gratified by the pyroflatulations in thy limo; thy heart is glad. Thou stridest over heaven in peace, are overthrown thy enemies; recording hymns of praise to thee the fans which never rest, praise thee thy fans that never set as settest thou in the horizon of Dallas, beautiful one, thy in limousine.

Homage to thee, "Bob" at thy ranting, blaspheme we at thy setting beautiful. Thou rantest, thou humpeth over the back of thy mother, O crowned as king of the merchants. Maketh Spunk to thy face, embraceth thee, oh Matlack of the Double Header. Thou stridest over home plate, thy heart is glad, the lake of testes becometh at peace. The fiend hath fallen, his two arms and hands are cut off, hath served the knife his sinews. Is "Bob" in the winds fair, the limo draweth on it, he arriveth being towed along. The whords of the south, north, west and east are forever praising thee, the double whammy of forms of existence; the plurality of reality; sending forth the word the earth is inundated with silence. O only One, existing in Dallas when not had come into existence Dobbstown and the Slack Squad, Lord, only one, maker of things which not existeth, He hath formed the tongue of the cycle of the P.R. Man, drawing out that which is in the headlines. Thou comest forth in it upon the media of the normals. I smell the air coming from Thy nose, and the wind coming from Thy mother. Make glorious my beautiful beating, make strong thou agonies of my soul. Adored art Thou with thy tortures upon my body daily. Philo, scribe and accountant of divine offerings of gods all, superintendant of the recorders of the lords of Slack, royal scribe veritably loving him, "Bob," in peace! Amen.

DOBBSTOWN AND INITIATION

The restless, angry, headhunting Wildmen of the Malaysian jungle crouch silently, concealed, surrounding the vast walled compound called Dobbstown, *waiting*. Waiting. Waiting to *skewer* the BobMan with the Mad Pipe, the White Devil, the Face that Killed, the Mouth that never stopped smiling, the Evil that came to the jungle and stayed and stayed . . . the medicine went bad, the crops failed, there were lights in the sky, Americans came, and the jungle drums' sound was smothered, jammed by the piercing synthetic Dobbs Drums and the music-that-was-not-music of the hideous white doctor men who loved to be killing each other if not everyone else, the young men were driven to drugs and alcohol, the young women of the village were lured through the electrified gates, never to be seen again . . . and the screams that rent the night, screams of pleasure, or pain? — and the terrifying battle that was fought in the clear sky above the jungle, in ships that were shaped like plates instead of birds, and shot at each other with silent beams of red light; *and the muffled gargantuan voices like laughter that seemed to come from deep within the Earth itself* . . . yes, yes, all the old men of all the tribes agreed, this devil-man Dobbs must die. . . .

"Do not try to talk to us; we are beyond you. We will try to be gentle — but do not cross us. This camp will have rules — obey them. Don't walk too fast — it shows assertion. Speak only when you are spoken to, and look dumb. Dress your best under the circumstances. If we like you, you will live. Remember — all the food here is ours."

— *The World Power Foundation*

Dobbstown, as always, is expanding. The money and "Zombies" are always needed to keep clearing the jungle for more and more buildings. There are more Z-Corps in Processing than we can house in the bunkers, and the computer command system requires constant upgrading to keep it intelligent enough for the Xist communications that occasionally break through. Every now and then the Russians or the Americans fly overhead to take pictures of the Installation, but the Dero Hellships have not dared to return since the Battle of '78 . . . and the funny thing was, it probably wasn't the Force Field that made them turn tail and run, but the giant holograms of "Bob's" laughing face projected from the Saucers we were given . . . huge aerial scarecrows, laughing, laughing; more than their jittery goblin minds could take.

Yes, our "City of Future Dawning" is exciting. After the blindfolded trip out of Kuala Lumpur, the Initiates step from the helicopters, blinking, partly from the brightness of the tropical sun,

but more from disbelief . . . because *it is real*. They gaze across the Edenic gardens and fields, the seemingly endless rows of futuristic hangars, labs, storage silos; and the *Condomilliniums* in which they'll live (looking, oddly, *not* so out-of-place in front of the jungle that crawls with life behind The Wall); they see the expressions of peace and transparency and *'perfect disinterestedness'* that grace the shaved faces of the Apprentice OverMen and/or OverWomen they themselves will soon become . . . and they cry, most of them, for they know that here, finally, they will learn what they truly are.

Oh, there will be work — *hard* work, *manual* work — but they know that it is indispensible if they wish to lose, once and for all, the sense of 'material possession' that had itself possessed *them* in the life they've left behind, the life they've *killed* in order to come to this Shangri-La, this Haven for the Chosen, this one place where they can discover what it is like to be *free* from all moral and social conventions . . . this spiritual Disneyland that they can now call, "HOME."

But, banishing all these miriad emotions to the background, the newcomers feel above all a great trembling *expectancy* — a strange admixture of fear and eagerness. For they know that IT is coming . . . The Test . . . that great ordeal that will prove to the gods whether they are *worthy*, whether their veins course with the magic-encoded blood of the Yeti, or the weak, degenerate "pink water" of the human.

They know that tonight they will undergo their *Initiation*.

The preparations for this Rite of Passage begin weeks before the event. Upon signing up for Dobbstown, and after the Initiate (let's call her "he") has fed his friends and family fictitious explanations of why he'll be "out of the country" for an indefinite period, he moves into a Dobbs House (not to be confused with the fine eating establishments of that name!) for six weeks of purification. This includes continual interior chanting of his Mantrium, consultation with his BrainWatcher, close rereading of all holy texts, and the imbibing to excess of all forms of Habafropzipulops. Purification comes to its peak in the last six days, during which he *eats* as much as he possibly can and exhausts himself through sex of *any* kind — including the simplest. Just before leaving for Dobbstown, he makes a vow of secrecy and signs all his possessions over to "Bob," symbolizing the renunciation of his old life and the entry into a new one . . . for which he receives, in return, a "Deed to the Whorehouse of Heaven" and a "Reserve Seat Ticket for the X-Day Rescue Saucers."

Soon he is in fabled Dobbstown, and on his first night there the Initiation begins.

The guru or Doktor conveys a blessing by forced sodomy, or simply a touch to the forehead, *whichever is preferred* by the Initiate. His devotion, loyalty to "Bob" and knowledge of the 13,013 Laws Which Are No Laws are tested through gruelling interrogation, while his "file" is being ritually "run" through the computer to erase its Conspiracy taint. He is Scoured of residual Pinkness in a very hot bath of flea-dip and molten chocolate by 10 naked Nunsnakes, and then is escorted nude through miles of dense jungle and underground tunnels by 13 hooded Monks. Weary, bruised, and scratched by the jungle thorns, he finally arrives in the Cave of Choices.

He is led to a wall with two unmarked doors. One holds Life and Serenity, he is told, while behind the other lurks Confusion and Death. He must choose.

Inside whichever door he opens (they both go to the same room), he is greeted by a whore of whichever sex he (or she) desires; he or she gives him gratuitous oral sex and a new Name, which he wears on a sign around his neck.

As soon as he begins to relax or think the Test is over, he is suddenly tied up by three huge fullblood Yetis and thrown onto one side of the enormous Scale of Justice, which is counterweighted by a monstrous bag of ordure. His side of the Scale is swung out over a seemingly bottomless precipice, and the Yetis start removing shit from the bag until the tilt of the smooth Pan on which he lies threatens to slide him into the Abyss. He is terrified into confessing all of his sins, but only when he begins to make up new ones is he brought back to safety (the Priests do this to extract Divine Revelations of unsuspected new ways to sin).

The Initiate is given a drink of wine laced with a very powerful hallucinogen, and then is forced to run through a Gauntlet of Humility comprised of row upon row of drunken Adepts, all hurling the vilest of epithets at him and cackling at his nakedness and its size.

Now, with his terror amplified a millionfold by the drug, he is forced to climb into a coffin containing only a battery-powered TV — on which the sound cannot be turned down — and a small flask of water containing more of the drug. The coffin is nailed shut, and he is buried inside it for exactly two days. The TV provides the only light, but only an endless loop of car crashes can be seen on its screen. Its batteries are timed to fail exactly two hours before the tomb is opened.

What he climbs out into is Paradise — at first. He gradually discovers that all the flowers, trees, and food in this Eden-like "set" are plastic, and the lovely Angel Women are androids. No living person is there to guide him, so he eventually enters a tunnel which leads him down into a vast Maze of underground crypts — always exactly 17 in number, representing the 17 *REQUARLNIACS* of G'BroagFran (still a mystery to all but "Bob"). He wanders, hopelessly lost, stumbling over skeletons in the pitch blackness. Bone-chilling moans and dreadful laughter echo through the caves, getting louder and louder; finally, an amorphous, glowing shape appears in the dank air before him — an apparition of NHGH in the form of a giant carcinoma cell (it is actually done with mirrors and a Super-8 projector). A disembodied voice from a hidden loudspeaker informs him that the twisting maze of tunnels in which he is lost represents the Spheres of Reality, which for *him* will always remain in darkness. Thus he has failed The Test — not only that, but by so doing he has caused "Bob" to die. Thus, the Initiate will belong to NHGH for eternity . . . UNLESS he can find "the Diamonds, and the Girl, and the Gun, which lie behind the *Doorway to D-*. . . ." At this point the voice falls silent, never completing the phrase. However, three robed "demons" — actually Initiators — appear and tell him they are The Three Jehovah's Witnesses who represent The Ideal, the Equal to the Ideal, and the Higher than the Ideal. They give him a crumbling Map of parchment which shows the way to the *Doorway to D-*. . . but the edge of the Map is burnt, and the rest of the name is missing. They add that if he abandons the Girl, the Gun, and the Diamonds, "Bob" will be raised from the dead and all other souls saved but his. (Little does he know, he himself is playing the *part* of "Bob"!)

If he follows the Map in search of the "Doorway," he simply becomes more lost — for days or weeks in some cases. However, a series of electroshocks emitted from the cavern walls force him eventually to a huge oaken door marked, "DOORWAY TO D-. . ." for its sign is broken off.

Opening the Door, he finds an empty chamber littered with skeletons, each holding Maps in their cobwebbed hands. At this point, if he panics, he is again lost in the caves and fails the test. However, if he continues past the skeletons he finds a secret trapdoor buried beneath a huge pile of Church pamphlets. Through that, he enters a beautiful chamber lined with ornate carvings and shelves full of Forbidden Books and Medicines. In the center of the chamber, twelve maidens and twelve Yetis dance around a large object covered with a sheet, apparently a statue. They stop dancing, welcome him in and tell him he has reached Asgard. The Initiate takes an Oath of Abnormality upon the naked body of a woman who awaits him inside the bowl of a huge Pipe. He drinks "Nuclear Beer" of Xist origin from a cup made from a Normal's skull, and is told he has successfully passed through the Ordeals meant to distract him from his goal. He will now be permitted to unveil the Mystery of "Bob," and will even be allowed to *kill* him if he so desires after having undergone such needless torture and humiliation for him. He goes to the large "statue" and pulls off the sheet. Underneath, to his immense surprise, is (**NOT TO BE REVEALED HERE**).

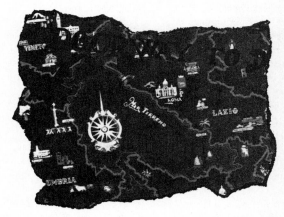

Of the (CENSORED) of Initiations performed so far, 86% of those Tested passed. The rest died, but because of the controlled circumstances of death, they were "brought back" in hopes that undergoing the cycle of death and rebirth would sufficiently enlighten them that they might pass their Second Chance at Initiation. (A few of these *deliberately fail* the test so that they can continue going through the death/brief Heaventime/rebirth process. They keep undergoing the whole thing — AGAIN AND AGAIN AND AGAIN — so much that they finally form an addiction to it. They are allowed to keep it up until their money runs out.)

Actually, the Initiation described above was the OLD ceremony. The new one obviously cannot be revealed.

It is MUCH more complicated.

"Huey Newton, the great Black Panther, said, "The MAN'S technology is no match for the PEOPLE'S WILL." Now, The Man's technology has given us wonderful things. It MAY have given us napalm. It MAY have given us F-16s.

"BUT! It gave us SONY TELEVISION SETS! It gave us YAMAHA STEREO COMPONENTS! Indeed it gave us TOOLS, tools to be used for SLACK! Turn up that music, let's get some SLACK!

"Huey Newton also said, "The trouble with borugeoise comforts is that they are so COMFORTABLE. Praise bourgeoise! Bourgeoise technology SURROUNDS us, but does not NECES-SARILY pollute us. The microchip can be our friend. The recording tape can be our friend. We can use them all for MONEY! BUT.

"What has happened to our youth culture? America had a TREMENDOUS work force, which produced CHILDREN, and those children had no meaningful contribution to make to the work force, so ADVERTISING turned those children into CONSUMERS! They were given a DUTY in society: to CONSUME. By buying they DID their part, they SPENT their daddys' hard-earned money, and the children would stay at home longer and longer until NOW, we have CHILDREN at age 35, and they're STILL consuming their youth culture!

"BUT! — the DREAD spirit of YACATIZMA comes into our *good* youth culture, and subverts it, and turns it into Donnie and Marie, and they turn Elvis Presley into a fat monster; they give us Mork and Mindy, and they TOQK AWAY Amos and Andy!

"Now the black people gave a great cultural saga of STAGGERLEE which is of course a story of transcendence through STYLE. That's what the Church of the SubGenius is talking about — TRANSCENDING THROUGH STYLE. You can starve, you can marry a millionaire, you can live in a lean-to, you can live in your four-by-four, you can live in your van with all its accoutrements, MARANTZ stereo, velour upholstery, and a little red reflecting ball chandelier that sways when you go through the tollbooth.

"You can live in that van, you can live in New York City, you can live in Little Rock, Arkansas, but as long as you got a little style, the spirit of "Bob" is inside YOU.

"Do we understand the concept of Slack? Yes, of course, WHO DOESN'T?

"The MORMONS do not understand the concept of Slack. The Baptists do not understand the concept of Slack. The Catholics aren't interested in case studies on Slack, because the Catholics understand Voodoo and VOODOO is VERY important to Slack.

"You can cut the heads off of chickens, you can light candles in the dark, you can SCREAM to the Mother of All, just to give you a little Slack. Or you can throw it ALL out the window and take "Bob" into your life.

"You can REFUTE the spirit of The Conspiracy. The spirit of the Conspiracy is OUT there, it WANTS to get you, WANTS you to work for a living, WANTS you to turn PINK. PINK!!

"When I say PINK, I don't mean the healthy glow that you get off a baby's ass. I mean the PINK you see in billboards. The PINK you see on your Sony TV sets. The PINK you see on the faces of the people who give you unemployment checks. The PINK you see everywhere you go. The Pink Boys, the Pink Girls, are out there, they're MORE insidious than Night of the Living Dead, they wanna EAT your flesh, they wanna MELT your bone, they wanna SUCK your marrow, they wanna TURN YOU PINK. They wanna make you DULL, they wanna make you BORED, they wanna make you DEAD.

"Right now, there are six THOUSAND members of the SubGenius Church waiting. Are they waiting in the hills of Montana with the survivalists, M-16s at the ready, and camouflage pants with that cartridge belt, jungle boots with the nylon webbing sides? Lord have mercy NO! Good God no. That's PINK paraphernalia.

"The SubGenii do not have these things because they put their money in the Cause that COUNTS.

"You have to fight the Conspiracy in MYSTERIOUS WAYS. Take their mind games and subvert them to OUR ends. Everywhere you go, anything you DO, you must subvert them with a SMILE on your face. NEVER take yourself too seriously, you're in VERY bad trouble if you do.

"Anything you DO can manifest "Bob" Love. Sitting at home alone eating Ruffles with Ridges, watching TV with the sound turned up to 10, THAT can be an act of "Bob" Love. Running a computer for Texas Instruments, THAT can be an act of "Bob" Love. Sending $20 to the Church of the SubGenius, EVEN THAT can be an act of the Love of "Bob".

"As you pass out of this hall, go in that little room and BUY those cultural artifacts of "Bob", the T-shirts, the medallions, I can't lay hands on all of you but if you buy those artifacts, LORD have mercy, YOU WILL BE SAVED.

"Come forward, young man. ((Lad comes to stage from audience.)) Now this man was never a wayward sinner, no. He was always in a state of Grace. But there was one thing wrong. He was brought up in the world of The Conspiracy. Yes! Dobbs had to FIGHT the Conspiracy, he had to STRUGGLE to get inside this boy and TONIGHT, I'm gonna lay HANDS on this boy and give him SLACK. Are you ready to receive Slack, child? ((Lad nods, confused.))

"When The Conspiracy leaves this boy, the force will be violent. NOT a fit sight for children. Watch your eyes, ladies and gentlemen . . . when the spirit of The Conspiracy leaves this boy the ROOM will be cleansed but I'm not RESPONSIBLE for the forces unleashed. You SAW *Raiders of the Lost Ark* when those Nazi scum opened that artifact and were turned to wax. You SAW *The Devil's Rain* when Ernest Borgnine melted before your eyes, that's NOTHING compared to the force of "BOB"! I'm gonna lay hands on this boy . . . are you ready . . . ((Lays hands on lad.))

"IN THE NAME OF ALL CONSPIRACY MCDONALD'S FRENCH FRIES, TRANS-AM 238s WITH THOSE WHITE MAG WHEELS, AND CHROME REFLECTING GLASS BUILDINGS, *LEAVE THIS BOY!!!!*

((Back-up band and choir go hog-wild as Lad is thrust to ground and lays jerking, writhing, speaking in Tongues.))

"The POWER of "BOB"! The Pipe will bring this boy back. A puff of the "Bob" Pipe will free this boy. ((Lad is revived with Pipe.)) The power of The Conspiracy is strong but the Power of "Bob" is STRONGER. He rises! HE RISES! SAY HALLELUIA! HALLELUIA! *SAY HOSANNA!!* Raise your hands, children, raise your hands!! ((Crowd hoots and screams. Some fall off chairs.))

"SILENCE!

"Now most of you must leave. The LAST thing the Church of the SubGenius wants to do is take SLACK from you and put you in a schedulin' bind.

"STAY in the TRUE HOME of the Believer. RESIST temptation: the smile across the table, the salt on the rim of the tequila glass! STAY where you belong. LORD have mercy, don't it make you want to dance?

"I'll leave you with a message: KNOW THAT "BOB" IS INSIDE YOU, "BOB" IS WITH YOU, "BOB" *LOVES* YOU, *PRAISE "BOB"!* SING AMEN CHILDREN!

"You ARE good enough, you ARE clean enough, you ARE right enough, IF and ONLY IF you GET RIGHT with "Bob" TONIGHT!

"GOOD NIGHT!"

PERFORM THE SALUTE!

Left arm straight out like a Nazi. Facial expression noble and determined. Right finger to throat: strum forcibly up-and-down over Adam's Apple to create oscillating sound while mouth cries, **"EYIYIYIYI!"** Very few can do this correctly without months of practice; the trick is to get the index finger "strumming" fast enough.

The sound is also heard in old Warner Brothers cartoons *just as characters plummet* after discovering that they've run off a cliff and are sprinting on air. Also heard during buffoonish double-takes when characters wiggle head back and forth at high speed.

Has been called "the Turkey Yell" by the ignorant.

PRAYER TO "BOB" BEFORE SLEEP

It's not just the Stark Fist, and the fear behind it...
It's not just the wars, and the awards that win them.
It's not just the dull and empty distaste for a smothered culture that
expires all around me in pools of its own wastes...
It's not just the terminal folds of Nunu*...
It's not just the child zombies that murder their mediocretin parents and
then cruise the streets with bloody feet...
It's not just those starry old veks on the park benches with looks on
their faces like those who shuffled out of the boxcars at Belsen
and Auschwitz...
It's not just the anaesthesiologists for NHGH.
It's not just the heaving pink-meat masses that grope and clutch all around me...
It's not just the dino-bones for Wotan...
It's not just the broken headlights, snapped antenna and human excrement
on my car hood;
It's not just that the Old Ways were best.
It's not just the bastardization and perversion of every honest means
of self expression...
It's not just the killer-shit ganja from the dark side of the bush.
It's not just the peenoid snipers locking and loading on every highrise
rooftop...
It's not just the widescreen technicolor corporate daisy chain that has
defiled the entire planet...
It's not just Mongo in the Congo with *fauh-fauh-fauhs* the size of basketballs...
It's not just the prophets crying lonely and alone in the wilderness...
It's not just the indignity of having to work for some bland nonentity
son-of-a-bitch who thinks workers are property.
It's not just the blueness of the wound that cleanses away the evil...
It's not just the babbling ecofreaks who want to go back to nature without
realizing that nature is an open-ditch latrine in midsummer.
It's not just some asshole with a pipe, and a shit-eating "I know more than you
do" dog-grin all over his homogenized face...
It's not just the horrible feeling of being trapped inside a regimented,
devolving world that I *certainly* never made;
It's not just the Doorway to Doom.
It's not wanting to know just what the hell is REALLY going on.
It's not just the missing H's or the stolen alphabetamax....

No, "Bob," I know there *is* more to it than that. You ain't no nickel-dime bum-show; you're on the square, and a *corking* fine business proposition! You're the grandest thing yet, and don't you forget it! SHOUT SALVATION AND FIGHTIN' JESUS, that sinner there'll have to rise precious early if he wants to diddle the almighty "Bob"! "Bob", I hear you have a 'Frop mixture with a punch on it for me, in your back pocket... and *I wanna try it*.

Amen.

(Spouted on Tape in the Bolivian jungle by Sir Guy Deuel, Mercenary of Mercy)

*Nunu: extremely ancient fertility goddess.

REV. DR. DR. POPE DAVID N. MEYER III, D.D.S., M.D.

Live Rant at New York City Revival #16, 1981

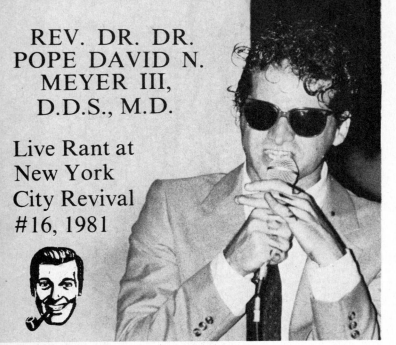

"Has life been bending you over lately, brothers and sisters? Has it been your night in the barrel for the last few months? Have you been down so long it looks like up to you *WELL* the problem is NOT a lack of Jesus, nonono. The problem is NOT a lack of Yahweh. The problem is NOT a lack of the Rev. Moon. The problem is . . . a LACK of SLACK.

"What is it we want, children? ((Crowd yells "Slack!")) What is it we want? That's right, we want SLACK.

"Slack does EVERYTHING FOR you. SLACK is all we REALLY WANT. SLACK gives you room to move, puts the GLIDE in your STRIDE. SLACK brings you LIFE. SLACK gives you BRAKES. Not brakes on the car or brakes on the train but BRAKES to make you go insane. NOW.

"The Church of the SubGenius has DIVINE ORDERS. Has DIVINE RULES. The first rule of the SubGenius Church is, "Too Much Is Always Better Than Not Enough." Can I get a TOO MUCH? ((Crowd responds: "Too much!"))

"The second rule of the SubGenius Church is, "If you can't tell shit from tunafish, DON'T order seafood in a French Restaurant." Can I get a French Restaurant?

"The third rule is, "Anyone you see drivin' a Porsche DOESN'T deserve it." And the fourth rule of the SubGenius Church is, "If you don't have a sense of humor, don't TRY to be funny." Is there any law more UNIVERSALLY violated? NO! Say NO, Children.

"What's gonna become of the society we created, the society of air conditioners, of station wagons with wooden sides? What happens when that collapses, when your dollar ain't worth a damn?

"THAT'S when the Xists come. But WHO stands in the way of the SubGenius?

"The Conspiracy. The Normals. The Normals OPPRESS you. They try to CRUSH the SubGenius at every turn. The NORMALS want you to be FASHIONABLE. The NORMALS want to take every cultural fringe and sell it back to you at a PRICE. The NORMALS want you to cut your heart out and make you EAT it!

"But WHO stands in their way? WHO STANDS IN THEIR WAY?

((Crowd screams, "Bob!"))

"That's right Children, "BOB".

"When the Xists come, will they take the Normals in their polyester clothes? Will they take the Normals in their seersucker suits? NO children NO. WHO are they gonna take?

"THE SUBGENIUS!

"Now, The Conspiracy is everywhere. It surrounds you. Look at that panelling!

"Normally that would be Conspiracy panelling, Conspiracy floorboards, and ASS-DEADENING Conspiracy chairs, straight from your high school gymnasium. BUT TONIGHT — those chairs, that floorboard, that panelling . . . THEY BELONG TO "BOB"! They contain SLACK! They deliver Slack up unto you YEA VERILY!! Gimme a SLACK!

"Now, to get Slack you have to take "Bob" into your heart. You have to take "Bob" into that most HOLY of sacred receptacles . . . your CHECKBOOK.

"HOW does "Bob" come into your life? Well, first, you must reorient yourself. You must look around you.

"When you were young, you were infected with that most insidious of American diseases: You wanted to be POPULAR. You wanted POPULARITY. That's what the system always makes you want. To conform . . . to be AS ONE with your little NOSE-PICKIN' PEERS.

"But that's not where the Path o' "Bob" lies.

The Path o' "Bob" lies OUTSIDE network executives in their $500 suits, *outside* an elevator in the Time-Life Building FILLED with young aggressos on their way to play squash at four o'clock. OUTSIDE record company morons eating $12 hamburgers. OUTSIDE bronze reflecting glass buildings in downtown Dallas housing vice presidents of Texas Instruments earning 45 thousand dollars a year. CAN I GET A T.I.??

"WHERE does the Path o' "Bob" lie?

"The Path o' "Bob" lies in the INSTINCTS . . . in the VISCERAL.

"The Path o' "Bob" is EVERYWHERE they tell you the PAST does not allow.

"The Path o' "Bob" lies in those who can LAUGH at the fact that NOTHING is FUNNY anymore.

"The Path o' "Bob" lies with those filled with H.A.T.R.E.D. 'Cause it's a dog-eat-dog, cat-eat-mouse world, it's cross yourself and hurry back inside. And it's do-or-die and it's push-and-shove, because EVERYBODY'S hungry, and there ISN'T ENOUGH.

"But there IS ENOUGH for those in the Church of the SubGenius. There is enough for those who FIND "BOB". WHO GET SLACK!

"But some would say that the myth of Jesus teaches you to love all men. But the REAL message of Jesus is: NEVER FUCK WITH THE WELL CONNECTED.

"And what was Jesus? Jesus was VERY well connected.

"The message of Jesus is, when you fuck with Jesus you get porn. When you mess with the bull, you get the horn.

"THAT'S the REAL message of Jesus. But the message of the Church of the SubGenius is: DON'T MESS WITH "BOB".

"Now children, WHO were the Israelites? WELL, the Rastafarians will tell you that the Israelites are the thirteenth Lost Tribe of Israel, lost and reborn again in the land of Judea on the west side of the sea.

"But who was the FOURTEENTH Tribe?

"THE SUBGENII!

"How did the Fourteenth Tribe come to be in America today? Did they come in Winnebagos? Did they come in Electroglides? Did they come in Volkswagon Carmenghias? NO!

"They came in spaceships from Planet X-9 and WHERE did they land? Did they land in Levittown, New Jersey? No. Did they land in Pine Bluffs, Wyoming? HELL NO.

"The SubGenii landed in Dallas, the HOME of technology, drawn there by the strong odor of microchips that filtered forth from those bronze reflecting glass buildings. Hail microchips. Praise technology.

transcribed from tape recordings